Repeal and revolution

Manchester University Press

Repeal and revolution
1848 in Ireland

Christine Kinealy

Manchester University Press
Manchester and New York

Manchester University Press
Manchester and New York
distributed in the United States exclusively by Palgrave Macmillan

Published by Manchester University Press
Oxford Road, Manchester M13 9NR, UK
and Room 400, 175 Fifth Avenue, New York, NY 10010, USA
www.manchesteruniversitypress.co.uk

Distributed in the United States exclusively by
Palgrave Macmillan, 175 Fifth Avenue, New York,
NY 10010, USA

Distributed in Canada exclusively by
UBC Press, University of British Columbia, 2029 West Mall,
Vancouver, BC, Canada V6T 1Z2

British Library Cataloguing-in-Publication Data
A catalogue record for this book is available from the British Library

Library of Congress Cataloging-in-Publication Data applied for

ISBN   978 0 7190 6516 3 *hardback*
ISBN   978 0 7190 6517 0 *paperback*

First published 2009

18 17 16 15 14 13 12 11   10 09   10 9 8 7 6 5 4 3 2 1

Typeset
by Action Publishing Technology Ltd, Gloucester
Printed in Great Britain
by CPI Antony Rowe, Chippenham, Wiltshire

Contents

Acknowledgements

It is with humility really unassumed – it is with a sentiment even of awe that I pen the opening sentence of this work: for of all conceivable subjects I approach the reader with the most solemn – the most comprehensive – the most difficult – the most august. What terms shall I find sufficiently simple in their sublimity – sufficiently sublime in their simplicity – for the mere enunciation of my theme? (*Eureka*, a Prose Poem by Edgar Allen Poe, 1848.)

The completion of this book has been one of the most challenging, yet interesting, projects with which I have been involved during my academic career. To some extent, this has been due to the subject matter itself. 1848 was a pivotal year in world history for a number of reasons. Events in Ireland, although often ignored in general historiographies, were also significant. The more research I did on this topic, the more I came to realize how important this year was both in the short term, and in Ireland's longer-term political and cultural development. The diversity and brilliance of the men and women involved in 1848, both individually and collectively, made this study fascinating. But so much happened and they each did so much worthy of note that it became difficult to know what to include and what to leave out. I hope I have done some justice to their contributions.

Writing is a solitary pursuit. Many years ago, I was berated by a far more senior historian for thanking my dog, who was my companion when I wrote in the early hours of the morning, in my acknowledgements. 'Trot', whom I had had since being a student at Trinity College Dublin, died a few months later. Perversely, the attack and my response achieved an unlooked-for notoriety for my book. I now have another dog, Guinness, who also has been my constant companion in the writing of this book. It would be remiss not to mention him, although by doing so, I know that I risk being criticized.

Amongst those who have supported, challenged or inspired me in other ways, are, notably, Ernst Wangerman, Fabrice Bensimon, Kay Boardman, Guy Thomas, Judith de Groat, Joe Lee, Roger Swift, John Walton and

Terry Eagleton. Although I never met him, John Saville's ground-breaking work has been particularly valuable. A number of colleagues and friends, including Bill Rogers, David Sexton, Susan Sydney-Smith, Jack Worrall, Honora Ormesher, Angela Farrell, Bernadette Barrington, Susan Bailey, Carol Russell and John Joughin, have encouraged and supported me in other ways. I would like to extend my gratitude to Emma Brennan at Manchester University Press, particularly for her patience when this book took longer to complete than I had anticipated. Thanks are also due to graduate students at Drew University where I taught a course on 1848 at the beginning of 2007, and again, in 2008. As is often the case with mature students, I learned much from them. They confirmed that interest in 1848 is strong, and not only in Europe. I apologize to those colleagues whose assistance or involvement I may have overlooked.

I have received help from archivists and librarians in a number of places, including the Working Class Movement Library, New York Public Library, the Bodleian Library, the Manuscripts Room in Trinity College, Dublin, the Public Record Office of Northern Ireland, the Royal Irish Academy, the National Library of Ireland, the National Archives of Ireland, the National Archives of England, the British Library and Windsor Castle. Special mention and thanks are due to Alan Delozier of Seton Hall Archive, Bruce Lancaster and Lois Sechchey of Drew University, Aidan Turner-Bishop, formerly of the University of Central Lancashire Library, and William Cobert of the American Irish Historical Society in New York. I am particularly grateful to the Duke of Clarendon for granting me permission to quote from the papers of his ancestor.

As usual, special thanks are due to those who have read and commented on portions of my work, including Francine Sagar, Barry Quest, Steve Butler and Ernst Wangerman, who have respectively provided a French, an English, an American and an Austrian perspective on my work. Both Siobhán Kinealy and Roger Swift kindly shared their research on 1848 in England. Clearly, any faults or omissions are my own.

Inevitably, my greatest thanks are reserved for my family who have tolerated my idiosyncratic lifestyle and obsession with 1848. My children have shared the vicissitudes that accompany the writing of any book, but especially as they have had to share their home and their mother with the extraordinary men and women of 1848 for many years. Their love, support, and frequent teasing, are deeply appreciated.

Finally, I hope that this small book does justice to a remarkable period in Irish history and the outstanding contribution of the men and women whose participation helped to shape it.

Introduction

1848 is frequently referred to as 'the year of revolutions' or, less prosaically, the 'springtime of the peoples'. Yet, despite the widespread challenge to the status quo throughout Europe, historians as diverse as G.M. Trevelyan and A.J.P. Taylor long ago averred that 'History failed to turn'.[1] Other historians have shown how, following an initial flurry of revolutionary activity, order was quickly restored and conservative governments and monarchies were re-installed.[2] Consequently, as Jonathan Sperber has noted, 'The European revolutions of 1848 have not always received the kindest of treatment at the hands of historians. Gentle mockery, open sarcasm and hostile contempt have frequently set the tone for narrative and evaluation.'[3] Nevertheless, 1848 was a pivotal year in the development of modern Europe. Its repercussions spread beyond the groups and the countries immediately involved, with revolutions and revolts occurring in places not generally considered to be directly included in the revolutionary loop. In the longer term, their legacy was evident in the emergence of nationalism and democracy, not only in Europe, but as far away as Australia and South America.[4]

The historiography of 1848 has focused overwhelmingly on revolutions in France, Germany, Italy and Hungary, while events elsewhere, notably in Britain and Ireland, have been marginalized. A widespread assumption has been that the United Kingdom remained untouched by the revolutionary fervour. Accordingly, the presentation of the Charter to the British government in April of that year has been frequently reduced to a comic act, thus rendering it worthless, even as a political gesture, while its Chartist supporters have been characterized as figures of fun.[5] Political upheavals in Ireland have been similarly ignored or ridiculed, despite an uprising taking place there in July 1848. Moreover, the rebellion in Ireland has been largely erased from histories of the period. In a one-thousand page history of the 1848 revolutions published in 2001, for example, only four pages were devoted to Ireland, while it is totally absent from many comparative studies of the uprisings.[6] Furthermore, general references to the Irish insurrection commonly suggest that it was unimportant, or constituted, in the words of the historian Robert Evans, a 'small and ill-conceived rising'.[7] More damningly, even Irish historians frequently refer to it as 'farcical' or as a 'shoot-out in a cabbage patch'; in fact, mention of the cabbage patch appears obligatory in accounts of this event.[8] Overall, derision, generalizations and omission are commonplace regarding the Irish involvement in the year of revolutions.[9] Nor is this approach of recent origin. In a series of contemptuous articles published in the weeks following the rising, the London *Times* contributed what was to become an enduring view of the 'ridiculous' rebellion in Ireland, with its leader referred to as 'the contemptible figure of Smith O'Brien crouching amidst Widow Commack's [*sic*] cabbages'.[10] In December 1848, the British journal *The Economist* described the previous twelve months as 'the most eventful year in the history of modern Europe'. Yet no mention was made of the challenge to the British state by Irish nationalists.[11]

These interpretations are both misleading and disingenuous. Both Britain and Ireland were individually and jointly caught up in the revolutionary momentum that swept Europe in 1848. In the wake of the February Revolution in France, when other European governments started to fall, 'No one was certain that Britain would remain immune.'[12] Yet publicly, both the government and the conservative press suggested that British people would not support a revolution because they were different from other Europeans. *The Times* explained it in this way: 'We possess those things which other nations are everywhere demanding at the gates of the palace or the door of the Legislature.'[13] It was therefore ironic (or significant) that Britain and Ireland both contained large and organized political movements even prior to 1848. Moreover, the revolutionary rhetoric of the new government in France alarmed the British government, particularly as it inspired Irish and British radicals, with representatives of both groups visiting Paris to offer their congratulations to the French people. While there was widespread sympathy in France for Ireland, the Provisional Government had no desire to go to war with Britain. It was not merely Irish links with France that worried British officials, but also the support for Irish independence expressed by Irish emigrants to Britain and to the United States. The concern increased when British radicals and Irish nationalists moved closer together at the beginning of 1848, even sharing public platforms and declaring a common interest.[14] Such an alliance was unwelcome to the British government, which acted ruthlessly to undermine and then arrest the leadership of both groups. Yet the British government had not been opposed to all revolutions. In 1847 Lord Palmerston, the British Foreign Secretary, had expressed his support for the rising in Lisbon.[15] Russell's government had monitored the events in France after February 1848 closely, and Britain was one of the first governments to recognize the new French republic. They were also sympathetic to the Hungarian uprising, helping Lajos Kossuth to escape from Turkey and welcoming him in England.[16]

The Irish rising was led by an eclectic group of middle-class intellectuals, known collectively as Young Ireland. They had left Daniel O'Connell's Repeal Association in 1846 and founded the Irish Confederation in January 1847, with the similar objective of repealing the Act of Union of 1800. At this stage, they did not support an armed uprising, but the deepening famine in Ireland and the February Revolution in France radicalized their aims. Unlike the other revolts in Europe, the Irish uprising did not commence in the capital city or any of the major towns, but took place near the small village of Ballingarry in County Tipperary. The location was chosen because Dublin was so heavily guarded that the insurgents realized they had no chance of success there. The timing of the rising was unfortunate. Since 1845, Ireland had been experiencing an extensive subsistence crisis, triggered by a lethal blight on the potato crop. Almost one million people had already died or emigrated and the numbers were still increasing. Hence, the leaders of the Confederation did not want an uprising to take place until the 1848 harvest had been safely gathered. Instead, the timing of the rebellion was precipitated by government repression, including the suspension of Habeas Corpus. The government also commenced a wholesale arrest of both the leaders and their supporters, thus provoking an uprising for which the insurgents were badly prepared, largely unarmed, and, in the case of the leader, William Smith O'Brien, reluctant. The rising lasted for less than two days and was easily defeated by the local constabulary, with few casualties. Nevertheless, the various repressive measures remained in place for many more months.

The short-lived nature of the uprising belied the fact that in the preceding months both the British government and some sections of the press had regarded the activities of Young Ireland as a serious threat to the state.[17] However, immediately after receiving news of the outcome of the Ballingarry rebellion, the danger to the state was minimalized and publicly derided. Clearly, the British government was anxious to play down the events of 1848 both at home and overseas. The Irish Confederation was dismissed by the government as not posing a serious threat, with Lord Clarendon subsequently boasting that he had 'known everything that passed in Dublin in 1848'.[18] Yet regardless of the widespread dismissal of 1848 and its leaders, it is clear from official reports of the time that Irish nationalism, and the support that it attracted outside Ireland, created major anxiety for the government. Nor did the defeat at Ballingarry mark an end to Irish revolutionary aspirations. Richard O'Gorman, one of the Confederate leaders, led an attack on a commissariat store in Rathkeale while on the run, and also robbed the local mail bags.[19] More localized uprisings took place in autumn 1848, centred on Carrick-on-Suir, while joint Chartist and Confederate insurrections, due to take place in London, Manchester, Liverpool and other British towns in August, were only prevented by wholesale arrests, followed by transportation of the leaders.[20] In September 1849, a more coordinated, but equally unsuccessful, rising took place in Cappoquin in County Waterford.[21] Further arrests and transportations followed. The leaders of these movements had realized that they stood little chance of success, but their determination to act demonstrated that defeat in July 1848 had not diminished the revolutionary fervour. Tellingly also, the importance of the gesture rather than of immediate success was a factor in nationalist aspirations in 1848. For the most part, these follow-up activities have been omitted from narratives of 1848 in Ireland.

Why has so little been written about Ireland in 1848 and its place in the spectrum of European revolutions? Unquestionably, the roots of Ireland's absence from the historiography of the revolutions can be found in 1848 itself. By the end of the year, both the Chartist and the Repeal threats appeared to have been vanquished and the British state had survived intact, unlike some European governments. Moreover, the twin threats posed by these movements were being characterized in the press as having been pusillanimous and farcical. O'Brien, the leader of the Irish uprising, was especially pilloried in the British press for his leadership skills, the method of his arrest and his conduct at trial. *Frazer's Magazine*, for example, portrayed his behaviour as 'infatuated obstinacy and quixotic exaltation which have marked his conduct through his life. Though it might be hard to prove him insane under an ordinary commission of lunacy, his conduct throughout has been such as to shew [*sic*] that, as a politician at least, he is *non compos*.'[22] A similarly unsympathetic judgment was made by a fellow nationalist, John O'Connell, a son of Daniel O'Connell, who described 1848 as 'that year of disgrace and dismay ... The effect on the Irish Catholic clergy can scarcely be exaggerated. It revived all the old distrust of insurrectionary movements.'[23] A number of disappointed participants were also harsh in their immediate assessments; Thomas Clarke Luby, for example, referred to it as a 'fiasco', while Joseph Brenan wrote, 'The attempt was desperate and its promoters were madmen.'[24] To what extent did either the disappointment of the participants or the anger of its opponents influence the later belief that the 1848 rising had neither support nor lasting impact?

The one-hundredth anniversary of the 1848 uprising was muted, although the University of Cork announced a project to open a Smith O'Brien Library.[25] The proposal was not followed through.[26] The sesquicentennial commemorations were more elaborate, although were mostly based in County Tipperary, the location of the rising. They were, however, overshadowed by the high-profile government-sponsored commemorations of the Great Famine (between 1995 and 1997) and of the 1798 Rebellion (in 1998).[27] An attempt by Labhrás Ó Murchú, an Irish TD (*Teachta Dála*, or member of the *Dáil*, the Irish parliament), to have Widow McCormack's house taken over by the state was resisted by fellow TD, Síle de Valera, who was the minister responsible for heritage and public monuments. Interestingly, during the parliamentary debate both ministers referred to the significance of 1848 in the development of Irish nationalism. Ó Murchú averred that:

> The risings of 1867 and 1916 would never have taken place but for the Young Irelanders' deep intellectual assessment of the Irish psyche and their right to full sovereignty. It was they who established the agenda and set down the parameters of nationhood.[28]

De Valera responded that, 'I agree that had there not been the Young Ireland movement we would not have had the Fenians of 1867 and the 1916 Rising.'[29] Ó Murchú also reminded his fellow TDs of the context in which the rising occurred, stating that:

> at the time of the Young Ireland rebellion – which occurred during the Famine – people's spirits would have been exceptionally low … The Young Irelanders remotivated and inspired the Irish people and helped them rise from the dungeon of depression imposed by the Famine. It is for that reason that the Young Ireland Movement is significant.[30]

Throughout this debate, the 1848 rising was categorized as something that was specifically Irish in origin and impact. This view was in marked contrast to the state commemorations of the 1798 rebellion which located the event firmly within its wider European and American framework. Although little government support was evident in 1998 for the events of 1848, on 21 July 2004, Widow McCormack's House was officially opened as a heritage centre.[31] Its designation as the 'Famine Warhouse', reinforced the link between the 1848 rising and the wider social devastation caused by the Famine.

If the two anniversaries of 1848 failed to capture the imagination of either the general public or of Irish politicians, what was more surprising was the scant attention paid to it by Irish historians. Writing on the centenary of the 1848 uprising, the Irish historian Denis Gwynn (a great-grandson of William Smith O'Brien, the leader of the uprising) suggested that, 'The failure of the attempted insurrection of 1848 was so complete and, it seemed, so ignominious that its history has never been fully written … It is usually dismissed as a deplorably incompetent adventure by a few earnest but incapable men.'[32] However, he disagreed with this accepted interpretation on the grounds that 'the facts are very different'.[33] As his various writings have shown, the men who led the 1848 uprising were widely respected, influential, and continued to influence Irish politics even after they had been transported to Van Diemen's Land. Moreover, their actions in the early months of 1848 were closely monitored and feared by the British government.[34] Gwynn, in fact, was echoing the assessment made by the *Launceston Times* upon the arrival of four of the insurgents in Van Diemen's Land at the end of 1849. The newspaper declared that 'in England, their efforts have been the subject of scathing sarcasm, and the individuals themselves have been ridiculed and made the objects of merriment. But this was after their failure.' Although the paper did not approve of the actions of the prisoners, the writer acknowledged that 'their motives were patriotic and cannot be disputed'.[35]

Sixty years after Gwynn's assessment, the historiography of 1848 in Ireland remains relatively small. Unlike the abortive uprisings of 1798 and 1916, the 1848 uprising continues to be largely unexplored, with most of the recent research coming from historians outside Ireland, particularly Australasia and Canada.[36] Moreover, recent publications have focused on individual leaders of Young Ireland, following the pioneering work undertaken by Richard Davis on William Smith O'Brien.[37] Very little research has been undertaken on the role of rank and file membership of the Irish Confederation and their role in the Confederate clubs.[38] The smallness of the literature is surprising given the resurgence of interest in Irish political history since 1995. Yet, if political change was the benchmark of significance and success, few European revolutions can be judged to be triumphant. As Sperber has noted in relation to the better-known European revolutions, 'It was all great and glorious, but primarily in gesture and pathos – whether it really achieved anything is quite another matter.'[39] His words have resonance in the Irish context. By 1849, the status quo had returned throughout Europe, even if some individual monarchs and politicians had disappeared. Even though little appeared to have changed in the short term, in the longer term, the political landscape in Europe had been irrevocably altered. This was the case also in Britain and Ireland. In the latter, modern Irish nationalism, with its roots in 1782 and 1798, became more firmly embedded and this in turn sowed the seeds of a more militant form of loyalty to the Union. Nor was the legacy of the 1848 uprising confined to Ireland. A similarly underestimated outcome of the events at Ballingarry was the effect on politics within Britain. John Belchem has suggested that, 'The volume and nature of anti-Irish propaganda underwent significant change once the events of 1848 demonstrated Irish "apartness". Paddy appeared in new and defamatory guise, denied his former benign and redeeming qualities.' This prejudice fed into the emergence of popular Toryism in Britain.[40] This revised view of the Irish was not just confined to Britain. John Belchem argues that, 'On both sides of the Atlantic, 1848 proved an important point of closure ... Through the misperceptions of 1848, the "outcast" Irish was deemed incapable of political and cultural conformity.'[41]

A publication that gave both Chartism and Irish nationalism their due recognition within the radical developments of 1848 was John Saville's ground-breaking study *1848: The British State and the Chartist Movement*.[42] Unlike many earlier accounts, which had marginalized the involvement of the United Kingdom, Saville 'located British domestic politics within the triangle of revolutionary Paris, insurgent Ireland, and a revitalised native Chartist movement in England, particularly London and the industrial North'.[43] Saville argued that the British press in 1848, encouraged by the government, deliberately played down the Chartist threat and systematically ridiculed its activities and leaders. Moreover, unlike many histories of British Chartism, Saville examined the links between Irish and British radicals, suggesting that fear of this alliance was a major preoccupation of the government in the early months of 1848.[44] He concluded that, following the French Revolution, 'The most important political question of the year ahead, although it was not recognised in these early weeks, was the relationship between the Irish Confederates, who were the most radical of the Irish Repeal movement, and the English Chartists.'[45] Belchem has extended Saville's revolutionary axis to include, in the case of Irish nationalism, support from the United States.[46] One of the themes of this book is the significance of the British, French and transatlantic connections with Irish nationalism in 1848, which help to explain why the British government reacted so vigorously to developments in Ireland.

Nonetheless, by mid-April 1848, when the revolutionary momentum was building up throughout Europe, the Chartist threat in Britain appeared to have been extinguished, largely due to the resolute interventions of the government. Why had such a large, populist movement been so easy to subdue? Leslie Mitchell has suggested that the defeat of Chartism was possible because, ultimately, it was never a serious danger and that 'the great Chartist demonstration of 10 April proved not that England was threatened by the same violence that disturbed Europe, but precisely the opposite'.[47] Mitchell additionally argues that from mid-April, when it had become clear that the English radicals were not going to revolt, the government's concern was directed increasingly at 'two groups only, the Irish and foreigners resident in London'.[48] A similar interpretation has been offered by Robert J.W. Evans who suggested that throughout 1848 'there was great concern about the Irish, as usual. Events in Ireland were closely monitored, and the Irish involvement in Chartism noted. Equally, the behaviour of foreign residents in London came under fierce scrutiny'.[49] Yet despite the assertion by the government and some sections of the press that the Chartist threat evaporated after 10 April (a claim repeated by a number of historians), Chartist activities actually increased in some parts of the country in the ensuing months.[50] The actions of the central government and the local authorities, especially in regard to the arrest of Chartist leaders and the banning of public demonstrations, suggest that they were not sanguine that the threat was over. Increasingly though, the British authorities were absorbed in countering the threat posed by Irish nationalism.

The seriousness with which the British government regarded the activities of the Chartists and Irish nationalists in 1848 can be gauged from the range and intensity of the special measures that were put in place in both Britain and Ireland. In addition to the highly visible presence of the volunteer militia, the police and the army, the authorities made more covert use of the press, the telegraph, and a network of spies and police informers.[51]

In order to quell any intended disturbance, public meetings were banned and those that went ahead were closely monitored. New repressive legislation, such as the Aliens Act in April 1848, was introduced, while additional coercive measures were put in place in Ireland, culminating in the suspension of Habeas Corpus in July. Furthermore, as Sperber has pointed out, by the 1840s, the proportion of constabulary to the population in Ireland far exceeded that of 'the absolutist "police state"', Prussia, while the police presence in England, especially London, was substantial. Consequently, 'The greater ability of the liberal state in Great Britain, with its parliament and legal system, to enforce its will, when compared with the surprisingly feeble forces of repression in the absolutist monarchies on the continent also helps explain why the United Kingdom rode out the revolutionary wave with little rocking of the boat.'[52] If, as has been suggested, the British state was not at risk, why were so many extraordinary measures necessary? Moreover, if the real threat to the British state came from Irish radicals, why has the Irish uprising been so widely disregarded by historians of 1848?

Despite 1848 and the events that led to it being ignored in general histories, the contemporary literature is extensive. Several of the 1848 leaders kept their own record of events, while many of the participants who spent time in exile were writers, who felt the need to explain their actions and left personal narratives of their involvement. Some accounts were penned by men who had not been present at Widow McCormack's house, most notably John Mitchel, who was not even in the country at the time. Nonetheless, Mitchel's *Jail Journal* remains the most famous and controversial chronicle of 1848 in Ireland, yet it was a second-hand account, written from his prison ship in Bermuda. The first eye-witness account by a participant was by Michael Doheny. He was one of the most radical of the insurgents and had led some guerrilla attacks after the failure at Ballingarry. In 1849, he had fled to New York to escape arrest and from there he wrote *The Felon's Track*, which was published in October of that year.[53] It covered the history of the repeal movement from 1843 to 1848, including the emergence of Young Ireland. Doheny said its main purpose was 'to show that Ireland's failure was not owing to native recreancy or cowardice'. The book was well received in the United States and praised for its 'passion and feeling'.[54]

The account of another leading participant who was transported to Van Diemen's Land, Thomas Francis Meagher, was serialized in the revived *Nation* after 1849, while his *The Legislative Independence of Ireland* was published in New York in 1853. O'Brien, the leader of the rebellion, although a reluctant revolutionary, spent his years in exile justifying and explaining his actions.[55] Charles Gavan Duffy, who was acquitted for this part in the uprising and so remained in Ireland, produced his restrained *Four Years of Irish History* in 1883.[56] It was a sequel to his previous book on the history of Young Ireland prior to 1845. Duffy, then aged almost

70, wrote with the benefit of thirty-five years' hindsight and when most of his former associates were dead. Duffy, who even in his youth had been a moderate, inevitably offered a more temperate view than some of the earlier accounts. At this stage also, he had gained respectability within the British establishment, having served as Prime Minister of Victoria in Australia, leading to his knighthood in 1873. Like Mitchel, Duffy was not present at Ballingarry, and he had played no part in any of the supporting actions as he had been in Newgate Prison at the time. His account of the uprising, therefore, was second-hand, based on written and verbal accounts given to him by the main participants and through access to many of the contemporary records that had been given to his care.[57] Moreover, as Richard O'Gorman, one of his sources of information, warned him:

> It is so many years since I was called upon to put my memory to the test ... I am not surprised to find it now scarcely reliable either as to the incidents themselves, or the exact order of time in which they took place.[58]

Nevertheless, Duffy, who outlived many of his former colleagues, became the primary custodian of the memory of Young Ireland and 1848.

Unpublished accounts of 1848 were produced by some of the lesser-known participants, including Patrick O'Donohoe and Terence Bellew MacManus (both of whom were convicted of treason, sentenced to death, but eventually transported), John Cavanagh and Richard O'Gorman.[59] Some of the junior participants who took part as young men, including John O'Mahony, Charles Kickham, James Stephens and Thomas Clarke Luby, left their own shorter versions of events. The politics of O'Mahony, Stephens, Kickham and Luby, who became leading Fenians, were clearly inspired by the writings and actions of Young Ireland. Jeremiah O'Donovan Rossa, a Fenian leader who had played no part in 1848, was influenced by the events of that year, particularly Young Ireland's fusing of cultural and political nationalism.[60] The life and writings of O'Donovan Rossa provided a link between the insurrection in 1848 and the republican risings in 1867 and 1916.[61] Moreover he, like so many of those involved in these three rebellions, spent much of his time in the United States, thus reinforcing the transatlantic support for Irish nationalism.[62]

There are inevitably differences in emphasis in the above accounts and even some contradictions.[63] A general point of agreement, however, concerns the role of the Catholic Church, with the consensus being that the Catholic bishops and clergy were opposed to a rising taking place, while some actively discouraged the participants with threats of eternal damnation.[64] John O'Mahony, a member of a Confederate club in County Tipperary who was closely involved with the rebellion, was unequivocal in condemning the role of the local Catholic priests who, until the eve of the rising, had professed their support for Young Ireland from the pulpit. Writing shortly after the rout, O'Mahony reflected that it would have been 'better if they had never come into it', such was their influence in persuading people not to support O'Brien.[65] An alternative contemporary view of these events was left by the Reverend Fitzgerald, the local parish priest at Ballingarry. In his personal recollections published in 1861, he drew on the uprising as a lesson to the people to 'inculcate rational obedience to constituted authorities, to dissuade them from secret societies and every illegal combination, and especially, that they may be never again deluded into any crude and abortive and foolish attempt at rebellion'.[66] No doubt his words were influenced by the revival of republican nationalism in the form of Fenianism after 1858.

One hundred and fifty years after the 1848 rising, views of the Young Irelanders remained divided. During a debate in the *Dáil* in 1998, one member referred to them as 'fine intellectuals [who] were not aggressive in any sense of the word'.[67] A number of historians, however, have characterized the leaders of the 1848 uprising as violent and 'sword-waving'.[68] However, the view of Young Ireland as fanatical revolutionaries who were committed to an armed uprising is retrospective. The path to attempted revolution was not inevitable. As late as 1847, each section of the Repeal movement hoped to win the support of the Irish landed classes for Repeal and they both eschewed violence, including agrarian agitation. They also opposed class conflict, and supported the rights of property. Essentially, the Repeal movement looked back at the Irish parliament that had been granted limited independence under Henry Grattan in 1782, rather than the republican ideals that had been promoted by Theobald Wolfe Tone in 1798 and Robert Emmet in 1803. At heart, Daniel and John O'Connell, William Smith O'Brien and Charles Gavan Duffy were moderates, who abhorred the idea of social revolution and advocated constitutional agitation. It was not until 1848 that the leaders of Young Ireland began to consider seriously the possibility of an armed uprising. Until that year, even John Mitchel, whose subsequent reputation was built on his radicalism, hoped for an alliance with the landlords, whom he believed would be the natural leaders in an independent Ireland. Clearly, the Famine radicalized the politics of some members of Young Ireland, most evidently those of Mitchel, Father Kenyon and Thomas Devin Reilly. They left the Irish Confederation a few weeks before the revolution in France, arguing that a political revolution alone would not solve the social problems of Ireland. Yet the majority of Young Irelanders still preferred to place their hopes in peaceful tactics. The overthrow of Louis-Philippe in February 1848 changed political dynamics within Europe, including Britain and Ireland. The French Revolution provided an example and an opportunity for an uprising; an example because it was virtually bloodless and it was achieved without exessive damage to property; an opportunity because the British government felt vulnerable, both as a consequence of increased Chartist activity and the prospect of having a hostile new government in France. In retrospect, the moderate Duffy blamed 'the disastrous results of the French revolution in Ireland' for precipitating the rising.[69]

Unlike the carnage that had accompanied the 1798 uprising, there were only two casualties in 1848. Significantly, therefore, all the leaders survived and were able to tell, and retell, their stories. The fact that they lived beyond 1848 and had careers that were longer than their lives as revolutionaries also meant that they were evaluated by what they did post-1848 as much as for their activities during that year. Within their lifetimes many of them attained celebrity status, although in some cases it was short-lived. More unusually, the exiled Terence Bellew MacManus achieved more notoriety for his funeral – which was orchestrated by Fenians in Ireland – than for anything he did during his life. Furthermore, many of the nationalists were also writers and poets, and their contribution to the emergence of cultural nationalism and the Irish Literary Revival was immense. W.B. Yeats was a great admirer of John Mitchel's style, power, and energy as a writer, describing him as 'the only Young Ireland politician who had music and personality'.[70] James Joyce regarded James Clarence Mangan as the most talented poet of his generation, claiming that, despite Mangan's short and tragic life, he 'sums up in himself the soul of a country and an era'.[71] Young Ireland, therefore, has been remembered for its contribution to Irish literature as much as its role in Ireland's political development.

The Young Irelander most associated with the 1848 rising is John Mitchel. In the early months of 1848, he, rather than O'Brien, Meagher, or any of the other nationalists, was the popular choice to lead the rebellion. Yet, at this stage, Mitchel had left the Irish Confederation and when the rising took place he was not in the country as he had been transported to Bermuda that May. Consequently, he played no part in its planning or execution. In fact, he only learnt that it had taken place from newspapers smuggled to him by sympathetic guards on board his prison ship.[72] Ironically, therefore, Mitchel, the quintessential rebel, promoter of physical force and implacable enemy of England, was denied the chance to take part in the actual rebellion. His enduring notoriety and zealous reputation was helped by the publication (and frequent reprinting) of his polemical *Jail Journal* in 1854. Its opening sentence was dramatic and uncompromising, thus setting the tone for much of the writing, stating that on 27 May 1848, 'I, John Mitchel, was kidnapped, and carried off from Dublin, in chains, as a convicted "Felon".'[73] The account ended in November 1853 when Mitchel arrived in Brooklyn, where he was met by his mother, following his dramatic escape from Van Diemen's Land.[74] Mitchel consolidated his position as historian of the 1840s with the publication in 1861 of *The Last Conquest of Ireland (Perhaps)*, which included an account of the 1848 rising, clearly based on second-hand reports.[75] Mitchel's influence was still apparent at the beginning of the early twentieth century, not merely amongst adherents of Sinn Féin, including Arthur Griffith; W.B. Yeats quoted Mitchel's condemnation of the Act of Union when Queen Victoria visited Ireland in 1900.[76] Modern historians have portrayed Mitchel's contribution in a more negative way, viewing him as a master of distortion and propaganda. His searing use of language when describing the response of the British government to the Famine has meant that, according to James Donnolly, 'he did more than any other nationalist writer to make the notion of an artificial famine a central part of the public memory of the disaster in Ireland and the Irish diaspora'. Furthermore, the vehemence of his language is often given as one of the reasons why Mitchel 'repels modern revisionist historians'.[77]

Inevitably, the achievements of Young Ireland have been measured against those of Daniel O'Connell, by contemporaries and, subsequently, by historians. Both William Daunt, a close ally of O'Connell, and John O'Connell, Daniel's son and political heir, almost totally ignored the role of Young Ireland and the uprising in their political histories of the 1840s.[78] Historians sympathetic to O'Connell have viewed the accounts written by members of Young Ireland as distorted and 'self-serving'.[79] For the most part, the leaders of Young Ireland acknowledged the achievements of O'Connell, despite disagreeing with his approach.[80] Successive generations of militant nationalists, however, were uneasy with O'Connell's open admiration for the monarchy and the British Empire, while his retreat at Clontarf became a yardstick for measuring his commitment to independence. An early comprehensive account of Young Ireland was produced in New York in 1856 and within a few months it was in its third edition. It lauded the rebellions of 1798 and 1848, but criticized O'Connell's form of constitutional nationalism as a 'distraction'.[81] The author, John Savage, concluded that O'Connell's whole career had been, 'to use the mildest term – a brilliant error'.[82] Clearly, the next generation of revolutionary nationalists were more influenced by Young Ireland than by either of the O'Connells. Moreover, nationalist writers regarded the Fenians and their republican followers as the 'spiritual offspring' of the 1848–ers, rather than the insurgents of 1798.[83]

The increasing appropriation of O'Connell's memory by the Catholic Church was in marked contrast to the Church's public disapproval (and occasional damnation) of other forms of advanced nationalism. Ironically, it was a British politician, William Gladstone, who towards the end of the nineteenth century, attempted to rescue O'Connell's reputation as a nationalist leader by juxtaposing his career with that of Charles Stewart Parnell.[84] In the early 1960s, O'Connell's constitutional approach was reappraised by a new generation of scholars, who were generally approving of his tactics.[85] More recent accounts of O'Connell have focused on the complexity, diversity and inconsistency of his political approach, while placing his achievements in a broader international context.[86] The debate about competing forms of nationalism became even more relevant when set against the backdrop of a fresh wave of republican nationalism in Ireland after 1969. The conflict in Northern Ireland had more in common with the nationalists who had led the risings in 1798, 1848 and 1916 that with the constitutional nationalism of Daniel O'Connell, Isaac Butt or John Redmond. In the late twentieth century, the debates between proponents of physical force tactics and of constitutional methods mirrored those that had taken place in the 1840s and continued into the following century.

For the most part, the historiography of the contribution of women to the Young Ireland movement has been slender. An exception is the work of T.F. O'Sullivan, published in 1944, which dedicates twenty-three pages to the role of various women.[87] More recently, biographies have been published on the lives of Jenny Mitchel and Jane Elgee (Speranza).[88] Following the arrest of Charles Gavan Duffy in July 1848, and the departure of McGee for Scotland, it was the intervention of the women, notably Margaret Callan and 'Speranza', which allowed the *Nation* to continue in production. Ironically, it was as a result of a passionate article by the latter, which amounted to a call to arms, that the *Nation* was suppressed by the British government.[89] The historian Jan Cannavan has suggested that not only did these women help to set the stage for the later generations of Irish republicans and feminists, but they also played an important part in helping to forge a positive view of national identity. Without their involvement, the political debates and cultural nationalism of this period would have been less richly textured.[90]

This book examines 1848 in Ireland in the context of the longer-term development of both nationalist and unionist ideologies in Ireland. In particular, it analyses the emergence of cultural nationalism, which became a powerful force in the late nineteenth century, but which had its intellectual roots in the contributors to the *Nation* newspaper. What is clear is that there were a variety of forms of nationalism, each vying for support throughout the course of the nineteenth century. Following and developing the model provided by Saville, Ireland in 1848 is placed not only within the Paris and London triangle, but also within its wider British, European and transatlantic contexts. Consequently, a key argument of the book is that, even before the rise of the Fenians, as early as 1848 Irish nationalism was being encouraged and assisted by external supporters. A further theme of this publication is to demonstrate the ways in which this support was manifested, how repealers in Ireland responded to it, and how it informed and alarmed the British authorities. The roles of leading Irish political leaders such as Daniel O'Connell, John Mitchel and William Smith O'Brien are considered, but their contribution to the uprising is placed alongside that of lesser-known groups and individuals. In particular, the role of women, Protestants, radicals and that of nationalists who lived outside Ireland is examined. Also, despite the non-sectarian approach of Young Ireland, and its rejection of O'Connell's close relationship with the Catholic Church, the clergy played a pivotal role in the events of 1848. Finally, the response of the British government to the revolutionary threat is re-appraised, especially the use of propaganda and the repressive measures introduced to defeat the rebels. A contention of this book is that the 1848 uprising in Ireland had a major impact on the subsequent development of Irish politics, not only in Ireland but further afield.

It is not possible to understand the events of 1848 in isolation, but they have to be placed in the longer-term struggle for Irish independence, especially the emergence of republican nationalism in Ireland in the 1790s. By the 1840s a new form of nationalism was taking shape in Ireland, which was largely the vision of one man, Daniel O'Connell. Unlike the struggle of fifty years earlier, it eschewed the use of physical force, endorsed links with the British Empire and viewed the Catholic Church as a valuable conduit for promoting its ideals. Chapter 1 commences with a brief look at Daniel O'Connell, the man who was inextricably linked with the nationalist movement in the early decades of the nineteenth century. It examines the key issues that shaped the policies of the Repeal Association after 1840, in particular the emergence of a dynamic group of writers who founded the *Nation* newspaper. The *Nation* embodied a new type of cultural nationalism that had its roots both in European romantic nationalism and in the political debates that accompanied the American War of Independence, the French Revolution and the 1798 uprising in Ireland. Despite the tradition of physical force, the *Nation* and its supporters were firmly committed to achieving independence though the constitutional methods advocated by Daniel O'Connell. The emergence of Young Ireland added a fresh dynamism to the Repeal movement, but its energy, popularity and strict code of behaviour brought it into conflict with O'Connell and his favourite son, John. These differences became more pronounced following O'Connell's retreat at Clontarf in 1843. The seeds, therefore, were sown for a battle, not with the British government, but between the two main sections of the Repeal movement. At the same time, the revival of a nationalist movement that was confident, organized, highly visible, and increasingly Catholic, alarmed a number of Protestants and, while Young Ireland actively sought to win Protestant recruits, a new form of militant loyalism was emerging simultaneously.

Chapter 2 demonstrates the complexity and porous nature of Irish nationalism and shows that, until 1848, neither revolution nor a violent uprising were the aims of any section of the Repeal movement, not even the radical John Mitchel. In 1846, O'Connell had engineered a public debate concerning the so-called 'peace resolutions', as a way of either taming Young Ireland or ousting it from the Repeal Association. The ensuing division in the Repeal movement between Young and Old Ireland was acrimonious. The split was welcomed by the Whig government, which had no majority in parliament, and therefore relied on O'Connell's support. Little was given in return for his cooperation and, like previous administrations, the Whigs continued to undermine Irish nationalism, oscillating between coercion and conciliation. The loss of Young Ireland weakened the Repeal movement, both in Ireland and overseas, and it demonstrated that O'Connell's long reign as the Liberator was almost at an end. More importantly, released from O'Connell's control, a new form of nationalism took root that was more inclusive, egalitarian and independent. The challenge, though, was to rebuild a united movement, which proved to be particularly difficult since the backdrop was a devastating famine. Moreover, despite the endeavours of Young Ireland, under John O'Connell's brief leadership, the identity of the Irish nation was increasingly being aligned with a Catholic Ireland.

The Irish Confederation was formed in January 1847 and Chapter 3 traces the challenges it faced in trying to rebuild a robust, united movement. Resistance was especially strong amongst members of Old Ireland, who, paradoxically, showed their readiness to employ physical force tactics against their former colleagues. By the end of the year, however, divisions were appearing in the Confederation. A small minority led by John Mitchel, angered by the famine polices of the British government and the indifference of many Irish landlords to the suffering of the poor, argued for a social revolution to accompany political independence. Consequently, at the beginning of 1848, the supporters of Repeal appeared to be more divided than ever and thus the likelihood of a revolution was remote. Moreover, despite bearing the main financial burden of famine relief, many landlords remained aloof from the Repeal movement, while the poor were still dealing with the day-to-day realities of starvation.

Chapters 4 and 5 survey the multiple dilemmas faced by the supporters of Young Ireland in the early months of 1848, especially in the wake of the French Revolution. Many Irish nationalists viewed themselves as being part of the revolutionary upheaval in Europe and they became caught up in the general mood of optimism that infected European radicals. From this point, a rising appeared inevitable. Ireland, however, was still in the throes of famine and the desire for political change had to be balanced against the need to feed the poor. Worryingly for the British government, support for the Repealers extended beyond Ireland. Not only was French intervention a possibility, but an alliance between British Chartists and Irish Confederates had taken place at beginning of the year. Support for Young Ireland was also spreading in the United States. Even before the exodus associated with the Famine, Repeal Associations had been established throughout North America. Following the split, they favoured the Irish Confederation over Old Ireland. Young Ireland, in turn, believed that if Irish independence was to be achieved it would probably require external assistance. The British government took the threat of a rising seriously and during the spring and summer intervened – both overtly and covertly – to isolate and weaken Confederate movement. The limited success of these measures resulted in even more repressive action being taken.

Chapter 6 is concerned with the events that led to, and followed, the small and unsuccessful rising in Ballingarry in July 1848. The role of key protagonists and antagonists is examined, in particular how their actions were informed by external events, notably in France and the United States. When it was clear that the rising had failed, the British government commenced a propaganda campaign which characterized the revolt as a farce and its participants as buffoons. The Confederate leaders, however, continued to have widespread respect and sympathy regardless of the unimpressive way in which their revolutionary aspirations had ended. Despite being routed at Ballingarry, the revolutionary threat was not totally extinguished. In 1849, a further uprising took place in Cappoquin in County Waterford. It too was easily defeated. By the end of 1849, as the old order was re-establishing itself throughout Europe, Ireland was coming to terms with not only a failed uprising, but with the loss of almost two million people as a result of mortality and emigration. Chapter 7 explores how the country adjusted to these changes.

After 1848, much political activity in Ireland was directed into the emerging struggle for land reform. Nonetheless, the ideology of the Confederation had taken root, although its strongest advocates were in jail or in exile in France and the United States. Chapter 8 moves the focus of Irish politics outside Ireland. Overseas involvement in the events leading to the 1848 rising was important, even if the much-vaunted Irish Brigade proved to be elusive (both to the authorities and to historians). As the chapter shows, following Ballingarry the centre of Irish nationalism moved outside the island of Ireland. The presence of so many Young Irelanders in the United States, particularly New York, and the transportation of the state prisoners to Van Diemen's Land, extended Irish political debate to three continents.

The transportation of six of the leaders of the Confederation to Van Diemen's Land (where they were later joined by John Mitchel) left Irish nationalists without leadership. Yet their absence from Ireland did not diminish their importance to the nationalist struggle. Their activities continued to be followed by the international press and British propaganda and opprobrium did little to diminish their heroic status. Moreover, the contribution of the Young Irelanders to a wide range of literary, cultural and political issues confirmed the fact that they were a remarkable group of men and women.

On 9 August 1849, the London *Times*, writing about the recent success-ful visit of Queen Victoria to Cork, Dublin and Belfast, averred, 'The Queen's visit to Ireland is the concluding chapter of the history of the Irish rebellion.'[91] Such a positive reading of events disguised the fact that some of the Young Ireland supporters, who were not in prison or exile, attempted a further rising in Waterford. It failed but, according to Joseph Brenan, one of the leaders, the motivation for this 'desperate' revolt was that 'the memories of the famine horrors were searing their hearts and inciting them to vengeance on the murderers of their kith and kin. They were tantalised by seeing the English Queen flouting their land by her presence at a time when her war-ship was conveying her victims to the antipodes – and this to make the world imagine that the Irish were loyal slaves at heart and will.'[92]

Chapter 9 examines the legacy of the *Nation*, Young Ireland and the Irish Confederation. It was considerable. The Fenian Brotherhood, the Home Rule movement, the Land League and the cultural revival of the late nineteenth century all had their roots in the writings or personal involvement of the leaders of the 1848 rising. This extraordinary group of individuals also inspired later generations of male and female radicals and revolutionaries whose prose, poetry, plays and political activities culminated in the Easter Rising. The participants in this rebellion made it clear that they were the latest phase of a revolutionary continuum that had commenced in 1798, resumed in 1848 and 1867, and was completed in 1916. What is apparent when looking at the legacy of the 1848 uprising is that the men and women who played a part in it left an intellectual and ideological legacy that continued to reverberate into the twenty-first century.

In the early years of the twenty-first century, the historiography of the 1848 revolutions has been moving from its traditional focus on parliaments, monarchs, cities, and national leaders to reassessing the impact of the revolutions on the wider populations and the deeper relevance of their political activities, whether peaceful or violent in intent, or revolutionary or otherwise.[93] A further aim of this book, therefore, is to show that the revolutionary experience of Ireland in 1848 was shaped by a number of factors, not simply by the patriotic fervour of the handful of leaders who were most closely associated with it. The varieties of nationalism (and, to a lesser extent, unionism) which emerged after 1848 grew out of the debates that had preceded the 1848 uprising and which continued even after many of the leaders of Young Ireland were in prison, in hiding or in exile. These debates were not restricted to any particular social group, gender, religion or location. Nor were they confined to the island of Ireland. For a short period, largely due to the vision of Young Ireland, Irish nationalism attempted to be truly inclusive, and this remains one of the most remarkable legacies of 1848 in Ireland.

Notes

1 George M. Trevelyan, *British History in the Nineteenth Century, 1782–1901* (London: Longmans, 1922), p. 292; A.J.P. Taylor, *Revolutions and Revolutionaries* (London: Hamish Hamilton, 1978), p. 3.

2 R. Gildea, *Barricades and Borders: Europe 1800–1914* (Oxford: Oxford University Press, 1996), p. 91.

3 Jonathan Sperber, *The European Revolutions, 1848–1851* (Cambridge: Cambridge University Press, 1994), p. 1.

4 Kay Boardman and Christine Kinealy, *1848: The Year the World Turned?* (Newcastle: Cambridge Scholars Press, 2007); Guy Thomson (ed.), *The European Revolutions of 1848 and the Americas* (London: Institute of Latin American Studies, 2002); Benjamin Vicuna McKenna, *The Girondins of Chile: Reminiscences of an Eyewitness* (first pub. 1876; Oxford: Oxford University Press, 2003); Miles Taylor, 'The 1848 Revolutions and the British Empire' in *Past and Present* (vol. 166, 2000), 146–80.

5 For example, William Simpson and Martin Jones, *Europe 1783–1914* (Oxford: Routledge, 2000), p. 156. They described the petition as having 'a touch of comedy about it'.

6 Dieter Dowe, Heinz-Gerhard Haupt, Dieter Langewiesche and Jonathan Sperber (eds), translated by David Higgins, *Europe in 1848: Revolution and Reform* (New York and Oxford: Berghahn, 2001).

7 R.J.W. Evans (ed.), *The Revolutions of Europe 1848–1849* (Oxford: Oxford University Press, 2000), p. ix.

8 Mike Cronin, *A History of Ireland* (Hampshire: Palgrave, 2001), p. 147. His brief account of the 1848 rising contains a number of factual inaccuracies.

9 In a chapter entitled '1848 in European Collective Memory' written in 2000, there is no mention of the Irish experience: see Robert Gildea, '1848 in European Collective Memory' in R.J.W. Evans and Hartmut Pogge Von Strandmann, *The Revolutions in Europe 1848–1849* (Oxford: Oxford University Press, 2000), pp. 207–35. Also, on a reputable website, *Encyclopaedia of 1848 Revolutions*, there is only one small entry concerning Ireland ('Young Ireland' by Richard Davis): http://cscwww.cats.ohiou.edu (accessed 24 January 2005).

10 *The Times*, 1 August 1848, 12 August 1848.

11 Quoted by Pádraig Ó Snodaigh, 'The Impact of the 1848 Insurrection' in Marcus Bourke (ed.), *Tipperary Historical Journal* (1998), 1.

12 D.N. Petler, 'Ireland and France in 1848' in *Irish Historical Studies* (vol. 24, no. 96, 1985), 501.

13 *The Times*, 21 March 1848.

14 Christine Kinealy '"Brethren in Bondage": Chartists, O'Connellites, Young Irelanders and the 1848 Uprising' in Fintan Lane and Donal Ó Drisceoil (eds), *Politics and the Irish Working Class, 1830–1945* (Houndmills: Palgrave Macmillan, 2005), pp. 87–112.

15 *United Irishman*, 18 March 1848.

16 *New York Times*, 8 October 1851.

17 *The Times*, 26 July 1848.

18 Quoted in Petler, 'Ireland and France', 495.

19 *The Times*, 16 August 1848.

20 Ibid., 17 August 1848.

21 Brendan Kiely, *The Waterford Rebels of 1849* (Dublin: Geography Publications, n.d.).

22 *Frazer's Magazine* (November 1848), 593.

23 John O'Connell, *Recollections and Experiences During a Parliamentary*

Career from 1833 to 1848 (London: Richard Bentley, 1849), p. 341.

24 Life of Joseph Brennan [*sic*] by Michael Cavanagh, NLI, MS 3225, n.d., p. 37. Tellingly, Brenan went on to say that 'They were mad because the memories of the Famine horrors were searing their hearts and inciting them to vengeance on the murderers of their kith and kin.'

25 *Irish Times*, 2 August 1948.

26 I am grateful to Carol Quinn, Archivist at Cork University, for clarifying this matter.

27 This is in contrast to the 150th anniversary of the Great Famine in 1995, the 200th anniversary of the 1798 rebellion, and the one hundredth anniversary of the 1916 Rising, each of which attracted considerable media support and the backing of the Irish government.

28 Labhrás Ó Murchú, *Seanad Éireann*, vol. 154, 4 March 1998.

29 Ibid., response by Síle de Valera.

30 Ibid.

31 Press Release by the Office of Public Works, Ireland, 12 July 2004.

32 Denis Gwynn, 'The Rising of 1848' in *Studies* (xxxvii, 1948), p. 7.

33 Ibid.

34 Denis Gwynn, *Young Ireland and 1848* (Cork: Cork University Press, 1949).

35 *Launceston Examiner*, 3 November 1849.

36 Richard Davis, for example, has written extensively on the impact of 1848, especially the role played by William Smith O'Brien: Richard Davis, *Revolutionary Imperialist: William Smith O'Brien* (Dublin: Lilliput Press, 1998).

37 More recently (2000), Robert Sloan has published on O'Brien and the 1848 rising, disagreeing with some of Davis's conclusions. Brendan Ó Cathaoir published a fine biography of John Blake Dillon in 1990, and more recently has edited the diary of a lesser-known Young Irelander, Charles Hart. In 2008, David A. Wilson published the first volume of an excellent biography of Thomas D'Arcy McGee.

38 Exceptions are research by a Japanese scholar, Takashi Koseki, who published a paper in 1992, mostly relating to the Dublin clubs, and Gary Owens, who wrote a chapter on the clubs, which adopted a more national approach, in 2001.

39 Sperber, *The European Revolutions*, p. 1.

40 John Belchem, 'Nationalism, Republicanism and Exile: Irish Emigrants and the Revolution of 1848' in *Past and Present* (vol. 146, 1995), 103–35.

41 Ibid., 135.

42 John Saville, *1848: The British State and the Chartist Movement* (Cambridge: Cambridge University Press, 1990).

43 Ibid., p. 1.

44 Saville is one of the few historians to explore this alliance.

45 Saville, *1848*, p. 72.

46 Belchem, 'Nationalism, Republicanism and Exile'.

47 Leslie Mitchell, 'Britain's Reaction to the Revolutions' in Evans and Von Strandmann, *The Revolutions in Europe*, p. 91.

48 Mitchell, 'Britain's Reaction', p. 94

49 R.J.W. Evans, 'Liberalism, Nationalism and the Coming of the Revolutions' in Evans and Von Strandmann, *The Revolutions in Europe*, p. 83.

50 Paul Pickering, *Chartism and the Chartists in Manchester and Salford* (Houndmills: Palgrave, 1995); Siobhán Kinealy, *1848 in Liverpool*, unpublished undergraduate dissertation, presented to Department of History, Essex University, 2007.
51 Evans and Von Strandmann, *The Revolutions in Europe*, p. 20.
52 Sperber, *The European Revolutions*, p. 242.
53 *The Irish American*, 7 October 1849.
54 Review in *The United States Magazine and Democratic Review* (vol. xxvi, no. cxl, February 1850), 133–42.
55 For example, Richard Davis (ed.), *'To Solitude Consigned': The Tasmanian Journal of William Smith O'Brien, 1849–1853* (Sydney: The Crossing Press, 1995).
56 Sir Charles Gavan Duffy, *Four Years of Irish History 1845–1849, Being a Sequel to 'Young Ireland'* (London and New York: Cassell, Petter, Galpin & Co, 1883).
57 Ibid., p. v. These documents include the minutes and letters of the Irish Confederation, which he eventually deposited in the Royal Irish Academy in Dublin. In 1853, Duffy printed a request in the *Nation* for documents concerning the uprising: ibid., p. vi.
58 Narrative of MacManus and O'Gorman, NLI, MS 5886, 23 May 1881.
59 Their personal accounts are held in the National Library of Ireland (NLI).
60 In 1856, Jeremiah O'Donovan Rossa (1831–1915) founded the Phoenix Society in Skibbereen, Co. Cork, which was a literary and political group. Rossa, *Rossa's Recollections 1838–1898: Memories of an Irish Revolutionary*, with an Introduction by Seán Ó Lúing (Shannon: Irish University Press, 1972), pp. 132–4.
61 T.C. Luby, *The Life and Times of Daniel O'Connell* (Glasgow: Cameron, Ferguson and Company, 1872).
62 Luby first published his reminiscences of 1848 in the *Irish Nation* (published by John Devoy in New York) between January and April 1882.
63 For example, Meagher and Duffy disagreed in their accounts about who was elected to the Council of Five in 1848.
64 For more on the role of the Catholic clergy see Denis Gwynn, 'The Priests and Young Ireland in 1848' in *Irish Ecclesiastical Record* (vol. lxx no. 38), 590–609.
65 Narratives of 1848, by John O'Mahoney, NLI, MS 7977.
66 Rev. P. Fitzgerald PP, *Personal Recollections of Insurrection at Ballingarry in July, 1848* (Dublin, 1861). Fitzgerald republished his narrative and included an account based on a diary by some of the leaders, including Meagher, written as when in hiding. They gave their account to Father O'Carrol who left it to Father Philip Fitzgerald, the parish priest in Ballingarry.
67 L. Ó Murchú, *Seanad Éireann*, vol. 154, 4 March 1998.
68 K. Theodore Hoppen, *Elections, Politics and Society in Ireland 1832–1885* (Oxford: Clarendon Press, 1984), p. 16.
69 Charles Gavan Duffy, *Young Ireland: A Fragment of Irish History. Irish People's Edition* (Dublin: M.H. Gill, 1884–87, 2 vols), vol. ii, p. 223.
70 Ibid., p. viii; quoted from *The Autobiography of William Butler Yeats* (New York: McMullen Books, 1953). Yeats met Duffy in the 1890s in London.

71 Quoted in Joy Melville, *Mother of Oscar: The Life of Jane Francesca Wilde* (Edinburgh: John Murray, 1994), p. 33.

72 John Mitchel, *Jail Journal* (facsimile of 1913 edition, published by Gill and Son, Dublin, reprinted with critical introduction by Thomas Flanagan, Dublin: University Press of Ireland, 1982). *Jail Journal* first appeared serially in the *Citizen* (New York) between January and August 1854.

73 *Jail Journal*, p. xv.

74 Ibid., p. 363.

75 John Mitchel, *The Last Conquest of Ireland (Perhaps)* (Glasgow: R and T. Washbourne, 1861).

76 John Kelly, *Collected Letters of Yeats* (Oxford: Oxford University Press, 1986), p. 503.

77 James S. Donnolly, *The Great Irish Potato Famine* (Gloucestershire: Sutton, 2001), p. 18.

78 For example, William O'Neill Daunt, Esquire, *Personal Recollections of the Late Daniel O'Connell MP* (London: Chapman and Hall, 1848, 2 vols).

79 See, for example, the articles by Maurice R. O'Connell (a descendant of O'Connell) in *O'Connell, Young Ireland, and Violence* (Bronx: Fordham University Press, 1972); Raymond Moley, *Nationalism without Violence: an Essay* (New York: Fordham University Press, 1974).

80 An exception was Father Kenyon who was vitriolic in his attacks on O'Connell; see Christine Kinealy, *Lives of Victorian Political Figures: Daniel O'Connell* (London: Pickering and Chatto, 2007). Also, W.J. Fitzpatrick (ed.), *Correspondence of Daniel O'Connell* (London: John Murray, 1888); Arthur Houston, *Daniel O'Connell: His Early Life and Journal 1795–1802* (London: s.n., 1906); Robert Dunlop, *Daniel O'Connell* (London: Putnam, 1900), amongst others.

81 John Savage, *'98 and '48: The Modern Revolutionary History and Literature of Ireland* (New York: J.B. Aldem, 1884).

82 Ibid., p. xiii.

83 A. Newman, *Why the Manchester Martyrs Died* (Dublin: Whelan and Son, 1915).

84 W.E. Gladstone, 'Daniel O'Connell' in James Knowles (ed.), *The Nineteenth Century: A Monthly Review*, (vol. xxv, January to June 1889, New York and London: Kegan, Paul, Trench & Co.), 149–68.

85 For example, A. Macintyre, *The Liberator: Daniel O'Connell and the Irish Party 1830–1847* (London: H. Hamilton, 1966); K.B. Nowlan, *The Politics of Repeal: A Study in the Relations Between Great Britain and Ireland, 1841–50* (London: Routledge and Kegan Paul, 1965), and for later, sympathetic, accounts, see, Maurice O'Connell, Mary Robinson and James Lydon, amongst others.

86 Kinealy, *Lives of Victorian Political Figures*.

87 T.F. O'Sullivan, *The Young Irelanders* (2nd edn, Tralee: The Kerryman, 1945), pp. 107–30.

88 Melville, *Mother of Oscar*; Rebecca O'Conner, *Jenny Mitchel: Young Irelander: A Biography* (Tucson, Arizona: O'Conner Trust, 1988).

89 Christine Kinealy, 'Invisible Nationalists' in Boardman and Kinealy, *1848: The Year the World Turned?*, pp. 131–9.

90 Jan Cannavan, 'Revolution in Ireland, Evolution in Women's Rights:

Irishwomen in 1798 and 1848' in Louise Ryan and Margaret Ward (eds), *Irish Women and Nationalism: Soldiers, New Women and Wicked Hags* (Dublin: Irish Academic Press, 2004).
91 *The Times*, 9 August 1848.
92 Cavanagh, Life of Joseph Brennan, pp. 37–8.
93 Sperber, *The European Revolutions*, pp. 2–3.

1

'Ourselves alone': Repeal, 1840–45

Political debate in Ireland in the first half of the nineteenth century was dominated by the imposing figure of Daniel O'Connell (1775–1847), a Catholic barrister from County Kerry. For three decades, he controlled Irish nationalist politics and his activities had significant repercussions not only on British political developments, but also within Europe and the United States. O'Connell used his oratorical and legal skills to maximum advantage within the hostile climate of Westminster, outlasting and outwitting a number of British political opponents. The timing of his birth was significant, enabling him to benefit from the relaxation of the Penal Laws in the late eighteenth century, in particular those reforms which allowed Catholics the right to vote, inherit land and join the professions. Consequently, he was one of the first Catholics to be called to the Irish bar. As a young man, he had been governed by an Irish parliament located in Dublin. In 1782, that parliament, under the leadership of Henry Grattan, had been granted more legislative independence from the British one. Although Grattan's parliament was exclusively Protestant, landlord-dominated, and of short duration (1782–1800), it provided the inspiration for much of O'Connell's subsequent views on Irish independence.

Despite O'Connell's fiery rhetoric, he resisted the use of physical force, hoping to bring about major political change by peaceful means. During the 1798 uprising, he opposed the United Irishmen, even joining the yeomanry in Dublin to make it clear that he did not support violent upheaval.[1] This experience shaped his subsequently political philosophy; he believed that if Irish people were to achieve self-government, they had to work within the limits of the law and the constitution.[2] Throughout the remainder of his life, therefore, he favoured a form of limited independence based on Grattan's Parliament, rather than the radical nationalism associated with Theobald Wolfe Tone and Robert Emmet. Although O'Connell's greatest triumph lay in marshalling grassroots support in Ireland to challenge the British government, he remained a constitutionalist who preferred to work with, rather

than against, the authorities. While he advocated social reform, his support
was selective and he frequently chose to ally with the Whigs (or Liberals)
rather than the radicals in British politics.[3]

O'Connell's most successful political struggle was in relation to
Catholic Emancipation, that is, the demand for Catholics to sit in parliament. Since 1801 the imperial parliament at Westminster had included
representatives from Ireland, but continuity had been maintained with the
exclusion of Catholic MPs. In 1823 O'Connell founded the Catholic
Association to rally Irish opinion in support of Emancipation. His tactics
were non-violent, based on the mass mobilization of a predominantly
agricultural society. Significantly, this movement was financed through
the collection of a weekly 'rent' that was paid for by his sympathizers, rich
and poor alike. Between 1826 and 1829, over £35,000 was raised in this
way, leading to accusations by his enemies that O'Connell was exploiting
the Irish poor.[4] In reality, the main contributors were the Catholic middle
classes, who had most to gain from Emancipation.[5]

In 1829, fearing civil war, the British government conceded
Emancipation. The relevant legislation was steered through parliament
by a reluctant Duke of Wellington, who was supported by Robert Peel.
Their intervention lost them personal support and created lasting bitterness within the Tory Party. Wellington was later to confide in Peel that
supporting Emancipation was 'the most painful act of my long life, as
well as yours'.[6] The achievement of the Catholic Association was
remarkable: it had transformed an illiterate, peasant people into a disciplined extra-parliamentary force that was confident enough to challenge
– and triumph over – the British state. O'Connell was the main beneficiary of this victory and the success earned him the title 'the Liberator'
in Ireland, while gaining him admiration throughout Europe and the
United States. Throughout his later life he often referred to his foremost
achievement, telling children, 'Do you know, my young friends, it was
I who emancipated you?', while admonishing Irish opponents with the
observation, 'Only for me, he would not have been emancipated.'[7]
However, Catholic Emancipation marked the apogee of O'Connell's
political career and his subsequent achievements were diminished by his
arrogance, political misjudgements and personal opportunism. Although
the rest of his career appeared to be devoted to the abolition of the Act
of Union, he intermittently used Repeal as a political bargaining tool.
In 1835 and again in 1846, he demonstrated that he was willing to
abandon this aspiration in return for increased personal influence and
the vague aspiration of winning 'justice for Ireland', which he defined
as being reforms that would reconcile Catholic opinion to being part of
the United Kingdom.[8]

Emancipation brought O'Connell and his supporters into mainstream
British parliamentary politics. At the same time, it disenfranchised
40–shilling freeholders – Irish men who met the property qualifications to

vote in the county and parliamentary elections – who were predominantly
Catholic. Initially, it appeared that O'Connell would use Westminster as
a platform to bring about a Repeal of the Union. In 1830, he wrote a
series of addresses to the people of Ireland, inviting the nation to combine
in order to return the domestic legislature, and he spoke on Repeal at
several meetings.[9] In that year, there were successful revolutions in France
and Belgium, and the example of using force to achieve political ends
encouraged some of O'Connell's followers to offer to take up arms at that
point to win Repeal.[10] O'Connell, encouraged by the success of peaceful
tactics in winning Emancipation, continued to believe that independence
could be achieved through constitutional methods alone. In 1834, he
introduced the Repeal question in the House of Commons, although even
his supporters felt it was not one of his better speeches, and the debate
was defeated by 523 votes to thirty-eight. Anticipating the tactics subsequently used by the British Chartists, he also presented a petition
containing half a million signatures in favour of Repeal.[11] In the 1835
General Election, O'Connell made Repeal the focus of his campaign,
despite the fact that the majority of Irish MPs continued to support the
Union. At this point, his strategy changed and he used his high profile and
political influence to win 'justice for Ireland', that is, concessions to Irish
Catholics that would make political union with Britain more acceptable.
To this end, he consented to the Lichfield House Compact by which he
promised support to the Whig Party.[12] The ambivalence of his political
stance had been clear as early as 1836 when he had spoken in favour of
the Union, arguing that Irish people were 'ready to become a portion of
the Empire, provided they be made so in reality, and not in name alone;
they are ready to become a kind of West Briton, if made so in benefits and
justice'.[13] He even stated that he was 'opposed to Repeal if justice is done
to Ireland'.[14] By allying so publicly with the British Whig Party,
O'Connell cemented his long-standing and implacable opposition to Sir
Robert Peel and the Tory Party, but he also relegated Repeal to the background of Irish political demands. The collaboration did bring about
some benefits, notably the softening of the relationship between the traditional symbol of the Protestant Ascendancy, Dublin Castle, and the
Catholic population. One consequence was that a number of Catholics
were appointed as magistrates.[15] Overall, the alliance yielded little lasting
benefit for Ireland or the Repeal movement. O'Connell later described this
phase to a close confidant as a 'six years experiment of trying to bring
"Imperial Justice to Ireland"; an experiment in working with the government that failed'.[16]

In 1840, in a further reversal of strategy, O'Connell founded the Loyal
National Repeal Association, which sought a Repeal of the Act of Union
of 1800. The title of the new Association reflected the paradox of
O'Connell's nationalism; namely, that he wanted independence for
Ireland within an imperial context and with links to the British monarchy

being maintained. His timing was deliberate; he formed the Association in
July 1840, in the wake of an attempt by Lord Stanley to limit the Irish
franchise, an action that had outraged Irish voters.[17] O'Connell, therefore, justified renewing the Repeal campaign on the grounds that equality
with Britain had been denied to the Irish voters.[18] In 1840 also, there was
a possibility of war between England and France – which O'Connell
hoped might play into his hands and help Repeal.[19] Like the Catholic
Association, the Repeal Association was organized on a national level,
with its headquarters in Dublin. Unlike many of his contemporaries,
O'Connell understood the value of imagery and historical symbolism,
creating memorabilia to promote the movement, including a Repeal
uniform and Repeal buttons. He also realized the value of publicity and
propaganda, and helped found a newspaper, the *Pilot*, to promote the
Repeal movement. Financial security was always a priority for O'Connell
and a large part of the new Association's income was derived from weekly
donations, in the form of 'Repeal Rent'. The purpose of the rent was two-
fold: it created an income for O'Connell and paid for the employment of
permanent administrative officers, while giving the subscribers a direct
stake in the movement. O'Connell had also created the 'O'Connell
Tribute', which was a fund collected annually not only to pay for election
expenses and petitions, but also for the upkeep of O'Connell's establish-
ments in Dublin, London and Kerry.[20] The fact that his lavish lifestyle
was paid for by the Irish poor was continually criticized in the hostile
sections of the British and Irish press. In this way also, his personal
fortunes became inextricably linked with those of the struggle for independence. Nonetheless, the creation of an efficient national organization
in a predominantly rural, illiterate society was one of O'Connell's greatest achievements, and it provided a model for other large political
organizations, including the British Anti-Corn Law League.[21] His tactic of
politically empowering deprived peoples was pioneering and won the
admiration of both radicals and liberals throughout Europe.[22] In reality,
the unity of Repeal movement was at times illusory, reflecting the lack of
homogeneity amongst the Irish population, especially Irish Catholics.[23] A
further achievement of O'Connell, therefore, was to make the disparate
social groups and their demands appear to be unified.

The return in 1841 of a Tory government led by Sir Robert Peel, a political and personal foe of O'Connell and an implacable enemy of Irish
independence, provided a fresh focus for Repeal agitation. However,
despite holding weekly meetings at the Corn Exchange in Dublin and
hosting a programme of lectures in Ireland and Britain, the new Repeal
movement did not have the force or vigour that it had possessed ten years
earlier. By the end of the year, the wife of a landowner in County
Wicklow, who deplored the belligerent tactics of Repealers, applauded the
impact of the new Tory government, writing in her diary:

This vigorous new government has brought peace already, agitation is now such a mere farce that it soon must cease altogether, everyone appearing tired of it, the rent too has been a perfect failure, smaller sums than usual collected in the most *Repealing* neighbourhoods, none in some places, in others a refusal to allow of it. There is a great change coming over the Irish minds most certainly.[24]

By 1842, O'Connell was privately admitting that the Repeal Association was suffering from apathy and needed to be energized.[25] The required vitality was provided by a group of young intellectuals of mixed religious origins who founded a new nationalist newspaper, the *Nation*.

The *Nation*

The origin of the *Nation* resulted from collaboration between three young writers: Thomas Davis, Charles Gavan Duffy and John Blake Dillon. In 1841, they decided to establish a newspaper that would support O'Connell's Repeal movement, while promoting the idea of the Irish nation. The men had diverse backgrounds: Davis was a Protestant lawyer from County Cork; Duffy was a Catholic journalist from County Monaghan, who had previously edited the *Belfast Vindicator*; and Dillon was a Catholic lawyer from County Mayo, who had initially trained for the priesthood at Maynooth College, and then studied at Trinity College. They were all members of the Repeal Association, and Davis and Dillon were members of its General Committee, which ran the weekly meetings. They each admired O'Connell,[26] but they disliked the way in which he harangued those who did not support him, especially when his scorn was directed against Protestants.[27] A primary aim of the new paper was to promote education and conciliation within Ireland, in an attempt to bring all classes and denominations together. In particular, it endeavoured to bring Ulster Protestants into the Repeal movement. From the outset, therefore, the *Nation* adopted an inclusive approach to Irish nationalism, the aim of its editors being to 'carry with us all the elements of a nation, its gentry and merchants, as well as its artisans and peasantry'.[28]

The *Nation* first appeared on 15 October 1842 and weekly thereafter. Duffy was the proprietor, and Davis its main political editor. Dillon and Davis had already, unsuccessfully, tried their hands at journalism, but Duffy had been successful in running the *Vindicator*, the first Catholic newspaper in Belfast. The three men were discouraged by other national-ist journalists from attempting the new venture, as the Repeal movement was already represented by the *Freeman's Journal* and the *Pilot*, and an additional nationalist journal was seen as unnecessary.[29] The Prospectus of the *Nation* countered such criticisms by pointing out that, 'The neces-sities of the country seem to demand a journal able to aid and organize the new movement going on amongst us ... Such a journal should be free from the quarrels, the interests, the wrongs and even the gratitude of the past. It should be free to apply its strength where it seems best; free to praise; free to censure, unshackled by sect or party.'[30] A policy of the new paper was not to engage with the group's opponents in its columns, preferring to pursue a policy of positive patriotism.[31] While Repeal was the main political focus of the *Nation*, it also supported social change in Ireland, but by gradual means. The editors believed that the economic transformation of Ireland would follow political independence as, 'Repeal would abolish absenteeism and foreign taxation, and would give Irish offices and rewards to Irishmen ... would secure peasants from oppression ... and, with justice, would bring order, industry and riches.'[32]

One of the achievements of the *Nation* was to successfully fuse political and cultural issues, thus bringing it closer to the romantic nationalism of many European radicals.[33] The paper aspired to be not merely the champion of the 'National Party', but also the voice of the 'Literary Party'.[34] The founders of the *Nation* were united by their passion for Ireland, particularly its history and culture, and they sought to familiarize Irish people with their history and literary achievements through the commissioning of a 'Library of Ireland', which made these texts cheaply available.[35] They also decided that only books about Ireland or the Irish were to be reviewed. To make both the *Nation* and other Irish publications generally available, they established Repeal Reading Rooms throughout the country.[36] A distinctive feature of the paper was the 'Poet's Corner', which proved universally popular. The songs and ballads that appeared were reprinted as a brochure, five months after the *Nation*'s first appearance. The instant success of the publication surprised even the editors. A second edition appeared a few months later, and both were reprinted as *The Spirit of the Nation*.[37] Unlike O'Connell, who on utilitarian grounds supported the decline of the Irish language, Davis recognized the place of language in forging cultural and political identity.[38] The fact that an English language newspaper was a tool for promoting Irish culture and Irish independence in a county where a large portion of the population were Irish speaking and illiterate demonstrated the complexity of Irish nationalism and Irish society in the 1840s.

The *Nation* brought together an eclectic collection of people, mainly professionals and students, who wrote for the paper in their spare time. Apart from sharing political convictions, the main writers became close friends, meeting for a weekly supper and socialising together.[39] Contributors included members of the discontented Protestant middle classes and the upwardly mobile Catholic middle classes. The *Nation* embraced poets and romantics, intellectuals, disgruntled Catholic priests, political radicals and social conservatives. Daniel O'Connell (anonymously) and his sons, John and Maurice, were occasional contributors during the early years of the *Nation*'s existence. John later explained that he had only contributed three poems that were 'prosaic and heavy'.[40] While the majority of the writers were drawn from the professional classes, a small number were from poor backgrounds, notably the talented poet James Clarence Mangan who died in poverty in 1849, from a combination of malnutrition and cholera.[41] A lesser- known, but equally impoverished poet was John de Jean Frazer, originally an artisan from King's County. He was a Presbyterian who in his youth had been an Orangeman, before becoming an impassioned nationalist.[42] Unusually, the regular contributors to the paper were paid generously, which was possible due to the high sales that the paper enjoyed. However, articles in the *Nation* were published either anonymously or under a pen-name although, occasionally, the writers' initials were used.[43] The most influential and respected contributor to the *Nation* was Thomas Davis, and his premature death in 1845 left a vacuum that no single person could fill.

Despite the extensive array of talent that was involved in the early issues of the *Nation*, according to Duffy, 'Among the new agencies which the *Nation* called into play, one subtle force was still wanting, the fertile brain and passionate soul of woman.'[44] This situation changed dramatically after 1845 when the influx of new writers included a high proportion of women. Before then, the female authors included Mrs Ellen Fitzsimons, who was Daniel O'Connell's eldest daughter. She contributed a small number of poems, writing as 'L.M. F.'.[45] A number of political articles were provided by Margaret Callan (née Hughes) whom Duffy referred to as the foreign correspondent for the *Nation* in 1843.[46] Callan was Duffy's cousin and the wife of Dr J.B. Callan, a Dublin apothecary.[47] Although the 'woman's question' was occasionally discussed in the paper, for the most part the focus of the female writers was on Repeal and related issues.[48]

The popularity of the *Nation* was instant. On the first day of publication, it sold out its print run of 12,000 copies and it quickly became the best-selling newspaper in Ireland, with an estimated readership of over one million people.[49] These sales were impressive in a country that possessed a small middle class and contained a large number of people surviving at subsistence level.[50] The timing of the launch of the *Nation* in October 1842 was propitious for O'Connell as the Repeal movement was languishing, with only twenty Repeal candidates being returned in the 1841 General Election.[51] Even his appointment as Lord Mayor of Dublin at the end of 1841 (the first Catholic one since the seventeenth century) was predominantly remarkable for its symbolic significance. The appearance of new journal, therefore, not only energized the political debate, but it attracted a new generation of young intellectuals to the nationalist cause. Thus the *Nation* was not only an important tool in promoting the history, culture and traditions of the nation of Ireland; it also broadened support for Repeal. Significantly, following its establishment, the Repeal movement enjoyed a resurgence in popularity.

The *Nation*'s success alarmed conservative opinion and the unionist press alike. The *Quarterly Review* described its literary contents as 'perilous and mischievous because they were the actual convictions of the writers'.[52] *The Times* opined that O'Connell's activities were 'as nothing compared to the fervour of rebellion which breathed in every page of these verses'.[53] The government realized the propaganda value for the Repeal movement in being supported by a strong nationalist press, especially one controlled by 'young men of talent'. The Lord Lieutenant, therefore, sought out people willing to condemn Repeal, 'to be applied in daily doses, and in the most pungent form, and this can only be done in the columns of a newspaper'.[54] The covert propaganda campaign commenced by the British government intensified as the popularity of the *Nation* increased. However, it was not just opponents of Repeal who disliked the journal's popularity. The youth of its contributors – who were initially all under thirty – led some of the older members of the Repeal movement to refer to them scornfully as 'Young Ireland'. Although both Davis and Duffy disliked this appellation, by 1845 the supporters of the *Nation* were using this name to describe themselves.[55] In contrast, close allies of O'Connell were increasingly referred to as 'Old Ireland', suggesting that there were two distinct groupings within the Repeal movement.[56] Following the public split in the Repeal Association in 1846, the term 'Young Ireland' was again used as a way of ridiculing the youthful group of intellectuals associated with the *Nation*.[57]

The political inspiration for Young Ireland lay in events both within and outside Ireland. Thomas Davis particularly admired the writings of the French historians Jules Michelet, Augustin Thierry and Jean de Sismondi.[58] Thierry, in turn, was an admirer of Ireland and had written enthusiastically about its history and culture. He had championed the French Revolutions of 1789 and 1830 and much of his work was concerned with how nations could achieve free government and independent parliament.[59] The Young Ireland movement also had roots in romantic nationalist movements in Europe, especially in Germany and Italy with their emphasis on 'cultural rather than constitutional distinctiveness; group or collective rather than individual rights, sympathies and antipathies rather than forms and institutions as the substance of political independence'.[60] The Young Italy movement (*Giovine Italia*) had been formed in 1831 by Giuseppe Mazzini. Nobody aged over forty was allowed to join. The statutes of the movement declared that, 'Young Italy is a brotherhood of Italians who believe in a law of Progress and Duty, and are convinced that Italy is destined to become one nation ... one independent sovereign nation of free men and equals.'[61] Within a year of its foundation, Young Italy had become the most influential nationalist organization in Italy, helped by the circulation of its newspaper, *La Giovine Italia*.[62] Mazzini believed that his movement was an international rather than a national one and he encouraged the formation of similar groups such as Young Switzerland and Young Germany. In 1834, he founded Young Europe, which was 'designed to help any people rising against their rulers to overthrow the government'.[63] Ireland, however, was not included in this pan-European movement, Mazzini arguing that the Irish were not a nation. Nonetheless, he admired O'Connell and his achievement in winning Catholic Emancipation.[64] Yet, as late as 1847 Mazzini criticized Repeal on the grounds that Irish people did not 'plead for any distinctive principle of life or system of legislation derived from native peculiarities or contrasting radically with English wants and wishes'.[65] His reasons for this stance probably had more to do with his desire not to affront the British government as he lived in exile in London between 1837 and 1848.[66] While there were a number of parallels between Young Ireland and Young Italy, Davis and Duffy believed that O'Connell's Repeal movement was politically more sophisticated than the relatively immature nationality movement in Italy.[67]

While European nationalists may have influenced Young Ireland, its inspiration also lay within Ireland's history. O'Connell's success in winning Catholic Emancipation had encouraged a generation of Catholics into believing that it was possible to achieve a political and moral victory against the British state. Moreover, the men and women who established and sustained the *Nation* were too young to remember the brutality of the 1798 uprising. According to Thomas Francis Meagher, who joined the movement in 1845, the radicalism of his colleagues was derived 'from the blood which drenched the scaffolds of 1798'.[68] He was also impressed by Belgium, which had won its independence from the Netherlands in 1830 and which he had visited during his Continental Tour.[69] Ironically, Belgian independence had only been achieved through the intervention of British ministers, notably the Duke of Wellington and Lord Palmerston, and the revolutionary struggle had been approved of by O'Connell.[70]

If Irish independence drew inspiration from European nationalism, European radicals, in turn, were encouraged by Ireland's example. O'Connell in particular was admired for winning Catholic Emancipation in 1829 and the following year three Belgian deputies voted to make him king of their newly independent state.[71] His career was followed closely in Germany, especially the Rhemish provinces, and his victories against the British government were reported and widely admired.[72] O'Connell's notoriety had spread to the autocratic Hapsburg Empire. The journalist Karel Havlicek, a leader of the Czech independence movement, believed that there were many parallels between Ireland and the situation in Bohemia. He was a 'passionate disciple of Daniel O'Connell ... [and] had recently electrified the public by using the Repeal movement as a transparent cover for criticism of Austrian constitutional arrangements and the Irish people as exemplar for the revival of oppressed and forgotten nations'.[73] Havelick believed that the Repeal movement was the most progressive and successful in Europe and, in 1847, he published a series of articles entitled 'Daniel O'Connell' in his radical paper *Prazske*

Noviny.[74] Young Ireland also had its admirers outside Ireland. The appearance of the *Nation* was welcomed by democrats and nationalists throughout Europe and even further afield and its format was emulated by radicals in France (*La Nation*), Italy (*La Nazione*), Buenos Aires (*La Nación*) and and it was read in North America and Australia.[75]

In the early months of 1843 there was a palpable political awakening in Ireland. Encouraged by the success of the *Nation* and the popularity of the Young Ireland group, O'Connell decided to introduce the Repeal question into Dublin Corporation, where it was endorsed, an action that was copied by other corporations in the provinces of Connaught, Leinster and Munster. Members of the middle class, landlords, Ulster Protestants, Catholic bishops and priests, joined the Repeal Association.[76] There was also a substantial influx of students, including R.D. Williams, who wrote in the *Nation* as 'Shamrock'.[77] The number of Repealers increased so rapidly that the Corn Exchange in Dublin became too small for their meetings. Consequently, O'Connell decided to build a hall especially for Repeal meetings that could hold 5,000 people.[78] The new meeting place, named Conciliation Hall, opened within a few months and one of the first things that O'Connell did was to call for cheers for Young Ireland.[79] O'Connell also announced that he would hold two weekly meetings in Dublin instead of one, and that public meetings would be held in every county in Ireland, commencing with Leinster and Munster.[80] The weekly income from the Repeal Rent, which was a barometer of public support, increased substantially: in 1842, it averaged from £60 to £700 a week, but in a single week at the beginning of 1843, it had reached £2,200.[81]

Under the influence of Young Ireland, the visual appearance of the Repeal Association changed, with Irish poetry and history adorning both the walls of Conciliation Hall and the previously plain membership cards of the Association.[82] O'Connell seemed revitalised by the new spirit of activity and proposed the creation of a Council of Three Hundred, the members to be selected not by election (which would have been illegal) but through the endorsement of their neighbours. The historical symbolism was important: in 1782 a Convention in Dungannon, attended by 300 delegates, had drawn up a programme asserting the legislative independence of Ireland. Shortly afterwards Ireland had achieved limited political autonomy. O'Connell hoped that his Council would provide the framework for a parliament in Dublin, which might be recognized by the Queen.[83] Due to the resurgence in Repeal activities, O'Connell felt confident enough to declare 1843 to be the 'Repeal Year', which would result in an Irish parliament sitting in Dublin again.[84]

Protestants

The leaders of the 1798 uprising had aspired to remove religion from Irish politics but, in the following decades, the demand for independence appeared to be moving closer to Catholicism. The winning of Catholic Emancipation in 1829 alarmed many conservative Protestants, especially as it was followed by the demand for Repeal. Although O'Connell claimed that he wanted the abolition of all sectarian divisions, during his career he did little personally to reassure Protestants that Irish independence would not result in the emergence of a Catholic Ascendancy.[85] Significantly also, in both the campaigns for Emancipation and for Repeal, O'Connell used the Catholic clergy as his local organizers and the churches as his campaign centres. While O'Connell's alliance with the Whigs in the 1830s yielded few significant benefits for Catholic Ireland, it brought about enough changes to alarm conservative Protestants, who believed that their traditional rights were being eroded. The founding of the Repeal Association did little to reassure them, particularly as Catholic priests were given a prominent position within the organization, O'Connell telling his campaign managers to 'be sure to have the approval of the Catholic clergy in every place you move to'.[86] His language, so often intemperate, was frequently misleading and insensitive to Protestant opinions. At the commencement of the Repeal campaign in 1840, he stated that, 'The Catholic Church is a national church, and if the people rally with me, they will have a nation for the church.'[87]

Although O'Connell frequently toured the country promoting Repeal, he rarely included Ulster in his schedule. In January 1841, however, at the invitation of the Belfast Repealers, O'Connell visited the north. Some Orangemen reacted angrily, threatening violence if he should 'invade' Ulster.[88] A poster in Lisburn warned that if O'Connell and his Repealers disturbed the peace 'we will treat them to a thunder of northern Repeal'.[89] O'Connell avoided bloodshed during his journey north by lying about his travel plans: he ordered post horses for 18 January but, under an assumed name, actually travelled to Belfast on 16 January. In Belfast, O'Connell spoke at an open air meeting, a dinner and a temperance soirée, the latter being hosted by 450 ladies of various religions. A small number of liberal Protestants attended the meetings but, overwhelmingly, his audience was Catholic.[90] Although local Orangemen attempted to disrupt these arrangements, serious violence was prevented by the presence of police and over 2,000 extra troops.[91] Nevertheless, wherever he spoke, stones were hurled at him, and the homes of Repealers were stoned.[92] Anger at O'Connell's visit was inflamed by Reverend Dr Henry Cooke, an evangelical minister in Belfast. He published a pamphlet addressed to O'Connell in which he stated, 'I believe you are a great bad man, engaged in a great bad cause.' He challenged O'Connell to a public debate on the question of Repeal.[93] O'Connell refused, but suggested that Cooke, 'the cock of the North', should come to Dublin to debate with him there.[94] Regardless of the banter, these reactions to O'Connell's visit suggested that there was a new spirit of Protestant militancy that associated Repeal with Catholicism, and could tolerate neither. Moreover, economic argu-

ments were marshalled to support political ones. Cooke and his supporters were attributing the prosperity of Belfast and other towns in Ulster to
the Union, while warning that a predominantly Catholic parliament based
in Dublin would be disastrous both politically and economically.[95]

O'Connell's inclusive approach to Repeal was short lived, thus allowing both him and the Repeal Association to become increasingly identified
with the hopes and aspirations of Catholic Ireland.[96] This led Duffy to
caution that a 'sectarian tone' was becoming apparent in Conciliation
Hall.[97] In 1842, O'Connell and his son John's ambivalent relationship
with both the north of the country and Protestants in general, became
apparent. In the autumn of that year, when a concerted effort was made
to promote the Repeal Association nationally, Ulster was not included in
the campaign. John O'Connell explained that this decision had been made
on the grounds of 'endeavouring to avoid what would endanger the shed-
ding of human blood'.[98] Later in the year, however, Daniel O'Connell
ventured to the north of the country but, according to his son John, 'it was
sorely against his will, as against his judgement and earnest counsel'.[99]
O'Connell had been invited to the north by local Repealers and although
he had tried to dissuade them 'they persisted, and at length became so irritated at his arguing the matter with them, that most reluctantly, and
entirely against his better judgment, as well as against the spirit of the
policy which had ruled his whole political life, he had to yield, and to
consent to visit'.[100] Privately, Daniel O'Connell's view of Irish Protestants
was even more bizarre. He confided privately to Paul Cullen, then the
Rector of the Irish College in Rome, that, 'If the Union were repealed and
the exclusive system abolished, the great mass of the Protestant community would with little delay melt into the overwhelming majority of the
Irish nation. Protestantism would not survive the Repeal ten years.'[101]
Predictably, many middle-class Protestants remained antagonistic to
Repeal. However, their dislike of O'Connell was almost matched by their
distrust of the Prime Minister, Sir Robert Peel, the politician who had
betrayed them through the introduction of Catholic Emancipation.[102] The
combination of Peel and O'Connell in central positions of power made
many conservative Protestants very nervous.

Unlike O'Connell, Young Ireland contended that it was important to
reach out to the people in the north of Ireland, including Orangemen, who
were traditional opponents of nationalism. The leaders of Young Ireland
included Anglicans and Presbyterians, as well as Catholics, and they
wanted the Repeal movement to cut across religious and geographic divisions. Duffy, an Ulster Catholic, believed that, 'Ulster, jealous and
froward as she was, influenced by bigots, led by a gentry who had a manifest interest in keeping her apart, might and must be won.' He also
pointed out that the 'national movements' of 1782 and 1798 had been
planned by Ulstermen. Young Ireland had more success with middle-class
Protestants in Leinster and Munster who believed they could benefit

financially from national independence.[103] The *Nation* was an important tool in forging a new spirit of cooperation amongst the different religious denominations, the founders realising that 'Repeal papers were for the most part as uniformly Catholic in their sympathies as if they were exclusively sectarian organs'.[104] The *Nation* sought to counteract this approach by addressing Catholics and Protestants alike. The appeal to Protestants was led by Thomas Davis, an Anglican, whose poetry included 'Orange and Green will carry the day' and 'A Nation Once Again'. He wrote a series of letters to the *Nation* entitled 'Letters of a Protestant on Repeal', which were subsequently reprinted in pamphlet form by the Irish Confederation.[105] From 1842, the *Nation* regularly printed letters from Protestant sympathizers who were trying to induce their co-religionists to support Repeal. Their justification was that they needed Protestant help to make Ireland free.[106] A regular contributor was Francis Davis, a Protestant weaver from Hillsborough in County Down, who identified himself as 'A Belfast Man'.[107] This approach did not have the full support of some Old Irelanders. However, the non-sectarian policy of the paper won the admiration of Samuel Ferguson, a barrister, poet and Protestant Unionist. He addressed a poem to 'The Gentlemen of the "Nation" Newspaper on their being censured for want of sectarian zeal'. While Ferguson made his support for the Union clear, he admitted that he admired their inclusive approach and their desire to teach 'national self-confidence':

> Brave youths, though much I prize the Union Act,
> And warm resent some marchings for Repeal
> Which I deem menaces, no less I feel
> How loving-brave, with manly minds erect,
> Ye toil to give the people self-respect.[108]

In May 1843, the *Nation* reported that £200 (over one-quarter of the Repeal Rent) had been raised in the north, which Duffy ironically referred to as 'the Protestant anti-Irish, black North'. In the same week, 225 new members were enrolled in Belfast and a smaller number of Protestants joined the Repeal movement in Derry. The paper regarded this information as a sign that the inclusive methods of Young Ireland were working.[109] By 1845, the continued influx of northern Protestants led Duffy, John Martin and Thomas D'Arcy McGee to suggest that it would be beneficial to have a separate newspaper, based in Belfast, for Protestant Repealers, which was sympathetic to their religion and interests. Mr Godkin, a Congregationalist minister, was to be the editor.[110] The plan came to nothing as the conflict with Conciliation Hall, which resulted in Young Ireland's secession, absorbed their time in the latter part of 1845 and early months of 1846.

The Repeal Year

O'Connell's declaration that 1843 was Repeal Year provided a clear challenge that the Prime Minister, Sir Robert Peel, could not disregard. Since
coming to power in 1841, Peel had adopted the tactic of ignoring the
Repeal Association or treating it with contempt, but after 1843 this was
no longer possible.[111] There was continuing debate within the British
parliament and British press as to whether policies of coercion or conciliation should be adopted in Ireland.[112] Nonetheless, tensions between the
British government and the Repeal movement had deteriorated largely
due to the illiberal attitudes of the Irish administration based in Dublin
Castle. The Lord Lieutenant, Earl Grey, had Orange sympathies and gave
little support to Catholics.[113] When it was suggested that he should
appoint more Catholics to legal positions he responded, 'Conciliation is a
chimera. I would not be deterred from doing what I thought right by any
fear of their anger.'[114] Peel, though, was adamant that conciliation was a
way of countering Repeal, arguing 'there must be many Roman Catholics
of intelligence, tired of excitement and agitation, on whom a favour of the
Crown bestowed on one of their body would have a beneficial effect'.[115]
He believed that agrarian poverty was a major source of discontent in
Ireland and so he and his Home Secretary established a Commission to
look into the relationship between landlords and tenants.[116] The Duke of
Wellington offered to take over the government of Ireland but Peel
declined, fearing that his draconian approach would inflame nationalist
opinion. Privately though, the Prime Minister regarded Wellington as an
asset if Ireland did threaten to rebel.[117] Although the Repealers were
angered by this treatment, O'Connell's response was to convene more
meetings, while re-iterating his opposition to physical force. Peel, who
favoured conciliation rather than force, preferred not to intervene on the
grounds that 'when a country is tolerably quiet it is better for a
Government to be *hard of hearing* in respect to seditious language than to
be very agile in prosecuting'.[118]

   O'Connell's success in winning Catholic Emancipation in 1829 led him
to believe that the same tactics would bring about a Repeal of the Union.
His main strategy, therefore, was to convene a series of 'monster' political meetings, similar to the ones that had proved successful in the 1820s.
However, O'Connell had underestimated Peel's determination and the
fact that, unlike Catholic Emancipation, within parliament and amongst
conservative Irish Protestants Repeal had little support. Nevertheless,
Grey was alarmed at the 'astounding' spread of Repeal agitation and
warned Peel:

> The Roman Catholic hierarchy support Repeal. Dr McHale remits subscrip-
> tions from nearly every priest in his diocese. America gives increased support
> to it. This can only be with *separation* in view. The corporations, following
> the example of Dublin, have nearly all declared for it. The Teetotallers are all

Repealers. All Ireland is organised by Repeal Wardens, sent down, appointed, and paid, by the head Association ... Our own professed friends are out of sorts, out of spirits, out of temper. They say they are neglected, their interests overlooked, their opponents fostered ... I would earnestly suggest that you look at this subject instantly.[119]

Peel heeded Grey's words and informed him that he, in the House of Commons, and the Duke of Wellington in the House of Lords, were going to 'declare our intentions to preserve inviolate the Union and to use all the authority of the Government in support of it'.[120] Ironically, in 1829 it had been Peel and Wellington who, under pressure from mass agitation, had agreed to grant Catholic Emancipation – a parallel that was probably not lost on O'Connell. Yet, despite O'Connell's repeated declarations of loyalty to the Queen and the Empire, the desire for Repeal was made to appear as an assault on the integrity of the British Empire. Peel's opposition was unequivocal: on 9 May 1843 he informed parliament:

There is no influence, no power, no authority which the prerogatives of the crown and the existing law given to the government, which shall not be exercised for the purpose of maintaining the union; the dissolution of which would involve not merely the Repeal of an act of parliament, but the dismemberment of this great empire ... Deprecating as I do all war, but above all civil war, yet there is no alternative which I do not think preferable to the dismemberment of this empire.[121]

This proclamation angered Repealers but was welcomed by conservatives in Ireland.[122] For O'Connell, it amounted to a challenge to his political leadership, especially if Peel was willing to match his words with action.[123] O'Connell responded with even more inflammatory language. Speaking in Mallow on 11 June 1843, he told his followers, 'The time is coming when we must be doing. You may have the alternative to live as slaves or die as freemen.'[124] The Repealers were further enraged when, without consulting his superiors in London, the Irish Lord Chancellor undermined the Catholic middle classes by removing magistrates who had attended Repeal meetings on the grounds that they were a danger to the public peace and could not claim to uphold the Union.[125] O'Connell, a renowned pacifist, was outraged by such 'absurd' claims, again restating his commitment to peaceful means and respect to the Queen of the 'brave, loyal and attached people of Ireland'.[126] By September, as Repeal agitation continued, the Duke of Wellington suggested that he should be sent to Ireland, because if there was rebellion 'his iron hand would crush it'.[127]

Opposition to Repeal had widespread support in the British parliament and amongst Irish Protestants, therefore a confrontation appeared inevitable. O'Connell provided the stage when he announced a monster meeting, the final one of the year, to be held at Clontarf, near Dublin, on 8 October 1843. People came from all over Ireland to attend, including 1,500 supporters from Britain. Peel banned the meeting on 7 October,

using the excuse that it was going to assume a military character, and he
sent troops to Clontarf to prove that he was in earnest. O'Connell
complied with the order by cancelling the meeting and sending messages
to the approaching crowds that they should return home. This action
pleased his moderate followers who continued to support constitutional
action, but it disappointed many of his rank and file followers who had
believed his defiant oratory. Following Clontarf, Repeal donations from
the United States decreased, although by this stage, the demand for Repeal
had become inextricably linked with the Abolition question, which had
also lost O'Connell support.[128] Clontarf was both a defeat and a watershed. From this point, O'Connell never commanded the same respect or
influence within the Repeal movement. Independence seemed more
ephemeral than at any time since 1829.

Disillusionment with O'Connell's actions was tempered by Peel's decision to arrest him and five of his close associates for inciting a
disturbance. Those arrested included Duffy, the proprietor of the *Nation*,
and O'Connell's son, John. The government hoped that if O'Connell was
safely convicted the threat of rebellion would disappear. Consequently,
the success of the trial was regarded as 'necessary for the safety of the
State'.[129] To achieve this end, the state's solicitors repeatedly used their
right to challenge jurors and dismiss them. Consequently, there were no
Catholics on the jury.[130] The actions of the government reopened a public
debate, which involved sections of the press in Europe and North
America, as to whether there could be a fair trial of nationalists in
Ireland.[131] To the relief of the government, O'Connell and his followers
were charged with seditious conspiracy and were imprisoned in
Richmond Gaol in May 1844. Their imprisonment was short lived as the
House of Lords overturned the conviction in September. O'Connell's
supporters viewed his release as a victory over the British government.
O'Connell himself, who was a master at exploiting publicity and propa-
ganda, used his release as an opportunity to win personal and political
sympathy.

An important outcome of O'Connell's arrest and imprisonment was
that William Smith O'Brien, an independent MP and landowner in
County Clare, joined the Repeal Association, to the dismay of his conservative family.[132] O'Brien's involvement delighted Daniel and John
O'Connell. It also pleased Davis and his associates in Young Ireland, who
had admired O'Brien's principled stand on Irish issues in the House of
Commons.[133] O'Brien's family was descended from Brian Boru, the hero
of the Battle of Clontarf in 1014. Like many liberal Protestants, he had
supported Catholic Emancipation. What made him unusual was the fact
that he had joined O'Connell's Catholic Association. He became a
Member of Parliament in 1828, initially supporting the Tory Party, but he
quickly became disillusioned with their Irish policies and, in 1832, he
supported the reform of parliament.[134] Although O'Brien promoted

justice for Ireland, particularly for Catholics, he did not join the Repeal Association. Nevertheless, he supported O'Connell in parliament on a number of issues, including opposition to the Arms Bill. By 1843 his sympathy with Repeal was becoming more pronounced, which paralleled his increasing disillusionment with the British parliament.[135] The banning of the Clontarf meeting and conviction of O'Connell proved to be the decisive factor in his joining the Repeal Association on 20 October 1843.[136] Like O'Connell, O'Brien was opposed to violence, believing that Repeal should be won by constitutional methods. Both men, however, had fought a number of duels, O'Connell even killing one of his opponents, indicating that their opposition to physical force did not extend to matters of personal honour.[137]

O'Connell chose O'Brien to manage the Association during his imprisonment. His enforced absence also allowed other people to be more involved in the day-to-day running of the Repeal Association. With O'Connell and his closest associates unavailable, O'Brien had freedom to impose his own views on the Association. Apart from the daily administration, he made plans for the long-term development of the movement, forming a parliamentary committee, comprising its most talented supporters, to advise on matters of policy. Part of its strategy was to contest every vacancy in Ireland for public office. Despite being a political moderate and aged forty in 1843, when acting as O'Connell's deputy, O'Brien increasingly worked with Young, rather than Old Ireland. He consulted Thomas Davis regarding the running of the Repeal Association and he established close personal relations with leading Young Irelanders, particularly Thomas Davis, Richard O'Gorman, Charles Gavan Duffy and, subsequently, Thomas Francis Meagher.[138] Moreover, O'Brien used the columns of the *Nation* to promote the winning of Repeal through education and reconciliation.[139] Nonetheless, he continued to shun any public identification with Young Ireland.[140]

During his short period in charge, O'Brien had considerable success: attendance at weekly Repeal meetings grew and the Repeal Rent increased; significantly, a number of northern Protestants, including John Martin, joined the Association. Meetings were held throughout the country to offer sympathy to the state prisoners, including one in Belfast, addressed by local Protestant landowners – a development that worried the British government. The Tory press was just as alarmed by O'Brien's management of the Repeal movement as they had been by the more public activities of O'Connell and the monster meetings. Their alarm resulted in a number of demands for Conciliation Hall to be closed down.[141] What this brief episode demonstrated was that the Repeal Association did not depend on O'Connell or his son for its existence. It was these experiences that gave a shape and direction to Young Ireland as a distinct political group within the Repeal movement. Moreover, as a result of their association with O'Brien they had found a leader of experience, integrity and credibility. However, these developments created disquiet within Old Ireland and the release of O'Connell and his son resulted in a direct assault on the honour of Young Ireland.

The Clontarf meeting in 1843 was a watershed in the Repeal movement. For O'Connell personally, despite widespread anger at his imprisonment, it was a major and irreversible setback. Although he retained the loyalty of the Catholic masses, he lost the trust of the energetic middle classes. The decline of the Repeal movement following his release was reflected in the rapid dwindling in Repeal Rent. Although during his confinement O'Connell had been treated as a guest of the governor rather than a dangerous prisoner, when he was released in 1844 he appeared to be broken in health and spirits and the Repeal movement seemed to lack strategy. At this stage O'Connell, who was almost aged 70, was slowing down physically. Moreover, Peel was determined to 'strike a blow at the influence and authority of O'Connell, and in the most vital part, the collection of Rent'.[142] Following his imprisonment, O'Connell's commitment to Repeal changed, resulting in a brief and unconvincing flirtation with federalism, which would provide for the establishment of a separate but subordinate parliament in Dublin, essentially to deal with local affairs. Overall, it was a narrower objective than Repeal of the Union. The idea had first been proposed by some Protestant Repealers from Ulster, led by William Sharman Crawford, a County Down landowner. It was supported initially by Davis as a first step in winning Repeal, but his view changed when O'Connell made it clear that federalism was to be an alternative solution to full independence.[143] O'Connell, who due to illness was spending an increased amount of his time in County Kerry, believed that this demand for limited self-government would appeal to the Irish upper and middle classes. He also regarded federalism, unlike Repeal, as an achievable goal. At the same time, he claimed that he was replacing force and intimidation with 'an appeal to reason and argument'. For Peel, O'Connell's new tactic presented a fresh challenge, which he determined to combat with as much force as was required. Privately, he was concerned about the implications of federalism for the unity of the United Kingdom, despairing that, 'If Ireland must have Federalism, so must Scotland. Why not Wales? Why not Wessex and the kingdoms of the Heptarchy?'[144]

To counteract the demand for federalism, the government secretly employed Isaac Butt to publish a series of refutations of the idea in the *Morning Herald*.[145] Ironically, in later life, Isaac Butt founded the Home Rule Association which laid the foundations for the Home Rule movement. The dislike of federalism was closer to home, with many supporters of Young Ireland disagreeing with O'Connell, believing that federalism would allow only limited responsibility to Irish men both in the domestic legislature and in the imperial parliament.[146] They doubted that it would satisfy supporters of Repeal, while allowing their enemies to accuse them of lacking consistency.[147] The disagreement became public when Duffy published an open letter to O'Connell disagreeing with federalism. The letter had the support of most of the younger members of the Association, including Davis.[148] The demand for federalism was short-lived and quickly abandoned by O'Connell, indicating his lack of clear vision for the future of Repeal. More seriously, it signified a growing rift within the movement over how the struggle for independence should advance. After 1843, the idealism of Young Ireland increasingly diverged from the more hard-nosed, pragmatic politics of O'Connell and his supporters. Relationships were strained by O'Connell's authoritarian style of leadership, his sloppy financial management, his willingness to exchange political favours in return for status, and the influence of the Catholic clergy in the everyday administration of the Repeal Association.[149] Moreover, he organized many of his public meetings on Sundays, which was distasteful to Protestant supporters, a fact that was pointed out to him by O'Brien in 1844.[150]

In 1844, there was short-lived unity, following the establishment of the '82 Club, which was inspired by the winning of legislative independence by the Volunteers in 1782. Unfortunately, this development could not counteract the growing antagonism between Old Ireland and Young Ireland. The rift widened following the publication of an article, probably written by John O'Connell, which appeared in many newspapers, accusing Young Ireland of being religious infidels. It suggested that the supporters of Young Ireland had abandoned Repeal and their loyalty to O'Connell. The article drew a response from Thomas MacNevin, a lawyer and regular contributor to all the nationalist newspapers, who vigorously denied both charges. He pointed out that even though the contributors to the *Nation* were overwhelmingly Catholic, the journal's policy had been to act 'with a respectful, conciliatory, and generous demeanour towards our mistaken and prejudiced Protestant fellow-countrymen'. By doing so, they had proved that they were 'incapable of uttering one word disrespectful even to their prejudices or entertaining one thought of hostility to men ... whom we unaffectedly regard for their firm and manly character'. At the same time, Young Ireland repudiated the existence of an exclusive state church 'looking upon it as a garrison of bad passions by which England has so long kept in Ireland political division and social derangement, for her own profligate and abominable purpose'.[151] The publication of these articles moved the disagreements between Young and Old Ireland into the public domain. O'Connell, encouraged by his son John, did little to heal the rift. Instead, he focused his attention on those whom he regarded as his enemies within the Repeal movement, rather than uniting his followers in order to achieve Repeal. An early indication of his desire to remove 'troublesome' elements was his decision to ban newspaper proprietors from membership of the Repeal Association, thus making a link between the nationalist press and his arrest. He threatened that unless they resigned, he would dissolve the Association. Duffy was one of the people affected by this decision.[152]

By the end of 1844, although O'Connell proclaimed that his main goal was Repeal, he appeared willing to abandon this aim in order to re-enter an alliance with the Whig Party. Initially, the leaders of Young Ireland maintained that their differences were with the Whigs and not O'Connell, but events in 1845 made this distinction increasingly difficult to sustain. The tensions were exacerbated by John O'Connell's actions. Since O'Connell's release from prison, he had effectively allowed control to pass to his son, John, whose management of the Association created an increasingly fractious atmosphere, Duffy accusing him of playing 'the part of dictator at that time with a dogmatism which his great father after a life of public services rarely assumed ... at every meeting there was some personal conflict or some gross violation of the neutrality on which the Association rested'.[153] Even more worrying for members of Young Ireland was the fact that he was moving the Association closer to the Catholic Church, thus turning the Repeal Association into an over-whelmingly Catholic organization.[154]

Repeal and Chartism

In the early months of 1843, the Repeal movement was expanding both in Ireland and overseas. The fact that Irish news, especially Repeal news, received so much positive coverage in Europe, led the *Freeman's Journal* to assert that, 'The question of Ireland has become European.'[155] Support for Repeal was especially strong in the United States, principally, but not exclusively, amongst Irish immigrants. Repeal organisations were also formed in some cities in Canada.[156] The groups in North America regularly sent donations to Ireland. Repeal also had supporters in Britain, particularly in London and the northern industrial towns, including Liverpool, Leeds, Manchester and Sheffield; areas with large Irish settlements and established radical traditions. As in Ireland and elsewhere, Repealers in Britain raised weekly amounts of money for the Repeal Rent. Young Ireland and O'Connell disagreed about the role of external help in any future struggle with the British government. Despite the setback of Clontarf, O'Connell believed that Repeal should be won through the constitutional efforts of the Repeal movement in Ireland, under his leadership. O'Connell publicly denounced aid from radicals in both France and the United States, and he rejected any alliance with the British Chartists.[157] Young Ireland forecast that 'it was under the pressure of foreign troubles their desire would be most speedily accomplished'.[158] Increasingly, Daniel and John O'Connell alienated much of the goodwill that existed overseas.

Support for Repeal was frequently tied in with the British Chartist movement, despite O'Connell's antagonism towards the latter. The

Chartist movement had originated in 1838 with the aim of bringing about political reform, including universal male suffrage, a secret ballot and payment for MPs. Its main strategy was the presentation of monster petitions to parliament: in 1839, 1842 and 1848. The Chartist leadership included several prominent Irishmen, the most influential of whom was Feargus O'Connor. He had been Repeal MP for Cork from 1832 to 1835, when he had failed to make the property qualification on a technicality. His focus then moved from Irish Repeal to British parliamentary reform. The Irish influence in Chartism was apparent in a number of local organizations in areas with large Irish populations, including Barnsley, Manchester, London and Lancaster. Many of the local leaders in these areas were Irish.[159] In Manchester and Salford, for example, where Irish people represented approximately ten per cent of the population, they accounted for almost twenty per cent of the Chartist executive.[160] Increasingly, Repeal was an integral demand of many local Chartist groups. O'Connor remained committed to Irish political independence and in October 1841 announced that 'henceforth he would go for the Repeal of the Irish Union along with the Charter'.[161] Consequently, the call for a Repeal of the Act of Union was mentioned in the preamble to the 1842 Charter.[162] A number of leading Chartists were opposed to this inclusion, because they did not want the Charter to be diluted with other demands.[163] Regardless of this fear, when Feargus O'Connor was elected MP for Nottingham in 1847, he openly supported the Repeal movement in parliament.

The main opposition to forming a partnership with Chartists came from Daniel O'Connell. On 13 September 1841, he had introduced a strongly-worded resolution in the Repeal Association, which was sent to supporters in Britain and the United States, 'cautioning them against any species of connection with the Chartists, and begging of them to exclude all known Chartists from their meetings'. If they did not obey this instruction, they would be expelled from the movement. His grounds for this directive were that the Chartists had supported the Tories in the recent elections, they used violence and they were not genuine supporters of Repeal but were 'the worst enemies of Ireland' and wanted to damage it; therefore, their intervention in the Repeal movement could only be 'evil'. He described their activities as equivalent to 'High Treason' and the 'peaceful, temperate, moral and loyal Repealers of Ireland' should have nothing to do with them. O'Connell pointed out that his followers were reformers, supporting 'general' suffrage for men aged over 21 and other parliamentary reforms. Consequently, there was no need 'for contaminating the pure and holy cause of Repeal with the torch and dagger turbulence of unprincipled Chartism'.[164]

O'Connell's antipathy to Chartism was intensified by his personal dislike of its Irish leader, Feargus O'Connor. In spite of O'Connell's objections to any alliance, O'Connor used the main Chartist newspaper,

The Northern Star, as a vehicle for promoting Repeal, frequently linking it with the demand for universal suffrage.[165] While a number of Chartist leaders believed that O'Connell had provided a model for building a mass movement, O'Connor regarded him as a traitor to the Irish people. As early as 1839, O'Connor sent a weekly letter to O'Connell, via the pages of the *Northern Star*, accusing him, amongst other things, of not supporting working men and doing little to win Repeal while simultaneously lining his own pockets with money raised from the Irish poor.[166] The antagonism was mutual. O'Connell had been an original signatory of the Charter, but his social conservatism was already becoming more noticeable after 1838, when, according to Dorothy Thompson, 'he made a sharp break with the English radicals, and endeavoured to take the whole of the Irish movement with him'.[167] From this point, O'Connell became an implacable enemy of the Chartist movement and he urged Irish people in Britain to stay away from it.[168] O'Connell's stance was strengthened by the fact that the Catholic Church was overwhelmingly opposed to Chartism, denouncing it from the altars of Ireland. Hence, they were using the tactics and language more commonly associated with their treatment of Fenians twenty years later.[169]

Regardless of the opposition of O'Connell and the Catholic Church, Chartism did spread to Ireland. In the summer of 1839 a Chartist Association was founded in Dublin by Patrick O'Higgins (1790–1854), a Dublin wool merchant. The Dublin police reported that the Association was spreading 'rapidly' in the city and, by 1841, had extended to other towns including Belfast, Newry, Drogheda and Loughrea.[170] Although Chartism was largely urban-based, a number of small farmers joined the movement.[171] Its early success led to the establishment of a coordinating body, the Irish Universal Suffrage Association in August 1841, with Patrick O'Higgins as the President. The Association's motto was 'Peace–Law–Order' and, like the Repeal movement, it supported moral and constitutional methods to win its aims, namely, by creating public opinion that was favourable to such changes and by getting supporters into parliament.[172] Building a base of working-class support was an important aspect of the Irish Chartist mission. Consequently, the rules of the Suffrage Association stated that the Standing Committee of thirteen members had to include seven 'working men', and that five members of the Committee made a quorum, but only if three of them were working men.[173] Nonetheless, a fee was charged, albeit a small one: every member had to pay an entrance fee of two pence and then to pay a weekly subscription of one penny. Clergymen of all religious denominations were given free membership.[174] Although the number of members probably never exceeded 1,000, this was not reflective of the full support for Chartism.[175] The Second Charter of 1842, for example, drew 2,000 signatures in Belfast alone.[176] The Irish Chartists were less visible than their British counterparts, as they 'did not take part in militant processions or public meetings, but they confined their activities to the distribution of Chartists periodicals and to holding weekly political discussions'.[177]

Inevitably, Irish Chartism remained overshadowed by the Repeal movement and was undermined by O'Connell's opposition. O'Connell's supporters even showed themselves willing to use violence in order to prevent leading English Chartists from speaking in Ireland.[178] Despite O'Connell's antagonism, Irish Chartists continued to be enthusiastic supporters of Repeal, especially in the exhilarating atmosphere of the early months of 1843, the 'Repeal Year'. During this period, they organized petitions that supported the demands of the Charter, called for a Repeal of the Union, and appealed for a union between the Irish Repealers and the English Chartist movement.[179] They also worked fruitlessly to bring about reconciliation between O'Connell and Feargus O'Connor, both of whom, nonetheless, continued to act separately.[180] O'Connell's retreat at Clontarf in 1843 not only disheartened Repealers, but Irish Chartists became less politically active following this. Regardless, therefore, of the attempts by Chartists to work more closely with Repealers, the partnership was short lived. Consequently, Repeal and Chartism continued to have an uneasy relationship, and this only changed in 1848.

The United States

The role of the United States proved to be both significant and controversial in the Repeal movement. Since 1840, donations had been sent to the Repeal Association from sympathizers in America, which included various Irish groups, such as the Association of Friends of Ireland. In New York alone, there were a number of different Repeal societies but at the end of 1842 they made a decision to unite.[181] Inevitably, support was most extensive in areas with large Irish immigration, notably New York, Boston and Philadelphia. However, interest in Irish Repeal was not confined to Irish-Americans. In 1842 Robert Tyler, son of the then American President, John Tyler, joined the Repeal movement in Philadelphia.[182] Some Irish landowners viewed the American intervention with dismay, and in July 1842 Lord Glengall informed Peel that 'fifty thousand men are ready to come over from the United States to aid the Irish patriots'. Peel, who had been Chief Secretary for Ireland for six years (1812–18) and therefore believed that he understood the Irish temperament, was sceptical. He publicly dismissed the information as exaggeration.[183] Privately though, British government informers were attending meetings of the American Repeal groups and their reports were assiduously followed by the British Home Office in London.[184]

As Repeal spread in the United States, attempts were made to create a more formal network, with a National Convention being held in Philadelphia in March 1842.[185] The following year, a three-day Repeal Convention was held in New York, presided over by Tyler. It agreed that organizations on behalf of Irish liberty should be established in each state of the Union. More significantly, in its wake 'large sums of money' were sent to Ireland; for example, Boston raised $10,000 on behalf of O'Connell.[186] Just as worryingly for the British authorities, the Repeal movement was receiving encouragement at the highest political level in the United States. One member of the Congress wrote to the *Nation* congratulating the Repeal movement on the progress that it was making, but warning that 'the right must either fail or triumph. It is up to the Irish people whether Ireland remains a province or becomes a nation.'[187] In summer 1843 also, the President, John Tyler, openly declared his support for Irish independence, stating that he was a 'decided friend' of Repeal.[188] On St Patrick's Day 1844, he sent a pro-Repeal letter to an Irish group in the United States.[189]

Peel's treatment of the Repeal movement in 1843, especially the imprisonment of O'Connell, angered sympathizers in the United States. This resulted in a six-day meeting being convened in New York, attended by United States senators, merchants, judges and clergymen. The tone of the meeting was belligerent, it resolving that if Britain 'invaded' Ireland the consequence would be 'the assured loss of Canada by American arms'. The meeting issued an address to the people of France asking them to intervene on Ireland's behalf. Smaller, but similarly enthusiastic, meetings were held in Boston, Philadelphia and Baltimore. Large sums of money for the Repeal Association were collected: in New York, over $5,000 was raised and over $2,000 in Philadelphia. The President, John Tyler, confirmed his support for Ireland's bid for independence, issued a declaration saying:

> I am the decided friend of a Repeal of the Legislative Union between Great Britain and Ireland. I ardently and anxiously hope that it may take place, and I have the utmost confidence that Ireland will have her own parliament in her own capital in a very short time.[190]

O'Connell, who was pragmatic in many aspects of his political life, was a consistent opponent of American slavery. This contrasted with the views of Young Ireland, whose attitude was more ambivalent.[191] Nonetheless, O'Connell was willing to accept financial contributions from sympathizers in the United States, even those who overtly supported slavery.[192] However, Daniel and John O'Connell's outspoken opposition to slavery lost them support, especially in some of the southern states where the Repeal movement had established strong roots.[193] Consequently, support for Repeal in the United States became enmeshed in the debate concerning Abolition. In 1842, O'Connell issued an address condemning American slavery, which was signed by thousands of Irish people. The reaction was not what O'Connell had expected: the Louisiana, Baltimore and Albany Repealers spoke out against the Irish Address, and the Philadelphia Repeal Association split into two groups. Even more signifi-

cantly, the Repeal Convention in New York in September 1843 refused to
discuss the slavery question, on the grounds that it was too controversial
and exposed newly-arrived Irish immigrants to doubts about their loyalty
to the country of their adoption. The most public challenge to O'Connell's
pronouncements came from Repealers in Cincinnati who wrote to him in
August 1843 saying that the future of the American Union depended on
the existence of slavery. Their letter included a donation towards the
Repeal Rent. O'Connell read his response to the Cincinnati Repealers in
Conciliation Hall. In it, he reaffirmed his opposition to American slavery,
even quoting the recent Apostolic Letter of Gregory XVI and reminding
them that the Pope had condemned slave traffic. O'Connell's unequivocal
statements caused an immediate reaction, with a number of American
Repeal societies dissolving. Although O'Connell's response won him
support amongst Abolitionists, the slave issue did not go away and was
only overshadowed by his arrest and imprisonment shortly after this.[194]

Overall, O'Connell's public denunciations of the institution angered
many in the United States, especially, but not exclusively, in the southern
states. One American commentator, Lewis Levin, publicly criticized what
he characterized as 'the fallacy of [Repeal] principles', and he denounced
O'Connell 'the slave and devotee of the Pope of Rome, [for] reviling the
Sons of Washington'.[195] The matter came to a head in late 1843, when
O'Connell refused to accept any further financial contributions from
American slave-holders.[196] A number of his supporters, including the
leaders of Young Ireland, were uneasy about his intervention, on the
grounds that the Anti-Slavery Society in Dublin was the place to condemn
slavery, not Conciliation Hall.[197] When they warned him that his outspokenness would lose influential support in the United States for the
Repeal movement, O'Connell responded, 'It is ourselves alone must work
out the Repeal.'[198]

John O'Connell was as vociferous as his father in supporting Abolition.
When a member of the House of Representatives asked the House to
consider making Ireland part of the American Union, John O'Connell
responded angrily, rejecting the alliance on the grounds that, 'I disdain the
attainment of selfish Irish nationality at the sacrifice of abandoning, even
for a moment, the sublime principle of universal liberty, religious and
civil, to every created man.' Furthermore, he added that he preferred to
continue the Union with Britain 'rather than see Ireland independent and
annexed to America, and polluted by sending representatives to sit in a
Congress that sanctions Negro slavery'.[199] Daniel and John O'Connell's
willingness to alienate American support troubled some of their younger
followers. As Duffy pointed out, O'Connell was content to be part of the
British Empire, but not an American one. Moreover, Duffy feared that
'our best allies, the American people, would feel outraged at being universally included in a reproach applicable only to a bare minority, and would
hold the Irish people responsible for language uttered in their name

without repudiation or dissent'.[200] O'Connell's position on the use of force disheartened some Repeal societies in the United States, many of whom favoured a more radical stance. Robert Emmet, President of the New York Repeal Association (and nephew of the leader of the 1803 rising), resigned when O'Connell made disparaging comments about the United Irishmen. The New York committee supported Emmet and passed a resolution disapproving of O'Connell's comments.[201] Nonetheless, in 1844, while the Repeal movement was languishing in Ireland, it was flourishing in many northern towns in the United States, especially in those areas where Abolitionism was most vibrant. Increasingly, O'Connell's churlishness and dogmatic approach to a number of issues reduced his popularity and provided a corresponding boost to that of Young Ireland.

France

Throughout Europe, O'Connell's winning of Catholic Emancipation gained him a mythical status, especially amongst Catholics and traditional enemies of Britain. One consequence was that Irish politics were watched and reported widely by the Continental press.[202] His imprisonment in 1844 was discussed and condemned in many European newspapers, to such an extent that O'Connell's international notoriety was debated in the British House of Commons.[203] While the conservative press in Britain and Ireland represented O'Connell as a political maverick and dangerous demagogue, within Europe, his commitment to peaceful, constitutional tactics was emphasized and praised. Outside of the United Kingdom, therefore, the British government appeared to be losing the propaganda war over the Repeal question.

In France, O'Connell was particularly admired: by Catholics for his winning of Emancipation, and by liberals for the fact that he had effected political change without recourse to revolution. Moreover, to the external gaze, O'Connell appeared as a cohesive force, and the embodiment of a revitalized, unified – and Catholic – Irish nation.[204] The place of Protestants within this nation was rarely addressed. Irish independence was championed by radicals, especially in Paris.[205] In 1843, in response to a request from the United States, a public dinner was held in the Bastille – ostensibly to commemorate its storming – but in reality to express sympathy for Irish Repeal. It was attended by leading members of the left, who were to play a prominent part in the Revolution five years later. This included Ledru Rollin, a prominent member of the French Chamber of Deputies, who stated:

> Let England understand that, if she attempts to overcome legitimate rights by violent and coercive measures, France is ready to lend an oppressed people, in their decisive struggle, experienced heads, resolute hearts, and sturdy arms.

In addition to promises of support, a collection was made for the Repeal funds.[206] Shortly afterwards, Ledru Rollin offered O'Connell French assistance to win liberty for Ireland. He and his friends sympathized with the demand for independence and he hinted that military aid might be provided should the British government seek to coerce the Repealers. O'Connell responded negatively, on the grounds that 'the contingency which we decline to discuss, because we deem it impossible it should arise, [that] the British government [utilize] every menace of illegal force and unjust violence'.[207] He was, however, willing to accept pecuniary aid – similar to that which was frequently received from the United States – but when the 'French gave nothing', O'Connell wondered if Rollin suffered from 'balderdashical vanity'.[208] Nonetheless, each of these decisions isolated the Repeal movement within Ireland. Clearly, by 1843, largely due to the achievements of O'Connell, the Repeal movement had attained international notoriety and support. Ironically, it was O'Connell's attitudes and actions that lost some of this support, especially amongst young radicals. Significantly, while O'Connell's post-Clontarf vacillations 'greatly impaired his influence' the *Nation* continued to attract support and while O'Connell's personal popularity declined, that of the Young Irelanders increased.[209]

Repeal divided

Following the conflict at Clontarf, Peel made maintaining the Union and conciliating Catholics the dual focus of his Irish policy. He attempted to take the sting out of his treatment of O'Connell by introducing a series of measures to appease Catholic opinion in Ireland – an early form of killing Repeal with kindness. To be successful, he realized it was necessary for him to undermine O'Connell's influence over Irish Catholics. In a secret memorandum, therefore, Peel informed his Cabinet that, 'Many we shall never reclaim or conciliate, but it is of immediate importance to detach, if we can, from the ranks of those who cannot be reclaimed or conciliated, all those who are not yet committed to violent counsels, and are friendly to the connection between the two countries.'[210] In a subsequent memorandum he admitted, 'I view our future position in respect to Ireland and the administration of affairs in Ireland with great anxiety ... I know not what remedy there can be for such an evil as this but the detaching (if it be possible) from the ranks of Repeal, agitation and disaffection a considerable portion of the respectable and influential classes of the Roman Catholic population.'[211] The Irish Administration at Dublin Castle was an important part of this new approach and significantly, the austere Thomas de Grey, the second Earl de Grey was replaced as Lord Lieutenant by the more temperate Lord Heytesbury. As a consequence, Catholics were promoted to more positions of power. Peel viewed this patronage, in the form of giving more responsibility to Catholics, as having a 'mollifying effect' in Ireland.[212]

Peel's conciliatory measures were mostly concerned with education and church matters. In 1844, he created a Board of Charitable Bequests that included five Catholic Commissioners, and which replaced a predominantly Protestant body. The Protestant domination of the previous Board had been a source of grievance to Irish Catholics yet the introduction of the act was vigorously opposed by O'Connell and many of the Catholic Church hierarchy, on the grounds that it would interfere with the Church's autonomy in fund-raising. The subsequent debate revealed divisions within the clergy between the majority, encouraged by Archbishop MacHale of Tuam, who favoured a no compromise approach to the winning of Repeal; and the minority, led by Bishop Murray of Dublin, who preferred cooperation. Its successful passage through parliament, therefore, was regarded by Peel as 'a signal triumph over O'Connell and MacHale'.[213] The Irish Administration was equally optimistic about the outcome of this disagreement and declared that 'O'Connell can no longer rely on the support of the Church'.[214] Even Prince Albert, who had been monitoring political affairs in Ireland closely, congratulated Peel, advising him to, 'Persevere in your cause, and I am sure that the good cause, that of moderation and impartial justice, must in the end remain victorious.'[215] The debate indicated that O'Connell was losing the support of some of his traditional, moderate followers, while alienating those who favoured more religious integration.

In 1845, Peel introduced more conciliatory measures. He increased the annual grant to Maynooth College, a Catholic seminary, from £9,000 to £26,000, which made its financial position more secure. In introducing this measure, he had the support of the Queen who averred that, 'the measure is so great and good a one, that people must open their eyes, and will not oppose it'.[216] Peel viewed education as essential to appeasing Catholics and so, in 1845, he provided for the establishment of three non-denominational universities, in Belfast, Cork and Galway.[217] A measure that was not passed by the British parliament was a Tenants' Compensation Bill, based on the findings of the Devon Commission. It had proposed to give tenants compensation for improvements that they made on their holdings, and its failure in parliament was a blow for Peel. He was, however, more successful in passing other measures that mollified a section of Catholic opinion in 1844 and 1845. Moreover, the introduction of measures that gave justice to Ireland by a Tory Party, which was doing it against the wishes of the Repeal Party, caused a dilemma for O'Connell. Increasingly, he was facing a choice between allying with more extreme members of the Repeal Association or damaging Peel by renewing his alliance with the Whigs. Whichever path he chose, he knew, would lose him support.

While Peel believed his policies were proving successful in conciliating moderate Catholic opinion, he had underestimated the anger that his measures would have amongst conservative Protestants. In 1845, in an attempt to conciliate popular Protestant opinion, Orange marches, which had been banned in 1832, were again made legal. Marches, notably the annual 12th July celebration of William III's victory at the Battle of the Boyne, resumed immediately and were larger than previous ones. They were also overtly political, with anger being expressed against both Catholics and nationalists, indicating that the Repeal movement had annoyed, rather than conciliated, some Protestants.[218] Consequently, Peel's main frustration at the end of 1845 was aimed at militant Protestants rather than militant Catholics, leading him to assert 'What shabby fellows those great Protestants are!'[219] Moreover, as his Home Secretary warned him, if they made more concessions to the Catholics, 'The Protestants of Ireland would resist them to the last extremity.'[220]

In 1845, O'Connell briefly attempted to revive Repeal agitation and he convened a number of monster meetings, although they were not on the scale of the 1843 ones. Because the meetings were peaceful, they were legal. Notwithstanding this, the political situation in Ireland was providing a quandary for Peel's government who, since the debacle caused by O'Connell's arrest and imprisonment in 1844, had adopted a policy of reconciliation. This policy did not have the support of all of the party. The Duke of Wellington was irritated with the passivity of the government, arguing that 'conciliation without coercion will be ridiculous'.[221] By this stage, divisions were widening in the Repeal movement. A major disagreement arose over the Colleges Bill in 1845. Prior to this, the only university in Ireland had been the Anglican Trinity College in Dublin. The Catholic Church objected to the fact that they were not to have charge of running the colleges, and that certain subjects, notably Catholic theology, would not be taught. Moreover, O'Connell's denouncement of the proposed universities, on the grounds that they would be 'Godless Colleges', demonstrated the limitations of his promotion of non-sectarianism.

By aligning himself with the Catholic hierarchy and asking for denominational education, O'Connell was re-affirming his role as defender of Catholic interests. In contrast, the Young Irelanders believed that the proposed Colleges Bill would help education become non-sectarian and that it would be a step in bringing the Catholic and Protestant middle classes closer together. Thomas Davis, a champion of mixed education, had already written an impassioned editorial in the *Nation* arguing that it was the mechanism for Irish people to escape from their 'rags and chains'.[222] The issue was debated in Conciliation Hall in May 1845. Religion was used to attack Young Ireland by stating that they were 'enemies of religion' and that the *Nation* was 'godless' on the grounds that it supported a non-denominational system of education.[223] The writers of the *Nation* were described as irreligious and infidels, which were labels that stuck with them.[224] Even Thomas Davis, who had worked tirelessly to inject an ecumenical spirit into the Repeal movement, was accused by O'Connell of being anti-Catholic; an accusation that reduced him to tears.[225] Ironically, Young Ireland, which had sought to promote a non-sectarian approach to politics, now found that religion was being used to damage their influence over fellow nationalists. Furthermore, the argument became personal, vitriolic and public. The writers in the *Nation*, who had helped to revive and expand the Repeal movement, were accused by Daniel and John O'Connell of being 'juvenile orators' and 'schoolboy philosophers', who wanted more than just a Repeal of the Act of Union.[226] By 1845, therefore, the Repeal question was still shaping Irish and British politics, although divisions had widened despite Peel's policy of appeasement. The Repeal Association was splitting over the question of religion, with O'Connell increasingly defining the Irish nation in Catholic terms. Despite the inclusive approach of Young Ireland, Peel's concessions to Catholics had alienated large sections of Protestant opinion. O'Connell was faced with a new political dilemma: how was he to react to a Tory Party, led by his long-term adversary Peel, which was passing more favourable legislation for Ireland than his former Whig allies had done? Furthermore, how was he to assert control over the Young Ireland group? O'Connell, who was approaching seventy, again changed direction, splitting the Repeal Association in the process.

Notes

1 Oliver MacDonagh, *The Hereditary Bondsman: Daniel O'Connell 1775–1829* (New York: St Martin's Press, 1987), p. 50.
2 Daunt, *Personal Recollections*, vol. i, p. 205.
3 Nowlan, *Politics of Repeal*, p. 7.
4 *Warder*, 3 January 1829.
5 Fergus O'Ferrall, *Catholic Emancipation: Daniel O'Connell and the Birth of Irish Democracy* (Dublin: Gill and Macmillan, 1985).
6 Duke of Wellington to Peel, 23 March 1844: Charles Stuart Parker, *Sir Robert Peel from his Private Papers* (London: John Murray, 1899, 3 vols), vol. iii, p. 109.
7 Daunt, *Personal Recollections*, vol. i, pp. 143, 280.
8 Nowlan, *Politics of Repeal*, p. 7.
9 Daunt, *Personal Recollections*, vol. i, p. 3.
10 Ibid., vol. ii, p. 137.
11 Ibid., vol. i, p. 14.
12 The Compact was a verbal agreement only and was never committed to paper.
13 Quoted in James Lydon, *The Making of Ireland from Ancient Times to the Present* (London: Penguin 1998), p. 293.
14 Ibid.
15 Daunt, *Personal Recollections*, vol. ii, pp. 158–64.
16 Ibid., vol. i, pp. 20, 35.
17 Ibid., vol. i, p. 59.
18 *Journal of the British Empire*, 17 July 1840.
19 Daunt, *Personal Recollections*, vol. i, p. 73.

20 Denis Gwynn, *Young Ireland and 1848* (Cork: Cork University Press, 1949), p. 2.
21 Peel to Sir James Graham, May 1843: Parker, *Sir Robert Peel*, vol. iii, p. 47.
22 Mary Robinson, 'Daniel O'Connell: A Tribute' in *History Ireland* (vol. 5, no. 4, Winter 1997), 30.
23 M. Cronin, 'Of one Mind? O'Connellite Crowds in the 1830s and 1840s' in p. Jupp and E. Magennis (eds), *Crowds in Ireland c.1720–1920* (Basingstoke: Macmillan, 2000), pp. 129–72.
24 27 November 1841: David Thomson and Moyra Gusty (eds), *The Irish Journals of Elizabeth Smith, 1840–1850* (Oxford: Clarendon Press, 1980), p. 40.
25 Daunt, *Personal Recollections*, vol. ii, p. 62.
26 Martin MacDermott, *Songs and Ballads of Young Ireland with Portraits of Authors* (London: Downey and Co, 1896), p. 344.
27 Gwynn, *Young Ireland*, p. 12.
28 Sir Charles Gavan Duffy, *Four Years of Irish History 1845–1849, Being a Sequel to 'Young Ireland'* (London and New York: Cassell, Petter, Galpin & Co, 1883), p. 23.
29 MacDermott, *Songs and Ballads*, p. xiv.
30 Prospectus of the *Nation* (8 October 1842). Two versions were published, in Dublin and Belfast respectively.
31 Duffy, *Four Years*, p. 59.
32 *Nation*, 30 September 1843.
33 Peter Ackroyd, *The Romantics* (Milton Keynes: Open University Press/BBC, 2006).
34 Duffy, *Four Years*, p. 96.
35 Young Ireland collaborated with the Dublin publisher, James Duffy, to produce these texts. Some of the Young Irelanders, including John Mitchel and Thomas D'Arcy McGee, contributed to the series.
36 Thomas MacNevin, *Young Ireland: A Few Words in Defence of the Party, its Principles and Practices* (Dublin: James Duffy, 1844), p. 13.
37 MacDermott's *Songs and Ballads of Young Ireland*, p. vii.-viii, which was published in 1896, was the fifty-fifth edition of *The Spirit of the Nation*.
38 Daunt, *Personal Recollections*, vol. i, p. 14. O'Brien viewed language as an important tool in creating a national identity and he took classes in Irish, but acknowledged that it was more difficult than he had anticipated. Ibid., p. 125
39 Duffy, *Four Years*, p. 78.
40 O'Connell, *Recollections and Experiences*, vol. ii, p. 215.
41 Christopher Morash, *The Hungry Voice: The Poetry of the Irish Famine* (Dublin: Irish Academic Press, 1989), p. 26.
42 MacDermott, *Songs and Ballads*, p. 356.
43 K.M. McGrath, 'Writers in the *Nation*', in *Irish Historical Studies* (vol. vi, no. 23, March 1949), 189.
44 Sir Charles Gavan Duffy, *My Life in Two Hemispheres* (London: T. Fisher Unwin, 1898), vol. i, p. 176.
45 McGrath, 'Writers in the *Nation*', 211, 277.
46 Duffy, *Four Years*, p. 89.
47 McGrath, 'Writers in the *Nation*', 191.

48 Christine Kinealy, 'Invisible Nationalists' in Boardman and Kinealy, *1848: The Year the World Turned?*, pp. 130–45.

49 National Library of Ireland website, www.nli.ie, December 2004; O'Connell's paper, the *Pilot*, had a weekly circulation of less than 2,000: Duffy, *Young Ireland*, vol. ii, Appendix, p. 227, provides a detailed break-down of sales. See also Rossa, *Rossa's Recollections*. He recounts how the *Nation* was read in public places in his small village of Skibbereen.

50 Hill estimates that the intelligentsia accounted for only one per cent of the Irish population: Jacqueline Hill 'The Intelligentsia and Irish Nationalism in the 1840s' in *Studia Hibernica* (no. 20, 1980), 73–109.

51 After 1832, Ireland returned 105 MPs to parliament. Candidates elected in various General Elections for the Repeal Party (which operated under various names): 1832 - 39 seats; 1835 - 60 MPs sympathetic to Repeal were elected; in 1841, 20 Repealers were returned.

52 Quoted in Melville, *Mother of Oscar*, p. 19.

53 Duffy, *Four Years*, p. 128.

54 Lord Heytesbury to Peel, 20 October 1844: Parker, *Sir Robert Peel*, p. 123.

55 Duffy, *Young Ireland*, vol. i, p. v. Not all Young Irelanders liked this sobriquet: Thomas MacNevin, for example, argued that it created a false division between 'the younger portion of a people, and the older and more experienced men'. Thomas MacNevin, *Young Ireland: A Few Words in Defence of the Party, its Principles and Practices* (Dublin: James Duffy, 1844), p. 5.

56 Duffy, *Four Years*, p. 21.

57 Nowlan, *Politics of Repeal*, p. 10.

58 Richard Davis, 'Young Ireland' in *Encyclopedia of 1848 Revolutions*: http://cscwww.cats.ohiou.edu (accessed 24 January 2005), p. 1.

59 Jacques-Nicolas-Augustin Thierry (1795–1856) was criticized by a later generation of historians for his romantic, literary style. He admired the Irish writer, Thomas Moore. See *Dix ans d'études historiques* (Paris, 1835, pub. in English, London: Whittaker and Co., 1845).

60 Oliver MacDonagh, *The Emancipist: Daniel O'Connell 1830–47* (New York: St Martin's Press, 1989), p. 224. MacDonagh suggests that, on each of these points, 'O'Connell differed from the Young Irelanders fundamentally'.

61 Arnold Whitridge, *Men in Crisis: The Revolutions of 1848* (New York: Charles Schribner and Sons, 1949), p. 122.

62 Ibid., p. 123. *La Giovine Italia* was founded in 1832 and described itself as a 'Series of writings for the regeneration of Italy's political, social, moral and literary conditions'.

63 Whitridge, *Men in Crisis*, p. 126.

64 Davis, 'Young Ireland', p. 1.

65 Quoted in Nowlan, *Politics of Repeal*, p. 9.

66 Priscilla Robertson, *Revolutions of 1848: A Social History* (Princeton: Princeton University Press, 1952), p. 408.

67 Davis, 'Young Ireland', p. 1.

68 W.F. Lyons, *Brigadier-General Thomas Francis Meagher: His Political and Military Career, with Selections from the Speeches and Writings* (London: Burns Oates, 1869), p. 220.

69 Duffy, *Four Years*, p. 8.

70 Philip Mansel, 'Nation Building. The Foundation of Belgium' in *History Today* (May 2005), 24–6.
71 Daunt, *Personal Recollections*, vol. ii, p. 10.
72 *Morning Advertiser,* quoted in Thomson and McGusty, *Irish Journals*, Appendix, p. 296.
73 Evans, *The Revolutions of Europe*, p. 190.
74 Barbara K. Reinfeld, *Karel Havlicek (1821–1856): A National Liberation Leader of the Czech Renascence* (New York: Eastern European Monographs, 1982), pp. 25–6.
75 Duffy, *Young Ireland*, vol. i, p. 128.
76 Duffy, *Four Years*, vol. i, pp. 86–7.
77 Ibid., p. 295.
78 Daunt, *Personal Recollections*, vol. ii, pp. 134–41.
79 *Proceedings of the Young Ireland Party at their Grand Meeting in Dublin, December 2, 1846* (Belfast: John Henderson, 1847), p. 11.
80 Duffy, *Young Ireland*, vol. i, p. 88.
81 Ibid., p. 114.
82 Ibid., p. 89.
83 Ibid., pp. 141–2. Duffy claimed that this was O'Connell's reason for choosing this number.
84 Daunt, *Personal Recollections*, vol. ii, p. 140.
85 Ibid., vol. i, p. 74.
86 Daunt to O'Connell, 9 September 1842: ibid., p. 82.
87 *Freeman's Journal*, 9 October 1840.
88 The phrase 'invasion' had first been used in 1828 by one of O'Connell's supporters, Jack Lawless, who had sought to win support for Emancipation in the province: see J. Bardon, *A History of Ulster* (Belfast: Blackstaff, 2005), pp. 245–7.
89 Henry Cooke, *The Repealer Repulsed! A Correct Narrative of the Rise and Progress of the Repeal Invasion of Ulster: Dr. Cooke's Challenge and Mr. O'Connell's Declinature, Tactics and Flight. With ... Illustrations. Also, an Authentic Report of the Great Conservative Demonstrations in Belfast, etc.* (Belfast: William McComb, 1841).
90 Bardon, *History of Ulster*, p. 255.
91 Daunt, *Personal Recollections*, vol. i. pp. 240–8.
92 Bardon, *History of Ulster*, p. 256.
93 Cooke, *Repealer Repulsed!*
94 Daunt, *Personal Recollections*, vol. i, pp. 246–8.
95 Bardon, *History of Ulster*, p. 257.
96 Nowlan, *The Politics of Repeal*, p. 4.
97 Duffy, *Four Years*, p. 24.
98 O'Connell, *Recollections and Experiences*, pp. 153–4.
99 Ibid., p. 155.
100 Ibid.
101 O'Connell to Cullen, 9 May 1842: Maurice O'Connell (ed.), *The Correspondence of Daniel O'Connell* (Shannon: Irish University Press, 1972–80, 8 vols), vol. vii, p. 158.
102 Duffy, *Young Ireland*, vol. i, p. 90.
103 Duffy, *Four Years*, pp. 23–4.

104 Ibid., p. 76.

105 Thomas F. Meagher (ed.), *Letters of a Protestant on Repeal by the Late Thomas Davis* (Dublin: The Irish Confederation, 1847).

106 *Nation*, 17 December 1842.

107 Morash, *Hungry Voice*, p. 285.

108 Quoted in Lady Mary Ferguson, *Sir Samuel Ferguson in the Ireland of His Day, etc.* (Edinburgh and London: W Blackwood and Sons, 1896), p. 138.

109 *Nation*, 27 May 1843.

110 Duffy, *Four Years*, p. 76.

111 Parker, *Sir Robert Peel*, vol. iii, p. 34.

112 Duffy, *Young Ireland*, p. 108.

113 Parker, *Sir Robert Peel,* vol. iii, p. 34.

114 Lord De Grey to Sir Robert Peel, 18 August 1843: ibid., p. 56.

115 Peel to Lord De Grey, 22 August 1843: ibid., pp. 58–9.

116 The Devon Commission published its findings in 1845, on the eve of the Great Famine. James Graham to Peel, 17 October 1843: ibid., p. 64.

117 Peel to Sir James Graham, 18 September 1843: ibid., pp. 63–4.

118 Peel to Sir James Graham, 19 December 1841: ibid., p. 37.

119 Lord De Grey to Peel, marked 'private', 6 May 1843: ibid.

120 Peel to Lord De Grey, 9 May 1843: ibid., pp. 47–8.

121 Quoted in J.H. White, 'The Age of Daniel O'Connell' in T.W. Moody and F.X. Martin, *The Course of Irish History* (Cork: Mercier Press, 1977), p. 43.

122 Elizabeth Smith, 14 May 1843, described the speech as '... exceedingly dignified. Not one unbecoming expression – calm, firm and perfectly conclusive': Thomson and McGusty, *Irish Journals,* p. 63.

123 Daunt, *Personal Recollections*, vol. ii, pp. 152–4.

124 J.C. Beckett, *The Making of Modern Ireland 1603–1923* (London: Faber & Faber, 1966), p. 326.

125 Peel to Sir James Graham, 1 June 1843: Parker, *Sir Robert Peel*, p. 51.

126 O'Connell to Sir Edward Sugden, 27 May 1843, ibid., p. 49.

127 Sir James Graham to Peel, 6 September 1843: ibid., p. 63.

128 *Boston Pilot*, 9 March 1844, 16 March 1844.

129 James Graham to Peel, 25 October 1843: Parker, *Sir Robert Peel*, p. 68.

130 Ibid., p. 124.

131 Duffy, *Young Ireland*, pp. 6–7.

132 Robert Sloan, *William Smith O'Brien and the Young Ireland Rebellion of 1848* (Dublin: Four Courts Press, 2000), p. 105.

133 Gwynn, *Young Ireland*, p. 21.

134 Sloan, *William Smith O'Brien*, pp. 17–19.

135 Ibid., p. 104.

136 *Freeman's Journal*, 6 December 1843.

137 Richard Davis, 'The Reluctant Rebel: William Smith O'Brien' in *Tipperary Historical Journal* (1998), 47–9.

138 Gwynn, *Young Ireland*, Preface.

139 Duffy, *Young Ireland*, vol. ii, pp. 49–50.

140 Duffy, *Four Years*, p. 144.

141 Ibid., pp. 51–5.

142 Peel to Heytesbury, 25 October 1845: Parker, *Sir Robert Peel*, p. 123.

143 Gwynn, *Young Ireland*, pp. 27–8. Federalism was supported by William Sharman Crawford, a liberal, Protestant landlord in County Down.
144 Peel to Heytesbury, 17 October 1844: Parker, *Sir Robert Peel*, p. 122.
145 Heytesbury to Peel, 20 October 1844: ibid., p. 123.
146 Duffy, *Four Years*, p. 22.
147 Duffy, *Young Ireland*, vol. ii, p. 108.
148 Gwynn, *Young Ireland*, pp. 30–1.
149 Nowlan, *Politics of Repeal*, pp. 11–12.
150 Gwynn, *Young Ireland*, pp. 22–3.
151 MacNevin, *Young Ireland*, pp. 5–6.
152 Duffy, *Four Years*, pp. 83–6.
153 Duffy, *Young Ireland*, vol. ii, p. 195.
154 Ibid., p. 196.
155 *Freeman's Journal*, 30 September 1844.
156 One of the most active was the Loyal Irish Repeal Association of the City of Toronto; see British Library, microfiche F.232, 22 September 1843.
157 Thomas C. Luby, *The Life and Times of Daniel O'Connell* (Glasgow: Cameron, Ferguson and Co., 1872), p. 536.
158 Duffy, *Four Years*, p. 33.
159 Dorothy Thompson, 'Ireland and the Irish in English Radicalism before 1850' in James Epstein and Dorothy Thompson (eds), *The Chartist Experience: Studies in Working-Class Radicalism and Culture, 1830–1860* (London: Macmillan, 1982), pp. 120–51.
160 Paul A. Pickering, *Chartism and the Chartists in Manchester and Salford* (Basingstoke: Palgrave Macmillan, 1995) p. 96.
161 *Manchester Times*, 2 October 1841.
162 Rachel O'Higgins, 'The Irish Influence in the Chartist Movement' in *Past and Present* (vol. 20, 1961), 89.
163 Anonymous, 'An Address to the Repealers of Ireland by a member of the Irish Universal Association' (Dublin, 1842), reprinted in George Claeys, *The Chartist Movement in Britain* (London: Pickering and Chatto, 1999), p. 4.
164 Letter from T.M. Ray to Charles O'Conor, a member of New York Directory, 13 September 1841, printed, Box Three, Folder 12, LN HSS, American Irish Historical Society (AIHS).
165 *Northern Star*, 27 July 1839, 10 July 1841, 24 August 1841.
166 Ibid., 26 January 1839, 16 February 1839.
167 Thompson, 'Ireland and the Irish', p. 133.
168 Anonymous, 'Address to Repealers of Ireland', p. 15; *Nation*, 27 May 1843.
169 Kinealy, 'Brethren in Bondage' in Lane and Ó Drisceoil, *Politics and the Irish Working Class*, p. 86.
170 Ibid., pp. 80–90.
171 *United Irishman*, 4 March 1848.
172 Ibid.
173 Rules of IUSA, in Appendix to 'Address of the Irish Universal Suffrage Association to the Most Reverend Roman Catholic Archbishops and Bishops of Ireland' (Dublin, 1843) reprinted in Claeys, *The Chartist Movement*, p. 17.
174 Ibid.
175 O'Higgins, 'The Irish Influence', 88.
176 Thompson, 'Ireland and the Irish', passim.

177 O'Higgins, 'The Irish Influence', 87.
178 Ibid., 89.
179 Ibid., 88.
180 Ibid., 89.
181 *Nation*, 14 January 1843.
182 Thomas D'Arcy McGee, *A History of the Irish Settlers in North America from the Earliest Period to the Census of 1850* (Boston: American Celt, 1851), p. 133.
183 Peel to Lord de Grey, 10 July 1842: Parker, *Sir Robert Peel*, p. 37. The post of Chief Secretary formed part of the Irish administration, which was based in Dublin Castle. It was under the authority of the Lord Lieutenant, who was appointed directly by the British government.
184 Many of the reports of informers were channelled through British consuls in the US to the Home Office, HO Papers, TNA, HO 45/2369.
185 Papers regarding Convention in Philadelphia, 22 March 1842: O'Connor Papers, AIHS, Folder 26.
186 McGee, *History of Irish Settlers*, p. 133.
187 *Nation*, 14 January 1843.
188 *Nation*, 22 July 1843.
189 John Quinn, 'The Rise and fall of Repeal: Slavery and Irish Nationalism in Antebellum Philadelphia' in *Pennsylvania Magazine of History and Biography* (vol. 130, no. 1, 2005), 14, suggests this may have been pragmatic as Tyler was switching his allegiance to the Democratic Party and wanted a nomination, and he realized the importance of the Irish vote.
190 Duffy, *Young Ireland*, vol. i, pp. 78, 149–50.
191 Kinealy, *Lives of Victorian Political Figures*, pp. 63–73.
192 Daunt, *Personal Recollections*, vol. ii, p. 168.
193 Ibid., vol. i, p. 284.
194 Hon. S.P. Chase, *Reply to Daniel O'Connell*, in Daniel O'Connell, *Liberty or Slavery? And Reply to O'Connell by Hon. S.P. Chase* (Cincinnati: Chronicle Print, 1863) [letters dated 11 October 1843 (Dublin) and 30 November 1843 (Cincinnati) respectively].
195 Lewis C. Levin, *A Lecture on Irish Repeal, in Elucidation of the Fallacy of its Principles, and in Proof of its Pernicious Tendency, in its Moral, Religious and Political Aspects* (Philadelphia, 1844), p. 13.
196 Luby, *O'Connell*, p. 536.
197 Duffy, *Young Ireland*, vol ii, p. 186.
198 Daunt, *Personal Recollections*, vol. i, p. 287.
199 Duffy, *Four Years*, p. 33.
200 Duffy, *Four Years*, p. 34.
201 Comments on Emmet's resignation by Thomas O'Connor, no date, Papers of Charles O'Connor, Box Two, Folder Four, AIHS, New York.
202 Geraldine F. Grogan, *The Noblest Agitator: Daniel O'Connell and the German Catholic Movement 1830–1850* (Dublin: Veritas, 1991); Pauline Collombier, *Le discourse des leaders du nationalism constitutionnel irlandais sur l'autonomie de l'irlande: Utopies politiques et mythes identitaires* (unpublished PhD, Sorbonne, Paris, 2007).
203 *Hansard*, vol. lxxii (House of Commons) 19 February 1844, State of Ireland debate, cols 1185–6.

204 Laurent Colantonio, 'Daniel O'Connell: un Irlandais au cœur du discours républicain pendant la Monarchie de Juillet' in *Revue d'Histoire du XIX siècle* (Varia, 2000 20/21). Colantonio has written extensively on this topic.
205 *Nation*, 27 May 1843.
206 Duffy, *Young Ireland*, vol. i, pp. 151–2.
207 Daunt, *Personal Recollections*, vol. ii, p. 168.
208 Ibid.
209 James E. McGee, *The Men of '48. Being a Brief History of the Repeal Association and the Irish Confederation; with Biographical Sketches of the Leading Actors in the Latter Organization, their Principles, Opinions and Literary Labours* (first pub. New York, 1874: Boston, 1881), *p.* 122.
210 Memorandum for the Cabinet, marked 'secret', 11 February 1844: Parker, *Sir Robert Peel*, p. 103.
211 Cabinet Memorandum, 17 February 1844: ibid., pp. 105–6.
212 Peel to Heytesbury, 5 September 1844: ibid., p. 120.
213 Peel to Mr Croker, 17 December 1844: ibid., p. 130.
214 Lord Eliot to Lord Heytesbury, 19 December 1844: ibid., p. 132.
215 Prince Albert to Peel, 22 December 1844: ibid., p. 133.
216 Queen Victoria to Peel, 9 April 1845: ibid., p. 173.
217 Lord Stanley to Peel, 18 February 1844: ibid.
218 *Belfast Protestant Journal*, 21 March 1846, 11 July 1846; *Freeman's Journal*, 11 July 1846.
219 Peel to James Heytesbury, 22 August 1845: Parker, *Sir Robert Peel*, p. 186.
220 James Graham to Peel, 2 October 1844: ibid., p. 188.
221 Graham to Peel, 3 October 1845: ibid., p. 190.
222 *Nation*, 17 May 1845.
223 Duffy, *Four Years*, pp. 26–7.
224 Ibid., p. 28.
225 Richard Davis, *The Young Ireland Movement* (Dublin: Gill and Macmillan, 1988), pp. 67–71.
226 Duffy, *Four Years*, p. 165.

2

'A death-dealing famine': conciliation and division

In 1845 an event occurred that, in the short term, pushed Repeal to the back of the political agenda and, in the longer term, transformed the social and demographic profile of Ireland. It also changed the political relationship between Ireland and Britain. In September of that year, a previously unknown blight appeared on the potato crop in Ireland and within a few months it had destroyed approximately half of the harvest. Food shortages were not unknown in Ireland, but the scale and longevity of this one made it unique. Many nationalists believed that if Ireland had been independent such a disaster would not have happened; others suggested that if the Repeal movement had been strong, as it had been in 1843, and the government had continued to export provisions, 'a food riot would have been the beginning of a revolution'.[1] According to Duffy, 'it was not the failure of the potato, but the failure of an all-wise and adequate government that was to be feared'.[2]

The onset of famine coincided with an increase in agrarian unrest, leading some conservative newspapers in Britain to renew calls for more coercive measures to be introduced. The *Standard* suggested that the recent creation of a railway network would greatly facilitate the subjugation of Ireland. Mitchel, who had replaced Davis as the chief writer for the *Nation* and was proving to be far more zealous in his condemnation of the British government than Davis had been, responded by writing an article on how railways could be sabotaged. He ensured the enmity of the more moderate section of the Repeal Association by suggesting that Repeal Wardens could lead the people in this act of subversion.[3] The article was not universally welcomed, even by his colleagues at the *Nation*, most significantly Duffy. The most vehement attack on Mitchel came from Daniel and John O'Connell, despite Mitchel's public acknowledgement that O'Connell had no control over the Repeal Wardens, which amounted to an implicit apology. In Conciliation Hall O'Connell suggested that the article had imperilled the existence of the Association.[4] To some extent he was correct as the British government used the article as a pretext for attacking the *Nation* and prosecuting Duffy, as proprietor, for publishing seditious libel.[5] Duffy's prosecution, which was eventually dropped, was widely condemned. O'Connell, however, through his silence, appeared to tacitly welcome it. Moreover, he tried to enlist William Smith O'Brien to condemn Duffy and the *Nation*, but O'Brien refused to do so.[6]

This public dispute coincided with the onset of widespread distress in Ireland. A series of relief measures introduced by Peel's government had ensured that nobody died in the first year of food shortages, but suffering was extensive. A number of people in Ireland believed that the impact of the shortages would be lessened if the Irish ports were 'closed' as a means of limiting the vast amount of food, particularly corn, that was continuing to leave Ireland.[7] Such a demand was concurrently being made by the Lord Lieutenant, Daniel O'Connell (who was a member of the Mansion House [Relief] Committee) and the leaders of Young Ireland. O'Brien used his position as an MP to advocate in the House of Commons that grain exports should be stopped and a tax placed on absentee landlords. He also opposed the Repeal of the Corn Laws, on the grounds that they would benefit Britain but not Ireland.[8] While his outspokenness was admired in Ireland, it annoyed members of the government, including Peel.[9] Revenge was exacted a few weeks later when O'Brien compounded his reputation amongst his fellow nationalists by refusing to serve on a parliamentary railway committee. Attendance was compulsory, but this rule had never been enforced. Nevertheless, on 30 April, charged with 'contempt of this House', O'Brien was taken into custody and imprisoned in a cellar in the House of Commons for three weeks. Significantly, Daniel O'Connell had participated in one of the railway committees. This episode divided opinion within the Repeal movement, with much admiration expressed for O'Brien. O'Connell belatedly capitalized on this support by treating O'Brien as a 'Repeal hero' on his release.[10] O'Connell's words were hollow, as he was involved simultaneously in negotiations with the Whigs that were once again to place Repeal in the background. Furthermore, as a result of his principled stand, O'Brien had not only consolidated his position as a leader of the Young Ireland group, but he was increasingly looking like a successor to Daniel O'Connell in the Repeal Association.

The potato blight in Ireland not only had a devastating impact on the poor in Ireland, but it indirectly resulted in the fall of Peel's government. Since 1842 Peel had been moving towards repealing the Corn Laws in the United Kingdom, but when he finally attempted to do so, he was regarded as a traitor by the Protectionist wing of his party, led by Lord George Bentinck and Benjamin Disraeli. Peel tied in his action with the potato failure in 1845, arguing that the removal of impediments to corn imports would help to end dependence on the potato crop in Ireland.[11] Privately, he admitted that this legislation would not help to alleviate Irish poverty in the short or longer term.[12] Peel did not have the support of either his

Cabinet or his party, making his political future as Premier untenable.[13] Consequently, when he introduced a Bill to Repeal the Corn Laws in December 1845, he simultaneously tendered his resignation. The premiership was offered to Lord John Russell, leader of the Whigs, but he did not feel strong enough to form a government and so declined. Russell's refusal meant that Peel remained in office as Prime Minister in the early months of 1846, and he used this time to oversee the Repeal of the Corn Laws in June 1846. Although Peel held on to the government, the political cost of his actions was high as it split the Tory Party into two sections: the Peelites and the Protectionists. The Protectionists used the first opportunity – ironically, the introduction of a new Irish Coercion Bill – to show their displeasure by voting against Peel, together with the Whigs and the O'Connellites. The Coercion Bill was defeated. Peel's administration could not withstand this onslaught and, in early July, the Whig Party took over the reins of government.

The Whig Party in the House of Commons, led by Lord John Russell, was weak, but this situation changed in June 1846, when Daniel O'Connell made it clear that he would be proud to support them.[14] Voting against the Peel government placed O'Connell in a strong position to renew his alliance with the Whigs. The Young Irelanders disapproved of this association, believing that it would mark an end to the demand for Repeal. When O'Brien protested, he was reassured by O'Connell that the Repeal Association would remain neutral as he was opposed to 'placing the Irish nation under the feet of the English Whigs'.[15] He further suggested that if the Whigs did come to power 'they would not be permitted to effect by corruption what the Tories had failed to effect by coercion'. Finally, O'Connell reminded O'Brien that his own motto was 'Repeal and no Compromise'.[16] O'Connell's assurances were meaningless. Only a few weeks later, he informed a meeting at Conciliation Hall that, 'The new administration will be wanting us, and they will have us, if they do good work for the Irish people.'[17] Furthermore, while his father was secretly negotiating with the Whigs, John O'Connell had commenced a 'whispering campaign against the *Nation*, on the grounds that ... [its] aims were incompatible with the traditions and the faith of Catholic Ireland'.[18] His actions were part of a longer-term strategy to undermine Young Ireland's position in the Repeal movement.

O'Connell's support made it possible for Russell to form a government. Peel regarded the defeat of the Coercion Bill and the alliance between the Whigs and the Repeal Association as a 'signal triumph of ... the promoters of assassination throughout Ireland'.[19] He mistrusted the motives of the Irish nationalists in assisting the Whigs, warning that:

> Their wish is to disgust England with Irish business and with Irish members, and to induce England, through sheer disgust, and the sense of public inconvenience from the obstructions offered to progress of all other business in Parliament, to listen to a Repeal of the Legislative Union for the purpose of

purging the House of a set of troublesome and factious members, who equally obstruct legislation for Ireland and for Great Britain.[20]

During early summer, parliamentary debate in Westminster was dominated by the fall of Peel's government and its replacement by a Whig administration. The fact that it was a minority government made an alliance with O'Connell more understandable. Russell, however, was anxious to draw a distinction between the two sections of the Repeal Party, publicly expressing his dislike of the *Nation* group while negotiating with O'Connell. In the House of Commons, he denounced Young Ireland, describing them as

> [a group] who, if I read rightly their sentiments as expressed in a newspaper – I will name it – called the *Nation*, which has a great circulation in Ireland, who go beyond that question of the Legislative Union – who would wish not merely to have such a parliament as that which it was the boast of Grattan to have found, and which legislated under the sceptre of the same Sovereign as the Parliament of Great Britain, but a party which exerts every species of violence, which looks to disturbance as its means, and regards separation from England as its end.[21]

At this stage, Young Ireland still supported O'Connell and opposed violence, thus suggesting that Russell's comments were disingenuous and politically motivated. Possibly also, the new Prime Minister was preparing for a split within the Repeal movement, from which he would benefit. The new Whig government had only been in office for a few weeks, however, when they were confronted by the prospect of a second subsistence crisis in Ireland, as the potato blight reappeared, earlier and more virulently than in the previous year. Distress, on an even more extensive scale, was inevitable unless the new government introduced comprehensive measures to alleviate the food shortages. Their failure to do so resulted in a devastating famine.

Death of Davis

As news of the appearance of blight was spreading, the Repeal movement received a major blow in September 1845 with the premature death from fever of Thomas Davis, aged only 30. His passing deprived Young Ireland of its most gifted and visionary writer. Davis's colleagues were devastated by his death. O'Brien described him as having 'united a woman's tenderness with the soul of a hero'.[22] Even the conservative *Dublin University Magazine* recognized his leadership qualities and his attempts to impart to the Irish people 'justice, manliness and reliance on themselves'.[23] Davis was mourned not only by nationalists in Ireland, but also by those further afield. In the United States, the New York Repealers wore a badge of mourning for thirty days, while the Boston Repealers discussed erecting a monument to his memory on Bunker Hill.[24] Davis's unexpected death also left the Young Ireland group without a leader. Duffy claimed that it 'threw upon me the task of reconstructing and directing the party he had created'.[25] Since 1844 though, when he had managed the Repeal Association during O'Connell's imprisonment, O'Brien had become more prominent within Young Ireland and his public stature had enhanced the reputation of the group. Consequently, he, rather than Duffy, became Davis's unofficial political successor. Davis had been a unifying force in the Repeal movement and his supporters regarded him as a natural successor to Daniel O'Connell, despite his being a Protestant. His death created an opportunity for John O'Connell to present himself as his father's political heir, regardless of the fact that he possessed little charisma or talent. Moreover, John was a devout Catholic who did little to promote non-sectarian attitudes within the Repeal Association.

Davis's death was a particular blow to his colleagues at the *Nation*, as, in the words of one of his colleagues, 'Davis was the *Nation* and the *Nation* was Davis.'[26] His passing coincided with the withdrawal of other regular writers, including John Blake Dillon and Thomas MacNevin (through illness), and O'Hagan and Pigot (who both moved to London).[27] Despite these losses, Duffy believed that it was the *Nation* that kept the Repeal movement alive at this period, as the O'Connells were still reeling from their imprisonment in the previous year.[28] The void was partially filled by two very different writers: Thomas D'Arcy McGee and John Mitchel. McGee was one of the youngest, yet most experienced, of the new contributors to the *Nation*. He had been born in 1825 to a poor family and so, from a young age, had needed to earn a living. Aged only 18, McGee emigrated to the United States where he got a job as a clerk for the Irish journal, the *Boston Pilot*, but he soon began contributing to it as a writer. He also became active in the American Repeal movement, quickly earning a reputation as a brilliant orator.[29] An article on Irish famines resulted in his being offered a position by the *Freeman's Journal* in Dublin, as their parliamentary correspondent in London. Secretly though, he was concurrently sending reports to the *Nation* for publication. Clearly, despite have great admiration for O'Connell, his sympathies lay with Young Ireland and when his employment with the newspaper was terminated, he was offered a job with the *Nation* by Duffy.[30] Another newcomer was John Mitchel, who replaced Davis as chief political writer of the *Nation*. He was the son of a Presbyterian minister, whose sympathies lay with the more tolerant section of the Church. Mitchel had grown up in Newry and was a barrister by training. Duffy had met him in Belfast and was impressed with 'the vigour and liberality of his opinions, as well as by his culture and suavity'.[31] He had persuaded him to contribute a number of articles to the *Nation*. In 1843, Duffy had invited Mitchel to be a northern delegate in the proposed Council of Three Hundred, but he had refused, saying 'I cannot afford to neglect my business. I have a wife and children. To devote myself to this cause would simply ruin me, and I cannot sacrifice my family.'[32] In 1845, though, Mitchel was persuaded by Duffy to replace Davis at the *Nation*. Mitchel quickly demonstrated that he was a talented writer and a brilliant polemicist, although he occasionally offended his colleagues by his outspokenness and frank criticisms of their work.[33] However, he was greatly admired by some of the younger writers, including the female contributors to the *Nation*.[34] Mitchel's wife Jenny played less of a public role in nationalist politics, but she supported Young Ireland and advised Mitchel on policy matters. She also allowed her home in Dublin to become a meeting place for political sympathizers.[35] Initially, Mitchel and Duffy, two Ulstermen, had a close personal and political relationship, but Mitchel's increasingly forceful writings went beyond the moderation preached by Duffy. Duffy and McGee, however, who had more in common politically, spent much time socializing and walking in each other's company.[36]

In addition to McGee and Mitchel, in the months following Davis's death, a fresh cluster of young writers and intellectuals became involved with the *Nation*. The new contributors included Thomas Francis Meagher, John O'Leary and 'Speranza' (Jane Elgee).[37] They revitalized the Repeal movement, more on the side of Young Ireland than the O'Connellites. Some of the most outstanding new recruits to Young Ireland were female.[38] Although women had attended meetings of the Repeal Association, until the appearance of the *Nation* they had few public outlets to be politically involved, even if they did so anonymously.[39] To disguise themselves, the women frequently used pen-names, some keeping their identity secret, even from the editors. A number of male writers used female pseudonyms, confusing even their colleagues as to their real gender.[40] Although approximately twenty women were involved sporadically with Young Ireland, only five were regular contributors.[41] They were overshadowed by their male counterparts, despite being no less patriotic, many of them admiring the outspoken radicalism of John Mitchel rather than Duffy's more moderate stand. In fact, the fervour of some women led to accusations that such militancy was unseemly for females.[42] Many were under 21 when they commenced writing for the *Nation*. While most were middle class, they were drawn from different religious traditions, with Protestant females finding a forum to express their patriotism and love for Ireland.[43]

One of the most prolific contributors of both poetry and prose was Jane Elgee, 'Speranza', whose family was Protestant and Conservative, her grandfather having been an Anglican bishop in Wexford. She claimed she had had no contact with Catholics until she became involved with the *Nation*.[44] Her association came about when she saw Davis's funeral procession in Dublin. She initially wrote under the pseudonym John Fenshaw Ellis, a play on her real name Jane Francesca Elgee. Speranza was a scholar and gifted linguist, leading Duffy to describe her as 'a woman of genius'. He particularly admired her because she wrote 'as a man'.[45]

Speranza's work first appeared in the *Nation* in 1846 and within a few months she had published one of her most famous poems, *The Famine Year*, which was a blistering attack on the inadequate relief policies of the British government.[46]

A number of the women were drawn from the Catholic middle classes. A regular contributor was Ellen Mary Downing of Cork. Her family were not nationalists. She had first published in the *Nation* in May 1845 when aged only 17. Initially she wrote as 'E.M.P.D.' but following Davis's death she became a more frequent contributor, writing as 'Mary'. Duffy described her lyrics as 'soft as summer rain, and as passionate, spontaneous, and native as anything'.[47] Her verses, however, were intensely patriotic and she sympathized with the more radical wing of Young Ireland, represented by John Mitchel.[48] Regular contributions were provided by 'Eva', who was, in fact, Mary Kelly from County Galway. She was a cousin of John Blake Dillon, who may have influenced her nationalist politics.[49] She was 15 when she started to write for the *Nation* in 1845. Collectively, 'Speranza', 'Mary' and 'Eva', were referred to as 'the Three Graces'.[50] Duffy regarded the poetry of the three women as 'some of the most original and popular' that was published.[51]

Interest in the *Nation* was not confined to women based in Dublin. Elizabeth Willoughby Treacy came from Ballymena in County Antrim. Her family had Orange sympathies, although she was a nationalist throughout her adult life.[52] She was only 16 when she commenced contributing to the *Nation*, a fact that was belied by the maturity of her topics.[53] She wrote under the pen-name 'Finola'. Two young sisters, who published under the pseudonym of 'Two Irish Girls', wrote letters to the *Nation*, appealing to other women to support the National Party.[54]

Despite the important contribution of women, they were not regarded as the equals of men and it was not until 1848 that the *Nation* started a series on *Illustrated Irishwomen*, to match its series on *Illustrated Irishmen*. One of the first women featured was Mathilda Tone, wife of Wolfe Tone.[55] The series ended abruptly with the suppression of the *Nation* in 1848. When the paper resumed publication in 1850, it had less input from females.

Apart from the involvement of women after 1845, the *Nation* attracted a number of gifted young men, who were influenced more by Davis than by O'Connell. Many were from the Irish professional classes and they had benefited from a more liberal attitude to Catholics evident since the 1780s, which had contributed to the emergence of an educated Catholic middle class. John O'Leary, who later achieved notoriety as a leading Fenian, had come across the poems and writings of Davis while recovering from fever. Even as an old man, he thanked Davis for awakening 'all that is Irish in me and, above all, for the inspiration that made me Irish'.[56] One of the most charismatic of the new intake was Thomas Francis Meagher, who was only 22 when he first became involved with Young

Ireland. His father was a wealthy Catholic merchant from Waterford, who had been a Repeal MP and supporter of O'Connell. Like many Catholics of his generation, he had not gone to the Anglican Trinity College, which was the only university in Ireland, but he had completed his education at the Jesuit Stoneyhurst College in Lancashire. According to Duffy, Meagher lacked true leadership skills but had risen quickly to prominence due to his powers of oratory, which exuded 'passion, poetry and imagination'.[57] Meagher's celebrity was copper-fastened by his famous speeches during the 'Peace Resolution' debates in 1846, which earned him the sobriquet 'Meagher of the Sword'. Overall, the new intake of writers and the loss of Davis's moderating influence moved the *Nation* in a more radical direction, which increasingly gave Daniel and John O'Connell cause for concern.

By the end of 1845, a new radical spirit had been awakened in the Repeal movement, which had re-energized it and broadened its appeal. The Young Ireland group wanted an Irish nation that appealed to both Catholics and Protestants, men and women, landlords and artisans. The broad church that formed the Repeal movement remained committed to constitutional tactics, hoping that by moral force alone they could win independence. Increasingly, O'Connell's autocratic style of leadership, his growing dependence on his son John, and his cavalier approach to the winning of Repeal, was alienating the Young Ireland group. The tension came to a head in the summer of 1846, in a dispute that was engineered by O'Connell and in which Young Ireland were reluctant participants. In the short term, the main beneficiary of the division was the British government. Consequently, less than a year after Davis's death, the Repeal Association had split into two distinct sections, and his aim of creating a unified, inclusive movement was in shreds. The backdrop to the political repositioning was the appearance of blight on the Irish potato crop. The expectation had been that good harvests would return in 1846. Instead, the blight marked the onset of a famine of unprecedented severity and longevity. At the same time, as O'Connell was placing his faith in the new Whig administration to give 'justice to Ireland', Young Ireland was becoming even more convinced that political independence was the country's only hope of achieving honourable government. The ongoing food shortages heightened political tensions, while intensifying disillusionment with the British government.

Secession

The summer of 1846 was dominated by a number of political struggles in Ireland. In the north of the country, the conciliatory policies of successive British governments to Catholics had led to the emergence of a more militant form of Protestantism and a consequent rise in sectarian conflict. Violence was most intense following the parades on 17 March (St

Patrick's Day, celebrated by Catholics) and 12 July (the anniversary of the Battle of the Boyne and celebrated by Protestants).[58] Peel had been unpopular with many Irish Protestants as he was indelibly linked with the granting of Catholic Emancipation, but the incoming Whig government was also mistrusted by some Protestants. The *Belfast Protestant Journal* explained that 'we expect no favour to the Protestants of Ireland. We have experienced their conduct in former times, their betrayal of principle, and their venal and corrupt practices.'[59] Protestant suspicions were exacerbated by O'Connell's overtures towards the new administration. But the divisions between Catholics and Protestants were overshadowed by the political tensions in Dublin where hostility was increasing within the Repeal movement, notably between O'Connell and the Young Irelanders.

While O'Connell claimed that the incoming Whig administration wanted to conciliate Repealers, the Young Ireland group believed that Irish independence had been sacrificed for promises of patronage and pensions.[60] O'Connell's intentions became apparent when, at the first meeting of the Association following Peel's resignation, a letter was read in which he outlined 'the opportunities a new Government would have to conciliate the Irish people', and exhorting the Association to 'discountenance the fomenters of dissension and destruction' in the Repeal ranks.[61] O'Connell sought approval from the Repeal Association for his proposed alliance with the Whigs, placing before the members a package of reforms, which included the return of denominational education. Accepting the association meant that the demand for Repeal would be replaced by a return to seeking reforms for Ireland, which now included providing relief for a second year of food shortages. However, Russell had made no firm commitment; and the fact that he did not have a parliamentary majority and was facing a General Election in 1847 made it even more unlikely that any substantial reforms would be made. Moreover, an aged O'Connell, who for twenty years had tormented British politicians, appeared to have lost direction. His health was also deteriorating which, according to Duffy 'paralysed his powerful will and rendered him an easy prey to sycophants and intriguers'.[62] In particular, it provided an opportunity for John O'Connell to assume additional control over the Repeal Association, and he, even more than his father, both disliked and feared Young Ireland. Young Ireland, rather than militant Protestants or intransigent members of the British government, were now the main enemy of the Repeal Association.

The leaders of Young Ireland were alarmed by O'Connell's renewed association with the Whigs, describing it as 'the fatalist stroke that fortune could strike against Ireland'. They believed that it would have a corrupting influence as O'Connell and his close allies would be given positions and pensions in return 'for silence or apostasy'.[63] Young Ireland believed that they had to oppose the alliance because 'the Irish cause was not the private property of the leader and his family, to be taken up and laid down at his individual discretion'.[64] O'Connell, who had initially welcomed the vigour that the *Nation* had brought to the Repeal movement, increasingly became critical of it and its young contributors. O'Connell's Federal Plan had produced a strain between the two groups. A further rift had occurred over the question of religion, exacerbated by disagreement over the Charities Commission and the University Colleges. During these debates, Young Ireland cautioned the Repeal movement that it must not be seen to be promoting a Catholic Ascendancy. They had also been critical of the way in which the Repeal Association was managed, especially the fact that its accounts were not properly audited and that important decisions were made without reference to the General Committee. O'Connell took these criticisms personally and informed Davis that this 'was far from the case although I have often felt amongst SOME of the Liberal Protestants I have met with that there was not the same soundness of generous liberality amongst them as amongst the Catholics'. He also warned that there was a danger of the *Nation* promoting 'Protestant monomania'.[65] Duffy believed that a serious problem for O'Connell was that, 'It was one of the fatal weaknesses of his life to surround himself by men whose chief characteristic was abject submission', and he was therefore unable to cope with the independent stance of Young Ireland.[66] Privately, O'Brien was concerned that O'Connell was becoming preoccupied with religious matters, having confided to him that he desired to retire to a religious establishment if he could 'extricate himself from the exigencies of his position as a political leader'.[67]

In the summer of 1846, Daniel O'Connell, encouraged by John, decided to reassert Old Ireland's authority within the Association, in order to demonstrate a unified front to the Whigs. Correctly, he anticipated that Young Ireland would be an impediment.[68] The mechanism for forcing obedience to his leadership was to demand that every member of the Association renounced the use of physical force in order to achieve their objectives, agreeing instead to the so-called 'Peace Resolutions'. The fact that no group within the Association was advocating violence suggested that the debate was a manufactured one. Although O'Connell disliked rebellion and denounced those who broke the law, he was not a pacifist.[69] The complexity of his outlook was indicated by his support for the Latin-American revolt against Spain in 1820 (when one of his sons fought on behalf of the rebel leader, Simon Bolivar) and his defence of the struggle for Belgian independence in 1830. In the same year, he had offered to raise 40,000 men to restore the Bourbon dynasty in France.[70] Within the Irish context though, O'Connell had always been resolutely opposed to violent tactics (despite the covert threats of his rhetoric) and the Repeal Association was committed to the use of legal and constitutional tactics only. Since the appearance of Mitchel's railway article, however, he had regarded Mitchel as an agitator who was a danger to the Association. He feared that the *Nation*, by printing such articles, was jeopardising his intended association with the Whigs.[71]

At first, it seemed that O'Connell would maintain his usual sway over the Association. Inevitably, the debate became tied in with O'Connell's longer term plans for it. At a meeting in Dublin on 6 July, only a few days after the Whigs had come to power, O'Connell expressed support for the new ministry and outlined twelve measures that he expected them to pass in return. While eleven of the measures were to be passed in the current parliamentary session, the twelfth demand, Repeal, he said, could wait for a later session. Mitchel in the *Nation* and Meagher in Conciliation Hall spearheaded an assault on the proposed alliance.[72] Mitchel wrote, 'let us not pretend to give up or postpone Repeal, in order that English ministers may more readily yield us that justice which they have delayed as long as they could; let no Repealer dare to hint that a "real Union" would satisfy us ... what we are determined to have now is, not "justice to Ireland or Repeal", but "justice to Ireland and Repeal"'.[73] But even Mitchel, who later became associated with the most extreme section of the nationalist movement, did not want either total separation from Britain or a republic.[74] Nor did he and his colleagues at the *Nation* want to establish a separate Repeal association. O'Connell's determination to please the Whigs became immediately apparent when he refused to select a parliamentary candidate to stand in Dungarvan, a Repeal stronghold. Consequently, a Whig candidate was returned unopposed.[75] When Young Ireland objected, O'Connell accused the dissenters of being 'juvenile orators', regardless of the fact that some of the main challengers to Old Ireland were 30 or over, notably John Mitchel (aged 30), Michael Doheny (40), Father John Kenyon (34) and O'Brien (42), each of whom enjoyed personal popularity within Young Ireland.

When the split came it was acrimonious and decisive, with individual members of Young Ireland being singled out for criticism. Ostensibly, it was over the use of physical versus moral force, although this disguised more immediate differences over university education, cooperation with the Whigs and O'Connell's willingness to accept public appointments and pensions for his family and close allies. Nonetheless, even at this stage, Young Ireland did not want a split. O'Brien, who since his imprisonment over the railway question had become the champion of Young Ireland, still admired O'Connell personally and he wanted to maintain the unity of the Repeal Association.[76] Daniel and John O'Connell were determined to draw a distinction between Old and Young Ireland. On 13 July 1846, John O'Connell brought forward a series of resolutions in Conciliation Hall by which members of the Association had to abjure violence in their efforts to gain national independence. The report outlining this proposal was embodied in the 'Peace Resolutions'.[77] The resolutions were debated over a number of days. Each member of the Association had to fully and unconditionally agree to them. At this stage, the use of physical force was not contemplated by even the most radical members of Young Ireland. The whole premise of the debate, therefore, was speculative and abstract. On principle, Young Ireland refused to accept the resolutions, while stating their support for the aims of the Repeal Association. Even Mitchel, who represented the more radical section of Young Ireland, professed his compliance with the rules of the Association and his desire to continue to work within it. He pointed out that 'he had no intention in the world of going to war himself or inciting anybody else to do so'. He went on to say that 'As far as the resolutions had anything to do with the practical working of the society, he applauded and approved of them most heartily. In as far as they conveyed, or seemed to convey, a general condemnation of other societies and other people, he altogether dissented from them.'[78] Mitchel also defended Duffy, who was not present, but had been accused of having 'last Saturday distinctly avowed an intention of doing the work of Ireland by physical force'. By the end of the meeting, the Young Irelanders felt that they had successfully resisted the Peace Resolutions and that the debate was at an end.[79] Their optimism was premature. The *Belfast Protestant Journal*, for example, warned that 'It is very currently reported that some members of the "Young Ireland" party have already received "notice to quit" the Association.'[80]

John O'Connell had not been present at the first meeting when the Peace Resolutions had been discussed. Some of the more moderate supporters of Young Ireland, including O'Brien and Duffy, had also been absent, leaving it to the younger, less experienced and less diplomatic members of Young Ireland to defend their position. Despite their optimism, the question had not been resolved. On 23 July, John O'Connell returned from London for the purpose of reopening the issue and drawing a 'marked distinction between Young and Old Ireland'.[81] Meanwhile, Daniel O'Connell had travelled to London, leaving John to act as his spokesman. O'Brien was present at the second meeting and he criticized the way in which the motion had been brought to the meeting, without going through the usual procedures of first presenting it to General Committee of the Repeal Association. It was the first time he had publicly and unequivocally sided with Young Ireland against O'Connell, but he said he could be 'no party' to the exclusion of the men associated with the *Nation*, describing such a move as 'suicidal'.[82] In rejecting the Peace Resolutions, Young Ireland were vehement, especially Mitchel, Meagher and Richard O'Gorman. At this meeting, the religious integrity of the Repeal Association was questioned, thus raising the important question of what sort of nation O'Connell and his supporters were seeking. Mitchel addressed the meeting as an Ulster Protestant, warning

this is our country as well as yours. You need not expect to free it from the mighty power of England by yourselves. Drive the Ulster Protestants away from your movement by needless tests, and you perpetuate the degradation both of yourselves and them. Keep them at a distance from you – making yourselves subservient to the old and well-known English policy of ruling Ireland always by one party or another – and England will keep her heel upon both your necks for ever.[83]

Mitchel's impassioned speech was overshadowed by Meagher's fiery rhetoric. During the main debate on 28 July he spoke after Mitchel. Like his colleagues, he denounced a proposed alliance with the Whigs, warning that, 'A Whig Minister, I admit, may improve the province – he will not restore the nation.'[84] He denounced the resolutions as unnecessary and impracticable, while emphasizing that he had joined the Association to achieve Repeal by peaceful means. He went on to say that, on occasion, 'force must be used against force ... The man who will listen to reason – let him be reasoned with, but it is the weaponed arm of the patriot that can alone prevail against battalioned despotism.'[85] Regardless of the quality and sincerity of the Young Ireland arguments, they were no match for the wiliness of John O'Connell and his supporters. Furthermore, the forcefulness of Young Ireland's response gave further ammunition to O'Connell, who interrupted Meagher when the latter was in full flow. He challenged Meagher with the choice of either leaving the Association or being responsible for its demise. O'Brien defended Meagher's right to speak, but John O'Connell threatened that if Meagher continued, the Association would no longer have a leader. He refused to allow Meagher to continue. At this point, O'Brien walked out of the Hall, followed by Meagher, Patrick Smyth, Father Meehan and Devin Reilly, amongst others.[86] Despite their treatment, the Young Irelanders did not wish to leave the Association, believing that 'to quit the Association meant to commit the public cause to Mr John O'Connell and speedy ruin'.[87] According to Meagher, they hoped the policy would be reversed when Daniel O'Connell returned to Ireland, and 'With this hope we refrained from the condemnation of that policy.'[88] Consequently, the *Nation*, speaking for the seceders, adopted the language of conciliation rather than rebuke. Nonetheless, their departure marked the demise of a united Repeal movement in Ireland. O'Brien, who had sided with the seceders despite his pacifist views, regretted that the debate 'on an abstract question' had diverted the public from what should have been its main objective, namely, a Repeal of the Union. Moreover, the anger of the Association had been directed at 'some of the most earnest and talented of the Repealers'. For him, the real decision within the Repeal movement concerned accepting public office from the government, especially as that government was opposed to Repeal. O'Brien appealed personally to Daniel O'Connell to 'exercise a sound discretion in trying to heal the wounds already caused'.[89] Yet O'Connell, who was old, infirm and increasingly under the sway of his son, John, did not intervene on behalf of Young Ireland.

John O'Connell exploited his friendship with some of the Catholic bishops to condemn physical force and those who supported it. He and his father also constantly referred to the seceders as 'infidels'. Thus, Dr Cantwell, the Bishop of Meath, warned that 'the Catholic members who would advocate a resort to physical force in the debates of the Association must be regardless of their duty as Christians, and insensible of their obligations as Roman Catholics'. Meanwhile Bishop Higgins of Ardagh went as far as to state that 'the *Nation* was the most dangerous publication that had ever appeared in Ireland'.[90] The assertive public support of some of the Catholic hierarchy was an important weapon for the Repeal Association, which Young Ireland found difficult to counter. In the week that followed the secession, Repeal Rent increased four-fold, largely due to the efforts of the priests who rallied around the O'Connells. The financial growth was used as proof that the separation was appropriate and that it had widespread support.[91]

The group that withdrew from the Association was quite small and, apart from O'Brien, they had little individual public profile, especially as many of the writers for the *Nation* had contributed anonymously. However, they included the most dynamic and talented people in Irish politics. The debate had given particular prominence to the young, charismatic, Thomas Francis Meagher, who had consistently opposed the Peace Resolutions with his fiery rhetoric. By losing control of this group, O'Connell lost the support of the *Nation*, and with it went much of the most incisive and influential writing on Irish affairs. Following this debate, two Repeal movements now existed in Ireland, united in their desire for Repeal, but divided on how that goal should be achieved. Although the division had been ostensibly on the question of physical force, and other disagreements had been raised, the differences between Young and Old Ireland were not as great as the schism suggested.

O'Brien and Mitchel, who since Davis's death had been the most prominent members of Young Ireland, approached the problem in contrasting ways: O'Brien felt that the clergy had to be respected and wooed, while Mitchel responded to their antagonism with corresponding hostility.[92] O'Brien's more cautious approach was based on his realization that his continuation as an MP partly depended on not alienating the Catholic clergy. There were, however, a number of priests who supported Young Ireland following the secession. The most famous, and militant, was Father Kenyon, a close friend and admirer of John Mitchel's.[93] He had first come to public notice in Conciliation Hall in June 1845 when he had criticized John O'Connell for adding a sectarian dimension to the debate over the Colleges Bill.[94] During the Peace Resolution debates, Kenyon spoke in favour of Young Ireland, declaring 'to say that no force but moral force should ever be employed was fanatical and ... in his opinion, monstrous folly'.[95] In Dublin, two priests, Father Meehan and Dr O'Carroll, continued to support Young Ireland and defend them from accusations of being religious infidels.[96] A few Catholic bishops did not side with the secession, including Dr Maginn, the Bishop of Derry, describing the resolution as a pointless abstraction.[97] Dr Blake, the Bishop of Dromore, to O'Connell's consternation, announced that the seceders should be recalled back into the Association.[98] Despite the activities of some Catholic priests, Duffy believed that Young Ireland would retain the support of Irish Protestants and of the younger Catholic clergy.[99]

Daniel O'Connell had been absent when the Repeal Association split. In general, his role in removing the Young Ireland group was ambiguous. Many Young Irelanders blamed John O'Connell for forcing the departure of Young Ireland from the Repeal movement. They believed that Daniel O'Connell was willing to consider reconciliation with Young Ireland, but that John was vehemently opposed to it.[100] Maurice O'Connell, a son of Daniel and brother of John, also blamed John for erroneously forcing the removal of Young Ireland and, following their departure, he refused to attend Conciliation Hall.[101] It was John, moreover, who oversaw the fragmentation of the Repeal Association into two factions, making it difficult for a reconciliation to come about.[102] In the remaining months before his father's death in May 1847, it was also John who managed what remained of the Repeal Association. Duffy attributed John's actions to 'the insensate ambition of Mr John O'Connell to succeed his father'. His father, in turn, who throughout his life had promoted the political careers of his sons, appeared motivated by the desire to create an O'Connell dynasty.[103] John rejoiced in his role leading the Association, but his father at times appeared despondent, a situation that was intensified by his rapid physical decline.[104] Daniel O'Connell's final months, therefore, were permeated with disappointment. The mass movement he had built up and led was fractured and in decline, and the controversial alliance with the Whig government had not materialized. Even more tragically, the country that O'Connell loved was undergoing a terrible famine, and the relief measures introduced by the Whigs were contributing to the suffering and mortality of the Irish poor.

Divisions

The contact between Young and Old Ireland in the months that followed the split was increasingly acrimonious. According to Duffy, this was because 'John O'Connell thought it necessary that the exclusion of the seceders should be justified by representing them as men of the worst principles, engaged in the worst designs, and that the *Nation* should be destroyed root and branch.'[105] Following the secession, all members of the Repeal Association were required to declare their support for the Peace Resolutions. Those who refused to do so were expelled. Protests from Young Ireland were silenced as the Repeal Reading Rooms were forbidden from taking their usual weekly free copy of the *Nation*, again, on threat of expulsion. At the same time, articles appeared in the *Pilot* and the *Freeman's Journal* attacking the seceders, in particular, O'Brien. In contrast, the *Nation* adopted a policy of not criticizing Daniel O'Connell or his role in the controversy.[106] Those who protested against the treatment of Young Ireland or the banning of the *Nation* were expelled from the Repeal Association. The first person to be formally expelled was John Martin, a Protestant landlord and a close friend of John Mitchel's. He had argued that while he was bound by the original rules of the Association, the new ones were unlawful. He suggested that northern Protestants had been wary of joining the Repeal Association because they feared it would result in a Catholic Ascendancy and religious liberty would be at the discretion of the Catholic clergy. The actions of Old Ireland during the recent debate, he believed, confirmed these fears. He attended a meeting of the Association to air his views, but he was not allowed to speak.[107] Like many Young Irelanders, he blamed John O'Connell for the split and the subsequent treatment of the seceders, describing his conduct as 'dictatorial'.[108] Martin's expulsion was followed by the exclusion of a number of other Young Irelanders, including Richard O'Gorman, Father Meehan and Thomas D'Arcy McGee.[109]

Other Young Ireland sympathizers wanted to resign in protest at these expulsions, but O'Brien advised that they wait for the Association to instigate action against them. More importantly, he urged those who supported Young Ireland not to attack the Association or its supporters, in order to allow the possibility of a future reconciliation of Repealers.[110] In the interim, he suggested that to distinguish themselves from the Repeal Association, the seceders should refer to themselves as the Irish Party. O'Brien believed that it was also necessary for Young Ireland to follow the secession by demonstrating that they had 'vitality', and he considered this was best done through the columns of the *Nation*. He feared that if they held a public meeting to discuss the split, it would end in an undignified way.[111] O'Brien had good reason to encourage Young Ireland to keep a low public profile because the division resulted in some violent assaults by members of Old Ireland on Young Ireland. This was particularly ironic as the ostensible reason for forcing a showdown with the *Nation* group was the issue of moral versus physical force, yet O'Connell's supporters showed themselves willing to physically attack their former political allies. Increasingly, Old Ireland's main enemies were members of Young Ireland rather than the representatives of British rule in Ireland.

Many of the women who wrote for the *Nation* continued to support the seceders.[112] Speranza, for example, wrote defending the carrying of arms and the use of physical force in certain circumstances.[113] The attack on the *Nation* and Young Ireland was also lamented by liberal Protestant opinion in Ireland. An editorial in *The Warder* referred to the 'caprice of the tyrant' and warned that 'If the *Nation* is crushed, it is clear there exists not a particle of independence in Popish Ireland'.[114] *The Morning Chronicle,* while describing the policies of Young Ireland as 'wild and mischievous', reminded its readers of the close alliance between them and O'Connell in 1843, adding that 'there is something disagreeable in hearing the hero of the Monster Meetings lay down the law of treason so very like a Tory Attorney-General'.[115]

Not all Repealers were happy with the autocratic methods of John O'Connell. A number of local Repeal Associations, including those in Cappoquin, Limerick, Loughrea, Drogheda, Templederry, Rathkeale, Rosbercon, Ballaghaderin, Kenmare, Newry, Belfast, Clare and Dublin, objected to the ruling that they could no longer take the *Nation* for their Reading Rooms.[116] In Cork, the opposition was so strong that no Repeal meetings were held and Repeal Rent dwindled.[117] The treasurer of the Mayo Independent Club resigned.[118] Even societies such as the Meath Repeal Club, whose members concurred with the Peace Resolutions, reported that there had been some dissenting voices.[119] The leaders of the Repeal Association responded to any dissension by warning that those who did not support the Peace Resolutions could no longer be members of the Association. They also persisted in a policy of not allowing the issue to be publicly debated.[120]

The Repeal Wardens were particularly distressed by John O'Connell's insistence that they should report the names of those who questioned the Peace Resolutions so that they could be expelled from the Association. Approximately 80 of the 120 Repeal Wardens and 400 members and associate members signed a Remonstrance protesting again this action. In Dublin, the protest was supported by members of the trade council, who had felt closer to Young than to Old Ireland. The Remonstrance was delivered personally to John O'Connell, who responded by ordering the document to be thrown into the gutter.[121] This action proved to be a watershed in the secession. According to Duffy, up to this point Young Ireland 'had endured whatever was done in the name of O'Connell with a forbearance which has few examples in the history of political contests ... But after the Dublin trades had to pick their Remonstrance out of the kennel it was no longer possible to prohibit retaliation.'[122] Following this action, the balance of power started to change in favour of the seceders, and this was accompanied by a dramatic fall in Repeal Rent.

The split in the Repeal movement had created two competing national-ist movements in Ireland. Overall, the public division within the Repeal movement demonstrated that O'Connell's long reign as liberator of the Irish people was at an end. Although he disliked the splintering of the Repeal Association, Daniel O'Connell publicly supported his son. In the months following the secession, he made a number of vicious and personal attacks on O'Brien. He also prohibited his followers from purchasing the *Nation*, in an attempt to destroy the financial base of Young Ireland. Ironically, in a number of places sales increased, including in the United States.[123] When O'Connell died in Italy in May 1847, there-fore, the Repeal movement was weak, while the Union appeared indestructible. Yet thousands of people were dying of hunger each month in Ireland. O'Connell's death in 1847 created a wave of sympathy for his family and Old Ireland, but this was short lived. His political heir, John, was too unprepossessing to fill his father's shoes, and too self-important

to take advantage of the atmosphere of sympathy to bring about reconciliation between Repealers. Instead, nationalist opinion slowly moved in
favour Young Ireland, who went on to dominate Irish politics in the
following year.

Overseas support

The activities of the Repeal Association were watched closely by Irish
nationalists overseas. Therefore it was inevitable that the secession would
have repercussions further afield. Young Ireland believed that amongst
Repealers in Britain they had more support that Old Ireland.[124] Within
Britain, O'Connell's actions were championed by the *Tablet*, a Catholic
newspaper. The paper blamed Young Ireland for the split, predicting that
the group would disappear into political oblivion. One editorial in the
Tablet cautioned that, 'Until peace is made with the "classes" of whom
John O'Connell is the chief political representative, the Confederation is,
and must be, a band of isolated politicians, surrounded by a very limited
audience, and for the most part preaching to deaf ears or stubborn recu-
sants.'[125] Many Repealers in Britain, however, while declaring support
for Daniel O'Connell, expressed their opinion that Young Ireland should
remain in the movement. In Manchester, 200 people sent a Remonstrance
to Dublin criticizing the actions that had led to the secession. Support was
also expressed by the Stalybridge and Liverpool Associations, with the
latter suggesting that more debate was needed in the Association. George
Smyth, the Treasurer of the Liverpool Repealers, resigned in protest.[126] In
London, a meeting of forty-five Repeal Wardens declared their support
for the seceders. Similar declarations were made by Repealers in Dundee
and Leeds. The response of the Dublin Association was that the names of
the people who had opposed the resolutions should be struck off the
Association's membership list.[127]

In the United States, where Repeal had established strong roots
amongst the Irish-American community, events in Ireland were watched
with interest. In the summer of 1846 Repealers in New York were heart-
ened by the defeat of the Irish Coercion Bill (which resulted in the fall of
Peel's administration) viewing it – incorrectly – as signifying the strength
of the Repealers in parliament.[128] At this stage, Repeal was still indelibly
linked with Daniel O'Connell, although the imprisonment of O'Brien in
the House of Commons had gained him recognition and admiration not
just in Ireland, but further afield. The United Irish Repeal Association in
New York adopted a resolution announcing their admiration of 'that
truly great and noble patriot William Smith O'Brien, who at every sacrifice of self, has upheld the interests and rights of his country, preferring to
suffer penalties and imprisonment, rather than accede to the unwar-
rantable demand of an imperial Parliament'.[129] Within the United States,
few Repealers remained neutral about the division, forcing a realignment

in Irish-American nationalism. In the ensuing reshuffle, the *Boston Pilot* supported Young Ireland while the *New York Freeman* remained loyal to Old Ireland.[130] Significantly, the *New York Freeman*, like the *Tablet* in England, was closely aligned with the Catholic Church.[131] As the Famine intensified in the winter of 1846–47 a more militant edge developed amongst Irish exiles, who regarded the British government's relief polices as ineffectual. The passive stance of the Repeal Association in Ireland was mocked, the *New York Weekly Herald* asserting that:

> If the part of O'Connell were not finished, or if some popular agitator were to take possession of the part which the Liberator has ceased to act, this social disease would soon be transformed into a rebellion. But by dint of amusing his countrymen with a chimera like 'the Repeal of the union' old O'Connell has made them lose the sentiment of reality. Instead of rising to a revolution, they will vainly agitate themselves in anarchy.[132]

Famine

The summer of 1846 was dominated by two political breakups – those of the Tory Party and the Repeal Association – both of which shaped the subsequent development of British and Irish politics. They were over-shadowed, however, by a second and more devastating failure of the potato crop. The food shortages in the previous year had been successfully met by Peel's relief measures and consequently there had been no excess mortality. There was no expectation that the blight would return, but a widespread belief that the short-lived crisis was over. This reappearance of the blight meant that the food shortages and hunger of the previous year could no longer be regarded as temporary. The fact that reports of misery being received from Ireland were not exaggerated was confirmed by Lord Lincoln, a former member of the Irish Administration, who warned that, 'The distress in many parts rather exceeds than falls short of the daily accounts in the newspapers.'[133] Clearly, without extensive government intervention, large-scale suffering was inevitable. While polit-ical divides were deepening in Ireland, the country was undergoing a devastating famine.

O'Connell was aware that the impact of potato failure would be disas-trous, especially as it was combined with a smaller than usual grain harvest. As early as July 1846, O'Connell wrote directly to the Prime Minister cautioning that the country was on the verge of a 'death-dealing famine'. He warned that without a large-scale relief programme 'there is the greatest danger of outbreaks in various parts of the county of Cork of the population driven to despair by want of food'.[134] Russell responded that his government was going to introduce public works as the main mechanism for providing relief, although they were to be less generously financed that in the previous year, with a higher proportion of their income coming from the local rates in Ireland rather than the central government. [135] The government had also decided not to import large amounts of food into Ireland but to leave food supply to market forces.[136] O'Connell was reassured, however, when Lord Bessborough, an Irishman and a personal friend, was appointed as the new Viceroy.[137] Despite Bessborough's good intentions, famine policies imposed from London demonstrated that a more stringent approach was being taken to relief provision in the second year of distress. Nor did O'Connell's offering to support the Whig Party mean that his demands for more government intervention were regarded with sympathy in London. Nonetheless, O'Connell, although clearly concerned at the condition of the poor, continued to place his trust in the government. At the end of October, he led a delegation to the Viceroy, Lord Bessborough, and reported that 'his Excellency was most anxious to do everything in their power to carry out their wishes ... [and] that the Board of Works were ready to work for Ireland to the utmost of their power'. He had even encouraged the Lord Lieutenant to adopt a system of payment on the public works by task, or piece-work, a measure that was adopted and proved to be disastrous.[138]

Within a few weeks of their introduction, it was clear that the public works were inadequate to deal with distress on the scale that was evident in Ireland. Additionally, the public works were heavily bureaucratic, slow to be implemented, expensive to manage, and the wages paid were so low that the people who were employed could not afford even a subsistence standard of living.[139] Moreover, large amounts of provisions, including grain, cattle, dairy products and alcohol continued to be exported from Ireland.[140] It was not only nationalists who were angry that while people died, large quantities of food were leaving Ireland. Even the Lord Lieutenant was concerned that the merchants were using the food short-ages to their advantage regardless of the suffering of the people, and in a private communication informed the Prime Minister that, 'I cannot make up my mind entirely about the merchants. I know all the difficulties that arise when you begin to interfere with trade, but it is difficult to persuade a starving population that one class should be permitted to make fifty per cent profit by the sale of provisions, while they are dying in want of these.' He added that the merchants had done little to get food to the poor, but at the same time, they had 'done their best to keep up prices'.[141] Although official mortality figures were not kept, the constabulary estimated that in the winter of 1846 to 1847, 400,000 people died or emigrated, either directly or indirectly through want of food.[142]

The *Nation* was critical of the government's relief polices, which they regarded as inappropriate and inadequate. Editorials in the papers also suggested that the political wranglings were shameful when the country was in the midst of a famine. Many of the writers, including John Mitchel, argued that food grown in Ireland should be kept in the country.[143] This demand had widespread support. During the previous year's shortages, O'Connell had been a member of the Mansion House Committee, which had rebuked Peel's government for allowing food to be exported 'thus inflicting upon the Irish people the abject misery of having their own provisions carried away to feed others, whilst they themselves are left contemptuously to starve'.[144] O'Brien recommended that the writers in the *Nation* should devote some of their energies to finding practical solutions for the distressed.[145] Following this, articles were published suggesting ways to alleviate the suffering, including proposals as to how owners of land could help the people, and ways to provide employment by establishing agricultural schools, reclaiming waste lands and building a national system of railways.[146]

By the end of 1846, as the condition of the poor deteriorated, some members of Old Ireland publicly criticized the British government's policies, and advocated a reunion of Repealers. The relief measures introduced by the Whig government had shown scant regard for either the needs of the Irish poor, the financial situation of the Irish rate-payers, or the aspirations of the Repeal Association.[147] In December 1846, as mortality and emigration rose sharply, O'Connell belatedly denounced the relief policies of the Whigs. Briefly, it appeared that the inappropriate relief policies introduced in 1846 might unite the disparate groups in Ireland and win the support of Irish landlords. This idea was disliked by John O'Connell.[148] Overall, his attitude to famine policies was passive, encouraging people not to protest on the grounds that this would ultimately help them in the winning of Repeal.[149] He and his father were also unwilling to deviate from his general support for the Whigs and therefore no reconciliation took place. Unification would have strengthened the Repeal movement and created a strong voice of opposition within parliament, which was particularly important given the disarray within the Tory Party. The tragic consequences of the relief measures introduced by the Whig government damaged O'Connell's political and personal credibility, a situation that was only reversed by his death in May 1847. By the close of the year, it was clear that the Irish poor were not the only victims of the Whig policies. Irish landlords were under increased financial pressure, which intensified in 1847 when the fiscal burden for famine relief was made their responsibility.

Regrouping

The British government hoped to be a beneficiary of the split within the Repeal movement. At the same time, it exploited the division. When, at the end of 1846, the Lord Chancellor announced that the Repeal magistrates who had been dismissed in 1843 could be re-instated, three supporters of Young Ireland – O'Brien, Dr Cane and Dr Geary – were excluded.[150] This action demonstrated that the government preferred a divided, rather than united, Repeal movement. Daniel O'Connell compounded this division by publicly denouncing the tactics and language

of Young Ireland, which pleased the British government.[151] At the end the
year, six months after the secession had taken place, Young Ireland
convened a number of public meetings in Dublin. These were well
attended, in contrast to the dwindling numbers that were present at
meetings in Conciliation Hall. The disparity in levels of support was
attributed by a Belfast Protestant newspaper to 'Mr O'Connell's waning
popularity'.[152]

A large public meeting was held on 2 December in the Rotunda in
Dublin, to coincide with O'Connell's visit to the city. It was Young
Ireland's first opportunity to put on record the history of the preceding
months. The meeting was attended by almost 3,000 men and women,
including approximately 2,000 'of the most intelligent of the artisan and
trading classes'.[153] O'Brien did not attend, still preferring to remain a
neutral observer, and Mitchel was absent due to illness (he frequently
suffered from asthma). Each of the Young Ireland speakers disavowed the
use of physical force. However, they explained their refusal to acquiesce
with the Peace Resolutions on the grounds that, 'they could not conscien-
tiously affirm a doctrine which they believe to be false in principle, servile
in spirit, and most mischievous in policy'.[154] They rejected the accusation
that they were religious infidels. Anger was frequently directed at Daniel
O'Connell for allowing the split to take place. John Blake Dillon, one of
the original founders of the *Nation*, asserted that, 'Mr O'Connell stands
charged with having deliberately broken up the Association, at the insistence of the present government.'[156] O'Connell's recent declaration that
reconciliation was impossible was frequently quoted. A particularly warm
welcome was given to Meagher, who outlined the history of the secession,
saying that he was now getting a chance to resume his interrupted speech.
He lamented the fact that, 'Through a fatal policy, the most powerful
confederacy that has ever yet been organised to win a nation's freedom is
broken up, its treasury exhausted, its influence blasted.' Yet Meagher
made it clear that, despite O'Connell's recent actions, he regarded him as
the liberator of the country, and believed that the Irish people would be
eternally grateful to him.[156] A number of priests attended, including
Father Meehan and Reverend Dr O'Carroll, both of whom spoke out
against 'the infidel cry'; Meehan cited the case of some Sisters of Charity
who enjoyed reading the poetry in the *Nation*.[157] Dr Hutchinson, chair of
the Liverpool Repealers, attended, promising that 'they will enter, heart
and soul, into the spirit of your agitation, and ... they will join you in
your efforts to establish a parliament in College-green'.[158] The suffering
caused by the Famine was referred to, allied with the suggestion that the
only way of averting continuing suffering was by having an Irish government.[159] At this stage, it was clear that many Young Irelanders still hoped
they could work with Irish landlords to bring about the necessary
changes. The meeting concluded with cheers for 'Repeal, Smith O'Brien,
the *Nation*, and Young Ireland'.[160]

The meeting's success upset Daniel O'Connell, and when his supporters tried to console him, he responded that 'it was a great meeting – they are a great party ... they are a powerful party and we must have them back'. John vehemently disagreed with any attempt at reconciliation.[161] Nonetheless, at the next meeting of the Association, while he attacked their violence, O'Connell announced that if the seceders complied with the demands of the Association regarding the Peace Resolutions, he would be willing to meet with O'Brien. If Young Ireland could pass the 'test', a reunion would be possible. Young Ireland believed it was a ruse, but felt they should meet as suggested. Before this could take place, they consulted with their supporters in the country. While most of the seceders desired a reunion, Mitchel and his close ally, Thomas Devin Reilly, disagreed, believing that such a merger would not work.[162] O'Brien refused to act as the spokesman of Young Ireland, preferring to see himself as a mediator rather than an activist.[163] He informed Duffy that although he supported the aim of the young patriots to win independence for Ireland, he continued to regard himself as belonging to 'middle aged Ireland'.[164] O'Brien was willing to return to Conciliation Hall but refused to do so if physical force was used as a way to get rid of troublesome members.[165] Despite the general mistrust of O'Connell's motives, the leading Young Irelanders realized that in the eyes of Irish public opinion they would appear to be the ones who did not wish for reconciliation. Consequently, a deputation consisting of Duffy, Dillon and O'Gorman offered to meet O'Connell and discuss whatever he desired. No agreement was reached, O'Connell refusing to read or accept the Statement of Reforms drawn up by the seceders. Despite the outcome, Young Ireland believed they had achieved their purpose of showing the country that they wanted reconciliation. They were praised by O'Brien for their actions.[166]

On 30 December 1846, Mitchel wrote to O'Brien saying that now a reunion seemed impossible, they could 'sweep away all the rubbish behind us and leave us free to look *forward* for the future ... I am heartily glad, as I think most of us are, that the "Reconciliation" is all over. I never for one moment believed the proposal to be *bona fide* (nor conceived it possible even it were *bona fide*) to make a sound safe working Association out of the present one.'[167] For O'Connell, the rupture was now final; he declared that:

> It is all over ... The Association will work on its way as well as it can without them, in total disregard ... of the paltry machinations and movements of the Little Ireland gang. I tell them this – I set them at defiance – and let them keep up as many dissensions as they please, and foment disaffection to no end, I shall still disregard them ... What crime has the Association committed that, in the first place, it should be condemned, and next handed over to such executioners as Duffy, Mitchel, and the other Young Irelanders? I would rather see the Association emptied of the last man than I would submit to their dictation.[168]

Nonetheless, the Repeal Association had clearly been weakened by the departure of Young Ireland. O'Connell's political ambitions in regard to winning concessions from the Whigs had not been realized, while famine policies had showed little sensitivity to the needs of either the Irish poor or of Irish landlords. Months of food shortages were having a disastrous impact on the income of the Repeal Association, which was dwindling.[169]

While Young Ireland had extensive support and was a serious rival to the Repeal Association, they remained without a leader or a coherent party structure. The need for a named leader was even more important as it was clear that O'Connell's health was deteriorating. In December, they had resolved to hold a meeting of all the seceders in January 1847, with the aim of forming a distinct party.[170] Despite O'Brien's sympathy with Young Ireland, he remained reluctant to accept a prominent role.[171] Duffy appealed to O'Brien to accept the position as leader of Young Ireland. Apart from O'Brien's many attributes, Duffy explained, 'The Protestants and the landed gentry must be won, and you, a man of property and family, and a Protestant, can and will win them. What chance of their listening to young men, most of whom are Catholics and all of them sprung directly from the trading class.'[172] The close of the year ended positively for the Young Ireland group with the Repeal Association losing support. The decline of the Association was expedited a few months later when it lost its leader, Daniel O'Connell.

The fifteen months since the death of Davis had witnessed major political upheavals in Irish and British politics. In Britain, the split in the Tory Party paved the way for a Whig government that could rely on the support of the Repeal Party. To facilitate this alliance, O'Connell manipulated a spurious quarrel between Young and Old Ireland. The withdrawal of Young Ireland from the Repeal Association divided the Repeal movement, just as it became inevitable that there would be a second year of food shortages. By the end of 1846, when a reunion appeared unlikely, Young Ireland began to reorganize, energized and angered by the government's relief policies. In January 1847, the Irish Confederation was formed, which rejected any future alliance with the British government while appealing to a wide spectrum of Irish people, including landlords, Protestants, women and trade unionists. The first year of its existence was set against a deepening national crisis caused by the Famine, which was not only killing the poor, but was causing massive social dislocation resulting from emigration, evictions, rising taxation and widespread landlord insolvency. Yet, in the autumn of 1847, the British government announced that the Famine was over and all future famine relief was to be paid for by Irish taxation, thus denying either British or imperial responsibility for alleviating the suffering. Far from delivering justice for Ireland, the Whigs appeared to have abandoned the country. Nevertheless, as the following twelve months demonstrated, building an inclusive Repeal movement remained an elusive goal, especially as, palpably, the Famine was not over.

Notes

1 Duffy, *Four Years*, p. 49.
2 Ibid., p. 41.
3 Duffy, *My Life*, p. 139.
4 Gwynn, *Young Ireland*, p. 58.
5 Duffy, *Four Years*, pp. 117–9.
6 *Freeman's Journal*, 3 July 1845.
7 Christine Kinealy, 'Food Exports' in Christine Kinealy, *The Great Irish Famine: Impact, Ideology and Rebellion* (Hampshire: Palgrave, 2002), pp. 90–116.
8 O'Brien, *Hansard*, lxxxiv, 16 March 1846, 30 March 1846, 31 March 1846.
9 Ibid., Sir Robert Peel, 13 March 1846.
10 Duffy, *Four Years*, p. 139; *Nation*, 9 May 1846.
11 Peel to James Graham, 13 October 1845: Parker, *Sir Robert Peel*, p. 223.
12 Ibid.
13 Memoir of Peel, 2 December 1845: ibid., p. 240. In December 1845, Peel offered to resign but Lord John Russell refused to take over the government, as head of a minority government.
14 Mr Arbuthnot to Peel, 7 June 1846: ibid., p. 351.
15 O'Connell to O'Brien, 18 December 1846: O'Connell, *The Correspondence of Daniel O'Connell*, vol. viii.
16 Duffy, *Four Years*, p. 36.
17 Ibid., p. 36.
18 Gwynn, *Young Ireland*, p. 57.
19 Ibid.
20 Peel to Wellington, 21 June 1846: Parker, *Sir Robert Peel*, p. 364.
21 John Russell, House of Commons, June 1846, quoted in Duffy, *Four Years*, pp. 148–9.
22 Duffy, *Four Years*, p. 209.
23 Ibid., p. 74.
24 Ibid.
25 Ibid., p. 4.
26 John O'Leary, *Recollections of Fenians and Fenianism* (London: Downey and Co., 1896, 2 vols), p. 5.
27 Gwynn, *Young Ireland*, p. 49.
28 Duffy, *FourYears*, p. 74.
29 David A. Wilson, *Thomas D'Arcy McGee: Passion, Reason and Politics, 1835–57* (Montreal: McGill-Queens University Press, 2008), pp. 74–97.
30 Duffy, *Four Years*, pp. 18–20.
31 Duffy, *Young Ireland*, vol. ii, pp. 191–2.
32 Ibid., vol. i, p. 145.
33 Duffy, *Four Years*, p. 96.
34 Karen Sasha Anthony Tipper, *A Critical Biography of Lady Jane Wilde, 1821?–1896, Irish Revolutionist, Humanist, Scholar and Poet* (New York: Edwin Mellen Press, 2002), p. 184.

35 Brigitte Anton, 'Women of the *Nation*' in *History Ireland* (vol. 1, no. 3, Autumn 1993), 36.
36 Wilson, *McGee*, p. 110.
37 Lyons, *Meagher, Speeches and Writings*, p. 13.
38 Duffy, *Four Years*, p. 90.
39 It was not only female nationalists who were interested in politics. The journals of Elizabeth Smith (Scottish-born but living in County Wicklow) show that she closely followed political developments in Ireland, although from a more conservative perspective. She responded to O'Brien's demand that only Irish people should legislate for Ireland with 'legislate for Ireland! A nation of lunatics! Reason with Irishmen! Every one of them stark staring mad from the peer to the peasant', 5 May 1846: Thomson and McGusty, *Irish Journals*, p. 95.
40 Duffy, *Four Years*, p. 89.
41 Anton, 'Women of the *Nation*', 34.
42 Tipper, *Lady Jane Wilde*, p. 52.
43 Kinealy, 'Invisible Nationalists', passim.
44 O'Sullivan, *The Young Irelanders*, p. 107.
45 Duffy, *Four Years*, pp. 94–5.
46 It was originally titled *The Stricken Land* and appeared in the *Nation* on 23 January 1847.
47 Duffy, *Four Years*, p. 92.
48 Anton, 'Women of the *Nation*', p. 34.
49 Ibid., p. 35.
50 Ibid., p. 34.
51 Duffy, *Four Years*, p. 70.
52 O'Sullivan, *The Young Irelanders*, p. 129.
53 Morash, *Hungry Voice*, p. 275. When she was only aged 21, a collection of her poetry was published – *Poems by Finola* (Belfast, 1851) – which included her renowned *The Irish Mother's Lament*.
54 This appeal appeared in the *Nation* on 23 May. The eldest sister married John Dillon.
55 Anton, 'Women of the *Nation*', 36.
56 O'Leary, *Recollection of Fenians*, pp. 2–3.
57 Duffy, *Four Years*, pp. 8–9.
58 *Belfast Protestant Journal*, 21 March 1846, 4 July 1846.
59 Ibid., 11 July 1846.
60 Gwynn, *Young Ireland*, p. 71.
61 Duffy, *Four Years*, pp. 172–3.
62 Ibid., p. 40.
63 Ibid., p. 38.
64 Ibid., p. 111.
65 Daniel O'Connell to Thomas Davis, 30 October 1844, quoted in Duffy, *Young Ireland*, vol. ii, pp. 231–3.
66 Duffy, *Four Years*, p. 114.
67 William Smith O'Brien, Cahirmoyle, marked private, 22 October 1847: NLI, MS 10515 (4).
68 Duffy, *Four Years*, p. 10.
69 Maurice O'Connell, *O'Connell*, p. 384.

70   Duffy, *Four Years*, p. 210

71   Ibid., p. 144–5.

72   *Belfast Protestant Journal*, 18 July 1846.

73   *Nation*, 13 May 1846.

74   Duffy, *Four Years*, p. 170.

75   Ibid., pp. 178–81.

76   Gwynn, *Young Ireland*, p. 72. Under the new rules of the Association as the proprietor of a newspaper, Duffy could attend meetings but could not be a member of the Association.

77   *Nation*, 18 July 1846.

78   Duffy, *Four Years*, p. 193.

79   *Proceedings of the Young Ireland Party*, p. 20.

80   *Belfast Protestant Journal*, 11 July 1846.

81   *Proceedings of the Young Ireland Party*, p. 20.

82   Michael Cavanagh, *The Memoirs of Gen. Thomas Francis Meagher, Comprising the Leading Events of his Career* (Worcester, MA: The Messenger Press, 1892), p. 57.

83   Quoted in Duffy, *Four Years*, p. 233.

84   Cavanagh, *Memoirs of Meagher*, p. 59.

85   Ibid., p. 65.

86   Gwynn, *Young Ireland*, p. 73–8.

87   Duffy, *Four Years*, p. 216.

88   *Proceedings of the Young Ireland Party*, p. 21.

89   Smith O'Brien Papers, NLI, MS 22345, n.d., probably late 1846.

90   Quoted in Gwynn, *Young Ireland*, p. 81.

91   Duffy, *Four Years*, p. 245.

92   Gwynn, 'The Priests and Young Ireland', 597.

93   Gwynn, 'The Priests and Young Ireland', 595.

94   Denis Gwynn, 'Father Kenyon and Young Ireland' in *The Irish Ecclesiastical Record* (vol. lxxi, no. 975, 1949) 231.

95   Duffy, *Four Years*, p. 204.

96   Ibid., p. 337.

97   Ibid., p. 256.

98   Ibid., p. 264.

99   Ibid., p. 259.

100   Savage, *'98 and '48*, p. 292.

101   Duffy, *Four Years*, p. 270.

102   John O'Connell has been defended by a descendant and historian of the family, Maurice O'Connell, who suggests that 'The assertion that John was instrumental in provoking the Young Irelanders into engaging O'Connell in a confrontation that might otherwise have been avoided, cannot be sustained': *O'Connell*, p. 389.

103   Duffy, *Four Years*, pp. 114–15.

104   Gwynn, *Young Ireland*, p. 84.

105   Duffy, *Four Years*, p. 242.

106   Ibid., p. 218.

107   Ibid., p. 251–3.

108   *Nation*, 2 August 1846.

109   Duffy, *Four Years*, p. 258.

110 Gwynn, *Young Ireland*, pp. 82–3.
111 Ibid., p.86.
112 Duffy, *Four Years*, p. 265.
113 For example in her articles 'Jacta Alea Est' and 'The Girondins', which was reprinted in Lady Wilde, *Notes on Men, Women and Books* (London: Ward and Downey, 1891), p. 42.
114 Quoted in Duffy, *Four Years*, p. 268.
115 Ibid., p. 265.
116 Ibid., pp. 282–5, 290, 294, 336.
117 Ibid., p. 300.
118 Ibid., p. 293.
119 Ibid., p. 96
120 Ibid., p. 292.
121 Gwynn, *Young Ireland*, p. 86.
122 Duffy, *Four Years*, pp. 307–8.
123 Ibid., pp. 324–5, 331.
124 Ibid., p. 259.
125 *New York Freeman*, 4 March 1848.
126 Duffy, *Four Years*, p. 293.
127 Ibid., pp. 284–7.
128 *New York Freeman*, 1 August 1846.
129 Ibid.
130 Ibid., 12 September 1846.
131 The *New York Freeman was* sponsored and controlled by Bishop John Hughes of New York.
132 *New York Weekly Herald*, 21 November 1846.
133 Lord Lincoln to Peel, 17 November 1846: Parker, *Sir Robert Peel*, p. 465.
134 O'Connell to Lord John Russell, 25 July 1846: Russell Papers, TNA, 30 22 5B.
135 Russell to O'Connell, 14 August 1846, ibid.
136 For a contemporary critique of the policy of non-intervention by a political economist who was conservative, Protestant, Unionist, see Isaac Butt, *A Voice for Ireland. The Famine in the Land* (Dublin: Thoms, 1847). Within parliament, George Bentinck, leader of the breakaway Tory Protectionists, also argued that 'under the circumstances it was the duty of a government not only to employ, but to feed, the people': see Benjamin Disraeli, *Lord George Bentinck: A Political Biography* (London: Archibald Constable, 1905), p. 233.
137 Lytton Strachey and Roger Fulford (eds), *The Greville Memoirs 1814–1860* (London, Macmillan, 1938), vol. v (January 1842 to December 1847), p. 447.
138 *Belfast Protestant Journal*, 7 November 1846.
139 For more on the relief measures introduced by the British government see Christine Kinealy, *A Death-Dealing Famine. The Great Hunger in Ireland* (London: Pluto Press, 1997), pp. 66–91.
140 *Account of the Number of Cattle Exported from Ireland to Great Britain from 1846 to 1849*, BPP, 1850, 423, lii. For debate on food exports, see Kinealy, *The Great Irish Famine*, chapter 5.
141 Bessborough, Dublin Castle to Russell, 23 January 1847: Russell Papers, TNA, 30 22 16A.

142 *The Times*, 12 March 1847.
143 Duffy, *Four Years*, pp. 314, 349.
144 Minutes of Mansion House Committee, 19 November 1845, quoted in Canon John O'Rourke, *The Great Irish Famine* (first pub. 1874, reprinted by Veritas, Dublin, 1989), pp. 41–2.
145 Duffy, *Four Years*, pp. 316–17.
146 Ibid., pp. 332–3.
147 Kinealy, *Death-Dealing Famine*, chapter 4.
148 Duffy, *Four Years*, p. 316.
149 Ibid., p. 314.
150 Gwynn, *Young Ireland*, p. 86.
151 A. Bannerman to Russell, 25 July 1846: Russell Papers, TNA, 30 22 5B.
152 *Belfast Protestant Journal*, 7 November 1846.
153 *Proceedings of the Young Ireland Party*, p. 3.
154 Ibid., p. 16.
155 Ibid., p. 11.
156 Ibid., p. 23.
157 Ibid., p. 27.
158 Ibid., p. 40.
159 Ibid., pp. 7–8, 45–6.
160 Ibid., p. 46.
161 Quoted in Gwynn, *Young Ireland*, p. 88.
162 Ibid., p. 90.
163 Duffy, *Four Years*, pp. 338–41.
164 O'Brien to Duffy, quoted in *Four Years*, p. 342.
165 Ibid., p. 343
166 Ibid., pp. 344–5.
167 Mitchel to O'Brien, 30 December 1846: Gwynn, *Young Ireland*, p. 92.
168 Daniel O'Connell quoted in Duffy, *Four Years*, p. 348.
169 Gwynn, *Young Ireland*, p. 69.
170 *Proceedings of the Young Ireland Party*, p. 39.
171 Duffy, *Young Ireland*, p. 132.
172 Quoted in Gwynn, *Young Ireland*, p. 93.

3

'Black '47': Repeal in retreat

Following the harvest of 1846, the deteriorating famine conditions in many parts of Ireland not only dominated Irish and British news, but were reported by the international press. The winter months were particularly awful, with the public works exacerbating rather than relieving the problems for many of the poor. The intentionally low wages meant that food prices remained out of the range of those employed on the scheme, which included an increasing number of women and children. At the same time, many merchants were making large profits, helped by the high demand for foodstuffs throughout Europe and a buoyant export market.[1] The various relief measures, despite being inadequate in scope and provision, placed a heavy fiscal burden on Irish property owners. Consequently, many landlords were beginning to feel financially squeezed as a consequence of two consecutive years of reduced rentals and increased taxation.

Not only did the public works fail in their primary purpose of saving lives, but they also proved to be cumbersome and expensive to administer. In January 1847, therefore, the Whigs announced major changes in their relief policies, in what amounted to an admission of failure of the measures introduced only a few months earlier. Following the harvest of 1847, an amended Poor Law was to be responsible for both ordinary and extraordinary relief. Until the appropriate legislation could be put in place, free food, in the form of soup, was to be provided in government depots. At the beginning of 1847, the public works were abandoned as the main vehicle for providing assistance and in the following months several changes were made in relief provision, with varying degrees of success.[2] The most efficient scheme in terms of saving lives and providing value for money was the Soup Kitchen Act, a temporary measure that contravened the government's guiding principle of not providing 'gratuitous relief to the poor'.[3] It was, however, an interim measure until permanent changes could be made to the existing Poor Law.[4] Despite a rigid means test and the frugality and low nutritional value of the food provided, by July over

three million people (almost forty per cent of the population) were
dependent on the scheme, compared with 750,000 people who had found
employment on the public works. Soup Kitchens were, from the outset,
intended to be a temporary measure until, following the 1847 harvest, an
amended Poor Law became responsible for providing all relief in Ireland.
The consequences of this policy were disastrous, both for the recipients of
the relief and for those who financed the system. And, in 1848 despite the
government's announcement that the Famine was over, over one million
Irish people relied on the Poor Law for survival.

The transfer to Poor Law relief signalled a draconian approach to
victims of the Famine: at the same time, it heralded a more punitive attitude to the Irish destitute and the landowners alike. Moreover, by making
relief a local charge paid for exclusively by Irish taxpayers, the Whigs
indicated that they were no longer interested in justice for Ireland, or even
pretending that the country was an equal partner within the United
Kingdom. The announcement of these new policies disappointed members
of the Repeal movement, while the proposed new Poor Law meant that
Irish landlords would be carrying the main financial burden for relief.
Many Tory MPs did not like the new Irish Poor Law, which would make
relief a local charge and allow outdoor relief, that is, relief given to people
within their own homes.

To conciliate Irish opinion during the second year of food shortages, the
Viceroy, Lord Bessborough,[5] had suggested that the government should
hand over some responsibility to Daniel O'Connell; an offer that
O'Connell was willing to accept.[6] Nothing came of this proposal and by
the beginning of 1847 there was widespread dissatisfaction with the Whig
administration amongst Repealers. Disillusioned with the Whigs' relief
measures, although not willing to make a formal break with them, Daniel
O'Connell convened a national convention in Dublin on 14 January 1847,
for Irish landowners to discuss how they should deal with the Famine. The
omens appeared good for a reconfiguration within Irish politics. The
meeting was attended by thirty MPs, twenty peers and almost 600 other
'gentlemen', drawn from all points of the political spectrum. William
Smith O'Brien attended, although some of his Young Ireland colleagues
did not approve. It was held at the Rotunda in Dublin, symbolically the
room in which the Volunteers had gathered in 1782. Unfortunately, the
attendees had little common ground in relation to the national question
and many were simply seeking changes in British government policy
during the Famine. Inevitably, they were concerned to protect the rights
of landlords.

The resolutions passed demonstrated that the tragedy was regarded by
many as an 'imperial calamity' and that the cost of the emergency relief
schemes should be borne by the Imperial Treasury. Far from seeking a
Repeal of the Act of Union, therefore, many at the meeting preferred to
seek more equitable treatment within it. The suggestion that relief should

be borne by the Empire ran counter to the government's philosophy of making relief a local charge on Irish taxpayers: a policy that was strengthened following the transfer to Poor Law relief in August. The meeting recommended that an Irish Party was needed to protect Irish interests. Its immediate demands included the suspension of the Navigation Laws (protective legislation that only permitted British-registered ships to bring goods, including foodstuffs, into the UK), the removal of remaining duties on corn imports, a request for the Navy to be used to carry food to Ireland, and a plea to expend whatever was necessary to save Irish lives. Auxiliary demands included recognizing a limited form of tenant right in terms of giving evicted tenants compensation for any improvements previously made to their property, and a special tax on absentee landowners.[7] Despite different political perspectives, the assembly was marked by its consensus. In the British press the meeting was denounced as an attempt by Irish landlords to protect their own interests.[8] The significance of this meeting, however, was that it marked a unique attempt by the Irish elite to act in unison and influence the government's relief policies. For the first time since the passage of the Act of Union almost fifty years earlier, it appeared that there was a possibility of forming an Irish parliamentary party. Sadly, the unity was short lived, partly demonstrating how deep-rooted the divisions were amongst the Irish elite, but also suggesting that O'Connell no longer possessed the ability to inspire and unite them, even when confronted with an overwhelming tragedy. Consequently, the government was able to ignore the recommendations that had been made.

For some Repealers, the suffering caused by the Famine provided incontrovertible evidence that only an Irish parliament could properly serve the needs of the Irish people. A repeated demand of many Irish people (including Old and Young Ireland and non-Repealers) was that food should not be exported from the country.[9] The Repeal Association, however, which was increasingly under the influence of John O'Connell, had virtually abandoned Repeal, devoting much of its energy to seeking personal advancement for its leaders.[10] Also, despite the inadequacy of the various relief measures, many Repeal MPs continued to support the Whig policies in parliament. In contrast, the continuation of famine radicalized the political outlook of the leaders of Young Ireland, who were progressively disillusioned with Irish landowners and British government alike. The Famine, therefore, rather than uniting political opinion in Ireland reinforced existing ideological differences, while causing realignment amongst Repealers who opposed the Whigs.

Ironically, at this stage the defence of Ireland was taken up by a small number of British politicians, notably the Protectionist group within the Tory Party, led by Lord George Bentinck and Benjamin Disraeli, members of a party that was not traditionally regarded as being sympathetic to Ireland or the poor.[11] In February 1847, Bentinck proposed a radical scheme for investment in Irish railways as a way of providing short-term employment and longer-term improvement. The railway proposal was supported by both O'Connell and O'Brien, the latter having suggested a similar scheme. It also had the support of George Hudson, the railway magnate, who believed that Bentinck's proposal could be completed without any cost to England.[12] The Whig Prime Minister, Lord John Russell, threatened to resign if the bill got a second reading.[13] O'Connell's frustration with the Whigs was evident in a letter to the secretary of the Repeal Association, written in response to Bentinck's proposal, averring that it was the best suggestion that had been made on behalf of Ireland. This view was particularly ironic given that throughout most of his political life he had opposed the Tory Party. Nonetheless, he confided to a close political ally:

> I am bound to forewarn the people of Ireland that, in my judgement, Parliament is not disposed to go far enough, that there will not be sufficient relief given by the Parliament, and that it will not be until after the decease of hundreds of thousands that the regret will arise that more was not done to save a sinking nation.
>
> How different would the scene be if we had our own Parliament, taking care of our own people, of our own resources! But alas, alas, it is scarcely permitted to think of these, the only sure instruments of Irish prosperity.[14]

In March, the Railway Bill was defeated in parliament by a Whig majority, supported by many Repeal MPs.[15] The mixed response of the Repealers, with many voting against the recommendation of their leader, confirmed that O'Connell's influence was declining, while for some Repealers, Repeal and saving the lives of the Irish poor appeared secondary to maintaining a political alliance with the Whigs and the personal benefits that the association had brought. For some members of Young Ireland, it was further evidence that justice for Ireland could not be expected from a British government.

Despite widespread dissatisfaction with Whig relief policies, and the growing disillusionment with the Repeal Association, in the early months of 1847 John O'Connell continued to support the Whigs and, in return, he became a regular guest at official functions in Dublin Castle. When O'Brien castigated him for being an 'ally of Whigs' and using his influence for his own personal benefit, John O'Connell responded by challenging him to a duel.[16] In contrast, Daniel O'Connell's private comments and actions in the early months of 1847 suggested that he was moving ideologically closer to the Irish Confederation and further away from the Whigs. However, O'Connell's political interests were being eclipsed by his religious convictions. In a private communication, O'Brien referred to 'the religious tendencies which during the last two or three years of O'Connell's life appear to predominate his mind'. He further explained, 'I have more than once heard him express a desire to retire into some religious establishment and I have no doubt he would have done so if he could have extricated himself from the exigencies of his position as a political leader.'[17]

Moreover, age and poor health meant that Daniel O'Connell was no longer the formidable political force he had once been. His declining physical condition may have contributed to his unwillingness to make a formal break with the Whigs. O'Connell spoke for the last time in the British parliament in February 1847, and asked for generosity for Ireland. In his speech, he gave support to the proposed new Poor Law, on the grounds that outdoor relief was necessary. Overall, O'Connell was careful not to be too critical of the party that he still supported, while making it clear that no blame was attached to the Irish landlords.[18] The deterioration in his appearance shocked his fellow parliamentarians.[19] Within three months of this attendance at Westminster, Daniel O'Connell was dead. Consequently, he did not witness the disastrous effect of the amended Poor Law on both the Irish poor and the landlords – two groups that he had sought to champion. The Whigs' polices after 1847 revealed that, despite O'Connell's loyalty, no concessions were made and relief continued on the lines already decided.

The Irish Confederation

Despite the continuing prevalence of distress amongst the poor and the repercussions of the potato blight on other groups in society, a number of significant changes were taking place in the political situation in 1847. At the same time that the Whigs were announcing new relief measures for Ireland, Young Ireland configured itself into the Irish Confederation. The party's public inauguration in January 1847 reduced the possibility of a reunion between the O'Connellites and Young Ireland. Notwithstanding periodic attempts to unite the two branches of the Repeal movement, the launch of the Confederation was a public admission that two rival nationalist organizations existed in Ireland.[20]

The first meeting of the Irish Confederation was held in Dublin on 13 January 1847, and was chaired by John Shea Lawlor, a landowner in County Kerry. Initially, 10,000 members were enrolled, but the leaders admitted they were disappointed because 'the gentry only furnished a few stray volunteers, the bulk of the middle class stood apart, the Catholic clergy were unfriendly, and the people in their suffering and despair scarcely knew what was going on'.[21] Nonetheless, the leaders applied themselves with vigour to creating an efficient and transparent political association. John Blake Dillon and Charles Gavan Duffy were appointed honorary secretaries of the new Confederation, but the latter was quickly replaced by Thomas Francis Meagher. To ensure that the body was representative, a Council of thirty-six men was appointed, most of whom were drawn from the professions (see Appendix). The composition of the Council reflected the diverse backgrounds and aspirations of the leaders of the new organisation, ranging from the aristocratic and socially moderate O'Brien, to the working-class democrat, Patrick O'Donoghoe, to the radical Catholic nationalist, Father Kenyon. In January 1848, the Council of the Confederation was reappointed and increased to 100 men, who included representatives from Birmingham, Liverpool, London and Manchester, demonstrating that support for Irish nationalism had spread beyond Ireland.[22] While the variety of political opinions gave the new organization much of its energy and made it attractive to radicals who had felt excluded by O'Connell's conservatism, it also meant that there was little consensus concerning the nature of an independent Ireland.

The policy of the Irish Confederation was based largely on the original aims of the Repeal Association.[23] Its central and incontrovertible aspiration was the demand for an independent parliament, believing, in the words of Duffy, that 'self-government was the only alternative to ruin'.[24] The Confederation emphatically rejected the acceptance of any favours from the government, especially in regard to taking official positions or pensions. Their focus was on positive aspects of their programme, based on the policy of 'no recrimination, no abuse of any person or anything belonging to the Association we have left. If the Liberator must be named, let the past be viewed with regret, but not in anger.'[25] From O'Connell, the Confederation had learned the importance of having a central administration and they opened an office at D'Olier Street, in the heart of Dublin. At times though, the paid secretary was overwhelmed by the task at hand, and was forced to apologize for the Confederation's slowness in responding to correspondence.[26] Like the Repeal Association, the Confederation held weekly meetings, while special gatherings were publicized by men who were paid to hold placards for two days.[27] Because the Confederation possessed no permanent meeting place, it rented the Music Hall in Dublin.[28] The close association of Young Ireland with the *Nation* continued, although O'Brien privately admitted that he occasionally found the writing in the paper to be too radical.[29]

Shortly after the formation of the Irish Confederation, a by-election was held in Galway and the Council had to decide whether they should support the Repeal candidate, Anthony O'Flaherty, whom many Young Irelanders liked and admired. Following lengthy discussions about whether to support him, the Election Committee finally decided to ask the people of Galway to unite and return a Repealer.[30] In February, they sent a deputation to Galway 'to use their best exertions for the return of a Repeal member'.[31] Their involvement in this election demonstrated that members of the Confederation were willing to support Old Ireland. Unlike the Repeal movement, however, the new Confederation sought no financial support from its members. Taking into account the poverty of the people, it was decided that all subscriptions should be voluntary and, if necessary, the founders should bear the whole cost of the organization.[32] Consequently, subscriptions raised at the weekly meetings were never large; in the third week of April, for example, only £9-3-6 was collected.[33] When Thomas D'Arcy McGee became Treasurer in June 1847, believing – as the government had stated – that the new harvest would mark the end of the Famine, he decided to introduce fees, from July onwards.[34] One of the grievances against O'Connell had been that there was no accounting or accountability in the Repeal Association regarding financial matters. Consequently, the Confederation made a point of having complete financial transparency, and details of their expenditure were scrupulously recorded, audited, and made publicly available.[35] While representatives were to be paid their entire hotel and travel costs, expenses did not include 'liquors'.[36] The design of the Confederation's membership cards was treated by the Council with its customary diligence. Some submissions for card designs were rejected on the grounds of being too expensive or too 'melodramatic'. The question of having the names of illustrious Irishmen on the card was debated, but was lost by one vote. In the end, it was decided to have a fairly plain card, with the motto of the Confederation printed in 'Irish characters', and with its ten principles printed on the reverse.[37]

Although the Repeal movement had split, its supporters still had a number of things in common, including respect for the rights of private property. The leaders of the Irish Confederation continued to hope that their moderate policies would enhance their appeal to landlords, clergy, Protestants and middle-class Catholics. Both Young and Old Ireland were anxious to win the landowners over to Repeal, viewing them as the natural leaders in an independent society. By the end of 1847, as the Famine persisted and landowners were responding with wholesale evictions, this proposition seemed less likely to the more radical members of the Irish Confederation. The determination of the Confederation to be constitutional was demonstrated by the fact that their constitution and by-laws were submitted to Jonathan Henn, QC, who pronounced them to be legal.[38] Also, at the first meeting of the Council, a committee was appointed to prepare a petition to parliament seeking a Repeal of the Act of Union.[39] In April, Isaac Varion, a Confederate in Cork, asked that 'strenuous measures' be taken to bring about Repeal of the Union, suggesting the adoption of a national address to the Queen.[40] Significantly also, the Council of the Confederation continued to refer to themselves as 'Repealers' throughout 1847, their main objective (like that of the O'Connells) being a Repeal of the Act of Union.[41] Demonstrably, the preferred tactics of the new Repeal society were the same constitutional ones that had been favoured by O'Connell. Nonetheless, some of the conservative press, notably the *Daily News*, continued to refer to the members of the Confederation as 'physical force men', thus associating them with tactics that were not part of their agenda.[42] Moreover, such a description suggested that their tactics had much in common with the more radical wing of the British Chartist movement.

Opposition to the famine policies of the Whigs gave the Irish
Confederation coherence in the first months of its existence. A frequent
demand, expressed in the columns of the *Nation*, was for food exports to
be stopped, based on the premise that there would be sufficient food in
Ireland if grain export could be halted.[43] Unlike the general perception in
Britain that Ireland was economically backward and producing insufficient food to feed its people, the Confederation believed that it was
'teeming with natural wealth'.[44] They predicted, though, that the
misguided policies of the government would result in the deaths of two
million people. Moreover, this mortality would take place 'while her soil
teemed with food, while she was partner in the richest nation in Europe,
while a single life was not sacrificed in any other country visited by
blight'.[45] Articles in the *Nation* repeatedly asked for the ports to be closed
and food to be kept within the country.[46] This sentiment was embodied
in a poem by Speranza, whose own family were wealthy and Protestant.
In January 1847, within a few months of first writing for the *Nation*, her
most famous poem, 'The Famine Year', appeared, combining poignancy
about the suffering of the poor with a searing indictment of the British
government's relief policies. Her contention that 'golden corn' was being
taken from the starving people in Ireland by 'the Stranger' was a theme
subsequently developed by John Mitchel.[47]

In the early months of 1847, although the condition of the Irish poor
was deteriorating, the Confederation seemed unable to capitalize on the
widespread anger against the British government. Despite having a
national organization and an energetic and active Council, the Irish
Confederation had little money. It also lacked direction and consistent
leadership. O'Brien spent much time in London on parliamentary business
and so he had little involvement in the day-to-day administration of the
Confederation. His prolonged absences allowed the initiative to pass to
some of the more radical members, and led Richard O'Gorman, a friend
and frequent correspondent, to observe, 'The Famine is a great fact, and I
do not think we have turned it to account as we ought.' He further
cautioned, 'My last word in this letter as my first is, Come Home as soon
as you can.'[48] A few days later, he warned that the Irish people were
'casting about for someone, and if *we* do not commence at once some
more decided and marked line of action than had hitherto marked our
policy, I fear the Irish Confederation will die a quiet death ... Believe me
you are badly wanting ... In my mind there never was such peril as now.
The Irish Confederation is working badly or rather, not working at all.
The Repeal Association is still alive and John O'Connell's presence may
give it a more nervous vitality.'[49] Patrick O'Donoghoe, a young legal
clerk, made a similar request, proposing in the Council of the
Confederation that O'Brien relinquish 'his present pursuit of vainly
endeavouring to awaken sympathy for Irish wrongs in a foreign legislature and resume his place as a leader of the loyal Irish millions'.[50] These

appeals coincided with O'Brien's disillusionment with the famine policies of the Whig government and strengthened his desire to retire from Westminster at the time of the General Election in August.[51] But as he was the only Young Irelander with a parliamentary presence, the majority of the Confederation did not support his wishes. The younger members of the Council, led by Duffy, Mitchel and Meagher, drew up a report stating that Irish MPs should not attend the British parliament in the current crisis.[52]

The Irish Confederation lacked coherence on a number of other issues. Two of the consequences of the prolonged food shortages were sharp rises in evictions and in emigration. Following the introduction of the new Poor Law in 1847, the steep increase in evictions swelled the already high levels of emigration. While some of the evictions resulted from the heavier fiscal burden on landlords, they also resulted from the fact that a number of landlords were using the dislocation caused by the crisis as an opportunity to clear their estates. The departure of so many people elicited divergent responses from members of the Irish Confederation. Duffy, Mitchel and Meagher opposed any schemes that attempted to alleviate the suffering caused by the Famine through a policy of large-scale emigration, equating it with transportation and colonization.[53] O'Brien, himself a benevolent landlord, regarded emigration, when benignly carried out, in a positive light. He feared that interfering in the process would alienate landowners from associating with the Confederation.[54] The emigration issue was taken up in the *Nation* by the radical James Fintan Lalor, who believed that the first duty of landowners was to feed their tenants, not to facilitate emigration. His writings won him the admiration of John Mitchel, who at this stage still hoped that landlords would support the Confederation, but was increasingly disillusioned by their treatment of their tenants during the famine crisis.[55] Prophetically, however, when writing to O'Brien on the topic of emigration, Mitchel concluded by stating, 'On reading over what I have written I find that I have expressed myself with rather more revolutionary vehemence than I really feel – *as yet*. I do think it is still in the power of the aristocracy to save this nation and themselves at the same time. And I wish and pray earnestly that they may find it in their hearts to do so.'[56] John Pigot, a young barrister who had been a close associate of Davis's, articulated the fear that the youth, inexperience and radicalism of some members of the Council of the Confederation might reduce the possibility of wooing moderate support. He advocated that the membership of the Council should be reserved for older, more conservative members of the Confederation. Pigot included himself in those to be excluded due to age and lack of experience. He felt that their intemperate language would alienate the support of 'the Protestant and conservative classes'. While Meagher approved of this proposal, O'Brien was reluctant to lose the enthusiasm and passion he believed that the younger members brought to the Council.[57]

The internal divisions within the Confederation were overshadowed by the public wrangles between Old Ireland and Young Ireland, especially those involving O'Brien and John O'Connell. Nonetheless, some negotiations continued with Conciliation Hall, although they came to nothing. John O'Connell's willingness to negotiate may have been rooted in the fact that the Repeal Association was in disarray with internal wrangling, and therefore he acted in order to appease some of the members.[58] At the end of April 1847, an overture was made to the Irish Confederation to explore a reunion, and the Council of that body agreed to negotiations on the grounds that they were 'anxious for a reorganization of the National Party'. It was decided that eight representatives from each side should meet.[59] John O'Connell, who was involved in the negotiations, had informed the Council that, 'On mature consideration I will not allow any objection (however strong it otherwise may be) that I can possibly waive to stand in the way of a friendly arrangement among Repealers.' The response of the Confederation made it clear that physical force was not of interest to them, but nor was it to be a condition of the negotiations. Their main demands were for the two organizations to be dissolved and a new body formed, committed to Repeal, which would 'be independent of all English parties' and not support anybody who was not pledged to support Repeal.[60] The talks foundered when John O'Connell refused to agree to dissolution of the Repeal Association as a condition of reunion.[61] The death of Daniel O'Connell on 17 May caused political opinion to swing back in favour of Old Ireland, a situation that was exploited by John O'Connell. Moreover, by refusing to allow members of Young Ireland to attend the funeral, O'Connell's sons made it clear that they wanted to distance themselves from the Confederation.[62]

For O'Brien, a strong impediment to a reunion was the fact that John O'Connell and many of his supporters were unwilling to criticize the Whigs, despite the palpable failure of their relief policies. In April, he publicly warned that it was crucial to know 'whether men are Whigs or Repealers', as he believed that it was not possible to be both.[63] Yet, regardless of the debates within all sections of the Repeal movement concerning the Famine, he realized that it was necessary to present a united front to the British government. In the summer of 1847, shortly after O'Connell's death, an Irish Council (Council of National Protection) was held in Dublin, in which the Confederation played a significant role. Some moderate members of Old Ireland also attended. Unlike the January meeting convened by O'Connell, it was attended by many members of the middle classes, but not the gentry. It was also religiously inclusive. Samuel Ferguson, a Protestant, and Colman O'Loghlen, a Catholic, were its honorary secretaries. Its avowed purpose was to suggest strategies to deal with the Famine, and the general feeling was that Ireland should not be treated as a separate entity during the tragedy if the Union meant anything. Representatives from Young Ireland participated in the committees, and their hard work won them respect from some of their critics, including Archbishop Murray of Dublin and William Monsell, a Catholic Unionist.[64]

A topic that dominated the work of the Council was that of food exports, with a sub-committee being formed to discuss 'the cardinal question of keeping the harvest in the country'. Mitchel chaired the sub-committee with his usual vigour, asking the management of each Poor Law Union to estimate food supplies in their area. On behalf of the Confederation, he made a special demand that all corn grown in the country should be kept in it. Many members of the Council were convinced that Ireland would have weathered the crisis more successfully if she had been legislated for by a native parliament.[65] Throughout the meetings though, the Confederation made their nationalism secondary to getting agreement on measures that would save the people. Both this and the January meeting demonstrated the paradox of Irish nationalism: namely, that it while it was seeking to sever the connection with the British parliament, it was asking the same government to give more relief to Ireland. The life of the Irish Council was short lived: because of the approaching General Election the committee adjourned until autumn.[66] Its advice was totally disregarded by the government.[67] By autumn, political factionalism had re-emerged within Ireland, particularly between Old Ireland and Young Ireland. Following the election, with a new Whig government supported by the Repeal Association in place, Duffy admitted that 'reunion with Conciliation Hall is no longer either desirable or possible'. Although he supported a reunion of Repealers, he believed it was not possible through Conciliation Hall and its new leader, John O'Connell.[68]

Confederate clubs and trade unions

The desire to be an inclusive movement sometimes created problems for the Confederation. One of their criticisms of the Repeal Association was that since its inception there had been a 'want of giving people higher pursuits than the mere gathering of money and attending public meetings'.[69] Moreover, whereas O'Connell had attempted to suppress working-class voices in the Repeal Association, the Confederation sought to embrace a wide variety of opinions. While trying to appeal to the moderate section of the Repeal movement, a more radical element was provided by the spread of political clubs affiliated to the Confederation. The clubs allowed popular participation in the political process, while giving the movement its grassroots support and energy. By 1848, they were also providing a vehicle for the mobilization of a broad section of Irish nationalists, dedicated to winning Irish independence.[70] Direct contact with the leadership of the Confederation was provided by many of the Dublin clubs having leading members of the Council of the Confederation acting as executive members.

The clubs provided an outlet for developing other aspects of the Confederates' programme. Since 1842, Young Ireland had used the *Nation* as a way of promoting education. The clubs were regarded by the Confederation as a tool for advancing this aim further. Duffy, who had been the key figure behind their founding, believed the clubs' main purpose to be 'Education, Conciliation, and Organization'.[71] The club structure was intended to recreate an organization which 'founded on the liberty of individual and local opinion, shall carefully substitute silent, progressive work, for clamour and idleness'.[72] Consequently, each club was to have a reading room that was stocked with nationalist newspapers and books. They were also expected to sponsor a lecture every two weeks. The fact that a large portion of the membership were drawn from the artisan or lower professional classes was suggested by the emphasis on improvement, with classes being offered in mathematics, grammar, book-keeping, literature and history.[73] The educational focus of the early clubs was so strong that John Mitchel, a member of the Swift Club in Dublin who was emerging as the radical voice within the Confederation, reminded his colleagues in October 1847 that the primary focus of the clubs should be 'to rid the island of English rule – how we should re-conquer this country from England'.[74] As Mitchel's radicalism lost him support amongst the leadership of the Confederation, he began to work more closely with the local clubs, especially those in Dublin.

The authorities in Dublin Castle probably had a better knowledge of the inner workings of the various local clubs than the leadership of the Confederation had. Since 1847, a number of Dublin clubs had been infil-trated with informers; men who were paid a small amount of money to provide detailed, and almost daily accounts of the activities of the members of the clubs.[75] These reports continued into late 1849. This action by the government demonstrates that they took the threat posed to the status quo by Young Ireland seriously, even after the uprising had been put down. The level of information demanded by the Castle author-ities, which is demonstrated by the following description of a newcomer to a club, further bears this out:

> A fashionable looking chap, about 22, named Owen Woods, wears a short pilot overcoat, silk hat, black trousers, neat shoes and white stockings, a shooting jacket inside, fashionable collar to his shirt and blue neck handker-chiefs, never shaved yet has a little hair under his chin. He told another tall looking thin chap (like a boxer) to call to him between 12 to 1 tomorrow and ask for Owen Woods at the Custom House. This is how I heard his name for he had to repeat it to the other who did not know him and thought he was in Maguires [sic] offices.[76]

The reports of the informers also reveal that most of the members of the Dublin clubs were predominantly ordinary working men – chimney sweeps, barbers, butchers, factory employees, shoemakers and tailors.

The subscription to the clubs – ranging usually from between 2d to one shilling – reflected the working-class composition of much of the membership.[77] Regardless of their relatively humble origins, the club members demonstrated an impressive knowledge of local, national and international politics. Information was exchanged between the various confederate members by visiting each other's club rooms, by reading the nationalist press, and through the use of political placards. By 1848, as the government introduced increasingly draconian legislation and an uprising appeared inevitable, club members became nervous that their meetings were being infiltrated. Their suspicions were correct.

Within six months of the establishment of the Irish Confederation, Duffy reported that 10,000 members had been enrolled into the clubs.[78] Coverage in the *Nation* suggested that the number might have been lower.[79] The death of O'Connell in May 1847, and the outpouring of grief for him, had limited the ability of the Confederation to win converts from the Repeal Association. It also kept anger with the Young Irelanders high. In Kilkenny, the local club rooms were physically attacked, with threats being made on the lives of the members by O'Connell sympathizers.[80] It is likely that these assaults were repeated in other parts of the country. Despite the optimistic predictions of the British authorities, the continuation of famine even after the harvest of 1847, while increasing popular anger with the system of government, clearly limited the Confederation's ability to recruit amongst a people whose main objective had become survival. Moreover, the impact of bad harvests had combined with an industrial downturn in Britain in 1847, which had repercussions in the towns of Ireland. Protestant workers in Belfast were affected particularly badly.[81] The prevailing economic conditions, and the social dislocation that they had engendered, made organizing an effective, national, political movement, a virtually impossible feat.

Despite the obstacles facing the Confederation, by spring 1848 almost 100 clubs, with an estimated membership of 40,000, had been formed in Ireland.[82] Moreover, while most of the clubs were concentrated in Dublin, large numbers were based in the provinces, especially counties Tipperary, Cork, Down and Galway, with strongholds in the towns of Belfast, Cork, Drogheda, Tullamore, Limerick, Wexford and Youghal.[83] These localities generally reflected the involvement of a national Confederate leader in their establishment. McGee, for example, who had family ties in Wexford, had travelled there in September 1847 and established clubs in Wexford, Enniscorthy, Taghmon and New Ross. He then, optimistically, informed O'Brien:

> On the whole I think I may safely say the County Wexford is more with us, *socially*, than with the others ... A little more success in other quarters ... and it will break out as suddenly and as strongly as it did in '98.[84]

Clubs were particularly popular with urban artisans and consequently

they increased links between the Irish Confederation and trade unions.
The Dublin shoemakers, for example, formed their own club, the
Molyneux Club, which met at the corner of George Street and Dame
Lane. Michael Crean was its president. Another local artisan, Edward
Doran, was a leading member of the Garryowen Club.[85] Many of the
early clubs took their name from famous Irish patriots and writers, but by
1848 the names were reflecting the more militant approach of the movement in general. As mentioned previously, the Confederate leaders were
unaware that some of the main Dublin clubs had been infiltrated by paid
informers, who provided daily written accounts of the comings and goings
of each of the members.[86] A similar practice had been established in
regard to Chartist meetings in Britain.[87]

Confederation clubs spread beyond Ireland.[88] In Britain, they were
established in Manchester, London, Birmingham, Sheffield, Liverpool,
and in the Scottish towns of Greenock and Airdrie. By the end of the year,
there were at least five Confederate clubs in London.[89] In these areas,
Repeal became fused with the more radical demands of trade unionism
and Chartism. They also provided an outlet for the working classes in
Britain to become involved in the Repeal movement. Significantly, in
August 1847 the Irish Democratic Federation, whose main purpose was
to achieve Repeal, was established in London.[90] Support spread further
afield. In July 1847, an Auxiliary Irish Confederation was formed in
Boston, Massachusetts.[91]

The influx into the clubs of working-class members, some of whom
favoured a radical social programme, took the Confederation in a direction with which the leaders were not always comfortable. Consequently,
the Council of the Confederation continually had to manage the conflict
between their aspirations of creating a representative, national movement
and their basically moderate agenda on matters relating to social reform.
The relationship between the Irish Confederation and other radical
groups in Ireland was at times uneasy, highlighting the essentially conservative leaning of some of the Young Ireland leaders. Since the 1830s, there
had been a strong tradition of labour unions in Irish urban centres. Apart
from protecting their working conditions, they petitioned for Repeal of
the Union, seeing it as a contributory cause to low wages and the decline
of Irish trade.[92] Skilled labour was particularly well organized in Dublin,
mainly through the Dublin Trades' Political Union, and later National
Trades' Political Union. The Dublin Trades' Political Union had been
formed in 1831 with the purpose of repealing the Union and promoting
the interest of Irish workers. They appealed to British workers to support
them.[93] O'Connell and some of his close associates joined the Dublin
Trades' Political Union in 1831.[94] But O'Connell's changing attitudes to
Repeal undermined the movement, as did his growing conservatism on
social issues. Despite cherishing his role as the champion of Repeal and of
the Irish working classes, he oscillated in his support for both issues.

O'Connell abandoned Repeal in November 1831, arguing that the British parliament would give the Irish people what they wanted and between 1834 and 1840, he officially supported the Whig Party. O'Connell also desired to limit Irish trade unionists' links with the British working classes, which annoyed many in the Dublin Trades' Political Union. In the 1820s, he had been a staunch supporter of the trade union movement, but by the late 1830s he had become hostile to their existence, viewing them as threatening 'the social state – the protection of property and the institutions of the country'.[95] The late 1830s, therefore, were marked by O'Connell's increasing social conservatism, when he tried to get rid of the unskilled and casual workers from the Irish trade unions by raising the annual fees, from one shilling to a pound, by moving meetings from evenings to afternoons (thus eliminating workers), and by getting the word 'Trades' removed from the title of the union. Although he was successful in undermining the radicalism of Irish trade unionism, O'Connell could not persuade the Trades' Union to abandon fully its commitment to Repeal. Nevertheless, within a few years of being formed, the Irish trade union movement had become 'dominated and subverted by O'Connell and his supporters' making it less effective both in achieving Repeal and in gaining benefits for workers.[96] The result was 'a difficult and complex relationship: on the general political issue of Repeal, they thought they had found a friend and champion; on the specific economic policies of trade unionism, they discovered that they had encountered a bitter enemy'.[97] In the face of such a strong opponent, the radical programme of trade unionists faded, not to reappear until the 1840s, with a monster demonstration taking place in 1843, the so-called Repeal Year.[98] Overall, O'Connell's attitude to trade unionism lost him support amongst both Irish and British radicals.

Inevitably, in the light of O'Connell's antagonism, after 1846 trade unionists, under the leadership of Patrick John Barry, moved closer towards Young Ireland. Moreover, when in the same year O'Connell renewed his alliance with the Whig government and turned his back on Repeal, the more radical programme of the Young Irelanders became increasingly attractive to labour activists. Trade unionists and Young Irelanders came together in autumn 1846 when they presented a Remonstrance to the Repeal movement, objecting to the Peace Resolutions, which was signed by 15,000 people in Dublin. The petition was supported by Thomas D'Arcy McGee, who was becoming one of the leading public figures within the Confederation.[99] John O'Connell's suggestion that it should be thrown into the gutter further alienated the trade unionists.[100] Significantly, by the end of the year, McGee had been appointed Secretary of the Dublin Remonstrants.[101] Following the formation of the Irish Confederation in January 1847, trade unionists in Dublin formed a sister organization, the Trades and Citizens Committee, led by Captain William Bryan and Michael Barry. This alliance indicated that, despite covering a wide spectrum of opinion, unlike O'Connell, Young Ireland was willing to embrace 'the trades'. The two organizations worked for closer cooperation between the Chartists and the Confederates, both in Ireland and in England. This alliance resulted in the spread of confederate clubs throughout Dublin, which were supported by working men.[102]

Chartism

Daniel O'Connell's relationship with British Chartism was fraught and reflected his changing political priorities. He had repeatedly ordered Irish immigrants in Britain to stay away from Chartism, although large numbers continued to join the movement while remaining loyal to him.[103] After 1845, the Repeal movement was losing support in England, with income from the Repeal Rent virtually disappearing in some places, including many parts of London. O'Connell's death in 1847 seemed, therefore, to pave the way for an alliance between the Chartists and Young Ireland.[104]

The attitude of the Irish Confederation to the British Chartist movement was initially ambivalent, with many of the leaders maintaining the antagonistic stance favoured by Daniel O'Connell. Like O'Connell, the leaders of the Irish Confederation had an uncomfortable relationship with Feargus O'Connor and with Chartism in both Ireland and Britain. When, in early 1847, Captain Bryan, a founding member of the Confederation, was asked to chair a Chartist meeting in Dublin, he offered to resign from the Council, fearing it might be 'injurious' to the Confederation to link them with such overtly radical demands.[105] The Council, however, agreed that the extension of the suffrage was an open question, to be decided upon by individual club members.[106] Nonetheless, the proposed appearance of Feargus O'Connor at a political meeting in Dublin caused consternation amongst some Young Irelanders. O'Gorman wrote to O'Brien, who was in London occupied with parliamentary business, warning him not to allow O'Connor to seize the political initiative in Ireland. O'Gorman advised O'Brien to spend more time in Ireland than in Britain on the grounds that, 'O'Connor is quite sharp enough to take advantage of the vacancy and turn it to account ... I fear it much. If we don't take care we shall find that we have broken one idol, but to find another and more degrading worship start up in its place.'[107] By the end of 1847, Feargus O'Connor was increasingly linking the issues of Repeal and Chartism together. In his capacity as MP for Nottingham, he introduced a motion for Repeal of the Union into the House of Commons. O'Brien considered that O'Connor had introduced the subject prematurely and in an 'injudicious manner'. Furthermore, he had brought it forward without consulting the Irish members. Consequently, the motion had little support, even amongst Repealers.[108] This incident revealed how far the Repeal Association had moved from seeing Repeal of the Union as a priority.

Support for Chartism also divided Irish Repealers. By the end of 1847, prominent Young Irelanders, including O'Brien and Thomas Francis Meagher, were affirming their opposition to universal male suffrage. Even John Mitchel, often regarded as the most radical of the Young Irelanders, publicly declared in August 1847 that:

> We desire no fraternisation between the Irish people and the Chartists, not on account of the bugbear of physical force, but simply because some of their five points are to us an abomination, and the whole spirit and tone of their proceedings, though well enough for England, are so essentially English that their adoption in Ireland would neither be probable nor at all desirable. Between us and them there is a gulf fixed, and we desire, not to bridge it over, but to make it wider and deeper.[109]

Within a few months, however, the Young Irelanders and the Chartists had become political allies in their struggle against the British state, and Repeal had again become a significant issue in British politics.[110]

Death of O'Connell

In May 1847, Daniel O'Connell died in Genoa, on a pilgrimage to Rome to meet the new Pope, Pius IX. The post-mortem revealed that he had been suffering from a congestion of the brain, which had contributed to his mental instability.[111] His remains were returned to Ireland for burial, but without his heart, which was taken to Rome and preserved in the Irish College. Despite his age and poor health, his death 'was a complete surprise to Ireland', as there had been a general expectation that he would resume active public life following his return from Rome. The fact that he had died so far away from home added to the sense of sadness at his passing.[112] He was mourned throughout Europe and in the United States.[113] O'Connell's death did not have a significant impact on Irish politics, signalling how much his influence had declined since 1843. Elizabeth Smith, the avid journal keeper, commented, 'It is odd how little stir there is about O'Connell's death. As little as about the approaching elections. The world is weary of politicks [sic].'[114] O'Connell's funeral on 5 August was a public spectacle and widely reported by media in Ireland, Britain and on the Continent, particularly Italy and France. Regardless of the public accolades and grief that attended his death, his later years had been marked by failures, and his alliances with the Whigs had brought little benefit to Ireland. Moreover, by promoting the idea that the Catholic majority was the Irish nation, he had added to the nervousness of many Protestants who wondered what their place would be in an independent Ireland.[115] Although he claimed that the Repeal Association was inclusive, in his later years he did little to win Protestant support.

O'Connell's alignment of nationalism with Catholicism and the Catholic Church had disastrous consequences in the decades following his death. His achievements, however, had been remarkable. He had created, in an agrarian society, two mass movements, which were disciplined and organized. His personal flamboyance made him difficult to ignore, but his intelligence, oratory skills and knowledge of the law meant that the British political establishment had to take him seriously. Much of the success and energy of the Repeal movement had been personal to O'Connell, making it difficult for any individual to replace him. What had been increasingly apparent throughout 1845 and 1846 was that John O'Connell was not adequate to fulfil the role that he so much craved as his father's successor. Nevertheless, O'Connell's death left a vacuum in the leadership of the Repeal Association that the uncharismatic John attempted, unsuccessfully, to fill. Moreover, by refusing to allow Young Ireland to attend his father's funeral, John O'Connell signalled his desire to maintain the division with them.[116] Control of the Association passed to John O'Connell, although he lacked his father's political skills, tactical sense, warmth or charm. John had masterminded the campaign against Young Ireland and he proved to be skilled at exploiting his father's death. Nonetheless, he was dismissed by many of his contemporaries and described by Duffy as 'feeble and trivial'.[117] The future of a united Repeal movement, however, lay in his hands.

The *Nation* was respectful about the death of a man who had once been the Repeal leader, framing all copies of the paper with a black border. Duffy wrote the leading article praising O'Connell's contribution to Irish politics and the young Devin Reilly wrote a reverential obituary notice.[118] O'Brien passed a resolution of sympathy on behalf of the Confederation and members were advised to wear black crepe as a mark of respect, for a month.[119] O'Connell's sons, however, used their father's death as an opportunity to reinforce divisions between Old and Young Ireland by refusing to allow the latter to attend the funeral.[120] This action appeared justified when a letter written by Father Kenyon criticizing the dead man was published in the *Nation*. In it, he claimed that O'Connell's death had not been a loss to the Irish nation as his actions before his death had resulted in 'very grievous injury to Ireland', adding that 'I deem him worthy of no respect from this nation. Whether he erred in ignorance or in malice, I believe that he has erred, grievously erred and I will not co-operate in the glorification of wrong.' Kenyon therefore refused to join in 'a tribute of national respect to his memory'.[121] His sentiments were not shared by other members of the Confederation; nonetheless, Duffy allowed his letter to be printed because the Confederation believed their members deserved the right to a hearing.[122] However, when Kenyon wanted to publish a second letter in the same vein, it was refused on the grounds that his objections had been aired, while further controversy would be 'unbecoming and untimely'.[123] The anger of Old Ireland was inflamed by Kenyon's letter, which they incorrectly attributed to the Confederation.[124] John O'Connell used Kenyon's criticisms to marshal opinion against Young Ireland, and so Kenyon's letter was frequently quoted as it kept alive anger against the Confederation.[125] Even more maliciously, it was suggested that if Young Ireland had not opposed O'Connell, he would still be alive. Thus, at a meeting in Cork on 20 September 1847, Meagher was greeted with cries of 'Who killed O'Connell?'[126]

The tributes that accompanied O'Connell's death disguised the fact that it coincided with a slump in support for the Repeal Association. A conference held in Conciliation Hall in May 1847 was not successful. According to Pigot, 'The Conciliation Hall is worse than ten Aegean Stables, and no Hercules could make it clean.'[127] The decline of the Repeal Association in the early months of 1847 had been expedited by the transfer of control from Daniel O'Connell to John O'Connell, who for a few months basked in his dead father's glory. John O'Connell deliberately delayed his father's funeral, from June to August, for his own political advantage, in order to maximize its impact on the General Election that month.[128] In the short term, O'Connell's death weakened the Confederation, and they were blamed for his demise, far away from home. Kenyon's attack and the protracted funeral arrangements fed these sentiments by increasing sympathy for the O'Connell family.[129]

O'Connell's death was viewed by political opponents in Britain with curiosity, rather than alarm. Greville, for example, writing in London, said that his passing:

> made little or no sensation here. He had quarrelled with half of his followers, he had ceased to be the Head of a Great Party animated by any great principle, or encouraged to pursue any attainable object; the Repeal cause was become despicable and hopeless without ceasing to be noisy and mischievous. O'Connell knew not what to say or do; he had become bankrupt in reputation and in power, and was no longer able to do much good or much harm; broken in health and in spirits, and seeing Ireland prostrated by famine and sickness, and reduced to a constitution of helpless dependence on England, having lost a great part of his prestige in Ireland without having gained respect or esteem in England, he went away unregretted and unnoticed to breathe his last in a foreign land.[130]

The London *Times*, which had opposed both Catholic Emancipation and Repeal, was dismissive of O'Connell's achievements. While O'Connell was frequently praised for his use of peaceful tactics, the paper averred that his name was 'the watchword of revolt'. They further suggested that O'Connell had outlived his usefulness and that he was 'dead to history before he left these shores'. Although *The Times* acknowledged that in the past he had been an influence in the British parliament, he was accused of never having shown any loyalty in return. Throughout the article, the rational, logical and reasonableness of English understanding was contrasted with O'Connell's unreasonableness, exaggeration, dishonesty – all characteristics that were regarded as essentially Irish.[131]

In many European countries O'Connell's passing was regarded as momentous. He was admired for his role in winning Catholic Emancipation in 1829 and his international profile had created widespread awareness of the Irish struggle for Repeal. Respect for O'Connell in France was evident following his death when a special funeral oration was held at Notre Dame, officiated by the Archbishop of Paris and organized by the Committee for the Defence of Religious Liberty. This form of honour was unprecedented, with similar ceremonies only ever having been accorded to kings and their offspring.[132] Many French nobles and politicians attended. A number of lavish banquets were also held to honour O'Connell, including one hosted by the Catholic youth of France. John O'Connell attended these ceremonies and sent back to Ireland detailed letters outlining the grandeur of the events, which were read at Repeal meetings and published in the Irish and American press.[133] By doing so, he reinforced the veneration for his father, he being the main beneficiary. In Rome, the fulsome funeral obsequies lasted for three days, with both his Catholicism and his commitment to constitutional, peaceful tactics being praised.[134] In an age of revolutions, O'Connell's tactics were widely admired by liberals and radicals throughout Europe, who failed to understand the social conservatism that underpinned much of O'Connell's politics.

The General Election

At the time of O'Connell's death, the Repeal Association was languishing, damaged by its dogged support for the Whigs and its refusal to denounce their policies. The grief caused by O'Connell's death and the public obsequies that followed briefly revived support for the Repeal Association – enough for it to benefit during the General Election in August 1847. John O'Connell exploited his father's death to reinforce public perceptions of divisions between Young and Old Ireland. This separation was consolidated by the Repeal Association's decision only to support Repealers from Old Ireland in the forthcoming election. In contrast, the Confederation felt that all sections of the movement should work together for the benefit of Ireland.[135] When it became clear, however, that Old Ireland was not willing to collaborate, a dilemma for the Confederation was whether to field candidates against a Repeal candidate and run the risk of splitting the Repeal vote. Moreover, apart from O'Brien, they had no members with parliamentary experience. During his absences from Dublin the younger members of the Council, led by John Mitchel, decided that they would not support John O'Connell in the forthcoming election, not because he was an Old Irelander, but because of 'his past conduct in allying himself with the English government and his recent declaration that he will continue to do so'. They went on to describe him as an 'anti-Repealer of the most dangerous and insidious kind'.[136] O'Brien disapproved of this decision, writing a public letter distancing himself from it and stating that John O'Connell was 'well qualified by industry and talents to become a very useful member of Parliament'. Significantly though, he went on to say that he hoped O'Connell would abandon 'the practice of soliciting places from Government'.[137]

Privately, O'Brien was less sanguine about John O'Connell's actions, believing that he would exploit his father's death and funeral to damage the Confederates. He therefore recommended that 'from the hour O'Connell is interred, there ought to be no measures kept with Conciliation Hall'. While the Confederates were not strong enough to field their own candidates, he suggested that they 'harangue' Association candidates and demand that they, 'earnestly seek to obtain domestic legislation ... not ally themselves with any English party, nor ask places for themselves or others ... sit in council in Dublin – to vote on measures necessary for the welfare of the country ... support the tenant right ... [and] do their utmost to sustain and create Irish manufactures and Irish industry'. Such interventions he believed would not only damage the Association, but raise the profile of the Confederation. He hoped that the measures would appeal to farmers and tradesmen. Moreover, despite their limited resources he believed that the agitation should not be confined to Dublin, but should extend to the provinces, where with 'great energy, rapid movement and skilful friendship' they could weaken Conciliation Hall.[138]

The public actions and words of the younger members of the Council estranged relations with Conciliation Hall further, and exposed a division between the members of the Confederation who continued to support a reunion and those who did not. The Council considered fielding John Mitchel to stand in Dublin against John O'Connell, but O'Brien thought that since Conservatives, Whigs and Repealers would all oppose him, it would have 'a very damaging effect'. He described the suggestion as being 'clean daft' but felt that it stemmed from the fact that 'intolerance of our Young Ireland friends and their consequent isolation disqualifies them in a great measure from forming a sound judgement in affairs of this sort'.[139] John O'Connell, however, threw down the gauntlet by deciding to stand in Limerick City, the heart of support for O'Brien. Richard O'Gorman stood against him. In the election, O'Connell received 581 votes to O'Gorman's thirty-eight votes, support for the Confederation in the city having been damaged by Kenyon's outburst.[140]

In the short term, the impact of O'Connell's death increased support for the Repeal Association. In the General Election in Ireland, thirty-seven Repeal candidates were returned, one Young Ireland member, forty-two Tories and thirty-five Whigs. Both John O'Connell and his brother Daniel were re-elected. Repeal candidates said they would make feeding the people a priority as another year of famine seemed certain.[141] Despite their consistent criticism of Whig policies, Young Ireland did not do well, with the O'Connellites cleverly exploiting the sympathy felt at the loss of their leader. Only O'Brien was returned as member of the Confederation, although the member for Youghal, Chisholm Anstey, was openly sympathetic to their principles.[142] Moreover, during the election debates, accusations that the actions of Young Ireland had hastened O'Connell's death became commonplace. The anger of Old Ireland also manifested itself by an increased number of physical attacks on leading members of the Confederation.[143] The Confederation blamed John O'Connell for fostering these divisions.[144] The failure of the Confederation to win electoral support disheartened some of its members, Richard O'Gorman confiding to O'Brien that 'I am every day convinced that it is our opposition that keeps up the Repeal Association'. Like other members of the Council, he was experiencing financial problems as a result of his political activities which were keeping him away from his profession.[145] Duffy was similarly dejected, claiming that, 'When the result of the dissolution was summed up, Conciliation Hall had gained something, the Whigs much, and the Confederates little or nothing.'[146]

The actions of the Confederation during the election resulted in their being criticized in the O'Connellite nationalist press. The *Freeman's Journal* condemned the Confederates for refusing to support the candidate of the Repeal Association, even though they were not standing in opposition. The paper called this policy 'reckless' and 'insane'.[147] The Confederates' stance was publicly defended by Richard O'Gorman, Thomas D'Arcy McGee and Michael O'Reilly. McGee pointed to the Remonstrance signed by 2,000 Repealers in Dublin, which stated that, 'an alliance with any English administration which does not make Repeal a central question is unbecoming to a Confederation which affirms as a vital principle that no foreign government whatever can rightly legislate for Ireland'. O'Brien's suggestion that candidates should be asked, amongst other things, to reject an alliance with the Whig Party was applied in all places where the Confederation organization existed, namely, Dublin, Kilkenny, Waterford, Cork, Limerick and Galway.[148]

Despite the Association's name, and regardless of the disastrous consequences of the Whigs' relief policies introduced in the autumn of 1847, the majority of Irish MPs, including John O'Connell, appeared to have abandoned Repeal. Moreover, notwithstanding the rise in evictions, emigration and excess mortality following the closure of the Soup Kitchens, they continued to support the famine policies of the Whigs. Consequently, despite having only one parliamentary representative, the Irish Confederation remained the main voice of opposition to government relief policies in Ireland. O'Brien's disillusionment with Westminster was so thorough that his colleagues feared he would refuse to take his seat, leading Mitchel to write to him saying 'we are all here unanimous in the which that you may feel yourself at liberty to accept the trust, now they have forced it on you ... In short, upon all public grounds my mind has quite changed as to this matter since I saw you. And provided personal impediments are removed and private feelings are satisfied (and only in that case) I hope you will consent to represent Limerick.'[149] Amongst other things, Mitchel's letter revealed that he still had confidence in the parliamentary process to deliver reforms for Ireland. O'Brien's disenchantment continued and in April 1848, due to a combination of disgust and frustration, he withdrew from parliament on the grounds that he was wasting his time trying to obtain justice for Ireland in London.[150]

Following the General Election, the Whigs continued to depend on collaboration with other groups, including the Repealers, who had increased their support in the election. Regardless of this alliance, Sir Robert Peel believed that there was 'little real sympathy' between Repealers and Whigs, and that the collaboration was pursued for selfish reasons on both sides.[151] For the Confederation, the results of the election suggested that they were making little progress, while O'Connell's death had rekindled antagonism towards them. O'Brien confided in his close ally, Dillon, that the mistake of the party had been to try to move forward so quickly and 'The more we push forward the more fixedly will the priests and people set their faces against us.'[152] Overall, the divisions apparent in the summer and autumn of 1847 weakened both Repeal groups, while showing that the Repeal movement was still bitterly divided. Tellingly, Conciliation Hall never lived up to its name.

O'Connell's death in May had overshadowed other news from Ireland. Another death that occurred in the same month, and which also changed the direction of Irish politics, was that of the Lord Lieutenant, Bessborough. The deaths of O'Connell and Bessborough took place within a few days of each other, thus depriving Ireland both of its Lord Lieutenant and of the leader of the Repeal movement. Bessborough was replaced by Lord Clarendon, who accepted the office of Viceroy reluctantly, out of a sense of duty rather than interest. Clarendon arrived in Ireland with preconceptions that Irish reports of the Famine had been exaggerated. He quickly realized that the situation in Ireland was worse that he had expected. Despite official, declarations that the Famine was over, Clarendon confided to a friend, 'I fear that the distress next autumn and winter will be greater than the last, and aggravated by the absence of that stream of charity, both public and private, which has flowed so liberally this year into Ireland.' Therefore, he was accepting the position 'without making to myself the smallest illusion as to the more than probability of failure that awaits me'.[153]

In addition to being dissatisfied with the famine policies of his government, Clarendon was concerned that Repeal agitation was reviving.[154] However, he was dismissive about the threat posed by the divided Repeal movement. In July, shortly after his arrival in Ireland, he confidently asserted that the Irish Confederation posed little threat to the government, informing Russell that 'Young Ireland has no money, some talent, very little influence, and is losing ground'.[155] He was also optimistic that he could exploit the divisions within the Repeal movement, noting with some satisfaction that, 'The physical force men, whenever they meet for spouting, have to be escorted home by two or three hundred police, or not one of them would escape alive from the moral persuasion party, who miss no opportunity of getting up a ferocious row. Moral persuasion always waylays physical force and beats it within an inch of its life.'[156] Furthermore, Clarendon believed that O'Connell's death made little difference to Irish politics, on the grounds that he had exerted little influence in his later years anyway. He was sceptical regarding O'Connell's motives, suggesting that, 'If he had ceased agitating when emancipation was carried, he would have been as great a man in his way as Washington; but ... his whole object was money and power; the latter in order to make it subservient to the former.'[157] Clarendon was even more disparaging about John O'Connell, the new leader of the Repeal Association, believing that under his management, support for Repeal would decline. Within a few months, however, when the mourning and inertia caused by O'Connell's death were over, his views had undergone a substantial change. In November 1847, he informed the Prime Minister that 'if the spirit of disaffection and insubordination spreads and the present anarchical tendencies increase, I must then ask for some extraordinary powers'.[158] The outcome was the introduction of another Coercion Bill for Ireland. John O'Connell, despite Clarendon's antagonism, continued with his father's policy of supporting the Whig government. His refusal to vote against the bill in December 1847 suggested that he was anxious not to alienate the Whigs, despite their mis-handling of the Famine. The introduction of another Coercion Act provided further confirmation to Young Ireland that there was no advantage to the Irish people in working with the British parliament.

Tenant Right and the land question

The Famine highlighted tensions within Irish society, especially in regard to the relationship between landlords and tenants. By 1847, a number of landlords were responding with widespread clearances of their estates and the scale of evictions increased when, in August, the Poor Law was made responsible for all relief. At this stage, even benign landlords such as Lord Sligo argued that the choice lay between evicting tenants or going bankrupt. The attitude of the Confederation to the land question was ambiguous, with many of its leaders hoping that they could win the support of landowners. Less than two weeks after the formation of the Confederation, John Mitchel had outlined his view of what he still referred to as Young Ireland, explaining that they were 'of no single school of politics; there are amongst them Conservatives, moderate Reformers, levelling Democrats; and ... they do not, as a body, consider the ruin of the landed gentry to be the best remedy, or any remedy at all, for the Irish ills'.[159] Old Ireland was also ambivalent about the support to be given to the issue of land reform. In 1846, when O'Connell had proposed a fresh alliance with the Whigs, he had suggested that, in return, Tenant Right would be granted, but when the Whigs returned to power, this promise was ignored.[160] John O'Connell did not oppose Tenant Right, but he never gave it priority or full support. However, the concept of Tenant Right, although not clearly defined, generally included compensation to tenants for improvements they had made to property if they were evicted or they left. This moderate view of reform was also referred to as the 'Ulster Custom' as it had become an established practice (although not law) in parts of Ulster.[161] Tenant Right had an influential champion in William Sharman Crawford, MP for Rochdale and a Protestant landlord in County Down. In 1846, Crawford had formed the Tenant Right Association in Ulster (sometimes referred to as the Tenant League).

Early in its existence, land reform entered the political discourse of the Irish Confederation, usually in the moderate form of the demand for an extension of the Ulster Custom. Land reform was given coherence and a radical dimension by a relatively unknown contributor to the *Nation*, James Fintan Lalor, who had been admitted to the Council of the Confederation in April.[162] Lalor had started writing regularly for the *Nation* in early 1847. Initially, he appealed to Irish landowners to lead a social transformation of the landholding structure in Ireland. The alternative, he warned, was revolution, in which changes would be forced upon them. Within a few months, Lalor's writings had become more radical, as he was angered by the indifference both of the British government and of Irish landlords to the suffering caused by the Famine. He suggested that, in the context of the food shortages, Repeal was not a priority for the Irish poor, a position he reversed intermittently.[163] Increasingly, he wrote about the need for a social revolution to accompany the political one, believing that without a reform of the land system, political change alone would be meaningless.[164] By mid-1847, he thought it unlikely that landlords might lead the revolution and instead put his faith in a strong farmer class to lead the new society. Lalor proposed that tenants mount a campaign of civil disobedience, which would include withholding rents, a strategy which he referred to as a 'moral insurrection'.[165] His suggestion was based on a conviction that the Irish people, not the landlords, owned the land. His programme was not as radical as this idea suggested since he continued to believe in the rights of private property, but not of absolute ownership. An integral part of the reforms would be that the rights of tenants would be protected, a philosophy that had much in common with that of the more moderate Tenant Right Association. The fact that Lalor signed his articles in the *Nation* gave him an identity and profile amongst the contributors, helped by the fact that his articles were often polemical and provided a clear strategy for change.

Initially, Lalor was not supported by the leaders of the Irish Confederation: even Mitchel's conversion to anti-landlordism was not complete until the end of 1847, although he was instantly captivated by Lalor's energy and vision.[166] From the outset, the land question was formally recognized as a concern of the Confederation, with the appointment of a Landlord and Tenant sub-committee.[167] In March, the Council also agreed to appoint a Land Committee to inquire into land tenure in Ireland.[168] In the following month, the Council passed a resolution supporting the Tenant League.[169] The approach of the Confederation to landlord–tenant relations was pragmatic, with the principle of Tenant Right increasingly viewed by Richard O'Gorman as a way of preventing the evils of the Famine occurring again. He proposed to the Council of the Confederation that they should support the formation and extension of a Tenant League in Ireland.[170] In a private letter to O'Brien written in the spring of 1847, he suggested that Tenant Right would take the Confederation in a new direction:

> ... by it we can go far to unite the *People* of the North and the South in the Association formed to support the tenant farmers' claims. The Tenant Farmers' League I believe to be the nucleus of a great movement. Our agitation so far had been a very elegant, eloquent, high-toned sort of business. I think it will have to become a more democratic style of work, and that at once too.[171]

O'Brien, however, remained unconvinced about adopting the principles of the Tenant League, as he was nervous about alienating landlords' support. He therefore encouraged the Confederation to seek more actively the involvement of Irish landowners.[172] In August 1847, he confided to Mitchel that he disliked the radical stance of some Confederates regarding the land question. Additionally, he was concerned that some of the attacks by Lalor and Kenyon were being directed against him personally. Mitchel replied that 'my doctrine is nearly identical with Lalor's', but he reassured O'Brien about the regard of the Confederation for him. He clearly hoped that the differences could be worked out, adding, 'I hope to see Lalor and Father Kenyon (neither of whom we can afford to lose) working cordially with us yet.'[173] Even at this stage, it was clear that Mitchel's views were becoming increasingly radical, but that he still hoped that landowners would support rather than oppose the need for social change.

Lalor's writings in the *Nation* won him some popular support. The third year of food shortages and the inappropriate relief policies of the government had resulted in some members of the Confederation adopting more radical policies, bringing them closer to his position. Father Kenyon and Michael Doheny (a radical barrister), who both had their own followings within County Tipperary, supported some of his aims. Doheny, in particular, appeared convinced of the importance of the land question in nationalist politics, and during the summer he had undertaken a tour in parts of the south, advocating the formation of a Tenant League. Yet his concerns about marrying the land question with the national question were evident in a letter to O'Brien, written in early September, confiding that:

> there is imminent danger if we take part in a struggle against the landlords (shape it how you will, it will come to that) if we do that the danger is that we extinguish thereby and perhaps for ever the spirit of nationality manifesting itself in that quarter. Then, on the other hand, if we keep aloof from this movement now, we will miss a great opportunity of taking the nation captive ... At the same time that I say this I don't think any of us ought to go out of our way to originate this movement or appear to lead it ... One thing I am almost certain of, that this League will succeed ... or be crushed.[174]

On 19 September 1847, Lalor held a public meeting in Holycross in County Tipperary, with a view to organizing a permanent Tenant Right Association in the area. Doheny spoke and, although not present, Mitchel gave his support to the aims of the meeting. Mitchel also wrote to O'Brien, warning him that although 'you will not quite approve of these proceedings', Lalor's ideas were winning converts within the Confederation. Mitchel's letter revealed that he still had faith in Irish landowners being won over to land reform, and that peaceful means would be successful in achieving the Confederation's goals, saying:

> I look to all this merely as a spur to the Irish Council and to the landlords generally. And there is no doubt, if they will be led or driven, to frame and propose a fair scheme of tenant-right, they will take the people out of the hands of Lalor and of all the revolutionists. But the time has nearly come when affairs must take a decisive turn either one way or the other. I sincerely hope it will be in the moderate direction.[175]

Approximately 4,000 people attended the Holycross meeting and the event was widely reported in the press. It ended in ignominy, with a public argument between Lalor and some of the other speakers.[176] The meeting, therefore, marked the end rather than the beginning of this phase of the Tenant Right movement in the south. Nevertheless, the debate highlighted – uncomfortably for O'Brien – that the majority of Irish landowners did not support a programme of either social or political change. Regardless of the fact that they too had been abandoned by the British government during the Famine, and the main burden of financing poor relief had been transferred to them, their loyalties overwhelmingly lay with the Westminster parliament. Despite Lalor's lack of influence on the main body of the Irish Confederation, his ideas for social change based on a reform of the land system would emerge again in the Tenant Right movement in the 1850s and during the turbulent decade of the 1870s, when they would provide a blueprint for the tactics employed by the Land League.

The debates about land tenure signified that a more radical social programme had become part of the Repeal question. Moreover, the discussion had been moved into the public arena through the columns of the *Nation*. Since the paper had been established in 1842, the context had changed greatly and this was reflected in the increasingly radical tones of its articles, notably those written by Lalor and Mitchel. Initially, most of Mitchel's anger was directed against the British government, rather than the Irish landowners. By the end of 1847, Lalor had converted Mitchel to his viewpoint. This was an important achievement as Mitchel was influential, both in his role as editor of the *Nation*, and as a leading member of the Council of the Confederation. He and his wife Jenny were personally popular, welcoming their political colleagues to their Dublin home. Ultimately, the land question contributed to a rift within the Confederation, only twelve months after it had been formed.

Protestant support

The Irish Confederation, like the United Irishmen in the 1790s, believed that nationality was more important than religion in defining Irish identity, and they hoped that religious and class divisions could be subsumed under the common banner of nationhood. Even before the inaugural meeting of the Confederation, they were concerned with making the organization inclusive but, throughout its existence, Protestants were especially targeted as welcome members. Before the first meeting of the Confederation in January, Dr Cane of Kilkenny wrote to Duffy, warning him that, 'The Protestants are bending their heads and opening their ears – we must draw them to us now or never.'[177] According to Duffy, himself a northern Catholic, the aim of the Confederation was 'to mould many hostile classes into a nation'.[178] Consequently, much of 1847 was spent reaching out to diverse social and religious groups. The leaders of the Confederation wanted particularly to win the support of Protestant landlords, without alienating moderate Catholic opinion. They also hoped that they could woo landlords who were dissatisfied with the relief measures introduced by the Whig government, as a large portion of the financial burden for providing this relief fell on owners of land.

The Confederation was supported by some Protestant intellectuals, notably Isaac Butt and Sir Samuel Ferguson, who did not totally agree with all the policies of Young Ireland, but hoped for a union of all patriotic Irishmen.[179] Winning of the support of less wealthy and educated Protestants proved to be more difficult, especially as there had been a revival of the Orange Order after 1845; partly in response to marches having been made legal, but also in reaction to Peel's decision to increase the grant to Maynooth College, the Catholic seminary.[180] However, poor Protestants, ranging from small tenant farmers to factory workers and independent weavers, had been affected by the combination of bad harvests and industrial recession in 1847. As a consequence, the work-houses in Newtownards and Lurgan, which were located in the industrial – and Protestant – heartland of Ireland, were amongst the most over-crowed and impoverished in the country.[181] Despite traditional Protestant support for the Union with Britain, the Famine was demonstrating that the British government had little sympathy for them, even at a time of national crisis.

Extending their support in the north-east of Ireland was a priority for the Confederation and John Mitchel, a Protestant from County Down and possibly the most charismatic of the leaders, was appointed Inspector of Clubs for Ulster. He held this position until he resigned from the Council in January 1848.[182] One of the first decisions of the Confederation was to visit the north of Ireland, an area neglected by O'Connell. O'Brien explained that because he had 'long been anxious to win over the north to the cause of Repeal', he proposed a 'mission' to Belfast.[183] The northern visit was proposed for the summer of 1847, but it was postponed due to O'Connell's death.[184] In the interim, 3,000 copies of an address from 'southerners to the men of Ulster' were circulated.[185] Duffy, a Catholic from County Monaghan, was optimistic about winning support from Protestants for the Confederation, claiming that 'nationality is now planted in the north more firmly than it was in Munster in 1842'.[186] John Martin, a Protestant landlord from County Down and a close friend of Mitchel's, was more cautious, describing the proposed visit as 'dangerous' but 'possible'.[187] Their conjectures were put to the test when the leaders of Old Ireland arrived in the north of Ireland.

The visit of the Young Ireland leadership to Belfast took place in mid-November 1847. Since the General Election in August, the Confederation had been in the doldrums, but the northern trip was carefully planned and gave the Council a fresh sense of direction.[188] O'Brien first spent a few days with Sharman Crawford, an advocate of Tenant Right, fellow MP and Protestant landlord, before proceeding to Belfast, where he was joined by John Mitchel, Thomas Francis Meagher and Thomas D'Arcy McGee. They had gone with the specified purpose of winning support from northern Protestants. They expected to be met with some opposition from militant members of the Orange Order, similar to that which O'Connell had experienced in January 1841, but much of the anger at their visit was generated by fellow Repealers, that is, supporters of O'Connell. The first meeting took place in the Music Hall in Belfast and even before they arrived, Old Irelanders were causing disturbances outside the theatre. Although the Music Hall was full, the audience consisted mostly of Old Irelanders. There were hundreds more outside, and they were only prevented from entering by the special constabulary (who had been brought into the town for the occasion) who were armed with bayonets, and local constables who had batons. Each of the speakers was greeted with a mixture of cheers and hisses and much of their address could not be heard. They were also heckled with shouts for 'John O'Connell' and accusations that the speakers had killed his father.

From an early stage in the proceedings, Old Ireland showed 'unequivocal signs that they were no longer bound by the all-endearing principles of "moral force", including the throwing of squibs and firecrackers'.[189] Those outside the hall assailed the locked doors of the hall and stones were thrown at the windows. A number of protesters mounted the stage and physically attacked the speakers. Meagher, who was held personally responsible for splitting the Repeal Association, was threatened with death.[190] He responded by saying, 'You may be able to kill me, but I do not leave this place except as a corpse', which won the admiration of Mitchel, who subsequently wrote, 'I admired him at that moment and felt that at any rate the Irish cause would never be disgraced by any lack of manhood in that man.'[191] The audience only calmed down when armed police removed the troublemakers, allowing Meagher to speak. He assured the audience that Repeal would not result in a Catholic Ascendancy. He constantly referred to the Protestant Volunteers of 1782 who had paved the way for the current wave of nationalism. O'Brien addressed the meeting as a fellow Irish Protestant: 'I am not forgetful of the fact that the intelligent and influential section of the inhabitants are Protestants; nor will I withhold from them my conviction, that after Repeal, they will enjoy as much protection for their peculiar privileges as before, and that then, they will not depend on the will of the English Legislature.'[192]

A second meeting was held four days later in the Belfast Theatre. The same speakers were present, but they were joined by John Martin. Earlier that morning, the Belfast magistrates had decided that the meeting could not go ahead and the speakers were barred from entering the theatre. O'Brien therefore addressed the crowd outside the building, but he was drowned by the crowds cheering for John O'Connell and shouting 'You killed O'Connell'. Two bulldogs were set loose to attack O'Brien. When it became clear that the speakers would not be given access to the theatre, O'Brien announced that he was going to go to Hercules Street, a notorious stronghold of Old Ireland. En route, he was attacked by missiles and more shouting. He and his entourage were only able to return to his hotel due to the presence of a police escort, although they continued to be attacked. A third meeting was attempted on the following day, in the same place. Again, Old Ireland turned out in large numbers. The speakers were constantly interrupted and taunted, but O'Brien managed to finish his speech. He pointed out that he had expected resistance but had come to remind Irish Protestants of their patriotic heritage. He also pointed out that although Ulster was represented to be the only flourishing part of the country, he had witnessed poverty and misery similar to that which existed in the south of Ireland. He added that this was the first time he had addressed Old Ireland since leaving Conciliation Hall and he asked that they should allow him free speech. Meagher delivered part of his speech before the tumult became too uncontrolled, while neither Mitchel nor Martin had any success in delivering their lectures.[193]

Despite their rough reception, O'Brien was pleased with the trip, which had brought him into contact with 'a considerable number of intelligent men' and given him a chance to inspect the industries and public institutions in Belfast. He did not believe that Orangemen were responsible for any of the violence, blaming it exclusively on Old Ireland in Belfast.[194] One of the main aims of the visit of the Confederation to the north was to reassure Protestants of their role in a united Ireland, but the meeting demonstrated that at the end of 1847 they still had to convince their fellow Repealers of the merits of their politics. Moreover, to Protestant onlookers, the internecine conflict between the two groups of Repealers may have provided compelling evidence that self-government was a very bad idea.

Black '47

At the end of 1847, the continuing distress in the country and rise in petty crime led Lord Clarendon to ask the Prime Minister for more coercive powers to be introduced. In addition to the suspension of Habeas Corpus, Clarendon wanted to limit the possession of arms and to impose a fine on any district where a crime was committed. Russell was unconvinced of the need for further powers, given the high police and military presence in the country anyway, and he responded that, 'I am not ready to bring in any restrictive law without at the same time restraining the powers of the landlord.' His preference was for 'leaving the law to its operation by the gradual influences of civilisation, by introducing and fostering education'.[195] Clarendon responded that he was 'surprised' and 'disheartened' by this answer, adding 'nor do I understand how any government can think it expedient to leave 300,000 arms in possession of some of the most ferocious people on earth, at the commencement of a winter when there will be great poverty and little employment'.[196] In a separate communication, he attributed the lack of response to the fact that 'the Cabinet has little or no confidence in my reports or opinions'. He also warned that if he felt unable to maintain the law, he would not 'remain here when I feel my power of usefulness is gone'.[197] Clarendon's persistence paid off and the next Queen's speech included a request to parliament for more legal powers, although he believed that the new Coercion Bill did not go far enough.[198] Ironically, after only eighteen months of being in power, the Whig government was introducing similar measures to those that had brought down Peel's administration in 1846. Moreover, the Repeal

Association's support for the Whig government seemed to have brought no benefit to either side.

Following the Confederation's visit to Belfast in November, O'Brien travelled to London to oppose the Coercion Bill being introduced by the Whig government. Despite suffering from influenza, he attended the third reading of the debate and spoke against the bill.[199] The majority of Irish MPs supported it, worried by the increased crime that had accompanied the food shortages. O'Brien, speaking on behalf of the Confederates, lamented that, in the midst of a famine, the Whigs remained primarily concerned with law and order, rather than with saving lives.[200] The bill provided for individual towns and counties to be 'proclaimed', which would result in a number of draconian measures including the compulsory disarming of the local population. The introduction of the new Crime and Outrage Bill further convinced O'Brien that justice for Ireland from a British government was not possible. A further outcome was that John O'Connell, by failing to consistently defend Irish interests during the passage of the Bill, brought his honeymoon period as leader of the Repeal Association to an end. Clarendon, who had closely followed the proceedings, warned the Prime Minster that:

> Young Ireland is very popular, the people of Dublin are all for getting the wonderful advantages they have been so long promised by force, and if J. O'Connell had come over the day after the Crime Prevention Bill was introduced, he would have been murdered for having *sowld his country*.[201]

By January 1848, Lord Clarendon was hopeful that the decline of the Repeal Association was being helped by critical articles in *The Times* and by the character and actions of John O'Connell. He was confident that, 'if we could knock up the Association it would be a heavy blow and great discouragement to agitation. With little money in their till, and that vapouring fellow, J. O'Connell, for their champion, such an establishment ought not to exist much longer.'[202] Privately, Clarendon acknowledged that the power balance was changing between Old and Young Ireland, with a majority of Repealers increasingly favouring physical force.[203] His comment revealed that, despite the moderate policies advocated by the Confederation, they were still tainted by O'Connell's accusations of violence.

In general, by the close of 1847 both sections of the Repeal movement seemed to have lost direction. Neither side had been able to win the support of landlords, despite the fact that the new relief policies, since August 1847, had placed a high financial burden on them for providing relief. Yet few believed that a better alternative lay in the Repeal of the Union. Neither Old Ireland, which had supported the policies of the Whigs, nor Young Ireland, who had consistently opposed them, had won the support of the majority of Irish landlords.

The electoral success of Old Ireland in the General Election disguised the fact that the party was in decline: despite the return of thirty-seven Repealers, the Repeal Association was inert and Repeal Rent had virtually disappeared.[204] Even their ongoing alliance with the Whigs had delivered little benefit to Ireland. The first twelve months had brought mixed fortunes for the Irish Confederation. Opprobrium had been heaped on them following O'Connell's death, but by the end of the year they were increasing in popularity. At this point, disagreement about the role of landowners in the Repeal movement was causing a rift in the Irish Confederation. The quarrel was led by John Mitchel, influenced by Lalor, both of whom were appalled by the continuing suffering in Ireland and the inertia of many landlords. Throughout 1847, O'Brien's disenchantment with Westminster had been increasing, and on a few occasions he had attempted to withdraw from parliament. Despite their disillusionment with mainstream British politics, neither section of the Repeal movement was any closer to building a national movement. Moreover, Ireland was entering its third year of famine, but the new Poor Law had demonstrated that the distress was to be treated as an Irish, and not a British or Imperial, responsibility. Members of the Irish Confederation overwhelmingly continued to support peaceful, constitutional tactics to bring about change. Ironically, it was Old Ireland who had most frequent recourse to violence in 1847, directed against their former colleagues in Young Ireland.

By the beginning of 1848 the two main Repeal organizations were more polarized than they had been twelve months earlier. The intermittent attempts to create a unified, inclusive Irish party had failed, while Daniel O'Connell's death signalled a new regime within Conciliation Hall. Apart from the political divergences between the two organizations, divisions were appearing within the two groups: some members of Old Ireland were disillusioned with the Whig alliance, while a small group within the Confederation had come to the view that Irish landowners could not be relied upon to protect Ireland's interests. While contact with the Tenant League broadened the appeal of the Confederation and gave it a more radical social agenda, it lost them the support of some landowners, who were increasingly squeezed by the pincer movement of increased taxation and diminishing rents. In the short term, therefore, the association of the national question with the extension of Tenant Right probably did more damage than good, especially in relation to the Confederation's relationship with landowners.

The year 1848 started badly for the Irish Confederation, with the departure of John Mitchel, John Martin and Devin Reilly from the Council of the Confederation. Events outside the country also provided a trigger for the development of a more radical programme. Irish nationalism continued to be inspired by what was taking place in Europe. The activities of Italian nationalists were watched with particular interest in the latter part of 1847. Meagher, in particular, used the Italian example to show that Ireland was not alone in its revolutionary struggle but referred to events in Italy saying 'Italy! The beautiful, the brilliant, and the gifted – Italy! Italy is in arms.'[205] Within a few months an even more significant revolution had taken place in France, which had a far-reaching impact on Irish politics. The Revolution in France opened the prospect that political change was possible in Ireland. However, as some sections of the Repeal parties moved closer together, they were watched by an increasingly nervous British government. The response of the British state to the growing nationalist threat helped to shape the progress of the Repeal movement in 1848.

Notes

1 Lord Bessborough, Dublin Castle, to Lord John Russell, 23 January 1847: Russell Papers, TNA, 30 22 16A.
2 See Kinealy, *Death-Dealing Famine*, chapters 5 and 6.
3 This principle had been the basis of the 1838 Poor Law and had governed relief provision in the early years of the Famine: see Kinealy, *Death-Dealing Famine*, passim.
4 The Poor Law Amendment Act of 1847 allowed outdoor relief – given to people within their own homes – to be provided in exceptional circumstances. Its introduction confirmed the principle that the Irish Famine should be supported by Irish taxation.
5 Bessborough and O'Connell had an amicable relationship, having worked together during various Whig/O'Connellite alliances.
6 *Nation*, 21 November 1846.
7 Duffy, *Four Years*, pp. 366–7.
8 Ibid., p. 369.
9 Gwynn, *Young Ireland*, pp. 98–9: Duffy, *Four Years*, p. 357.
10 Gwynn, *Young Ireland*, p. 98.
11 For more on the parliamentary debates between the Whigs and the Protectionists, see Kinealy, *Great Irish Famine*, chapter 1.
12 Duffy, *Four Years*, p. 374.
13 Donnolly, *The Great Irish Potato Famine*, p. 195
14 O'Connell to Ray, quoted in Gwynn, *Young Ireland*, p. 99.
15 Ibid., p. 100; Daniel O'Connell was too ill to attend parliament, but wrote a letter in favour of the bill, and his sons, John and Daniel, voted for it, but it did not have unanimous support amongst Repealers who decided to follow the ministerial whip: Duffy, *Four Years*, pp. 374–5.
16 *Mercury*, 20 April 1847.
17 Private letter from O'Brien, Cahirmoyle, 22 October 1847: NLI, MS 10515 (4).
18 Duffy, *Four Years*, p. 278.
19 W.F. Monypenny and G.E. Buckle, *The Life of Benjamin Disraeli, Earl of Beaconsfield* (London: John Murray, 1910–20), vol. iii, p. 325.
20 In April, for example, John O'Connell made overtures to the Confederation for a reunion: see Minutes of Council of the Confederation, 6 April 1847.
21 Duffy, *Four Years*, pp. 361–2; Duffy notes that more people were employed

in administering the public works (11,000) than initially enrolled in the Confederation.

22 Council of Confederation for Year 1848, in Correspondence of Confederate Clubs, RIA, MS 23.H.41, n.d., early 1848.

23 Duffy, *Four Years*, p. 360.

24 Ibid.

25 Dr Cane to Duffy, *Nation*, correspondence, quoted in Duffy, *Four Years*, p. 360.

26 Irish Confederation Council Office to Sheffield Confederate Club, 23 June 1847: Correspondence of Confederation, RIA.

27 The cost of 100 placards being displayed for two days was 8 shillings: Book of Expenditure of Irish Confederation, RIA, 23.H.43, 15 March 1848.

28 Ibid., 4 March 1847.

29 Memorandum of Smith O'Brien on 1847 and 1848, Smith O'Brien Papers, NLI, MS 442.

30 Book of Expenditure of Irish Confederation, RIA, 23.H.44. 25 January 1847.

31 Ibid., 9 February 1847.

32 Duffy, *Four Years*, p. 361.

33 *Mercury*, 20 April 1847.

34 Wilson, *McGee*, p. 165.

35 Book of Expenditures of Irish Confederation, RIA, 23.H.43, 1847–1848.

36 Ibid., Minutes of Council, RIA, 23.H.44, 9 February 1847.

37 Ibid.

38 Duffy, *Four Years*, pp. 360–1; The Confederation paid £3 3s. For this legal opinion, Book of Expenditures of Irish Confederation, RIA, 23.H.43, 23 January 1847.

39 Minutes of Council of Irish Confederation, RIA, 23.H.44, 19 January 1847.

40 Ibid., 3 April 1847.

41 Ibid., 9 June 1847.

42 *Daily News* quoted in *Nation*, 23 January 1847.

43 *Nation*, 28 August 1847.

44 Duffy, *Four Years*, p. 360.

45 Ibid., p. 373.

46 Ibid., p. 277.

47 *Nation*, 21 January 1847.

48 O'Gorman to O'Brien, quoted in Gwynn, *Young Ireland*, pp. 105–6.

49 O'Gorman to O'Brien, ibid., p. 108.

50 Minutes of Council of Confederation, RIA, 23.H.44, 18 March 1847.

51 He was proposed as a candidate in his absence and elected for County Limerick, despite a stiff contest.

52 Gwynn, *Young Ireland*, p. 109

53 Ibid., p. 109.

54 Ibid., p. 110

55 Mitchel to O'Brien, ibid., pp. 110–11.

56 Mitchel to O'Brien, ibid., p. 111.

57 Ibid., p113.

58 Ibid., p. 110.

59 Minutes of Council of Confederation, RIA, 23.H.44, 30 April 1847.

60 Ibid., 3 May 1847.
61 Ibid., 5 May 1847.
62 Ibid., 7 June 1847.
63 *Nation*, 10 April 1847.
64 Matthew Potter, *A Catholic Unionist: The Life and Times of William Monsell 1812–1894* (Limerick: The Press, n.d.), pp. 19–34.
65 Lady Ferguson, *Sir Samuel Ferguson*, p. 245.
66 Duffy, *Four Years*, pp. 404–6.
67 Lady Ferguson, *Sir Samuel Ferguson*, p. 245.
68 Duffy, *Four Years, pp.* 420–5.
69 Charles Gavan Duffy, *Report of the Organization and Instructions for the Formation and Government of Confederate Clubs* (Dublin: William Holden, 1847), p. 4.
70 *Nation*, 8 July 1848.
71 Charles Gavan Duffy, *The Use and Capacity of Confederate Clubs* (Dublin: James Charles, 1847), p. 16.
72 Duffy, *Organization ... and Government of Clubs*, p. 4.
73 Ibid.
74 *Nation*, 2 October 1847.
75 The copious notebooks of one of these police informers, 'CD', are held in Trinity College, MSS 2037–40.
76 Reports of CD, 5 February 1849: TCD, MS 2039, p. 206.
77 3 February 1849: ibid., p. 205.
78 Duffy, *Organization ... and Government of Clubs*, p. 3.
79 *Nation*, 15 January 1848.
80 *Nation*, 2 October, 9 October 1847. The paper included regular reports on club activities in both Ireland and Britain.
81 Christine Kinealy and Gerard MacAtasney, *The Hidden Famine: Poverty, Hunger and Sectarianism in Belfast c.1840–50* (London: Pluto Press, 2000).
82 List of Confederate Clubs, Correspondence of Irish Confederation, RIA, MS 23.H.41; Gary Owens, 'Popular Mobilization and the Rising of 1848: The Clubs of the Irish Confederation' in Laurence M. Geary, *Rebellion and Remembrance in Modern Ireland* (Dublin: Four Courts Press, 2001), p. 51.
83 Correspondence of Irish Confederation, RIA, MS 23.H.41, 29 May 1847, 4 June 1847, 7 June 1847, 3 March 1848.
84 McGee to O'Brien, 1 and 9 October, 4 and 6 October, quoted in Wilson, *McGee*, p. 167.
85 Rachel O'Higgins, 'Irish Trade Unions and Politics, 1830–50' in *The Historical Journal* (vol. 4, issue 2), 117.
86 Reports of CJ (informer), TCD, MS 2038/2039.
87 Reports of informers at Chartism meetings, TNA, HO45, OS 3136, 1848–1850.
88 Addresses of Confederate Clubs in Correspondence of Confederate Clubs, RIA, MS 23.H.41.
89 Ibid., Correspondence of Irish Confederation, MS 23.H.41, 29 May 1847, 3 June 1847, 7 June 1847, 12 June 1847, 18 June 1847, 23 June 1847.
90 Saville, *1848*, p. 72.
91 Minutes of Council, RIA, 23.H.44, 3 August 1847.
92 O'Higgins, 'Irish Trade Unions', 211.

93 The links with British radicals fluctuated, although initially the possibility for a strong alliance seemed good, with a large Repeal meeting being held in Manchester in January 1831: see F.A. D'Arcy, 'The National Trades' Political Union and Daniel O'Connell 1830–1848' in *Eire-Ireland* (xvii), 10; also *Freeman's Journal*, 31 January 1831.

94 D'Arcy, 'The National Trades', 11.

95 Quoted in O'Higgins, 'Irish Trade Unions', 214.

96 D'Arcy, 'The National Trades', 7.

97 Ibid.

98 O'Higgins, 'Irish Trade Unions', 215.

99 Wilson, *McGee*, p. 138.

100 The Dublin trades were represented by Martin Crean, a shoemaker, and Edward Holywood, who escaped to France in 1848: O'Higgins, 'Irish Trade Unions', 216.

101 Wilson, *McGee*, p. 139.

102 Ibid.

103 Asa Briggs, *Chartist Studies* (London: Macmillan, 1967), p. 51.

104 David Goodway, *London Chartism, 1838–1848* (Cambridge: Cambridge University Press, 1982), p. 65.

105 Minutes of Council of Confederation, RIA, 23.H.43, 12 May 1847; the Council decided that chairing the Chartist meeting did not disqualify him from being a member of the Council, ibid., 19 May 1847.

106 Minutes of Council, RIA, 23.H.44, 14 July 1847.

107 O'Gorman to O'Brien quoted in Gwynn, *Young Ireland*, p. 108.

108 Memorandum of Smith O'Brien on 1847 and 1848, Smith O'Brien Papers, NLI, MS 449, n.d.

109 Duffy, *Four Years*, p. 450.

110 Saville, *1848*.

111 Gwynn, *Young Ireland*, p. 114.

112 Duffy, *Four Years*, p. 393.

113 See Kinealy, *Lives of Victorian Political Figures*.

114 14 June 1847: Thomson and McGusty, *Irish Journals*, p. 151.

115 Beckett, *The Making of Modern Ireland*, p. 346.

116 Memorandum of Smith O'Brien, on 1847 and 1848, Smith O'Brien Papers, NLI, MS 449, n.d.

117 Duffy, *Four Years*, p. 26.

118 Gwynn, *Young Ireland*, p. 114.

119 R. Hamill, Council Rooms of Irish Confederation to James Cantwell, Correspondence of Irish Confederation, RIA, MS 23.H.41, 2 June 1847.

120 Maurice O'Connell to O'Brien, 7 June 1847: Minutes of Council of Confederation, NIA, 23.H.44.

121 Kenyon to O'Brien, 4 June 1847: Minutes of Council of Confederation, NIA, 23.H.44.

122 Duffy, *Four Years*, p. 402.

123 Ibid., p. 403.

124 Ibid.

125 Gwynn, *Young Ireland*, p. 239.

126 Lyons, *Meagher. Speeches and Writings*, pp. 53–5.

127 Pigot to Dillon, 8 May 1847: Dillon Papers, TCD, MS 6457 (f.33).

128 Gwynn, 'Father Kenyon', 239.
129 Duffy, *Four Years*, p. 409.
130 June 1847: Strachey and Fulford, *Greville Memoirs*, 7 p. 449.
131 *The Times*, 25 May 1847.
132 *New York Freeman's*, 26 February 1848.
133 Ibid., 25 March 1848.
134 Padre Gioacchino Ventura, translated by William B. McCabe, *The Funeral Oration on Daniel O'Connell Delivered at Rome on 28 June 1847* (Dublin: J.H. Scott, 1847).
135 Minutes of Council of Confederation, RIA, 23.H.44, 9 June 1847.
136 Ibid., 29 June 1847.
137 Gwynn, *Young Ireland*, p. 120.
138 William Smith O'Brien Papers, NLI, MS 22345, n.d., 1847.
139 O'Brien to Dillon, 23 August 1847: Dillon Papers, TCD, MS 6457 (f.56).
140 Gwynn, 'Father Kenyon', 240.
141 *The Times*, 6 October 1847.
142 Anstey stood as a Repeal candidate but informed the Council of the Confederation in August that although he admired them, he was not free to join them yet. Minutes of Council of Confederation, RIA, 23.H.44, 23 August 1847.
143 Gwynn, *Young Ireland*, pp. 121–2.
144 Nowlan, *Politics of Repeal*, p. 140.
145 Quoted in Gwynn, *Young Ireland*, p. 123.
146 Duffy, *Four Years*, pp. 430–5.
147 *Freeman's Journal*, 2 July 1847.
148 Ibid., 2 July 1847.
149 Mitchel to O'Brien, quoted in Gwynn, *Young Ireland*, pp. 134–5.
150 Kinealy, *Great Irish Famine*, chapter 1.
151 Peel to the King of the Belgians, 27 January 1847: Parker, *Sir Robert Peel*, p. 479.
152 O'Brien to Dillon, 23 August 1847: Dillon Papers, TCD, MS 6457.
153 Letter of Lord Clarendon to unidentified correspondent, 29 June 1847: Right Honourable Sir Herbert Maxwell, *The Life and Letters of George William Frederick, Fourth Earl of Clarendon* (London: Edward Arnold, 1913, 2 vols), pp. 277–8.
154 Ibid.
155 Clarendon to Russell, Bodleian Library, Clarendon Letter Books, 1 July 1847, 17 July 1847.
156 Quoted in Maxwell, *Life and Letters*, pp. 278–9.
157 Clarendon to unnamed friend, July 1847: ibid., p. 278.
158 Lord Clarendon to Lord John Russell, 10 November 1847: ibid., p. 281.
159 *Nation*, 23 January 1847.
160 Duffy, *Four Years*, p. 376.
161 A reform of the landholding system had been an unfulfilled aim of Sir Robert Peel's Premiership (1841–46). He had appointed the Devon Commission. Following its report, Peel had attempted to introduce some moderate land reforms, but they had been defeated due to the strong opposition of Irish landowners.
162 James and Richard Lalor were proposed by John Mitchel for admission to

the Council on 13 April and formally admitted on 17 April: Minutes of Council of Confederation, RIA, 23.H.44, 13 April 1847, 17 April 1847.

163 *Nation*, 17 July 1847.

164 Unlike many of the writers for the *Nation*, Lalor had never been a supporter of Daniel O'Connell, despite the fact that his father had been a Repeal MP. Lalor disliked O'Connell and his constitutional politics so much that in 1843 he wrote to the Prime Minister, Sir Robert Peel, offering to inform on the actions of the Repealers: see Mary E. Daly, 'James Fintan Lalor and Rural Revolution' in Ciaran Brady, *Worsted in the Game: Losers in Irish History* (Dublin: Lilliput Press, 1989), pp. 112–13.

165 *Nation*, 17 July 1847.

166 Gwynn, *Young Ireland*, p. 133.

167 Minutes of Council of Confederation, RIA, 23.H.44, 30 March 1847.

168 Ibid., 30 March 1847.

169 Ibid., 20 April 1847.

170 Ibid., 30 March 1847.

171 O'Gorman to O'Brien, quoted in Gwynn, *Young Ireland*, p. 107.

172 Minutes of Council of Confederation, RIA, 23.H.44,6 April 1848.

173 Mitchel to O'Brien, Gwynn, *Young Ireland*, pp. 133–4.

174 O'Doheny to O'Brien, 7 September 1847: ibid., pp. 135–6.

175 Mitchel to O'Brien: ibid., pp. 136–7.

176 Davis, *The Young Ireland Movement*, p. 189.

177 Duffy, *Four Years*, p. 360.

178 Ibid., p. 361.

179 Dr Cane to Duffy, *Nation* correspondence, quoted in Gwynn, *Young Ireland*, p. 109.

180 The *Warder*, 14 July 1845, 15 July 1847. Also see Christine Kinealy, 'Les marches orangistes en Irlande du Nord. Histoire d'un droit', *Le Mouvement Social* (no. 202, janvier–mars 2003).

181 For more on the impact of the Famine on Protestants, see Kinealy and MacAtasney, *Hidden Famine*, chapters 3 and 4, and Gerard MacAtasney, *'This Dreadful Visitation': The Famine in Lurgan and Portadown* (Belfast: Beyond the Pale, 1997).

182 *United Irishman*, 12 February 1848.

183 Memorandum of Smith O'Brien on 1847 and 1848, Smith O'Brien Papers, NLI, MS 449, n.d.

184 Minutes of Irish Council, RIA, 23.H.44, 31 May 1847.

185 Ibid., 4 June 1847.

186 Duffy, *Use and Capacity*, p. 7.

187 Martin to O'Brien, quoted in Gwynn, *Young Ireland*, p. 138.

188 Ibid. p. 138.

189 *Belfast Protestant Journal*, 20 November 1847.

190 Ibid., 20 November 1847.

191 Mitchel, *Shamrock*, July 1867.

192 *Belfast Protestant Journal*, 20 November 1847.

193 Ibid., 20 November 1847.

194 Memorandum of Smith O'Brien on 1847 and 1848, Smith O'Brien Papers, NLI, MS 449, n.d.

195 Russell to Clarendon, 15 November 1847: Maxwell, *Life and Letters*, p. 282.

196 Clarendon to Russell, 17 November 1847: ibid., p. 283.

197 Clarendon to Russell, 18 Nov 1847: ibid., p. 284.

198 Clarendon to G.C. Lewis, 2 December 1847: ibid., p. 285.

199 Memorandum of Smith O'Brien on 1847 and 1848, Smith O'Brien Papers, NLI, MS 449, n.d.

200 *Hansard*, lxxxxv, 13 December 1847.

201 Clarendon to Russell, 18 December 1847: Bodleian Library, Clarendon Papers.

202 Clarendon to Reeve, 21 January 1848: John Knox Laughton, *Memoirs of the Life and Correspondence of Henry Reeve* (London: Longman, Green and Co., 1898, 2 vols) p. 194.

203 Clarendon to Russell, 18 December 1847: Bodleian Library, Clarendon Papers, II.

204 Beckett, *The Making of Modern Ireland*, p. 246.

205 Lyons, *Meagher, Speeches and Writings*, pp. 53–5.

4

'Disunited Irishmen'

At the beginning of 1848, the likelihood of either reuniting the Repeal movement or of achieving a Repeal of the Union appeared doubtful. Divisions had hardened between Old and Young Ireland, with the death of O'Connell reinforcing, rather than healing, the rift. Moreover, although the Irish Confederation had won some popular support via the clubs, it had made little impact at the General Election and its attempts at wooing Irish landowners had been largely unsuccessful. Yet disillusionment with the British government remained high as Ireland endured its third consecutive year of famine, and the government was determined to make all poor relief a charge on Irish property. Paradoxically, despite the fact that the fiscal burden for famine relief fell almost exclusively on Irish landowners, they remained overwhelmingly loyal to the union with Britain.

The first year of existence of the short-lived Irish Confederation was eventful. Within a few months of its formation, differences emerged as some of the younger members championed a more sweeping social agenda, principally in regard to land reform. The Famine also proved to be a catalyst for a radical programme to develop within the Confederation. The spread of Confederate clubs in the towns resulted in an influx of urban artisans and workers to the Confederation, which not only broadened the social base of its support, but also increased the demand for universal suffrage. Apart from internal divisions, the summer of 1847 went badly for the Confederation, especially following the death of Daniel O'Connell, when the political pendulum swung in favour of Old Ireland. Nonetheless, by the beginning of 1848, there were some signs of disillusionment with the Repeal Association.[1] A further indication of growing interest in, and support for, the Irish Confederation, was the increased amount of newspaper space devoted to the activities of the Confederation rather than those of the Repeal Association.[2] Public interest in the Confederation was monitored closely by the British government, through its informers.[3]

Young Ireland had long been disillusioned with the government's response to the food shortages in Ireland, and throughout 1847 their anger had intensified, with the *Nation* becoming an important vehicle for expressing their dissatisfaction. The first edition of the paper to appear in 1848 referred to the famine deaths as 'massacres', which set the tone for its unrelenting censure of the British government in the subsequent months.[4] Some members of the Confederation were becoming more critical of the role of Irish landowners. When the Confederation had been formed, its leaders had hoped that Irish landowners would support them and take their place as leaders in an independent Ireland. The meeting convened by O'Connell in January 1847 had raised expectations that the Irish gentry were beginning to recognize their interests as being distinct from those of the British government. This hope was short lived. By the end of the year, it was clear that many landowners wanted to maintain their allegiance to the government and to remain within the United Kingdom. Their stance was particularly surprising as changes to the Irish Poor Law in August 1847 had transferred the fiscal responsibility for famine relief to Irish taxpayers, thus placing a large financial burden for famine relief on the landlord class.[5] The final months of the year, therefore, were characterized by increasing disillusionment with the Irish landlords and a growing realization by some supporters of Young Ireland that if a nationalist challenge took place, it would be independent of their support. The role of landlords in the Confederation – and questions relating to landlords and tenants in general – became a major factor in a public disagreement that took place in the Irish Confederation at the beginning of 1848, when these ideological divisions came to a head.

The debate was led by John Mitchel who had, in common with other members of the Confederation, initially hoped that landowners would lead the political revolution in Ireland. Even the militant James Fintan Lalor had written that 'it would be undoubtedly wise to compromise with the landlords . . . if the landlords could only rise to the height of their true calling and duty'.[6] The suffering in 1847, particularly the rise in evictions, led Lalor to lose faith in the willingness of Irish landlords to look after the needs of the Irish poor. Instead, he proposed that a social revolution was needed to accompany the political one. Mitchel, who was influenced more and more by Lalor's writings, supported this position and used the columns of the *Nation* to advocate social disobedience by tenants, in the form of a rent and rate strike.[7] Both men though, continued to support the rights of property.[8] Mitchel hoped that the Confederation would adopt a more radical social programme, and he put his proposals to a public meeting in January 1848. He was opposed by Duffy and O'Brien who continued to believe that the future direction of the Confederation should include landlords and that any political activities should be by constitutional means only. O'Brien threatened to leave the Confederation if Mitchel's 'dangerous doctrines' were adopted.[9] Consequently, less than a year after the Confederation had been formed, Mitchel was attempting to radicalize the programme of the body that he had helped to create.

The debate opened on 31 January and lasted for three days. Eventually, Mitchel was outvoted by 317 votes to 188 – a result that suggested that he and his views had extensive support amongst the rank and file of the Confederation.[10] As a consequence of his defeat, Mitchel retired from the Council of the Confederation and from his role as editor of the *Nation*, although he continued to be an ordinary member of the organization. Mitchel's followers included Father Kenyon, the radical priest from Templederry, John Martin, a small landowner from County Down, and the young journalist, Thomas Devin Reilly, all of whom were close personal friends. He was also supported by Eugene O'Reilly, Andrew English and John Fisher Murray.[11] Reilly, like Duffy, came from Monaghan, and had studied at Trinity College. Initially, he was a follower of Duffy's temperate approach to nationalism, but his anger at the government's response to the Famine radicalized his politics and he became a devoted friend and champion of Mitchel's. Duffy subsequently attributed Reilly's behaviour to the fact that he suffered from nervous headaches 'and this malady disturbed his judgement and even distorted his affections'.[12] Reilly and Mitchel remained devoted friends, until the former's premature death in exile in the United States.

Even before the split occurred, O'Brien, himself a Protestant landlord, had been uncomfortable with Mitchel's overt criticisms of Irish landowners. He was unequivocal in believing that a public debate on the issue would damage the Confederation. He wrote that, 'Serious dissentions now began to prevail in the Council of the Confederation, Mr Mitchel having endeavoured to make the Confederation an organ for the propagation of his views, which appeared to me to be very dangerous in their character – both in regard to the interests of the Repeal cause and in regard to the general well being of society. I felt it my duty to obtain from the Council a distinct disclaimer of participation in these views.' O'Brien also warned that if the Council supported Mitchel in this issue, he would withdraw 'from all further co-operation'.[13] His intervention undoubtedly influenced the action of some of his fellow Young Irelanders. The division also coincided with the publication of a Rescript from the Pope to the Catholic Prelates of Ireland. In it, he reprimanded them for allowing their churches and pulpits to be used for 'secular purposes'. It called on Archbishops to 'admonish the clergy' and to forbid them from involvement in politics.[14]

Disillusionment with Irish landowners increased palpably in the early months of 1848, as the new relief measures were accompanied by a further rise in evictions, emigration and mortality. Despite the optimistic assertions of the government, the Famine was far from over, with over one million people depending on the draconian Poor Law for survival in 1848. Even the moderate O'Brien appeared to be losing faith in members of his own social class. At a meeting of the Irish Confederation in March, he stated that 'with regard to landlords, I was in hope from the manner in which they came forward at a great meeting that was held in January 1847, that they were disposed to throw themselves among the people, but I regret to say these hopes have been to a considerable extent miserably disappointed'. Nonetheless, he recommended that, despite their recent experience, the Irish Confederation should continue to woo Irish landlords, together with members of the British army, and Orangemen and Protestants in the north.[15]

Regardless of the divisions taking place concerning the role of landowners in achieving independence, all sections of the Confederation remained committed to winning the support of Protestants, rich and poor alike. In addition to wooing landowners, involving artisans and tradesmen in their movement, especially those in the north-east of the country, continued to be a priority of the Young Ireland leaders. Despite their reception in Belfast in the previous year, O'Brien was sanguine that the famine policies of the British government, which had ruined a number of Protestant farmers in the north, would make Orangemen more willing to assist the Confederation.[16] Moreover, unlike Old Ireland, an attempt was made to appeal directly to Orangemen, who since 1845 had been growing in numbers and anti-Catholic militancy. Hence John Mitchel, a Protestant from County Down, had written a series of appeals to 'the Protestant farmers, labourers and artisans of the North of Ireland'.[17]

The response of northern Protestants was varied. Northern Orangemen, including a corps of yeomanry, offered their services to the Lord Lieutenant, which he refused. [18] Nonetheless, he boasted that, 'I needed only to hold up my finger to have had 50,000 Orangemen in arms, marching on the South, leaving everywhere traces of blood and sectarian hate that our grandchildren would not have seen effaced.'[19] Privately though, he was aware of the danger of giving such power to the Orange Order. On St Patrick's Day 1848, there were clashes in Belfast between the Young Ireland supporters and local Orangemen.[20] Most of the violence was perpetrated by the latter, leading Clarendon to admit, privately, that it was necessary to curb 'these furious Orangemen who, with their principles and their parsons, are quite as subversive of law and order as the priests and Young Irelandism'.[21] Undaunted, in March 1848, a deputation from Young Ireland undertook a second visit to Belfast, with a third one planned for June.[22] Notwithstanding the actions of the Orangemen, there were some signs that ordinary Protestants were alarmed by the continuing economic situation in the country. On 13 April 1848, about 150 Protestants attended a Repeal meeting in Drogheda to decide how to respond to 'this alarming crisis'. They affirmed their loyalty to the Queen but passed a resolution (with only three dissenters) stating that, 'viewing with alarm the increasing misery and destitution of our country, our trade and manufactures almost extinct, [we] are of [the] opinion that a local legislature would give stability to trade, and increased confidence to men of capital, and restore peace and order to our country'.[23]

An undoubted success for the Confederation was the establishment of the short-lived Protestant Repeal Association in May 1848. At its first meeting, Samuel Ferguson, a Protestant barrister and poet and member of the Council of the Confederation, stated that Irish self-government was required 'to counter the anti-national and servile spirit in the land'.[24] At a meeting in June, the meeting decided that the first object of the Association was 'to gain a domestic legislature' for Ireland. To achieve this end, it was willing to cooperate with other groups that shared the same aim. At the same time though, special consideration was given to protecting the rights of the Protestants in the north of the country, it being agreed that 'we are an independent Association, being determined to guard the just rights and privileges of the Protestants of the North'. They further added that 'to convince and coerce, the judgement, is our aim; and we shall yield no weapons, in endeavouring to advance our cause ... to raise and regenerate Ireland is our grand object; but Ulster, our birth place and our home, has a special claim on our sympathies. Fondly attached to it, we shall protect its interests as the apple of our eye.'[25] The determination of the Protestant Repeal Association to be part of an inclusive national organization was demonstrated by the decision at the end of June to send two deputations to Ulster taking two different routes – one to Dundalk, Newry and Belfast; the other to Monaghan, Armagh, Tyrone. They viewed their purpose as being to 'make Ulster part of a nation and Ireland a whole one'.[26]

The *United Irishman*

The departure of Mitchel from the *Nation* caused a vacuum in its editorial board while depriving the paper of one of its most radical and talented voices. Mitchel was admired by many of the female contributors to the paper and, in February 1848, 'Mary' (Ellen Downing) left the *Nation* and followed Mitchel to his new paper, the *United Irishman*.[27] The *United Irishman* first appeared on 12 February and it became the public manifestation of the new split in the Repeal movement. Its Prospectus claimed that it would provide a 'bolder voice' than those 'obsolete and superannuated' voices of both Young and Old Ireland.[28] More controversially, it asserted that Irish people who wanted to be free 'ought to have ARMS, and to practice the use of them'.[29] Although the name, *United Irishman*, paid tribute to the insurgents of 1798, Mitchel was keen to explain that 'we differ from the illustrious conspirators of ninety-eight, not in principle, no, not an iota, but as I shall presently show you, materially as to the mode of action. Theirs was a secret conspiracy – ours is a public one.'[30] The *United Irishman* included a weekly letter to Lord Clarendon written by Mitchel. In it, Mitchel deliberately taunted and goaded the Lord

Lieutenant, daring him to arrest him. In order that Clarendon (and the readers) should have no doubt of the author's feeling, the letter usually concluded with the salutation, 'I remain, your enemy, John Mitchel'.[31]

The new paper initially cost 5d. a copy (1d. less that the *Nation*), but demand proved to be so great that its presses were kept going for three days and copies sold for five times their original price. Subsequent editions were sold for as much as 1/6 and 2 shillings.[32] Within a few weeks, sales of the *United Irishman* in Dublin had risen to 12,000, with additional purchases in the rest of Ireland and in England.[33] This success was unprecedented in Irish journalism.[34] From the outset, the tone of the paper was more militant than either the *Freeman's Journal* or the *Nation*. The inflammatory tone of the first edition of the paper caused alarm within the British government. It was also the subject of an extensive discussion within the House of Lords. Lord Stanley, who led the debate, described the function of the paper as being 'for the purpose of exciting sedition and rebellion among Her Majesty's subjects in Ireland'. Quoting the letter addressed to Clarendon, he averred, 'This is not a mere casual article in a newspaper – it is the declaration of the aim and object for which it is established ... that object being to drive the people of Ireland to sedition, to urge them into open rebellion, and to promote civil war for the purpose of exterminating every Englishman in Ireland.' He justified his anxiety on the grounds that:

> If such a publication had appeared in England, I should have been very much inclined to think the good sense and sound judgement of the people would have rejected the article at once as seditious and coarse invective, whose very invective, like an over-dose of poison, prevented its effect, and in the minds of all rational beings rendered it utterly inoperative. But this language is addressed not to the sober-minded and calm-thinking people of England, but to a people, hasty, excitable, enthusiastic and easily stimulated, smarting under great manifold distresses, and who have been for years excited to the utmost pitch to which they could go consistently with their own safely, by the harangues of democrats and revolutionists ... With the people of Ireland, my Lords, this language will tell; and I say it is not safe for you to disregard it.[35]

Stanley believed Mitchel and his supporters to be particularly dangerous because, 'These men are honest; they are not the kind of men who make their patriotism the means of barter for place or pension. They are not to be bought off by the government of the day for a colonial place, or by a snug situation in customs or excise. No, they honestly repudiate this course; they are rebels at heart and they are rebels avowed, who are earnest in what they say and propose to do.'[36]

It was not only the government who disliked the radical politics of Mitchel and his followers. His former comrades in Young Ireland were critical of his approach. The belligerence of the *United Irishman* was particularly disliked by O'Brien, who worried that Mitchel's stance was damaging to the whole of the Repeal movement. He accused him of using 'language of a very vehement character', which had 'alienated from the course of Repeal and from the Confederation an incalculable number of young persons belonging to the higher and wealthier classes of society'. Whereas previously they had wished the Repeal movement success, the opinions expressed in the *United Irishman* had alienated their sympathies because, 'The revolutionary views put forward by Mr Mitchel and Mr Reilly in language which, while it was often very powerful, was frequently revolting to men of fastidious taste, had excited no little alarm and disgust among them who had something to lose. They interpreted the doctrines of the United Irishmen as stimulants to plunder; they now began to regard agitation for Repeal as synonymous with confiscation of property.'[37] Even Meagher – one of the most sympathetic former comrades of Mitchel and Reilly – maintained that 'their principles are unsound and their policy anti-national'. Writing in the middle of February, he warned Mitchel that an insurrection was neither 'probable nor practicable'.[38] However, events in France only two weeks later changed political interactions throughout Europe, including in Ireland.

The impact of Mitchel's writings was heightened by a revolution in France on 24 February, only twelve days after the first edition of his paper. In the eyes of the authorities, Mitchel's writings now amounted to a clear call to take up arms against them. A Dublin man who was charged in April with purchasing six pikes 'for the express purpose of using them against the constituted authorities' said he was inspired by reading the *United Irishman*. At the same time, Mitchel's exhortation to arm was used to defend the prisoner.[39] Nonetheless, the government did not intervene immediately, waiting until the thirteenth edition of the paper to confiscate it and to arrest Mitchel. At the same time, the authorities committed to bail O'Brien and Meagher for use of treasonable language. Regardless of his arrest, Mitchel appeared unrepentant, claiming that one of the aims of his paper had been 'stimulating the just dissatisfaction of the people to the point of insurrection'.[40] He also admitted that he had under-estimated 'the vigour and zeal of the British government in carrying out the designs of Providence'.[41] Retrospectively, O'Brien took a more cynical view of the actions of the British authorities, believing that they could have prose-cuted John Mitchel sooner, but had chosen not to. Instead, by simultaneously acting against him, O'Brien believed they had tried 'to implicate me in a concurrence with doctrines which I abhorred'. By pros-ecuting the three men at the same time, the authorities were deliberately linking their politics together.[42] This example of government intervention and manipulation in Irish politics was an early indication that the govern-ment were taking the Repeal threat seriously and that winning the propaganda war was an important part of their strategy.

France

The debates taking place between the various sections of the Repeal movement were overshadowed by external political events. On 24 February 1848 a revolution took place in France, which deposed King Louis-Philippe. Within only two days, he was in exile in England and the Second French Republic had been proclaimed. The information from France was disseminated rapidly, helped by the presence of electric telegraphs and railways, which linked the main cities of Europe. News of the revolution sent shock waves throughout Europe, including Ireland. It was welcomed widely, by political moderates, radicals and nationalists alike. Support for the French Revolution was made easier by the fact that the removal of Louis-Philippe had been accompanied by relatively little bloodshed or destruction to property. Consequently, the regime change was seen as a harbinger of a new type of revolution that even liberals and some conservatives believed they could support. The new provisional government in France, despite the inclusion of some radical members, appeared determined to balance workers' rights with the rights of property.

The French Revolution energized European politics, reinvigorating demands for universal suffrage, national independence, socialism and republicanism and, even occasionally, women's rights.[43] The weeks that followed the February Revolution witnessed a series of political upheavals throughout Europe. Within a few weeks of the French Republic being declared, uprisings had taken place in a number of European cities and revolution seemed a possibility in others. Symbolically, Prince von Metternich, an Austrian politician and a symbol of the Old Regime, fled from Vienna in March.[44] The victories were generally short lived. Many European nationalists and radicals believed that the new French government would give them assistance, similar to the military support that had been offered by the First Republic in the 1790s. However, France had no involvement with any of them, largely because it was anxious to avoid war with Britain. Furthermore, many of the revolutions relied on large-scale popular support, which embraced a wide spectrum of diverse demands and within a few weeks of the uprisings taking place, divisions had emerged amongst some insurrectionists.[45] Consequently, governments who had initially made concessions to the revolutionaries quickly started to regroup and reassert themselves. In the early months of 1848, however governments and monarchs throughout Europe were fearful for their political survival.

In both Britain and Ireland, the impact of the French Revolution on radical movements was dramatic.[46] The United Kingdom, so often held up as an example of good government, did not escape the revolutionary wave, but faced challenges from both the Chartists in Britain and the nationalists in Ireland. While publicly denying any danger to the British state, in private the government was alarmed at the political agitation unleashed by the French Revolution. The government feared there might be an outbreak in Dublin on St Patrick's Day and, in preparation, on 15 March two fully-equipped steam frigates, the *Gorgon* and the *Birkenhead*, were dispatched to Ireland. Supporting actions were also anticipated in Liverpool.[47] At the end of March, Clarendon warned London that although Ireland appeared tranquil, there was widespread discontent, particularly with the famine policies of the government, which had increased support for Young Ireland. He cautioned that 'the public mind is in a state of feverishness and excitement and any untoward act would start an insurrection, especially in Cork'.[48] Ironically, the British government's response was more rapid and repressive than the initial reaction of many European governments.[49] In addition to using its legislative powers to defeat the radicals, it employed more covert means to undermine the nationalists, including a network of government informers in Ireland, Britain, France and the United States, together with a powerful propaganda campaign in the British and Irish press. The latter tactic included the surreptitious employment of the writer William Cooke Taylor to publish alarmist articles concerning the views of Young Ireland in general and John Mitchel in particular.[50]

The French Revolution captured the popular imagination in Ireland, despite the backdrop of famine and large-scale emigration. All sections of the Repeal movement welcomed it, suggesting that an alliance might be possible between Young and Old Ireland. Developments in France were watched with particular interest by members of the Irish Confederation. The relationship between France and Ireland was traditionally close, forged by the 1798 uprising and consolidated by the Catholicism of both countries. Consequently, public meetings were held in many Irish towns, which were reminiscent of those convened by the Repeal movement at its height. Bonfires were also lit throughout the countryside. In Cork, a meeting was convened to congratulate the French people on achieving their liberty. French and Irish flags were flown from many ships in harbour, as well as in some factories and the windows of the local Confederate clubs. Confederate members were kept closely informed of developments within France, with extracts of the letters of Ledru Rollin, Louis Blanc and Lamartine being read at their weekly meetings.[51] The Council of the Confederation responded to news of the Revolution by issuing a formal address to the new French Republic, written by John Blake Dillon. He referred to nationalities that had been long oppressed in Europe, namely Italy, Poland and Ireland, the first two of whom had already begun to stir. He asked, 'Shall Ireland alone remain buried in darkness when her sisters are emerging in liberty and light and courage, forgiveness and fraternity? – these are the virtues of the hour.' He also recommended that the address should be accompanied by a silver pike head, the symbol of the 1798 uprising.[52] In the weeks that followed the Revolution, large meetings were held in parts of the north, including at

Cookstown, Dungannon, Omagh, Beragh and Belfast.[53] The largest meeting was held at the North Wall in Dublin, on 20 March, organized by the Irish Confederation, to send to the French people an address of congratulations, which was read by John Mitchel.[54] An estimated 4,000 people were present (although some reports suggested it was 10,000).[55] The meeting was closely watched by the authorities, with the military and the police being held in readiness in case of trouble.[56]

The rhetoric of the leaders of the Irish Confederation changed in the wake of the Revolution, which alarmed Clarendon.[57] Even the language of the *Nation* became uncompromising in the early months of 1848, notably in regard to the famine policies of Whigs. In April 1848, the paper declared the suffering to be 'a fearful murder committed on the mass of the people'.[58] O'Brien, the usually temperate leader of Young Ireland, seemed particularly impressed by events in France, believing that 'a passionate enthusiasm for liberty was preserved from excess by a love of order ... all Europe felt the electric sensation'. Furthermore, the Revolution had forced Irishmen to accept the fact that 'We are weak because we are divided.'[59] Although O'Brien continued to emphasize the legality of the actions of the Confederation, his language suggested that Repeal was inevitable. He thought that the French Revolution had increased the 'sense of self reliance and intrinsic power' of the Irish who had come to realize that the time was not far distant 'when Ireland would be able to regain her national rights by force ... I concurred with the Council of the Confederation in inviting the people to immediate action in order to win their liberties by those securities which the Bill of Rights or the British Constitution provide as the guarantee of national freedom'. He knew he spoke with a more war-like tendency 'than previously and this made grounds for sedition'.[60] At a meeting of the Confederation on 15 March, primarily for the purpose of congratulating the new French Republic, O'Brien predicted that there would be an independent Irish parliament within twelve months.[61] He resurrected an idea that had been mooted by O'Connell in 1843 but abandoned following his arrest, namely, that a Council of 300 should be elected, with representatives from all parts of the country. However, he believed that it should not sit until after the harvest was in. More controversially, he called on the Irish people to form a militia to be known as the National Guard, primarily to defend their country and their rights.[62] O'Brien envisaged that the Guard would only be used for defensive and not offensive purposes. Even at this stage, and despite their increasingly militant rhetoric, Young Ireland, with few exceptions, did not want a physical confrontation with the government. Inevitably, Clarendon was alarmed at the creation of a National Guard, especially when he was advised that such a body was not illegal.[63] A week later, on 22 March, O'Brien, Meagher and Mitchel were held to bail and told that they were to appear before the court of the Queen's Bench on 15 April. The men were, respectively, Anglican, Catholic and Unitarian.

The French Revolution offered opportunities for a reunion within the

Repeal movement, with Young Ireland making overtures to Old Ireland. Accordingly, O'Brien wrote to Lord Cloncurry and invited him to reconstruct the Repeal party.[64] However, the publication on 10 March of a Manifesto by John O'Connell, which exhorted the people to be wary of any violent talk, suggested that he was not anxious for a reunion.[65] And, as O'Brien later acknowledged, 'subsequent events showed that the wounds produced by our divisions could not be healed as speedily as I anticipated'. Nonetheless, he hoped that they could share the same platform in congratulating the French. Again, he was disappointed as 'the participation of Mr Mitchel in the preliminary arrangements was made a pretext by the O'Connellites for withdrawing all whom they could influence'. Therefore, the meeting held at the North Wall on 20 March, which O'Brien hoped would be a gathering of all Repealers, was attended by Confederates only. Despite the rebuff by Old Ireland, thousands of people were there and O'Brien admitted that it 'formed a display of popular strength which was by no means insignificant'.[66] John Mitchel approved of the new programme of the Confederation, but O'Brien, despite supporting a more radical agenda, was reluctant to ally with Mitchel and his promotion of physical force tactics.[67]

While the French Revolution inspired radicals, nationalists and republicans, it simultaneously alarmed governments and conservatives throughout Europe. Governments, monarchies and church leaders were pessimistic about the impact of the upheaval, informed by memories of the aftermath of 1789. In the wake of the Revolution, Clarendon felt a heightened sense of danger, informing the Prime Minister that, 'No Tipperary landlord ever received more threatening notices than I do, or more warnings as to when and how I am to be assassinated.' As a precaution, he went out little, which he believed had made him 'nearly a state prisoner'.[68]

The British government watched developments in France closely. Even before the Revolution, some British politicians, including the Duke of Wellington, had warned that the French government continued to harbour hopes of an invasion of England, and these would be put into operation following the death of Louis-Philippe. In particular, the government viewed any closeness between Irish and French radicals with suspicion. Invoking French interference had become commonplace during periods of perceived nationalist threat. An Aliens Act had been introduced in the 1790s, out of fear that the United Irishmen would win French or American support.[69] In 1843, O'Connell's 'Repeal Year', Sir James Graham had warned Queen Victoria of the threat of foreign interference, on the grounds that, 'Several Frenchmen have lately made their appearance in different parts of Ireland.'[70] Victoria believed that her subsequent visit to France, which had forged close relations with Louis-Philippe, 'has put to an end to *any* hopes of assistance from France, which he [Daniel O'Connell] pretended there would be'.[71] The overthrow of Louis-Philippe changed the relationship. In 1848, as had been the case in the 1790s, Ireland was viewed by the British government as a fertile ground for French invaders. Clarendon, who shared Wellington's concern about a possible French invasion, used the threat to request further powers of coercion, arguing in January 1848, that 'if the French were to land in Ireland, rely upon it, they would meet with a friendly reception from the people, who would obstruct the Queen's forces in every way they could'.[72]

News of the French Revolution alarmed some people in Ireland and fears of an uprising led to counter-insurgency forces being organized in a number of locations. On 14 March the heads of the University of Dublin (Trinity College) informed the Lord Lieutenant of their objection to any outside interference in the affairs of Ireland. A few days later a similar address was made by the College of Surgeons in Dublin.[73] Support for the British authorities also came from an unexpected source. John O'Connell informed Lord Normanby, the British Ambassador in Paris, privately that it was his 'great desire to join with the govt. in any step which might pacify Ireland, and resist with a strong hand any treasonable intentions'.[74] In fact, Clarendon was overwhelmed by offers of support, notably from northern Protestants, leading him to confide to his friend, George Cornewall Lewis, that 'I have been almost as troubled by the exuberance of loyalty as by the excesses of sedition'. He added, 'I had only to hold up my finger to have re-embodied all the Orange yeomanry and to have them set in march against the south.' Clarendon did not feel that their support was necessary, but he did not want to offend them, believing that, 'It is clear that in any real danger we have only the Protestants to rely on.'[75] Unfortunately, while the Irish Confederates were preaching a policy of non-sectarianism, the forces of opposition were aligned along traditional religious divisions.

Paris

In the weeks following the February Revolution, the situation in Europe had become more fraught with numerous upheavals, notably in Italy, Germany and Hungary, while in Britain the Chartists were preparing for the presentation of their Third Charter in London. In this revolutionary atmosphere, with many governments making concessions to the insurgents, there was no guarantee for Britain that the initially friendly overtures of the French Provisional Government would not change as their support and influence increased elsewhere. An early declaration made by Alphonse de Lamartine, the Secretary of Foreign Affairs, stating that France would help people seeking to win political freedom suggested that the Revolution might not remain within the French borders.[76] Yet, Lamartine's 'Manifesto to Europe', despite the ambiguousness of some of its content, essentially outlined his desire to maintain peace in Europe. His subsequent actions and speeches also did little to suggest that the new republican government intended to intervene in the affairs of other nations. Lamartine, although the most famous, was one of the most moderate members of the French Provisional Government. From the outset, the government in Paris was nervous that anti-republicans or pro-monarchists would wrench power from them, possibly leading to civil war.[77] They were also concerned about the response of other European powers to the overthrow of the monarchy and were particularly anxious not to offend Britain. Although leading members of the new French government disliked Lord Palmerston, the British Foreign Secretary, they felt they could work with Lord Normanby, the British Ambassador, and welcomed his approaches to them.[78] Yet, while Lamartine appeared responsive to the entreaties of the British government, his colleagues Ledru Rollin and Louis Blanc were regarded as being more radical.

Unaware that the French government was secretly negotiating with the British government, at the end of March six members of the Confederation travelled to Paris. They were O'Brien, Thomas Francis Meagher, Martin MacDermott, Richard O'Gorman, Edward Hollywood and Eugene O'Reilly. O'Brien and Meagher had to arrange bail prior to leaving Ireland. O'Brien considered that an aim of the visit was to direct the sympathies of Europe to Ireland. Before he left Ireland, O'Brien had composed an official address for this purpose, which was approved by the Confederation. When he arrived in Paris, he described it as being 'in a state of absolute intoxication from the excitement produced by the Revolution. The whole population appeared to be playing at soldiers ... good humour appeared to prevail.'[79]

The Irish Confederation was one of many delegations visiting Paris in the spring of 1848. Between 27 February and 28 April, the Provisional Government received twenty-one foreign deputations. As the revolution-ary fervour spread throughout Europe, the dilemma for Lamartine was what the response of the new government should be to the various dele-gations; that is, how to express sympathy with radical movements, but not alienate their rulers. He tried to balance these competing needs by seeming to give encouragement to various delegations, while making it clear that France would not take aggressive action against any other country.[80] This was possibly most difficult in relation to Ireland and Poland, as both countries had aroused much sympathy in France even before 1848.[81] Consequently, the British government was more apprehensive about the delegation from Ireland than that of the earlier visit of the Chartists. Moreover, Lamartine's refusal to support Polish national aspirations had lost him considerable support in France.[82]

The Confederation was not the first Irish group to meet the French government. On 17 March, a deputation of the Irish community in France, fronted by Monsieur John Patrick Leonard, had been received by Lamartine at the Hotel de Ville. Leonard, an Irish nationalist, had been born in Cork and was professor of English at the University of Paris. He was President of the United Irish Club, for Irishmen living in Paris.[83] This organization was regarded as particularly dangerous by Lord Normanby, and he impressed on Lamartine at this stage that no help was to be given to Ireland, even indirectly.[84] The meeting with Leonard, which was reported in the French, British and Irish press, suggested that Lamartine had expressed considerable sympathy for the Irish desire for independence. Yet his praise was directed at the achievements of the dead Daniel O'Connell and his attempts to obtain Repeal.[85] Nonetheless, Normanby was horrified by what appeared to be a message of support from Lamartine to the Irish people, particularly as Lamartine was reported to have accepted an Irish flag.[86] When confronted, Lamartine denied that he had done so or had offered any support to Irish hopes of independence. The outspoken Palmerston responded by threatening the closure of the British Embassy in Paris.[87] The uncompromising stance of the British government was probably exacerbated by the news of the imminent departure of a Young Ireland delegation to Paris, which was leaving Ireland on 22 March. Although the main purpose of the visit was to offer congratulations, within the British government more sinister motives were attributed to it. Clarendon's directive to Normanby was unequivocal: 'You must endeavour to defeat them.'[88] Lamartine's response following his meeting with Leonard provided an early insight into the fact that not alienating Britain was of more importance to the Provisional Government than assisting other countries, even Ireland. It also meant that before the Young Ireland delegation had set foot on French soil, the response to the Irish delegation had been decided upon, due largely to British intervention in the affairs of France.

In addition to making overt protestations to the French ministers, the British government employed tactics that were an integral part of its response to the Young Ireland threats, that is, the employment of spies and informers. Ironically, the agent employed to watch Young Ireland in Paris was so inept that even Palmerston expressed reservations concerning the accuracy of his reports.[89] At the same time, the British government continued to exert pressure on Lamartine, employing the bluff tactics of Palmerston in preference to the more diplomatic approach of Normanby. The Irish delegation met Lamartine and Ledru-Rollin at the Hotel de Ville on 3 April. In addition to the address of the Confederation, three other Irish addresses were presented.[90] The meeting took place two days later than had originally been intended. The delay occurred because, according to supporters of the Confederation, the Provisional Government were divided concerning the reply they should give: Ledru-Rollin wanted to offer immediate assistance, but Lamartine disagreed. His answer to the various addresses was to say that he desired to remain at peace with other nations, thus implying that the Irish delegates were seeking support from him.[91] The constant pressure from Britain, therefore, appeared to have been successful, with Lamartine treating the Irish delegation with caution. Regardless of Lamartine's reserved response, O'Brien remained in Paris and dined with him privately.[92] O'Brien also visited a number of political clubs while there, where he received a 'rapturous' welcome. All of his actions were carefully monitored by the British Cabinet.[93] Despite achieving little, the delegation placed a positive interpretation on their reception in France. The *Nation* even reported that military assistance had been offered, but turned down.[94]

Although the Young Irelanders were disappointed by Lamartine's response, they were more angered by his subsequent suggestion, made in writing, that they had asked for military support from France – which they insisted they had not.[95] O'Brien pointed out that, 'I carefully abstained from soliciting armed succour from France. The address of the Confederation speaks for itself.' He also pointed out that 'the written answer differed materially from the speech made by Mr Lamartine ... [and] created an impression for really there was no foundation; that we had gone to France to seek armed succour'. He believed that this claim had damaged the Irish Confederation as they had incurred 'the hostility of England' which was able to accuse them of encouraging civil war.[96]

Lamartine, on the other hand, believed that he had made the correct response to the Irishmen. He knew that his actions were being monitored by the British government, and that the Irish delegation was popular in France, but he was positive that his reply would have the support of the French people. A subsequent account referred to

> The reception Lamartine would give the Irish insurgents, who had set out from Dublin to come and demand encouragement and arms of the French republic. [O'Brien denied in his journals that they ever asked for arms]. The old national hatred between France and England favoured their cause; the party of the demagogues, the military and the Catholic Party, united in France in considering the Irish insurrection the cause of liberty, the church and France. Lamartine was not blind to the clamours these parties would raise against him, if he dared refuse the aid of the republic to a civil war against England. He dared to do so nevertheless, resting on the loyalty of the republic. He wanted to strengthen the ties between England and France.
>
> Cries of 'Long live the Republic' and 'long live Lamartine' form the immense multitude that surrounded the Irish, welcomed these words. These words showed them that the refusal of the minister on these grounds was even more popular than their cause, and they did not persist. They feigned to be satisfied with this language. The next morning their leaders dined, as private individuals, with the minister, and made no reference to the session of the preceding evening.[97]

The British authorities were delighted with the outcome of the meeting, Normanby telling Clarendon that Lamartine's reception had given 'the Irish deputation a good slap in the face'.[98] Clarendon was so delighted with Lamartine's response that he decided to have it printed and displayed throughout Ireland.[99] The following appeared on placards posted throughout the country a few days later:

Reply of the French Government to the Irish Deputation.

Paris, Monday 3 April, 1848 – This being the day fixed by the Provisional government for the reception of the members of the Irish deputation, Mr Smith O'Brien and other members of the Irish confederation went to the Hotel de Ville today at half past three to present their address. They were received by Mr Lamartine alone; none of the other members of the Provisional government being present. Besides the address of the Irish Confederation, addresses were presented at the same time by Mr R. O'Gorman, JR., from citizens of Dublin; by Mr Meagher from the Repealers of Manchester; and by Mr McDermott from the members of the Irish Confederation resident in Liverpool. M Lamartine replied to the whole of these addresses in one speech as follows:

Citizens of Ireland! – If we required a fresh proof of the pacific influence of the proclamation of the great democratic principle, this new Christianity, bursting forth at the opportune moment, and dividing the world, as formerly into a Pagan and Christian community – we should assuredly discern this proof of the omnipotent action of the idea ... We are not astonished to see today a deputation from Ireland. Ireland knows how deeply her destinies, her sufferings and her successive advances in the path of religious liberty, of unity and of constitutional equality with other parts of the United Kingdom, have all at times moved the heart of Europe!

We said as much, a few days ago, to another delegation of your fellow citizens. We said as much to all the children of that glorious Isles of Erin, which the natural genius of its inhabitants, and the striking events of its history render equally symbolic of the poetry and the heroism of the nation of the north. Rest assured, therefore, that you will find in France, under the Republic, a response to all the sentiments you express toward it.

Tell your fellow citizens that the name of Ireland is synonymous with the name of liberty courageously defended against privilege – that it is one common name to every French citizen. Tell them that this reciprocity which they invoke – that this hospitality of which they are not oblivious – the Republic will be proud to remember, and to practice invariably toward the Irish ... As regards other encouragements it would be neither expedient for us to hold them out, nor for you to receive them. I have already expressed the same opinion with reference to Germany, Belgium and Italy, and I repeat it with reference to every nation which is involved in internal disputes- which is either divided against itself or at variance with its government ... We belong to no party in Ireland or elsewhere, except to that which contends for justice, for liberty, and for happiness of the Irish people. No other party would be acceptable to us in time of peace. In the interests and the passions of foreign nations, France is desirous of reserving herself free for the maintenance of rights for all.

We are at peace and desirous of remaining on good terms of equality, not with this or that part of Great Britain, but with Great Britain entire. We believe this peace to be useful and honourable, not only to Great Britain and the French Republic, but to the human race. We will not commit an act – we will not utter a word – we will not breathe an insinuation ay variance with the reciprocal inviolability of nations which we have proclaimed, and of which the continent of Europe is already gathering fruits ... We should be insane were we openly to exchange such a diplomacy for unmeaningful and partial alliance with even the most legitimate parties in the countries which surround us. We are not competent either to judge them or to prefer some of them to others; by announcing our partisanship of the one side we should declare ourselves the enemies of the other. We do not wish to be the enemies of your fellow countrymen. We wish, on the contrary, by a faithful observance of the Republican pledges, to remove all of the prejudices which may mutually exist between our neighbours and ourselves. This course, however painful it may be, is imposed on us by the law of nations, as well as by our historical remembrances.

Do you know what it was which most served to irritate France and estrange her from England during the First Republic? It was the Civil War in a portion of her territory, supported, subsidized, and assisted by Mr Pitt. It was the encouragement and the arms given to Frenchmen, as heroical as yourselves, but Frenchmen fighting against their fellow citizens. This was not honourable warfare. It was Royalist propagandism, waged with French blood against the Republic. This policy is not yet, in spite of all our efforts, entirely effaced from the memory of the nation. Well. This cause of dissension between Great Britain and us, we will never renew by taking any similar course. We accept with gratitude expressions of friendship from the different nationalities included in the British Empire. We ardently wish that justice may be found, and strengthen the friendship of races: that equality may become more and more its basis; but while proclaiming with you, with her (Great Britain), and with all the holy dogma of fraternity, we will perform only acts of brotherhood, in conformity with our principles, and our feelings towards the Irish nation.[100]

The young nationalist, Jeremiah O'Donovan Rossa, later recalled finding a large printed bill on the shutters of his family's shop near Skibbereen in west Cork, which the police had posted during the night. It outlined 'the unfavourable reception the delegation of Young Irelanders had met with in Paris'. He recounted that 'My mother read it, and after reading it, she tore it down'.[101] In general though, the effect of this information was that it 'disheartened and weakened the ranks of the young Irelanders [*sic*] and England scored: substituting confidence for uncertainty and uneasiness – Lamartine, her ally – not her enemy'.[102]

In the short term, not only did French involvement in Irish affairs appear neutralized, but a rift had emerged between Lamartine and O'Brien. The failure of the Chartist demonstration in London on 10 April was a further blow to the aspirations of the Confederates. At this stage, O'Brien continued to hope that Repeal would be achieved without war, 'but we thought our countrymen ought to hold themselves in readiness to die for their country if necessary'.[103] Within the space of a few weeks, events in France, which had initially given him hope that Repeal could be achieved peacefully, suggested that the British government would not grant Repeal without a struggle.

Despite the outcome of the Irish Confederation's visit to Paris, it caused 'great indignation' in England and following it, O'Brien was advised not to attend the House of Commons. Nonetheless, he returned to Ireland via London, where he spoke, for the last time, in parliament on the evening of 10 April. During his speech, he denounced the Crown and Government Bill that was being introduced. He was booed when he spoke.[104] For O'Brien the timing was injudicious; the third Chartist petition had been presented that day and was deemed to be a failure for the movement. This easy defeat of the Chartists allowed many British MPs to vent their scorn at the demand for Repeal. Moreover, his report from France allowed his opponents to categorize him as a traitor.[105] It was an inglorious ending to an impressive parliamentary career spanning over twenty years. Poignantly, he believed that his time there had been wasted. But he was also concerned that if he was not in Ireland more permanently 'the guidance of the Confederation would fall into the hands of men who were desirous to produce an immediate collision between the Irish people and the English government'. He believed that if a conflict took place before harvest, the impact on the poor would be disastrous as 'a large portion of the population were dependent for food upon supplies imported from abroad, the stoppage of which for a single week would have produced the utmost public distress, amounting in many cases to absolute starvation'.[106]

It was generally agreed that Young Ireland's visit to Paris changed little. Clearly, the republican government had no intention of intervening in the affairs of Ireland.[107] The combination of the 'failed' French venture and the lack of success of the Chartist day of action were encouraging signs for the British government. Within the space of a few weeks the view of the February Revolution as the harbinger of universal uprisings no longer seemed so threatening in Britain. The British press rallied around the government and portrayed both Chartism and Repeal as defeated. Their response may have been premature, but was also part of a calculated propaganda offensive of the British government, in which they constantly exaggerated the extent of their victory in order to deter any further revolutionary actions.[108]

Meanwhile, developments in France continued to have an impact on Irish politics. In June 1848, political divisions within Paris resulted in an outbreak of violence. Following the June Days, the political uncertainty and retributions resulted in the political renaissance of Louis Napoleon. The fragility of his position meant that he was eager not to offend Britain. At the same time, the murder of Denis-Auguste Affré, the Catholic Archbishop of Paris, was a grim warning to the Catholic hierarchy in Ireland of a possible outcome of a republican insurrection. Within a few months, therefore, the optimism that had accompanied the February Revolution had largely disappeared. Ironically, events that had triggered such an optimistic and heady response in February 1848, only a few months later played a significant part in alarming Irish Catholics. The onset of violence in France coincided with challenges to the temporal authority of the Pope, which 'sent a shudder of dismay through the whole Catholic world'.[109] The effect in Ireland was to harden the opposition of the Catholic Church to the activities of the Irish Confederation.

Chartism

At the beginning of 1848 a number of local authorities in Britain noted a decline in support for Chartism as a result of the arrest and conviction of some of the leaders. Their complacency was short lived. The events in France in late February 1848 contributed to a revival of Chartism in both Britain and Ireland. Within a few weeks, local magistrates in Britain were warning of a revival 'stimulated by the late revolutionary movement in France and Germany'. Additionally, support for the new republic in France, and demands for a Charter for Britain, were being intertwined with a call for Repeal for Ireland.[110] A number of authorities responded by making all public meetings illegal. In the case of the Glasgow Chartists, they ignored the ban and met anyway.[111] A widespread response was the signing in of special constables, not only in London and the major cities, but in all parts of Britain.[112] The 'Specials' had been deployed by the authorities in previous periods of Chartist agitation, notably in 1839 and 1842, but it was in the spring and summer of 1848 that the highest numbers were enrolled.[113]

Chartist and Young Ireland leaders travelled separately to Paris to welcome the new republican government. The revolution also brought the two movements closer together. To some contemporaries it was natural that Chartism and the Confederate movement should unite. Lamartine, a leader of the February Revolution in France, when describing the impact of revolution in France said, 'Irishmen, united with English chartists, rushed to the continent, and sought insurrectionary complicity in France, both among the demagogues in the name of liberty, and among the Catholic party in the name of Catholicism.'[114] The British authorities were worried that a triangular relationship might develop between French republicans, British Chartists and Irish nationalists. Even if they did not act jointly, there was a belief that their separate actions would be mutually reinforcing, the Repealers sharing 'the popular assumption that the Chartists might seize power in London and this would facilitate the independence of Ireland'.[115] But some British supporters of Chartism disliked the alliance, the *Leeds Times* warning that 'the wilder and more extreme Irish elements' would ruin the good sense hitherto shown by the British Chartists.[116]

Regardless of Daniel O'Connell's opposition to Chartism, the Irish presence in the British movement was important and disproportionate to the size of the immigrant community. One historian has even suggested

that it was within this movement that, 'the Irish made their most important contribution to the growth of political radicalism among the working
classes in nineteenth century Britain'.[117] The attitude of Young Ireland
towards Chartism, and working-class movements in general, was more
ambivalent. In 1847, the Trades and Citizens Committee was formed by
tradesmen within the Confederate Party, although few of the leaders were
involved. Even before the Revolution in France, there were some signs of
growing cooperation. In January 1848, the Confederates and Chartists
held joint meetings in Dublin. A further one was held in April. This
alliance was consolidated by the visit of leading Young Irelanders to
Britain in the spring of 1848 when they shared platforms with leading
Chartists and vowed mutual support. This latter development was particularly worrying for the British government, who put elaborate security
arrangements in place, most notably in London and in northern towns
with a large Irish presence. On St Patrick's Day, in anticipation of a joint
outbreak in Liverpool, 3,000 Special Constables were sworn in to support
the existing police and military forces. The number of Specials in
Liverpool rose to 12,000 in the succeeding months.[118]

On 17 March 1848, Meagher and some other leading Confederates
shared a platform with Chartists in Manchester and Oldham. Their
comments were revealing, in the light of the Repeal movement's earlier
antipathy to democracy, demonstrating how much the French Revolution
had radicalized politics in Ireland and Britain. They also demonstrated
that a new alliance was being forged, which cut across previous antagon-
isms. When a leading Confederate, Michael Doheny, appeared alongside
Feargus O'Connor at Oldham Edge, he proclaimed himself to be, 'an Irish
Chartist'.[119] More tellingly, Meagher admitted to the 8,000 people who
were gathered in the Free Trade Hall in Manchester that he had previously
been wrong in his political stances, stating:

> We have confused the English government with the English people ... The
> disfranchised millions have been held responsible for the privileged hundreds
> ... We retract every word that has galled your manly pride; and here, in the
> name of the Irish people, we claim an alliance with the democracy of England
> ... I do not disguise my true sentiments, I renounce my false ones ... the
> revolution of Paris has made me a democrat.

A few days later, O'Brien and Meagher visited Liverpool, with the express
purpose of consolidating links between local confederates and Chartists.
According to J. Balfe, an informer who attended a number of the meetings, O'Brien had said that 'The die is cast' and suggested that English
towns should become scenes of 'flames and devastation' to ensure the
success of the Irish Confederation. He also talked of his intention to create
an Irish League in America.[120] On his return to Ireland, Meagher
addressed a mass meeting in Dublin where he declared that, 'we have
been guilty of sad injustice in our abuse of the English democracy. The

democrats of England are brave, intelligent, noble fellows and they will stand by you in the worst extremity.'[121]

Similar sentiments were being expressed by John Mitchel, although with an even more radical edge. On 16 April, he spoke alongside O'Higgins, the leading Irish Chartist, at the Princess Theatre in Abbey Street, Dublin. At this stage, however, British Chartism had suffered a major setback which was exploited by the conservative press to suggest – incorrectly – that the Chartist movement was dead.[122] Less than a week earlier, the Third Charter had been presented by Feargus O'Connor to the British government. Despite the involvement of a large number of 'physical force men' in the Chartist movement, the main mode of agitation continued to be the presentation of the Charter to the British parliament – a procedure adopted unsuccessfully in 1839 and 1842. At a meeting in London in March, Ernest Jones announced a mass meeting to be held at Kennington Common on 10 April, to be followed by a procession culminating in the presentation of the Third Charter to parliament. A mass meeting had taken place in Kennington Common in London on that day, but O'Connor had agreed to cancel the march to parliament. Despite the lack of success of the Charter, Mitchel no longer dismissed the demands of the Chartists, explaining that, 'it would be a small matter to gain Repeal if the people were not permitted to have a finger in the pie'.[123] At a further joint meeting at the same venue a week later, attended by a deputation of English Chartists, Mitchel said the Kennington Common affair had proved that constitutional agitation was pointless, adding, 'I hope the English Chartists have learned this lesson – never to petition again ... there is only one thing essential, and that is, to take up arms.' Mitchel's overt support for violent tactics was out of line with the constitutionalism that was favoured by the other leaders of the Confederation. The tensions were evident when, on 3 May 1848, Mitchel resigned formally from the Confederation. At this point, Mitchel appeared to be creating a fusion of the Irish national and the British democratic movements. His popularity and fame in both countries made it inevitable that he would come to the attention of the British authorities. The alliance that O'Connell had bitterly resisted appeared to becoming a reality in the spring of 1848. Clearly, Irish nationalism was moving beyond the island of Ireland, with Britain, France and, increasingly, North America, being involved in the revolutionary axis. Furthermore, in the spring of 1848 as governments throughout Europe continued to fall or to grant political concessions the power of the people appeared unstoppable.

There was a large Confederate presence on the day at Kennington Common when 5,000 Irishmen marched behind a green banner with Irish harp insignia.[124] In anticipation of violence, the government put in place elaborate security measures, orchestrated by the aged, but efficient, Duke of Wellington. These included the removal of Queen Victoria to the Isle of Wight.[125] At the last minute, it banned the mass procession to parliament: an order that the hitherto militant Feargus O'Connor acceded to meekly. His response was simultaneously a moral victory for the British government and a damning blow for the Chartist movement. The mood in the Houses of Parliament was jubilant and when later that day O'Brien spoke in support of Chartism in the House of Commons, he was treated with derision. He also argued against the latest coercion bill for Ireland. O'Brien's subsequent absence from the House of Commons meant that both the Repeal and the Chartist movements lost a champion in parliament, at a time when the British state was mobilizing its forces against them.

The fact that the day ended ingloriously for the Chartists was regarded positively by the British authorities. Lord John Russell informed the Queen that 'the Kennington Common Meeting has proved a complete failure', and added, 'A quiet termination of the present ferment will greatly raise us in foreign countries.'[126] The implications for the agitation in Ireland were also regarded positively, Sir George Grey opining in the evening that 'the manner in which this day has, up to the present time, proceeded here will have a good effect in Dublin'.[127] A few days later, Clarendon informed Russell that he feared an outbreak in Dublin on the night of 15 April, although he was confident that the troops would remain loyal and could suppress it. Again Russell emphasized the fact that the success of the British government in resisting unrest would benefit monarchs and governments throughout Europe.[128] Hearing the news from Ireland, Queen Victoria, who was closely monitoring the political unrest, wrote to Russell that, 'The state of Ireland is most alarming and most anxious; altogether there is so much inflammable matter all around us that it makes one tremble. Still, the events of Monday must have a calming and salutary effect.'[129] Overall, the fiasco of the Third Petition weakened Chartism, especially in the London area, while reassuring the British government. It also meant that Ireland again became the main focus of British apprehension.

While the collapse of the Third Petition was a significant victory for the British government, the Chartist threat had not disappeared. It did not, as the government and conservative press asserted, mark an end to Chartism. In fact, in the months after April, 'demonstrations grew in number and size'.[130] Nonetheless, the news that the latest Chartist petition had failed disappointed many local supporters, particularly in areas where the movement had become allied with Repeal. A further affect of the defeat of the Chartist meeting on 10 April was that it confirmed in the minds of some Chartists and Repealers that constitutional tactics were ineffectual.[131] In Manchester, at a meeting held on 10 April it was proposed that if the news was disappointing from London, the people should prepare to arm. At a further meeting only four days later, despite knowing that they were being watched by the police, one of the speakers, Thomas Roberts, a factory worker, suggested that they should arm, adding 'I will either live

a free man or die like a slave.'[132] The failure of 10 April had also diminished O'Connor's personal reputation with the Manchester Chartists who
were determined to challenge him on his forthcoming visit to the area. The
three Irish Confederate leaders though, who had recently been arrested by
the British government, were rising in esteem. The Manchester Chartists
had been asked to elect four representatives to the National Assembly,
which was to meet in London on 1 May. They proposed Mitchel and
O'Brien as two of their representatives, describing the latter as 'one of the
noblest men' because he not only defended his country 'but the liberties of
the universal world in the face of the tyrants that were facing him in the
House of Commons'. Sympathy was also expressed with the people of
Ireland because the Prime Minister had done so little to help the starving
poor in Ireland.[133] There were even more joint meetings in May, June and
July. The Irish Confederation also sent Michael Doheny to represent them
at the Chartist Convention and to convey their support for Chartist
demands. A new newspaper was founded, called *The English Patriot and
Irish Repealer*, published by James Leach, an English supporter of the
alliance, which encouraged an even closer union.[134] The Irish leaders
though, were preoccupied with events in Ireland, including the imminent
trials of Meagher, Mitchel and O'Brien in May for treason.

Despite public claims that Chartism was dead, privately it continued to
be regarded as a threat by the authorities. The government continued to
make plans to curb any Chartist uprising in Britain while closely monitoring the activities of its leaders in both Britain and Ireland. Over the
summer a number of these men were arrested, including Ernest Jones who
was subsequently sentenced to two years imprisonment, and Patrick
O'Higgins in Dublin, the latter for possessing arms. He was held in prison
without trial until March 1849 and his release was only due to public
protest. This marked the end of Chartism in Ireland.[135]

In the spring and summer of 1848, the British authorities turned their
attention to Ireland and the Confederate challenge. They introduced a
series of repressive measures, which demonstrated that, in private, they
were not sanguine about the threat posed by Young Ireland. The Treason
Felony Act that O'Brien had spoken against was the latest of a series of
coercion acts used in Ireland. It made it a crime, punishable by transportation, to write or say anything critical of the monarch, or which
might incite others to 'levy war against Her Majesty'. Furthermore,
treason was extended to include 'open and advised speaking' in such a
way as would encourage rebellion. Despite O'Brien's opposition, the bill
had an easy passage through parliament.[136] A draconian Removal of
Aliens Act was also introduced, which was similar to legislation passed in
1793. It was a response to a widespread belief that French republicans
would help the Chartists, although the legislation could be invoked
against any foreign national. The government was forced to reassure
Frenchmen living in Britain that it would 'in no way affect foreigners who

have been domiciled in the country for the last seven years and upwards', but it was intended to 'apply to those who it may be proved have come here for unlawful purposes'.[137] The wife of the American Ambassador in London sardonically observed, 'If the Alien Bill passes, our American friends must mind their p's and q's, for if they praise the "model republic" too loudly, they may be packed off at any time.'[138] Radical Members of Parliament also criticized the repressive nature of the Act. Despite opposition, it received a large parliamentary majority and remained on the statute books until 1850.[139] The Aliens Act was never utilized. And, as *Frazer's Magazine* pointed out in July 1848, 'Like the chartist mob, the French Republican propagandists have appeared not.'[140] According to the historian D.N. Petler, 'the danger from foreign revolutionaries did not materialize and, despite the suspicions of the government, had probably never existed'.[141]

Clearly the possibility of an alliance between French radical and Irish nationalists was short-lived.[142] Although the association between Repeal and Chartism apparently achieved little and dissolved in the face of government repression, the Irish presence in Chartism strengthened the physical force element. It also kept English working classes informed about the situation in Ireland and, possibly, made them more sympathetic.[143] Clearly, it was an alliance that the British authorities abhorred and feared.

The disarray of the Chartist movement following the aborted London meeting on 10 April, and the internecine conflicts among the revolutionaries in France, left the Irish Confederates without their political allies overseas. Support for Young Ireland in the subsequent months came from much further away, but was no less fervent. Prior to 1848 American supporters had expected O'Connell and the Repeal Association to bring about Irish liberty. According to McGee, 'Up to this time, the Young Ireland party had not attracted American sympathy, but no sooner did they move with the revolutionary momentum, than they found new and powerful friends in America.'[144] Just as the British government was confident that they had defused support from France, the transatlantic involvement in the affairs of Ireland increased.

Regrouping

The French Revolution had awakened hopes that a similarly quick and bloodless revolution could take place in Ireland: hopes that underestimated the determination of the British government to keep the Empire intact. The visit to Paris in April made it clear that no help could be expected from there, but a new development in Irish nationalism was the support it was evoking in the United States. Just as worrying was the alliance between radicals in Britain and Ireland, linking Chartism with Repeal and democratizing both movements in the process. But the springtime of peoples seemed to have had less success in Ireland and Britain than elsewhere in Europe. The Repeal movement had become more divided than ever. The government had in place draconian legislation, a network of informers and a large military and police presence within Ireland. The Chartist petition had ended in fiasco, the Irish delegation to France was rebuffed, and the most radical political figure in Irish politics was about to be successfully convicted and transported to Bermuda. Within the space of six months Mitchel had gone from radical seceder to international hero. The Repeal movement now had a martyr and, ironically, a man who had been a divisive force in the Confederation, as a result of his treatment by the government, was again uniting various factions together. If support for Irish Repeal neutralized in Britain and France, in the summer months a new threat emerged in the United States over which the British authorities held no sway.

Despite the mixed fortunes of the previous few months an insurrection was being openly talked about by the leaders of the Confederation, although it was not to take place until the harvest was in.[145] The government, therefore, had a deadline to work towards and to prepare its counter-offensive in the months between May and August.

Notes

1 *Tyrawley Herald*, 6 January 1848, 13 January 1848.
2 Ibid., 18 May 1848, 25 May 1848.
3 Reports of CJ, TCD, MS 2038/9.
4 *Nation*, 1 January 1848.
5 Christine Kinealy, *This Great Calamity: The Irish Famine 1845–52* (Dublin: Gill and Macmillan, 1994; reprinted with a new Introduction, 2006), chapter 5.
6 Quoted in *Nation*, 28 January 1882.
7 Lalor's ideas were most clearly formulated, following the arrest of Mitchel, in the columns of the *Irish Felon*, on 24 June, 1 July and 8 July.
8 *Irish Felon*, 24 June 1848.
9 O'Brien, Memorandum, Smith O'Brien Papers, NLI, MS 449, n.d.
10 Ibid.
11 Cavanagh, *Memoirs of Meagher*, p. 84.
12 Duffy, *Four Years*, p. 16.
13 Ibid.
14 Circular Addressed by Holy See to Catholic Prelates of Ireland, reprinted in *Northern Journal*, 16 March 1848.
15 *United Irishman*, 18 March 1848.
16 Ibid.
17 Reprinted in John Mitchel, *An Ulsterman for Ireland, Being Letters to the Protestant Farmers, Labourers and Artisans of the North of Ireland*, with a foreword by Eoin MacNeill (Dublin: Candle Press, 1917).
18 Clarendon to Grey, 27 March 1848: Clarendon Papers, Irish Box 33.
19 Clarendon to Reeve, 10 May 1848: Laughton, *Memoirs of Henry Reeve*, p. 200.

154   Repeal and revolution

20 From (London) *Morning Chronicle*, reprinted in *New York Freeman and Catholic Register* (hereafter *New York Freeman*), 15 April 1848.
21 Clarendon to Henry Reeve, 17 December 1848: Maxwell, *Life and Letters*.
22 Book of Expenditures, RIA, 23.H.43, 3 March 1848.
23 *New York Freeman*, 13 May 1848.
24 *Warder*, 13 May 1848.
25 *Nation*, 1 July 1848.
26 Ibid., 3 July 1848.
27 Anton, 'Women of the *Nation*', 34.
28 *United Irishman, Prospectus*, 12 February 1848.
29 Ibid.
30 Ibid.
31 *United Irishman*, 11 March 1848.
32 Ibid., 4 March 1848.
33 *New York Freeman*, 6 May 1848.
34 Cavanagh, *Memoirs of Meagher*, p. 99.
35 House of Lords, 24 February, *United Irishman*, 4 March 1848.
36 Ibid.
37 O'Brien, Memorandum, Smith O'Brien Papers, NLI, MS 449, n.d.
38 *United Irishman*, 12 February 1848.
39 *Tyrawley Herald*, 6 April 1848.
40 Mitchel, *Jail Journal*, p. lii.
41 Ibid.
42 O'Brien, Memorandum, Smith O'Brien Papers, NLI, MS 449, n.d.
43 Boardman and Kinealy, *The Year the World Turned?*
44 Ibid., Introduction, pp. 1–19.
45 Charles Crouch, 'The Myth of the Dem-Soc Coalition: France in 1848' and Ernst Wangerman, '1848 and Jewish Emancipation in the Hapsburg Empire' in Boardman and Kinealy, *The Year the World Turned?*, pp. 36–47 and 70–82.
46 Clarendon to Grey, 27 March 1848: Clarendon Papers, Irish Box 33.
47 *New York Freeman*, 15 April 1848.
48 Clarendon to Grey, 27 March 1848: Clarendon Papers, Irish Box 33,
49 Boardman and Kinealy, *The Year the World Turned?*, Introduction, pp. 1–19.
50 William Cooke Taylor to Clarendon, July 1848: Bodleian Library, Clarendon Papers, Irish Box 33.
51 *United Irishman*, 18 March 1848.
52 Handwritten Address of Council of Irish Confederation, TCD, Dillon Papers (f.61b) n.d., 1848.
53 *New York Freeman*, 15 April 1848.
54 Ibid.
55 Clarendon to Grey, 27 March 1848: Bodleian Library, Clarendon Papers, Irish Box 33. For example, the upper figure was provided in many Irish and American newspapers including the *Clare Journal* and the *Northern Journal*, 18 April 1848.
56 Cavanagh, *Memoirs of Meagher*, p. 114.
57 Clarendon to Earl Grey, 27 March 1848: Bodleian Library, Clarendon Papers, Irish Box 33.

58 *Nation*, 29 April 1848.
59 O'Brien, Memorandum, Smith O'Brien Papers, NLI, MS 449, n.d.
60 Ibid.
61 *United Irishman*, 4 March 1848, 11 March 1848.
62 *Nation*, 11 March 1848.
63 Clarendon to Home Secretary, 27 March 1848: Bodleian Library, Clarendon Papers, Irish Box 33; Davis, *Young Ireland*, p. 150.
64 O'Brien, Memorandum, Smith O'Brien Papers, NLI, MS 449, n.d.
65 Reported in *New York Freeman*, 15 April 1848.
66 O'Brien, Memorandum, Smith O'Brien Papers, NLI, MS 449, n.d.
67 *United Irishman*, 18 March 1848.
68 Clarendon to Russell, 30 March 1848: Maxwell, *Life and Letters*, p. 289.
69 McGee, *History of Irish Settlers*, p. 131.
70 Sir James Graham to Queen Victoria, 24 June 1843: Arthur Christopher Benson and Viscount Esher (eds), *The Letters of Queen Victoria. A Selection from Her Majesty's Correspondence between the Years 1837 and 1861* (London: John Murray, 1908, 3 vols), vol. i, p. 484.
71 Queen Victoria to the King of the Belgians, 17 October 1843: ibid., p. 496.
72 Clarendon to G.C. Lewis, 3 January 1848: Maxwell, *Life and Letters*, pp. 286–8.
73 *New York Freeman*, 15 April 1848.
74 Normanby to Palmerston, 4 March 1848: Maxwell, *Life and Letters*, p. 288.
75 Clarendon to G.C. Lewis, 4 May 1848: ibid., p. 289.
76 Comité National du Centenaire de 1848, 2 March 1848: *Documents Diplomatique du Gouvernement Provisoire et de la Commission du Pouvoir Exécutif* (Paris, 1953), vol. 1, p. 8.
77 Alphonse de Lamartine, *History of the Revolution of 1848* (London: Henry G. Bohn, 1849), part I, p. 85.
78 Helen Castelli, 'Alphonse de Lamartine', *Encyclopaedia of 1848 Revolutions: www.ohiou.edu/~chastain/index.htm* (accessed 10 June 2007).
79 Smith O'Brien Papers, NLI, MS 449, 1848, n.d. He travelled via London and Southampton and Rouen and then on to Paris.
80 Whitridge, *Men in Crisis*, p. 73.
81 Lamartine, *History of the Revolution*, Part II, pp. 144–6.
82 Castelli, 'Alphonse de Lamartine'.
83 Cavanagh, *Memoirs of Meagher*, pp. 120–4.
84 Whitridge, *Men in Crisis*, p. 73
85 Reported in *The Times*, 20 March 1848.
86 Earl of Normanby, Constantine Henry Philip, *A Year of Revolution: From a Journal Kept in Paris in 1848* (London: Longmans, 1857), pp. 243–5.
87 Petler, 'Ireland and France', 499.
88 Clarendon to Normanby, 23 March 1848, quoted in Petler, 499.
89 Ibid., 500.
90 Cavanagh, *Memoirs of Meagher*, p. 120.
91 Ibid., p. 120
92 Smith O'Brien Papers, NLI, MS 449, 1848, n.d.
93 Petler, 'Ireland and France', 502.
94 *Nation*, 8 April 1848; *Hansard*, xcviii, pp. 75–6.
95 Smith O'Brien Papers, NLI, MS 449, 1848, n.d.

96 Ibid.
97 Lamartine, *History of the Revolution*, part II, pp. 148–9.
98 Normanby to Clarendon, 3 April 1848: Bodleian Library Clarendon Papers, Box 20.
99 Duffy, *Four Years*, pp. 568–9.
100 Reprinted in Rossa, *Rossa's Recollections*, pp. 136–9.
101 Ibid., p. 132.
102 Charles G. Doran to O'Donovan Rossa: ibid., pp. 134–6.
103 Smith O'Brien Papers, NLI, MS 449, 1848, n.d.
104 *Hansard*, lxxxxviii, 10 April 1848. A poignant criticism was made of the proposed new sedition bill by an Irish member, Mr Reynolds, in the House of Commons on 11 April. He reminded them of a case in Galway where a starving woman had eaten the flesh of her dead child. He denied that Ireland was disturbed, saying it was just starving, and accused his fellow MPs of knowing more about New Zealand than they did about Ireland: *Northern Journal*, 20 June 1848.
105 *Hansard*, xcviii, pp. 78–83.
106 Smith O'Brien Papers, NLI, MS 449, 1848, n.d.
107 Petler, 'Ireland and France', 504.
108 Goodway, *London Chartism*, pp. 136–8.
109 Gwynn, 'The Rising of 1848'.
110 M. Meyricke, Merthyr, to Secretary of State For Home Department, f.922, TNA, part four, HO 45 2410, 6 April 1848.
111 Proclamation of Glasgow Magistrates, TNA, HO45 2410, part four, f.792, 7 March 1848.
112 For details on the names and locations of the Special Constables see, TNA, HO45 2410, which deals with Chartist disturbances in 1848 and the payment of Special Constables.
113 Roger Swift, 'The "Specials" and the Policing of Chartism in 1848' in Boardman and Kinealy, *The Year the World Turned?*, pp. 48–59.
114 Lamartine, *History of the Revolution*, part II, p. 87.
115 Petler, 'Ireland and France' 494.
116 *Leeds Times*, quoted in Briggs, *Chartist Studies*, p. 95.
117 O'Higgins, 'Chartist Movement', 83.
118 John Belchem, 'Liverpool in 1848: Image, Identity and Issues' in *Transactions of the Historic Society of Lancashire and Cheshire* (vol. 167, (1998), 1–26.
119 *United Irishman*, 25 March 1848.
120 J.B. Balfe to William Somerville, n.d. [late March 1848]: Irish Box 53.
121 Cavanagh, *Memoirs of Meagher*, pp. 115–6.
122 See Saville and Pickering for a analysis of the government's deliberate public undermining of the Chartist and Confederate threat throughout 1848.
123 United Irishman, 22 April 1848; *Nation*, 15 April 1848.
124 *Nation*, 15 April 1848; *The Times*, 11 April 1848.
125 The private journals of Queen Victoria, held in Windsor Castle, reveal how concerned she was about the events following the February Revolution in France. See also Yvonne Ward, 'Queen Victoria and the *Cabinet d'Horreurs*, in Boardman and Kinealy, *The Year the World Turned?*, pp. 173–89.
126 Lord John Russell to Queen Victoria, 10 April 1848: Benson and Esher,

Letters of Queen Victoria, vol. ii, pp. 168–9.

127 George Grey to Prince Albert, Royal Archives C.56, quoted in Briggs, *Chartist Studies*, p. 395.

128 Russell to Queen Victoria, 15 April 1848: Benson and Esher, *Letters of Queen Victoria*, vol. ii, pp. 169–70.

129 Queen Victoria to Lord John Russell, 16 April 1848: ibid., p. 170.

130 Saville, *1848*, p. 132.

131 Meeting at Smithfield Market, Manchester, TNA, TS 11, 21 April 1848, at which some of the speakers said they would never sign another petition.

132 Ibid., Meeting at People's Institute, Manchester, 14 April 1848.

133 Ibid., Meeting at Smithfield Market, Manchester, 21 April 1848.

134 O'Higgins, 'Chartist' Movement, 91.

135 Ibid., 89.

136 *Hansard*, lxxxxviii, 10 April 1848.

137 Denis le Merchant, Whitehall to Mr Boiteaux, 14 April 1848: TNA, HO 5 21, f.368.

138 14 April 1848, Elizabeth Davis Bancroft (Mrs George Bancroft), *Letters from England, 1846–1849* (London, Smith Elder & Co. 1904), p. 177.

139 *Hansard*, xcviii, pp. 268–71, 562–72, 574–7, 579–84, 852–4, 857–60.

140 *Frazer's Magazine*, June 1848, p. 727.

141 Petler, 'Ireland and France', 503.

142 Goodway, *London Chartism*, pp. 136–8.

143 O'Higgins, 'Chartist Movement', 92.

144 McGee, *History of Irish Settlers*, p. 133.

145 Letter of Balfe to Somerville, 17 April 1848: Clarendon Irish Box 53.

5

'The springtime of the peoples'?

Regardless of the draconian legislation being put in place by the government, and the fact that Mitchel, Meagher and O'Brien were awaiting trial for sedition, throughout April and May the language and behaviour of the three men became ever more militant and reckless. Rebellion was openly talked about, although the majority of the Confederates preferred that no uprising should take place until harvest.[1] In the interim, the clubs were encouraged to acquire arms and to practise military drilling. And, according to the informer John Balfe, Eugene O'Reilly and Richard O'Gorman were travelling to Paris to learn military tactics.[2] Nonetheless, the leaders of the Irish Confederation continued to pursue a constitutional approach. A proposal that Meagher should stand in a by-election in Waterford was welcomed by O'Brien as a success would be 'of infinite value to the Confederation'.[3] Mitchel disagreed, believing that involvement in the election would give more credibility to the Westminster parliament.[4] Despite Meagher's popularity with members of the Confederation, he polled weakly and split the Repeal vote. In contrast, during this period, Mitchel unequivocally, through the columns of his paper, taunted Clarendon, referring to him in a series of open letters as 'Her Majesty's Chief Butcher and Executioner-General'.

The trial of the three men was scheduled for May. While waiting for his court case, O'Brien decided to visit the south and west of the country. Upon hearing that Mitchel was also going south, 'I frankly told him that I disagreed so much with his views that I could not appear on the same platform with him without doing violence to my feelings.' O'Brien wanted to distance himself from the radical rhetoric that appeared weekly in the *United Irishman*. Mitchel, who was still a member of the Confederation, initially agreed that he would go to England and the north of Ireland instead but he changed his mind when he received an invitation to attend a soirée in Limerick, being held to honour the three 'prosecuted patriots'. O'Brien, who had also agreed to attend the occasion, was unaware that he would be seen in public with Mitchel.[5]

O'Brien's welcome in the south of the country was so enthusiastic that he feared it might be detrimental to the forthcoming trials by angering the government. The Limerick soirée, a highlight of his tour, was to take place on 29 April. When he arrived in Limerick he learned that Mitchel had been invited and had accepted. Mitchel's reception in the city was mixed: he was 'hooted' by the O'Connellites who were angered by an article in the *United Irishman* in the previous week, which was disrespectful to the memory of Daniel O'Connell.[6] Consequently, O'Brien feared the soirée would increase rather than heal the rift between the Repealers. He asked the local committee to postpone the meeting, but they insisted that it should go ahead. During it, an effigy of Mitchel was burnt outside – and the mob used a battering ram against the door. When the reception was over, O'Brien had to escape through the angry crowd, whom he tried to unite by shouting 'a cheer for Repeal', but he was hit and struck in the face. He did not stay in Limerick, but left by the night mail. When O'Brien next appeared at a meeting of the Council of the Confederation, he had a wounded face and pain in the side of his body. Besides, he felt so 'wounded' by the conduct of the people that he contemplated retiring from public life, but the leaders of the Council 'begged with great earnestness', that he continue, which he agreed to do. During this time, he received many messages of sympathy from Old and Young Irelanders throughout Ireland and even from republican admirers in France.[7] Yet the Limerick riot showed, as had been evident in the previous year, that some members of Old Ireland were not averse to using physical voice against their fellow Repealers. Moreover, it brought the relationship between O'Brien and Mitchel to a head.[8] Clarendon was delighted at the continuing divisions amongst the Repealers, although he was apprehensive that O'Brien's injuries might win him sympathy in the imminent trial. However, support for O'Brien amongst Limerick Repealers increased, although according to a local member, John O'Donnell, their new-found enthusiasm was because they were 'ashamed' at the riot.[9]

Overall, the incident crystallized the rift between O'Brien and Mitchel further, the former believing that 'Mr Mitchel had broken faith with me in regard to arrangements connected with my visit to the south'. He believed also that the incident had damaged Young Ireland 'by his [Mitchel] being identified in the judgement of the public mind with the Confederation. It was true that I had formerly protested against his doctrines, but his reappearance at the meetings of the Council and of the Confederation and his subsequent visit to Limerick made it impossible for me to disconnect myself from him in public opinion.' O'Brien recuperated slowly from his injuries. He believed that Mitchel's behaviour had almost cost him his life and he made it clear that Mitchel and his close ally, Reilly, had to retire from the Confederation, which they did. O'Brien considered publishing a letter denouncing Mitchel's actions, but he was persuaded by other Young Irelanders that it would damage Mitchel at his approaching trial so he left the letter in his portfolio and did not publish it.[10] However, Mitchel's resignation letter was reprinted in the *United Irishman* on 6 May. He explained that he had sought to give the Repeal movement a democratic character and a republican tendency, adding that, 'I believe that "rights of property", as they are termed, must be invaded ... I believe the national movement must become a class movement also – or it will stand still.'[11] The Limerick riot demonstrated the fluidity of the Repeal movement in 1848, with allegiances and loyalties frequently shifting. In the short term though, the outcome of the soirée was to leave the Repeal movement more divided than before, just as three of its most famous leaders were about to face trial.

The continuing schism between Old and Young Ireland reassured the British government about the prospects of any insurrectionary action. In May 1848, Clarendon informed a close friend in England that he believed he had averted the threat posed by the Irish Confederation. He wrote from Dublin, 'Here, the stream is going down wonderfully, and I have no reason to regret the course that has been taken ... Nothing would have been so easy as to produce insurrection by too severe an application of the law ... the great object, therefore, was to avoid collision anywhere, and that was best to be obtained by the imposing exhibition of force, and letting the evil-disposed see that we were thoroughly prepared for whatever they might attempt. This was really done without swagger and without fear, and the result has been that Dublin is almost the only capital of Europe where during the last two months there has not been a broken head or a broken window.'[12] In regard to Young Ireland he opined, 'The Confederates are all quarrelling among themselves, and Smith O'Brien, with his patched face and broken ribs, cuts a sorry figure.'[13]

The meeting in Limerick, at which O'Brien had been badly beaten and Mitchel and Meagher had been forced to flee to escape a similar fate, not only pleased the British government. *Frazer's Magazine*, which had despaired of the apparent inaction of the government for months, ridiculed the Repealers and the government equally, describing the response of the latter to the meeting thus:

> It was made the subject of a childish boast by the Dublin Government, that the avowed rebels should have required and received the aid of the queen's troops against their brother Repealers: and when the news arrived in England, Lord John Russell smirked and Sir Charles Wood strutted more than ever ... the House of Commons laughed, as it always does nowadays at a crisis ... The Irish question was settled for ever. No concession: no just government: above all, no Repeal.[14]

The trials

In April 1848, the government had seized the initiative against the Irish Confederation by prosecuting O'Brien and Meagher for inflammatory speeches and Mitchel for sedition. They were all to be tried under the newly-introduced Treason Felony Act, which had extended the coercive powers of the state even further. Mitchel believed that the new Act was passed 'with a special vow to crush the *United Irishman*, and to destroy its Editor'.[15] As the trials of Meagher, O'Brien and Mitchel approached, the government faced the dilemma of how they could rely on having a trial by jury in a country where the majority of the population was opposed to the law. This was not a new concern. In 1844, Peel, who had recently overseen the conviction of O'Connell, admitted to the Lord Lieutenant that, 'One consideration which presses most strongly on my mind ... [is] ... How will you administer the law in a country in which the vast majority regard the law with disfavour?'[16]

Isaac Butt, previously a champion of Protestantism, defended O'Brien and Meagher and his defence was an early indication that his pro-Union sympathies were undergoing a dramatic change.[17] O'Brien's speech on 15 March was used as the basis of the indictment against him. In his defence, Butt claimed that the later part of his speech was explicitly opposed to any form of rebellion.[18] To the chagrin of the authorities, both O'Brien and Meagher were acquitted as the juries could not reach a unanimous decision to convict. The release of Meagher and O'Brien was a psychological blow for the government. It also confirmed to the authorities that they could not rely on Irish people in any future legal proceedings. Privately, they asked the Duke of Wellington, who was Irish-born, to consider security arrangements in Dublin. He responded with a Memorandum in which he warned that:

> As the operation of the law in Ireland is nugatory, and it appears impossible to obtain the conviction by a Court of Justice of any of those whose seditious, felonious and treasonable efforts are unceasingly directed to disturb the public peace, to attack H. M. Castles, Forts and troops, and to obtain by force a separation of the kingdoms, we must continue to consider seriously our military position in Ireland and secure against an attack by surprise.[19]

He believed that an assault on Dublin Castle was inevitable and so he made plans to buy the houses and buildings surrounding it. If attacked, the Castle was to be surrounded by sand bags and the Lord Lieutenant removed to the Vice-Regal Lodge, approximately two miles away.[20] Troops were also placed in a state of readiness for any such attack. The elaborate military preparations indicated the importance of the outcome of Mitchel's trial to the government.

Following the acquittal of O'Brien and Meagher, the authorities were even more careful in choosing the jury for Mitchel. Despite O'Brien's falling out with Mitchel and the latter's departure from the Confederation, Mitchel had widespread support amongst rank-and-file Young Irelanders, particularly in Britain and America. The way in which the government conducted Mitchel's trial increased sympathy and support for him. Before his court case, Mitchel had argued that no jury that was fair and representative would convict him. The authorities, however, hand-picked a jury that was comprised of conservative Protestants. The fact that the jury was 'packed' to reach the desired conclusion was widely acknowledged.[21] That the Whig government acted in such a way could have been a sign of the desperation they were feeling as, when in opposition, they had vehemently attacked the Tory Party's use of jury packing.

Mitchel was defended by the octogenarian Robert Holmes whom, he believed, 'had the tongue of men and of angels'.[22] Baron Thomas Lefroy, an Orangeman and former Conservative MP, was the judge.[23] A few days before Mitchel's conviction, a poster had appeared addressed to the jurors of Dublin, which claimed that 'God's truth has been spoken and written by John Mitchel ... that innocent man of truth'. It claimed that if they pronounced against Mitchel then 'The curse of God will fall upon you. The fate of perjurers and assassins await you. Attend to your oaths and a true verdict give.' The fact that a copy of the poster was sent to the Prime Minister by the Dublin authorities suggests that they regarded the handling of the trial as politically significant.[24] A group in Dublin warned that they would rescue Mitchel if he was convicted, which would mark the start of a general insurrection.[25]

On 25 May, Mitchel was found guilty of felony. Two days later, and after two weeks in Newgate Gaol, he was sentenced to fourteen years' transportation. He was then taken in leg chains and under armed guard to the Dublin Quays and put on board the government steamer, the SS *Shearwater*. From there, he was taken to Spike Island, the convict prison in Cork Harbour. At Cork, on 31 May, Mitchel was informed that the following day he was to be transported to Bermuda. He was also told that Dublin Castle had decided that he was not to be treated as 'a common convict' but as 'a person of education and a gentleman'; a judgment that in Mitchel's opinion was ridiculous and confirmed his innocence.[26]

Mitchel believed that his treatment and harsh conviction would convince the people of the duplicity of English law.[27] He hoped that it would end constitutional and moral force agitation thus provoking the rising that he had been promoting for weeks. Despite his disagreements with some of the leading Confederates, Mitchel hoped that they would act honourably and courageously in the coming months. He regarded Meagher as 'eloquent and ardent – brave to act; brave, if need be, to suffer' but believed that he allowed himself to be led too easily by others; while he regarded O'Brien as 'bold and high-minded'.[28] He described Dillon and O'Gorman as 'good and brave, but not sufficiently desperate'.[29] Instead, he placed his 'chief trust' in John Martin and Thomas Devin Reilly.[30]

The blatant jury packing and the severity of the sentence created much sympathy for Mitchel and his family and elevated him to a heroic status that he had not achieved in his diatribes against the government. An early indication of this was given when Mitchel was at Cork awaiting his departure to Bermuda and he was asked for his autograph by some of the women in Cove.[31] His conviction also raised his standing to the unofficial leader of the nationalist movement. Moreover, the sympathy and admiration was not confined to his former colleagues in Young Ireland, but cut across all factions within the nationalist movement. Following Mitchel's conviction, there was a plan in Dublin to rescue him while he was being transported to the convict ship. This scheme had the support of many of the Dublin Clubs and even of some of the leaders of the Irish Confederation, who had adopted a vote of censure of the government. Meagher had even suggested that, 'if the worst befell us, the ship that carried him away should sail upon a sea of blood'. But the Council of the Confederation opposed such an intervention and told club members not to attempt a rescue, re-iterating their belief that no uprising should take place until the harvest was safely in. Meagher, there-fore, retracted his decision saying no action should be attempted due to 'the concentration of 10,000 troops upon the city – the incomplete organization of the people – the insufficiency of food, in case of a sustained resistance – the uncertainty as to how far the country districts were prepared to support us'.[32] Mitchel, however, continued to encourage a rescue, believing that it would mark the beginning of a more general insurrection. Consequently, he refused a sign a paper that was brought to him in Newgate, condemning any attempt to liberate him.[33]

When O'Brien heard of the outcome of the trial, he wrote, 'I could not refrain from sharing the indignation created by the violation of all the principles.' He wrote of his admiration for a man with whom he had publicly been at odds, saying, 'I believe him to be an enthusiastic lover of Ireland – a warm friend – an excellent husband, father and brother – amicable in all the domestic arrangements of life – and truthful though wayward and capricious.' Conversely, he argued that there was not enough support for Mitchel to ensure the success of a rescue or rising and that, even if there was, it was not a good time for the country to rebel as they were dependent on imported food until the next harvest. He also used his influence within the Confederation to induce them to put a stop to the idea.[34] Admiration for Mitchel came from more unexpected sources. Following his arrest, Clarendon had read through the prisoner's confiscated personal papers and as a consequence revised his opinion of him, informing the Prime Minister privately that he believed Mitchel to be both brave and sincere – which, in his view, made him an even more dangerous adversary.[35] The Protestant *Warder* newspaper, despite having advocated his arrest, believed he had been ill-served by the Whig govern-ment. They also praised his behaviour throughout the trial as being 'noble and heroic'.[36] On 1 June Mitchel left Cobh for Bermuda, to commence his life as a prisoner and an exile. To the relief of the British government, an uprising had been averted largely due to the intervention of O'Brien, who, ironically, was now their main adversary in Ireland.

Mitchel's conviction aroused sympathy outside Ireland, provoking an immediate response in Britain, where massive processions took place, especially in London and some of the industrial towns in the north.[37] News of Mitchel's sentence resulted in a week of mass meetings and processions in the capital, with the largest – but not the most violent one – taking place on 29 May when an estimated 80,000 people marched through the streets.[38] As the *Northern Star* pointed out, the conviction of Mitchel demonstrated not only support for him personally, but for the Repeal movement as a whole.[39] A number of Chartist leaders, including Ernest Jones, were arrested for their part in these demonstrations, most receiving a sentence of two years' imprisonment. Francis Looney, a prominent London Confederate, also received a two-year custodial sentence.[40] The government, the Queen and the press, however, were alarmed by the fact that Chartism was clearly not a spent force, but had been re-energized by its alliance with the Confederates.[41] In early June, in response to news of a mass Chartist meeting, all assemblies were banned in London and police, military and Special Forces were amassed on a scale similar to that in April.[42] But support for Repeal was not confined to the capital: it was also becoming more visible in the north of England and the towns of Scotland. At a meeting in Manchester in early June, Mitchel was eulogized and described as 'one of the best men in the world'. It was suggested that if he was allowed to be transported 'we are indeed a mean cowardly cringing set of slaves'.[43] A number of political clubs, which combined Chartist and Repeal demands, and named after Mitchel, were formed in England and Scotland.[44]

Similar meetings, which the British Consulate monitored closely, were taking place in the United States. At the beginning of July, they sent details of a report that had appeared in the *Globe* newspaper, stating that 2,000 'friends' of Mitchel in the United States were chartering three or four vessels and equipping them with munitions, with a view to carrying off John Mitchel from the prison hulks in Bermuda.[45] The British consul apprized James Buchanan, the American Secretary of State, of the rumour that the Irish Republican Union in New York was coordinating the rescue. Buchanan suggested that Mr Barclay, the British Consul at New York, should contact the District Attorney in New York 'in order to frustrate any attempt of the kind being made'.[46] Unknown to the British government though, Buchanan was personally sympathetic to Irish Repeal and had even attended some of the meetings in a personal capacity. While the government took the threats seriously, Mitchel was unconvinced. At Bermuda, Mitchel got to hear of the planned rescue from the United States when he slept in a prison cell on land, rather than in his usual accommodation on board the convict hospital ship. He had been moved to hospital due to his frequent attacks of asthma.[47] Mitchel was sceptical about plans to rescue him, on the grounds that 'words being cheap', he believed that no action would be taken.[48] The government, however, fitted the surveying steamer with guns.

The arrest and conviction of Mitchel changed politic debate in Ireland, helping to unite and radicalize the disparate nationalist groups. One of the consequences of Mitchel's arrest and the suppression of the *United Irishman* was the appearance of even more radical newspapers, which continued in the tradition of Mitchel. John Martin, a Protestant landowner who was Mitchel's close friend and was renowned for his gentleness and restraint, moved from his farm at Loughorne in County Down to Dublin to help Reilly edit the *Irish Felon*. Two young medical students, Kevin O'Doherty and Richard D'Alton Williams, started their own paper, the *Irish Tribune*. The two papers were produced in adjoining offices in Dublin. From the outset, they made it clear that their form of nationalism was derived from Wolfe Tone, not from the men of 1782 or O'Connell. They also advocated a physical force approach: a method that was promoted even by the two leading female contributors, Mary and Eva.[49] By early July though, Reilly admitted to feeling disillusioned and he informed Martin that he would have nothing more to do with politics until 'I see it will produce other effects than cowardice in the people, or till I can utter it with arms in my hands'.[50] Only a few weeks later, as the rising in County Tipperary got under way, he briefly got the opportunity to carry arms. The consequence of his action was that he was forced to seek exile in the United States.

James Fintan Lalor, possibly the most radical and original of all the intellectuals attracted to Young Ireland, had been increasingly irritated by Mitchel's adoption of his ideas without acknowledgement. Nonetheless, he assisted Martin and Reilly in founding the *Felon* on 24 June, which was intended to be a tribute to Mitchel.[51] It only lasted for five editions, its demise resulting from determined government intervention. He also contributed to the *Tribune*, which had a similarly short life. During these weeks, Lalor laid out his strategy for social and political revolution. It was based on his belief that:

> The entire ownership of Ireland, moral and material, up to the sun and down to the centre of the earth, is vested as of right in the people of Ireland. The soil of the country belongs as of right in the people of Ireland ... one condition being essential, that the tenant shall bear true and undivided allegiance to the nation whose land he holds, and owes no allegiance whatsoever to any other prince, power or people.[52]

A similar scheme was later adopted by Michael Davitt as his Plan of Campaign during the Land War.[53] By this stage, Lalor was convinced that Irish landlords would not take a leadership role. Unlike Mitchel, Lalor believed that the best way to get rid of the British government was not through 'agitation or military insurrection' but by asserting their 'moral right' to independence. The actions he proposed included 'refusal of obedience to usurped authority ... maintaining and defending such refusal of obedience ... taking quiet and peaceable possession of all the rights and powers of government and in proceedings quietly to exercise them'.[54] In the final edition of the *Irish Felon* he developed this programme further, advocating 'as the mode of reconquest' a refusal to pay rent and resistance of the process of ejectment.[55] Despite its short-lived existence, the *Felon* was influential outside Ireland, especially in Edinburgh where it was read by local Chartists 'with avidity and hailed with rapture and enthusiasm'.[56]

Propaganda and informers

Throughout spring and early summer 1848, newspapers in Ireland, Britain and the United States carried numerous reports outlining the activities of the Confederation, particularly the clubs. The conservative press in Britain was particularly alarmist about their activities. Articles in the *Morning Chronicle* suggested that rifles, muskets and pikes were plentiful and that the clubs were meeting regularly in order to have rifle practice. *The Times* warned that the clubs were meeting nightly in order to drill. However, it also pointed out that, including artillery, there were 31,000 British troops in Ireland with more en route.[57] For the government, a worrying aspect of the news from Ireland that it was anxious to minimize was the frequent reports of a number of British troops showing sympathy with the Repealers. In Dublin, some members of the 31st fought amongst themselves over the Repeal question; Repeal sympathies were manifested by the 2nd dragoons in Ballinasloe, the 7th regiment in Waterford, the 13th light infantry in Birr and the 57 regiment in Dundalk, Drogheda and Armagh. All Roman Catholic members of the 47th regiment who were stationed in Clonmel signed the petition for Repeal on St Patrick's Day. The government informer, John Balfe, also confirmed that soldiers in the 48th and 57th regiments were supporters of the Confederation.[58] The response to these actions was to move the regiment and to flog or court martial the individuals involved.[59] Increasingly though, the government responded to the spread in nationalist activities with a number of covert measures.

The influence of the nationalist press alarmed the Whig government, and the emergence of even more radical newspapers after the suppression of the *United Irishman* was especially disturbing. Clarendon believed that the *Nation* – and thus the ideals of Young Ireland – had an undue influence on Irish public opinion. To counteract its influence, Clarendon approached a number of writers, including William Cooke Taylor, to publish articles likening the activities in Ireland to those in France in the revolutionary period of the 1780s. Additionally, James Birch, the editor of the journal *The World*, agreed to promote exclusively the policies of the government in return for payment. This role was particularly important in the early months of 1848, which had witnessed the emergence of a number of new radical papers in Ireland, notably, the *United Irishman*, the *Tribune* and the *Felon*, each of which was more radical than the *Nation*. Birch further agreed, again for payment, to secretly employ agents in the country towns to champion the government. Because no public money was available for such a purpose, Clarendon paid Birch £300 from his own income. Initially, this plan seemed to be successful as the circulation of *The World* increased and Clarendon believed that the articles were doing some good. Birch received further money amounting to £1,100, over the course of two years, from secret service money, which was topped up from Clarendon's private income. Birch, however, was not satisfied with this amount, and in September 1850 he demanded that he be paid an additional £4,700 for his part in 'suppressing the Irish rebellion and other services rendered to the Government'. Birch threatened to sue unless the amount was paid. Clarendon took legal advice and was advised that in order not to embarrass the government he should pay Birch off. Clarendon reluctantly acquiesced in the blackmail in order to protect the government, and he paid Birch a further £2,000 from the Secret Service Fund. As a result of this episode Clarendon believed 'so great a scoundrel as he turned out I never had the misfortune to meet with'. Clarendon concluded 'It is a pleasant scrape to have got into for the public service.'[60]

John Mitchel's justification for his public challenges to the government had been that secrecy was counter-productive. To some extent he was correct because spies and informers were an integral part of the government's response to both the Chartist and the Confederate threat. Spies, who acted as agents provocateurs, were particularly disliked by the public.[61] *The Times* even suggested that God approved of using them on the grounds that, 'Treachery is the natural and providential antidote for treason.'[62] In Dublin, a number of working men who were members of the clubs provided in-depth reports of the meetings held. The notebooks of one, known as 'CD', ran into numerous volumes providing the names, addresses and backgrounds of those who attended the meetings.[63] The government received information about the activities of the leaders of Young Ireland from John Donnellan Balfe, a member of the Council of the Confederation, although his information became more sporadic after March 1848 when he was observed by a fellow Confederate going into the Irish Office. Following this, Balfe publicly denied to his colleagues that he was a government agent.[64] The rewards for his services were dubious. In his letters to the government Balfe frequently made requests for more money, suggesting that the government had paid him little for his services. At one point, he even asked if the government would provide him with ink. Despite receiving only sporadic and little payment, Balfe assured his go-between that he considered it to be his 'sacred duty' to continue to supply information.[65] Informers were also employed in Britain and the United States. In the latter, a number were employed, the most active of whom was Joseph Pinkerton. He later complained of the government's failure to pay the money that it owed him after they had made use of his services. Overall, even if some of the information proved inaccurate or exaggerated, the British government was well informed as to the key developments and the names of the most militant nationalists. In addition to using informers, the government made effective use of new technology, including railways for the rapid deployment of troops and, increasingly, the recent telegraph system. The first public telegram had been sent in 1844, although initially the service was too expensive for widespread use. The British government however realized its potential and installed communications in Liverpool and Dublin, which were both centres of Confederate activities.

The transatlantic threat

While French intervention in Irish affairs appeared to have been neutralized after April 1848, the developing relationship between British Chartists and Irish Repealers concerned the government. Just as worryingly, the early months of 1848 witnessed growing support for Irish independence in the United States, which added a dimension to Irish Repeal that the British authorities found difficult to control. Moreover, support for Ireland was voiced by a wide spectrum of people, including politicians. A meeting held in Washington in March, presided over by George Washington's nephew, was attended by Senators Cass, Alen, Hannegan and Curtis. They were joined by a relative newcomer to the Senate, Abraham Lincoln.[66]

Even before the February Revolution in France there was support in America and Canada for an armed uprising, especially in New York City where a committee had been formed by John Van Buren (the son of a former president), Benjamin Butler and Horace Greeley (of the *Tribune*), all of whom were supporters of Young Ireland. Irish emigrants within New York were also raising money on behalf of Ireland, although the Repeal donations inevitably became mixed in with famine relief.[67] In Boston, in January 1848 a Confederate Association had established an American Emergency Fund to raise money for an armed struggle, on the grounds that the moral force approach had failed.[68] When news of the Revolution in France reached America, therefore, a number of nationalists had already decided – however hazily – that an armed struggle was necessary in Ireland. The subsequent news from France and other parts of Europe resulted in meetings being held to offer congratulations to the revolutionaries and many became a platform for simultaneously expressing support for similar success in Ireland.[69]

A meeting of the Friends of Republican Liberty, chaired by the politician Fernando Wood who, significantly, was a career politician and not an Irish immigrant, demonstrated that support for Ireland had spread beyond the immigrant community. At the meeting it was decided to form an association 'having for its object the redemption of Ireland'. The anti-British tone of much of the rhetoric was helped by the fact that in the preceding decade, diplomatic relations between Britain and America had been tense, especially over land rights in the border areas of Canada. In 1840 some Americans had occupied parts of Canada and their actions were backed by the legislature in Maine. Within the British parliament these actions led to calls for military intervention. Britain was also believed to have meddled in American affairs especially with regard to the territorial claims over Canada, Oregon and Texas, and the war in Mexico.[70] Consequently, attempts were made to involve the American government in achieving their objective, claiming that 'the repeated attempts of Great Britain to interfere with the domestic affairs of this country, not only by secret diplomatic intrigue, but open incendiary action, fully justifies the government of the United States in respectfully remonstrating with that power against her continued oppression of Ireland'. Support for an armed insurrection was also evident in a collection being made to purchase ammunition for Ireland.[71]

Nationalists within Ireland, however, continued to disagree regarding the involvement of America in a future struggle. O'Brien in particular remained ambivalent on this issue. As early as 1845 he had suggested that an uprising would require external assistance in order to succeed, which would include the involvement of Irish emigrants in Britain (including, they hoped, members of the British army) and fleets of men from France and America, the latter carrying 'regiments of Irish emigrants enrolled, armed and disciplined, ready to land on Irish soil to defend the rights of their native soil'.[72] At this stage, he still hoped that Irish independence could be won through constitutional methods. In March 1848, imbued with revolutionary zeal following the overthrow of the French monarchy, O'Brien outlined his hopes for the coming rebellion in Ireland – stating the need to have support of the Irish members of the British army, the Irish police and of the new French government. He again recommended 'the formation of an Irish brigade in America, composed of Irish emigrants, who might, subsequently, serve as the basis of an Irish army'.[73] Yet despite the revolutionary intent that appeared to underpin his public statements, privately O'Brien was less willing than his other colleagues to enlist either financial or military aid from America.[74] In exile, he claimed that he had wanted only the 'sympathy' of France and America as he remained hopeful that armed resistance would not be necessary to bring about an independent Ireland.[75] John Mitchel, as early as April 1848, had suggested that 'a deputation should be *immediately* sent to America for the purpose of organizing an artillery corps'. This plan was, according to a government agent, opposed by Charles Gavan Duffy on the grounds that it would be impossible for such a body to enter Ireland secretly and because 'America would never go to war for *our sakes* – they were too commercial, and such a nation of people was always selfish'.[76]

Unaware of the arrests, plans were being made for a mass convention of 'Friends of Ireland' in America and 'the two Canadas' to be held in Albany on the third Monday in July 1848. But the arrests of Meagher, Mitchel and O'Brien alarmed the leaders of the Confederation, who realized that they needed to act sooner rather than later against the British government. Consequently, on 22 April, McGee wrote to the Friends of Ireland in the United States urging them to meet earlier on the grounds that 'events in Ireland will not allow us to wait for your aid until late in August'. He went on to explain that 'we do not want you to fight our battles – we have men enough still for that. But we – I unhesitatingly ask you to put whatever share of your wordy goods is superfluous to you, at the service of Ireland'. In a postscript, he added:

> The Council of Three Hundred which will assemble here before many weeks elapse, will constitute a power with which you can properly correspond. During its sitting it will be the supreme popular power in this kingdom, and as such will be entitled to your confidence, and worthy of your support. This is another motive to hasten your convention.[77]

McGee's letter was widely printed in newspapers in North America, usually accompanied by the preparations being made by the people of Ireland to arm in readiness for an uprising. These reports probably raised hopes amongst Irish nationalists overseas that plans for the future rebellion were more advanced than they in fact were. A report in the *Evening Journal*, which was reprinted in other American newspapers, stated that 'the revolutionary train has been fired' and it called on the friends of Ireland in America to 'give all the aid and comfort in their power'.[78]

Mitchel's conviction in May signalled a more draconian approach by the British government, and resulted in envoys being sent by the Confederation to America. At the beginning of June, the Irish Confederation issued an address stating that in the approaching period 'armed resistance to the oppressors will become a sacred obligation'. It was to be supported by diversionary outbreaks in parts of Britain. This address was printed in newspapers in Ireland and Britain.[79] Initially, it was suggested that either Thomas Francis Meagher or Father Kenyon should travel to America in order to win 'money and sympathy' for Ireland, but it was decided that they would be more useful remaining in Ireland to help to counter the activities of the government.[80] Instead, two lesser-known Young Irelanders were sent secretly to America, with a letter signed by four Young Irelanders – their documents were smeared in gunpowder and carried in a loaded pistol so that it could be fired if they were arrested. In addition, coded messages were inserted in copies of the *Nation* and the *Felon* to prove that the instructions were authentic.[81]

The French Revolution galvanized the formation of additional Repeal committees in the United States, which were even more imbued with revolutionary rhetoric. In March, the Irish Republican Union, which viewed itself as being distinct from the existing New York Repeal Confederation, was founded in New York. Its chairman was Robert Emmet, who had been named after his uncle, who had been executed in 1803. His father was Thomas Emmet, one of the leaders of the 1798 rebellion. Both his name and his family history gave the new organization a direct link with an earlier period of republican agitation. At its first meeting, support was declared for the establishment of republican governments throughout Europe, but especially in Ireland. The Executive Committee of the Republican Union was comprised of many wealthy businessmen, including Thomas O'Connor, a prominent lawyer, and Horace Greeley, a newspaper owner. They decided to put pressure on the American government to intervene, by exploiting the forthcoming presidential election at the end of the year. They were assisted by the fact that in New York, which had become the centre of Irish republican activity, a third of the electorate was Irish. The meeting closed with a collection being made to supply Ireland with arms for the uprising.[82] In addition to raising money for an armed struggle, the Republican Union was also planning direct military involvement in Ireland. They urged that 'every true friend of Ireland and republican liberty' should enrol at once, or if this was not possible, should make a collection for the purchase of arms. Although their initial goal had been to enlist 1,000 men, some of their more enthusiastic followers suggested that their ambition was to enlist 10,000 recruits.[83]

The movement did not remain confined to New York, but the proposals and methods of the Irish Republican Union were adopted by other nationalist organizations including the Boston Confederation, and Emmet Associations in cities as far apart as Newark and New Orleans.[84] The latter group sent O'Brien a donation of £140, praising his 'glorious attitude' and adding that 'the firm and determined spirit of the Confederation excites among the friends of Ireland in this country the deepest interest and most intense solicitude'. The American League of the Friends of Ireland was also active during the summer weeks, making their own plans to send military assistance to Ireland. The American example of republicanism was frequently held up as an example for Ireland to follow.[85] Yet these groups were hopeful that they could expect help from France, unaware that the Provisional Government there had already made up its mind not to intervene.[86] Without support from France, the American intercession gained more significance.

Although the lines between Repeal and republicanism appeared to be increasingly blurred a number of supporters of Repeal, including the Boston Repeal Association, were uncomfortable with the adoption of republican aims and the rapid shift from moral to physical force tactics.[87] Moderate nationalists also opposed the formation of the Irish Brigade, on the grounds that it was unconstitutional to intervene in the affairs of a foreign power.[88] Following such criticisms, the Committee of the

Republican Union moderated its language and its terms of reference, suggesting that the Irish Brigade would act as 'citizen soldiers ... [as] there was nothing to prevent them going forward afterwards as private citizens and going over to Ireland as mere passengers, to aid in her struggle, and in such a manner as would not give offence to America, or involve her in any way whatever'.[89] Nonetheless, at a meeting in Tammany Hall in New York in May there was clear evidence of a more militant approach by Irish-Americans: when the question of Repeal versus republicanism was debated, references to the former approach were greeted with cries of 'Too late, too late'.[90]

Throughout June and July 1848, meetings in support of Irish independence proliferated in the United States. Despite the militant assertions being made by many of the speakers, the press were allowed to attend and newspapers in Britain and Ireland, as well as the United States, gave extensive coverage of the discussions. In turn, despite a time lag of approximately four weeks, the Americans showed that they were following events in Ireland closely. The American League of the Friends of Ireland was particularly active, with branches in many cities on the east coast and stretching as far west as Cincinnati. At their first meeting in New York, it was agreed that 'this organisation was found with no other purposes than those of aiding Ireland to establish her independence, by sending her men, arms, and money, and then we will still continue our organisation for that purpose'. Richard Ryan, a member of the Bar and a Deputy from Cincinnati, urged his countrymen to show their devotion to Ireland. While he spoke, he held a pike in his hand from the '98 rebellion in County Wexford. The main discussions revolved around two issues: rescuing Mitchel from Bermuda and sending an Irish Brigade to Ireland. Another speaker, Mr O'Connor, a successful New York lawyer, criticized the British government for abolishing trial by jury. He informed the meeting that the Friends of Ireland were going to send 'within ten days, the first of the fighting deputation to Ireland; that their passage would be paid, and that they should have money to support them for one or two months; but ... there was no provision made for their return, for they should either conquer or die'. The second meeting of the organization, like the first, was held in the Shakespeare Hotel, but the room provided proved to be too small for the numbers attending. At that meeting, it was resolved to form a committee 'to bring Mitchel from Bermuda to America'. James Bergin, one of main speakers, described how easily it could be done.[91] Shortly after these meetings, both Bergin and Ryan travelled to Ireland to assist in the uprising, and both were arrested by the British authorities.

The size of the meetings meant that they were increasingly held outdoors. The press, employing language redolent of the activities of Daniel O'Connell, described these gatherings as 'monster meetings'. More worryingly for the authorities, they reported that smaller, secret meetings were being convened by this group.[92] At a public meeting held at Fort Green in Brooklyn on 21 June, 5,000 people were present. The Executive of the Irish Republican Union was called on 'to adopt an address to Mrs Mitchel'. Overall though, the tenor of the meeting was overwhelmingly bellicose, with a resolution to 'adopt the necessary steps to forward the cause of the Irish people in the present hour of their difficulty'. American military intervention appeared to be taken for granted. A resolution by Thomas Mooney claimed that, 'The real wants of Ireland at this moment are, a want of republican spirit and a want of military science' was adopted, as was one stating that 'the object of the Irish Republican Union is to supply her with those requisites in the persons of a few thousand Americanised Irishmen, who are ready and willing to embark in her battle'. Members of the newly-formed militia, to be known as the Irish Volunteers or Irish Brigade, were present, and they paraded, led by a brass band. O'Connor, a frequent speaker at these gatherings, informed those present that the first deputation of the Irish Brigade would assist in 'putting down British flag and tearing it to pieces'. Money was collected for this purpose and, according to one paper, 'Subscriptions came pouring in so fast that the secretaries could scarce perform their business.'[93]

Even larger meetings were held in New York. One convened at Niblo's Gardens, chaired by Robert Emmet, was attended by an estimated 15,000 people. William Mitchel, John Mitchel's brother, who had recently arrived in the United States, spoke at it and was 'rapturously cheered' by those present.[94] The fact that these meetings were being reported in the Irish and British press inevitably raised both expectations and apprehensions about Irish-American involvement in any uprising in Ireland. Furthermore, it was hard to ignore this information when, at the beginning of July, the New York correspondent of the *Nation* reported that a fleet of fast-sailing schooners was being fitted out in New York with experienced officers at the head of the expedition. Moreover, one schooner was said to have sailed in June, commanded by Richard T. O'Connor of the Irish Volunteers. Another was expected to be ready for departure at the beginning of July under the command of Robert Emmet and Robert Tyler.[95] As similar reports were being provided by their informers and by their Consul staff, the British government had no reason to doubt the veracity of such information. Clearly though, Irish nationalist aspirations were no longer confined to the island of Ireland.

Ironically, the debates taking place amongst nationalists in America were regarded as time-wasting by Confederates in Ireland who urged them to settle their internal differences as 'events in Ireland will not allow us to wait for your aid until late in August'.[96] The American League of Friends of Ireland responded to this plea by coordinating an attempt to 'purchase the best war steamers that can be obtained, have them fitted out, armed and equipped in the most effectual manner and sent forth in the service of the Irish republic'.[97] News of Mitchel's dubious conviction helped to unite the various groups within America, especially following the arrival of his brother, William, in the country.

Events in Ireland, however, were changing rapidly and nationalists in America were finding it difficult to keep pace with the developing situation. Following Mitchel's conviction the Irish Confederation claimed that the country was on the verge of an uprising, but they urged patience until the harvest period, thus allowing the people to obtain food. In America, however, the news of his conviction, and the British government's use of a packed jury, resulted in meetings being held in a number of cities in the United States to express sympathy with Mitchel and his family. William Mitchel attended some of them.[98]

The mood of the meetings was generally angry. In Philadelphia, for example, pikes and tricolour flags were carried and much anger was evinced against the British government.[99] Meetings were also held in Canada and Irish citizens in Quebec vowed that they would not enter the British army until 'Mitchel shall have recovered his liberty'.[100] At this stage, Mitchel was en route to Bermuda, and this led to schemes to rescue him from his imprisonment there.[101] Again, New York took the lead with the Irish Republican Union making a plan for 100 men to rescue Mitchel from Bermuda and bring him to America. Samuel Saunders, an Irish immigrant who was also an informer, was present at the meeting and the British government was therefore fully informed of the rescue mission and arranged for a British warship to proceed to Bermuda.[102] The plan to rescue Mitchel exposed divisions within the Repeal movement in America – the Repeal Association in Boston did not support the action and made their disapproval public. The Irish Repeal Association, although angry with the Boston Repeal Association, decided to call off the mission.[103] Nonetheless, some members of the rescue committee continued to meet privately throughout July. The incident revealed both that significant divisions remained within nationalist groups and that few of their discussions were secret.[104]

In June a large meeting was held at the Broadway Tabernacle in New York. The meeting was attended by over 5,000 people including a number of Mayors, Aldermen, Members of Congress and even a former American President. The chairman, Horace Greeley, called for all American citizens to express their sympathy with John Mitchel whom the British government had unjustly sentenced to 'fourteen years banishment in Bermuda ... chained like a wild beast to be 14 years the mate of the thief and the murderer'. He also added that the arrest of Mitchel had 'led many Americans to feel and sympathize now for that brave and heroic people' concluding that, 'We shall be able to contrast and prize American liberty, when we see it side by side, compared with the conduct of the British government to the Irish people.' Pledges were also made to stop using British goods.[105] The main speaker was Robert Emmet, the chairperson of the Irish Republican Union. He described the political activities that were taking place as marking the marriage of Irish and American republican-ism, and forging an alliance of immigrant and native. Emmet was opposed to seeking merely a Repeal of the Union, arguing that it alone could not address the political or social problems of Ireland.[106] A number of speak-ers, including John Van Buren, renewed calls for the formation of an Irish Brigade. It was suggested that 'the [United States] government can't fight for Ireland, but there are thousands of strong arms and hearts here, that may go where they please'.[107] At the meeting, Emmet was appointed to chair a new Provisional Committee, which was to unite the various Irish organizations. This proposal indicated that many supporters of Repeal in the United States were now willing to accept a more radical agenda for Irish nationalism. Moreover, the involvement of a number of prominent citizens in the Committee demonstrated that Irish republicanism had widespread support, which extended beyond the immigrant community. A report of the meeting was sent to all members of Congress.[108]

In addition to discussions about rescuing Mitchel from Bermuda and boycotting British imports, the Irish Republican Union also decided to take military action.[109] At a meeting of the Republican Union on 13 June it was agreed that military intervention from America was necessary 'to lead the people'. The skills and fearlessness of the American intervention were regarded as being of more value than the provisions of arms. At a recruiting meeting a week later, it was stated that 'the real wants of Ireland are the want of a Republican spirit ... the object of the Irish Republican Union is to provide her with those requisites, in the person of a few thousand Americanized Irishmen, who are now ready and willing to embark in her battle'.[110] Consequently, it was decided that 'squads of tens and twenties of well-drilled and scientific military men be sent off every ten days to Ireland, from all parts of the United States, going without arms, to educate the men of Ireland in the America principles of victory and independence'. Moreover, once in Ireland they would not leave until 'we plant the Republican tree of America on the Hill of Tara'.[111] Following the decision to abort the rescue of Mitchel more concerted efforts were made to win recruits for the Irish Brigade. Again, these events were public and were covered by the local press, and reprinted in Irish and British newspapers.[112]

The fact that support for Irish independence extended beyond the immi-grant community, attracted people with political influence, and cut across party allegiances, worried the British authorities but was regarded with scepticism by some newspapers. The New York correspondent of the *Manchester Guardian*, for example, viewed the public sympathy for Ireland as being tied in with the forthcoming presidential election, report-ing that 'Sycophantic meetings being held by all parties, Whigs, democrats, loco-focos, barn-burners etc., seek to win the Irish vote for their respective candidates for presidency. The last thing on the carpet is to send money, men and arms to Ireland. But don't be alarmed. The men will certainly drill for they are fond of playing soldiers – but money and arms, that's another matter.' Traditionally, Irish voters sided with the Democrat Party but the refusal of that party to contribute half a million dollars to famine relief in the previous year (even though it had the support of the Senate) had alienated some of them and so the Democrats felt it was necessary to win them back. The newspaper also believed that 'knowing the gullibility of poor Paddy, they are cramming him full of sympathy for Ireland'; concluding that the Irish people would wait a long time to get more than sympathy from America and even sympathy would dry up in December when 'the presidential agony is over'.[113] Similar sentiments were expressed in the States. The *New York Herald* described the meeting in June 1848 as 'a regular action for Presidential votes; and ... all there, bidding each other for the Irish vote'.[114]

Regardless of these divergent viewpoints, the British authorities took the threat of military intervention from America very seriously, especially when they received information regarding the travel plans of the Irish Republican Union. Men were to travel in groups of ten to fifteen to Liverpool or Ireland and, if questioned, they were to pretend to be 'disappointed emigrants'. The leaders had written instructions which were sewn into their waistcoats. The expected uprising would take place when the harvest was completed.[115] The authorities were informed that the first representative of the Irish Republican Union, who was a former lieutenant in the Prussian army, had left for Ireland as early as May and that he intended to travel to Ireland via Liverpool. Consequently, the authorities in Liverpool were alerted to the possibility that their port would probably become the main place of entry for members of the Irish Brigade and so a series of precautionary measures were put in place.[116] Liverpool, therefore, which already possessed a network of Confederate clubs, became involved in the revolutionary axis of London, Dublin and New York, with the local authorities watching anxiously for their arrival. They were helped by the fact that Saunders, who attended private meetings of the Irish Republican Union, provided physical descriptions of some of the members of the Brigade who left New York.[117] A number of American newspapers were also providing details regarding the activities of the Irish Brigade, reporting that fifteen men had sailed for Ireland at the beginning of July, although no evidence was found of their arrival.[118] Another informer, Joseph Pinkerton, warned the government in early July that over 1,200 men had already departed for Ireland and 5,000 more were ready to follow.[119]

The news from America alarmed the authorities in Ireland. By summer, the coast of Ireland was being patrolled by a squadron of 11 ships, with 456 guns and 3,900 officers and men.[120] Customs officials were told to search all vessels that arrived from the United States.[121] More controversially, the Inspector-General of the Irish Constabulary issued a memorandum stating that, 'All persons coming over from America are to be immediately arrested and searched for treasonable papers.'[122] Support for Irish Repeal – and increasingly Irish republicanism – in Ireland, Britain and the United States meant that a showdown between Irish nationalists and the British government was inevitable.

The Irish League

Concurrent with preparations being made for a violent uprising, the leaders of the two Repeal movements in Ireland were involved in discussions for a reunion, to be formalized in a body to be known as 'The Irish League'. Negotiations had first commenced at the end of 1847, but had foundered on O'Brien's insistence that the Repeal Association should be dissolved.[123] They resumed in the summer of 1848 when it was clear that the Irish Confederation was the most influential political organization in the country. The government was alarmed by the possibility of a reunion between Old and Young Ireland. The authorities believed that whilst Irish nationalists could not reach any consensus on their tactics, they posed little threat. But the creation of the Irish League in June 1848, which appear to favour the militant tactics of Young Ireland rather than the moderation preached by John O'Connell, caused concern.[124]

The discussions about amalgamation took place over a two-week period in the offices of the *Freeman's Journal*, with Dr Gray acting as an impartial facilitator.[125] Hardliners on both sides of the movement disliked the alliance but more moderate voices believed it was necessary in order to advance the cause of Repeal. Throughout the discussions, John O'Connell, the chief negotiator for Old Ireland, oscillated, intermittently threatening to resign if such a union took place.[126] At one point, the *Nation* suggested that if John O'Connell had scruples about joining the League, he should retire from the Repeal Association.[127] Many Old Irelanders, possibly out of residual loyalty to his father, felt that O'Connell should be allowed to make the final decision.[128] The Catholic Church hierarchy was also divided on the question of the Irish League, with Archbishop Murray of Dublin stipulating that chapels were not to be used for public meetings, except for charitable or religious reasons.[129] Dr Browne, the Bishop of Elphin, also distanced himself from the extremity of the League.[130] Nonetheless, the union had widespread support. On 24 June, a meeting of the United Repealers was held on Donnybrook Green in Dublin, comprising all religions and members of both Old and Young Ireland. Nearly 4,000 people attended.[131]

For moderates in the Repeal Association though, a sticking point to the union was the question of the use of physical force: the issue that had created the original secession two years earlier. Although the League was officially a constitutionalist organization, the creation of a National Guard by the Irish Confederation and the open support for military preparations via the club organization, meant that they unofficially sanctioned the use of physical force. Initially, this question was avoided but, at what was to be the final meeting, O'Connell resurrected the Peace Resolutions of 1846. By doing so, he may have hoped to create an insep-arable division amongst the negotiators. However, a compromise was reached with it being decided that the clubs could arm, but the League would not advocate physical force. Consequently, the reunification was not, in the first instance, to include the clubs.[132] On 11 July the first offi-cial meeting of the Irish League took place in Dublin. Both the Irish Confederation and the Repeal Association were to have wound up in advance of this meeting. It remained doubtful though, if O'Connell would bring to a close the Association that his father had founded. Only four days later, the Repeal Association officially withdrew its earlier agreement with the League, stating that it would only join if the League was commit-ted to constitutional means exclusively and that the clubs be disbanded.[133] Therefore, within less than two weeks of the inaugural meeting O'Connell had withdrawn from the League and, on 22 July, he publicly denounced it. [134] The short-lived attempt at union had failed, but by this stage the British government had initiated its own plan of campaign against the Irish Repealers.

By the beginning of July 1848, despite the creation of the Irish League, deep divisions remained in the Repeal movement. John O'Connell's lack-lustre performance and John Mitchel's transportation had left O'Brien the leader of a fractured, but increasingly desperate, movement. Moreover, his influence extended beyond Ireland, with support in the United States that mostly supported an armed insurrection. To what extent would O'Brien, a reluctant leader of the Irish Confederation, be able to control the disparate forces that had been unleashed in the previous three months? At this stage, the British government intervened to precipitate a rising for which the Irish people were unprepared and about which its leaders were undecided. But the Repealers had to deal with an enemy that wielded more power than the British government. At the end of June, news was received in Ireland that there had been a challenge to the Provisional Government in France which had ended in bloodshed. The news of the death of Archbishop Affré while trying to negotiate a truce shocked public opinion. In June also, there were riots in Rome that ultimately resulted in the Pope fleeing from the Vatican City. For the Catholic hierarchy the descent into violence was a reminder of the anti-clericalism of the original French Revolution and the violence of the 1798 uprising. The events of the early summer of 1848 confirmed the Irish Catholic Church in Ireland in their opposition to an uprising. The precautions being made by the British government in the previous three months now found an important ally in the shape of the Catholic Church.

Notes

1 Report of John Balfe, March 1848: Bodleian Library, Clarendon Papers, Irish Box 34,
2 Ibid., 17 April 1848.
3 O'Brien to John Dillon, 14 February 1848: Dillon Papers, TCD (f.62).
4 *United Irishman*, 19 February 1848.
5 O'Brien, Memorandum, Smith O'Brien Papers, NLI, MS 449, n.d.
6 *United Irishman*, 22 April 1848.
7 Club de l'Union a la Sorbonne, Paris, to O'Brien, 6 May 1848: NLI MS 442 f.2448.
8 Smith O'Brien Papers, NLI MS 442, n.d.
9 J. O'Donnell to O'Brien, 19 May 1848: Smith O'Brien Papers, NLI, MS 442, f.2457.
10 O'Brien, Memorandum, Smith O'Brien Papers, NLI, MS 449, n.d.
11 *United Irishmen*, 29 April 1848, 6 May 1848.
12 Clarendon to Reeve, 10 May 1848: Laughton, *Memoirs of Henry Reeve*, p. 200.
13 Clarendon to G.C. Lewis, 4 May 1848: ibid., p. 289.
14 'Ireland: Advance of Treason and Defeat of the Law' in *Frazer's Magazine* (June 1848), 728.
15 Mitchel, *Jail Journal*, p. li.
16 Peel to Lord Heytesbury, 8 August 1844: Parker, *Sir Robert Peel*, pp. 116–17.
17 In the 1860s, Butt defended a number of Fenians. He later founded the Home Government Association.
18 Davis, *Revolutionary Imperialist*, p. 252.
19 Papers of Duke of Wellington in relation to defence of Dublin Castle, Memorandum, Bodleian Library, Clarendon Papers, Irish Box 45, 21 May 1848.
20 Ibid.
21 *Frazer's Magazine* (June 1848), p. 729; William S. Balch, *Ireland: As I Saw It. The Character, Condition, and Prospects of the People* (New York and London 1850), p. 384.
22 Mitchel, *Jail Journal*, p. lii.
23 Lefroy and Jane Austen had been youthful lovers. He opposed Catholic Emancipation in 1829.
24 'Address to the Jurors of Dublin', TNA, 30 22, f.2, n.d.
25 O'Brien, Memorandum, Smith O'Brien Papers, NLI, MS 449, n.d.
26 Mitchel, *Jail Journal*, pp. 12–13.
27 Ibid., pp. 4–5.
28 Ibid., p. 7.
29 Ibid., p. 7.
30 Ibid., p. 7
31 This matter was transacted by the surgeon of Spike Island who acted on behalf of the women. Mitchel provided six autographs. Mitchel, *Jail Journal*, p. 13.
32 Meagher, 'Speech on the Transportation of Mitchel, 1848' in Lyons, *Meagher, Speeches and Writings*', pp. 216–17.

33 Mitchel, *Jail Journal*, p. liii.
34 O'Brien, Memorandum, Smith O'Brien Papers, NLI, MS 449, n.d.
35 Quoted in Introduction to Mitchel, *Last Conquest*, p. xiii
36 *Warder*, 3 June 1848.
37 See, for example, TNA, HO 45 2410, Part 2.
38 Goodway, *London Chartism*, pp. 80–4.
39 *Northern Star*, 3 June 1848.
40 Goodway, *London Chartism*, p. 84.
41 Ibid., pp. 80–4.
42 Ibid., p. 85.
43 Meeting at Stevenson's Square, TNA, TS 11, 12 June 1848.
44 Alexander Wilson, *The Chartist Movement in Scotland* (New York: Augustus M. Kelly, 1970), p. 239; Goodway, *London Chartism*, p. 80.
45 *Globe*, 4 July 1848; Mr Crampton to Foreign Office, 7 July 1848: TNA, FO 115/99, f.70.
46 Draft letter books of Mr Crampton, FO 5/483, 12 July 1848.
47 Mitchel, *Jail Journal*, p. 45.
48 Ibid., pp. 45–6.
49 *Irish Felon*, 26 June 1848.
50 T.D. Reilly to John Martin, 7 July 1848: Papers of John Martin, PRONI, D. 3127/1/12.
51 Davis, *Young Ireland*, p. 155.
52 *Irish Felon*, 24 June 1848.
53 *Irish World*, 29 January 1887.
54 Ibid., 1 July 1848.
55 Ibid., 8 July 1848.
56 Wilson, *Chartist Movement in Scotland*, p. 239.
57 *New York Freeman*, 29 April 1848.
58 J. Balfe to Henry Southern, April 1848: Bodleian Library, Clarendon Papers, Irish Box 53.
59 Reported in *New York Freeman*, 6 May 1848.
60 Clarendon to Wood, 29 November 1850: Maxwell, *Life and Letters*, pp. 317–18.
61 John Belchem, 'The Spy System in 1848: Chartists and Informers – An Australian Connection' in *Labour History* (vol. xxxix, 1980) 15–27.
62 *The Times*, 29 September 1848, 2 October 1848.
63 Reports of CJ, TCD, MS 2038/9/, 1848.
64 Report of Balfe, 17 April 1848: Bodleian Library, Clarendon Papers, Irish Box 53.
65 April 1848: ibid., Box 33. 17
66 *Nation*, 22 April 1848.
67 *Northern Journal*, 13 June 1848.
68 *Boston Pilot*, 12 February 1848.
69 Report of John Crampton, British Chargé in Washington, 2 April 1848: TNA, FO 5/485; *New York Herald*, 22 March 1848.
70 One of the most vociferous supporters of British retaliation was O'Brien: see Sloan, *O'Brien*, pp. 76–7.
71 *New York Herald*, 22 March 1848.
72 *Freeman's Journal*, 29 April 1845.

73 *Nation*, 18 March 1848.
74 Sloan, *O'Brien*, p. 215.
75 O'Brien's Journal, part four, 20 April 1852, in Davis, *'To Solitude Consigned'*.
76 These comments were attributed to Duffy by the government informer J.D. Balfe. This version does not appear in Duffy's account of 1848. Reports of Balfe, 21 April 1848: Clarendon Papers, Irish Box 53.
77 *Northern Journal*, 16 May 1848.
78 *Evening Journal* quoted in *Northern Journal*, 16 May 1848.
79 *Liverpool Mercury*, 6 June 1848.
80 Duffy, *Four Years*, p. 610.
81 Ibid., p. 609
82 Reports in TNA, FO 5/488 and HO 45/2391.
83 *Boston Pilot*, 13 May 1848, 20 May 1848.
84 *United Irishman*, 13 May 1848.
85 Mr Germori, Secretary of Emmet Club, New Orleans, to Irish Confederation, Dublin, 2 June 1848, *New York Herald*, 5 July 1848.
86 *Boston Pilot*, 8 April 1848.
87 Ibid., 6 May 1848.
88 Ibid.
89 *New York Herald*, 10 May 1848 (a copy of this article was sent to Lord Palmerston), FO 5/488.
90 *New York Herald*, 10 May 1848.
91 *Nation*, 15 July 1848.
92 *New York Herald*, reported in *The Tablet*, 8 July 1848.
93 *Nation*, 3 July 1848.
94 Ibid.
95 Ibid.
96 *Boston Pilot*, 13 May 1848.
97 Ibid.
98 Ibid., 8 July 1848.
99 Ibid., 1 July 1848.
100 *Wexford Independent*, 22 July 1848.
101 *Liverpool Mercury*, 14 July 1848.
102 Samuel Saunders (informer) to Lord Grey, 13 November 1848: Home Office, TNA, HO 45 2369.
103 *Boston Pilot*, 22 July 1848.
104 *New York Herald*, quoted in *The Tablet*, 8 July 1848.
105 *Armagh Guardian*, 10 July 1848.
106 *Boston Pilot*, 20 May 1848.
107 *Armagh Guardian*, 10 July 1848.
108 Greeley and Van Buren were involved with the Provisional Committee: see TNA, FO 5/488.
109 *Boston Pilot*, 24 June 1848, 1 July 1848.
110 Cited in the *Nation*, 22 July 1848.
111 *Boston Pilot*, 24 June 1848.
112 *Nation*, 22 July 1848.
113 *Manchester Guardian* cited in *Liverpool Mercury*, 14 July 1848.
114 *New York Herald*, 6 June 1848.

115 Barclay to Palmerston, 4 July 1848: TNA, FO 5/488.
116 Report of Edward Rushton, Stipendiary Magistrate, Liverpool, 28 June 1848: TNA HO 45 2416A.
117 Saunders to Barclay: ibid., HO 45 2369.
118 *Boston Pilot*, 8 July 1848.
119 Joseph Pinkerton (informer) to Lord Palmerston, Foreign Secretary, 11 July 1848: TNA, HO OS 2391.
120 *Wexford Independent*, 22 July 1848.
121 *Liverpool Mercury*, 15 August 1848.
122 Home Office Memorandum, TNA, HO 45 2416A.
123 William O'Neill Daunt, *Eighty-Five Years of Irish History, 1800–1885* (London: Ward and Downey, 1888), p. 276.
124 *Frazer's Magazine*, July 1848, pp. 119–20.
125 Davis, *Young Ireland*, p. 156.
126 *The Tablet*, 1 July 1848; *Nation*, 1 July 1848.
127 *Nation*, 1 July 1848.
128 Ibid.
129 *The Tablet*, 8 July 1848.
130 Ibid.
131 *Nation*, 1 July 1848.
132 Davis, *Young Ireland*, p. 157.
133 *Nation*, 15 July 1848.
134 Davis, *Young Ireland*, p. 157.

6

'A sacred obligation': July 1848

The potato blight reappeared in Ireland in July 1848, but its arrival was overshadowed by political unrest throughout Europe.[1] Within Ireland, an uprising appeared inevitable. The transportation of Mitchel had energized the Repeal movement, opening up the possibility of a reunion with the faltering Repeal Association that for two years had proved to be elusive. At this stage, Conciliation Hall was not doing well and Repeal subscriptions, which were a telling financial barometer, had fallen to almost zero.[2] In contrast, Mitchel's removal from Ireland had revitalized O'Brien, both personally and politically. However, managing a fast-growing movement whose members had been led to expect that unless Repeal was granted, a rising would take place at harvest, created a dilemma for O'Brien, who remained at heart a constitutionalist. Nevertheless, following Mitchel's deportation, he issued an 'Address to the Irish people on behalf of the Council of the Confederation'. In it, he warned that 'these indignities and wrongs are rapidly bringing us to that period when armed resistance to the oppressors of our country will become a sacred obligation'.[3] Additionally, O'Brien spent the early part of the summer touring the country, encouraging the clubs to prepare for a showdown with the British government. Privately, he hoped that any future engagement by the clubs would be purely defensive, and not offensive. Mitchel's departure had also paved the way for a reorganization of the administrative structure of the Confederation. Its Council was reduced in size, to now comprise twenty-one elected members. The radical Father Kenyon and the young, but charismatic, Thomas Francis Meagher received most votes. They instantly began preparing for an uprising, in which they believed their supporters in both America and Britain would play a role. According to Duffy, O'Brien was excluded from these discussions due to his moderation and continuing, if fading, hope in his fellow landowners.[4]

Young Ireland and the Irish Confederation had been consistent advocates of Protestants and Catholics working together in order to achieve an independent Ireland. Despite some setbacks, their persistence and vision

was rewarded with the establishment of a Protestant Repeal Association
in 1848. Its first meeting was held in Dublin on 15 May and it was
attended by both men and women who were described as 'eminently
respectable'. Overwhelmingly, the members of the new Association were
drawn from the urban professional and artisan classes, with little landlord
involvement, although they were supported by William Sharman
Crawford MP, a Protestant landlord in County Down who was a champion of tenant rights, and Samuel (later Sir) Ferguson, an antiquarian and
poet. These two men were sympathetic to Repeal, but they were both
constitutionalists.

One of the first actions of the meeting was to condemn the deportation
of John Mitchel, while pointing out that they disagreed with his politics.
Ferguson informed the meeting that he had attended despite 'social coercion ... of encountering cold looks from many of whom I esteem and
from some of whom I love'.[5] His comments suggest that the Repeal question was creating new political divides in Irish society. At their meeting on
30 May, the Protestant Association issued a public appeal to 'the
Protestants of Ulster'. It stated that the time had arrived to demand an
independent legislature. It appealed particularly to members of the
Orange Order, citing William of Orange's defence of Flanders in the face
of Spanish tyranny. It also sought to reassure members of the Order that
they had nothing to fear from an association with Catholics, accusing the
government of promoting mistrust for its own ends. It concluded by
pointing out the government's unjust treatment of an Ulsterman, John
Mitchel, 'with whom we disagree, yet from whom we cannot withhold
our sympathy'.[6]

A further meeting of the Protestant Repeal Association was held in the
Music Hall in Dublin on 12 July, and was well attended by both men and
women. The date was particularly significant as it was the day on which
the Orange Order celebrated the anniversary of the Battle of the Boyne,
by holding large parades and festivities throughout the country. Daniel
Sullivan, a paper manufacturer, was in the chair. He produced an orange
lily, an emblem used by Orangemen, and suggested that it should no
longer be viewed as a symbol of discord, but one of unity. Some of the
men present were wearing orange sashes, to show that the two traditions
could exist together. One speaker asserted that Orangemen would no
longer support the Union, 'which had reduced their country to their
present miserable condition'. Inevitably, there were cheers for John
Mitchel and for Martin, Duffy, Williams and O'Doherty, who had
recently been arrested for publishing subversive newspapers. Seventy-
seven new people joined the Association.[7] However, at the same time that
this meeting was taking place, Orange marches were being held, which
were not only the largest for years, but also some of the most overtly anti-
nationalist and violent.[8]

Shortly after the foundation of the Dublin Association, a Protestant

Repeal Association was established in Belfast: an occurrence that the Catholic *Tablet* paper described as a 'remarkable sign of the times'.[9] Smaller associations were formed in Drogheda and Lurgan.[10] At the beginning of July, the Belfast Association appealed to the Orangemen of Ulster to join them in calling for a Repeal of the Act of Union. They accused the Orange Order of allowing themselves to be used as 'mercenaries, garrisoning your own country for the benefit of strangers'.[11] Their call for unity had the opposite effect by further exacerbating existing tensions. Declarations were made that rebuffed any alliance and rejected Repeal. A common theme of the objections was to depict Repeal as a dangerously Catholic movement. One Orange lodge issued a public statement that declared:

> The Protestants of Ulster have everything to fear from an Irish legislature. In the first place they have to dread the ascendancy of a system the most intolerant that ever made its appearance on the face of the earth; secondly, they have to dread the influx of Jesuits; thirdly, they know well that they could not have a fair representation in the senate; and lastly, they believe that the liberty of conscience that they can now have under a British government would be taken from them.[12]

The local Protestant press was similarly vehement. The *Warder*, which had been founded to promote Protestantism in Ireland, congratulated the unswerving loyalty of the Orangemen. It suggested that Repeal was an exclusively Catholic plot, warning that, 'A vast and infernal conspiracy is gradually organizing the popery of Ireland for a savage revolution.' They called on all Protestants to use the forthcoming twelfth of July commemorations to show that they were willing to fight to defend the Union.[13] The paper quoted one Orange lodge who had informed the Queen that they would 'die rather than submit to a repeal of the Union'.[14] The *Belfast News-Letter* congratulated the local Orangemen for their stance, pointing out that 'popery won't change its spots'. At the same time, it accused Protestant Repealers of disgracing the name of Protestantism.[15] It further warned that all that Repeal agitation had done was to give the Orangemen 'more ardour'.[16] The paper also reminded its readers of the willingness of all Orangemen to act as a 'native garrison' in defence of the Union.[17] Nonetheless, twenty-nine Orangemen were expelled from their lodges in Belfast for openly advocating Repeal.[18]

The twelfth of July gatherings provided a public platform for Protestants not only to affirm their loyalty to the Crown and the Union, but to attack the Repeal agitation. Inevitably, Repeal was portrayed as having support only amongst Catholics and in the south of the country. It was also characterized as being ridiculous. The Revd McIlwaine, who addressed the Belfast lodges, began by asking his audience if there were any Protestant Repealers present because, if there were, they should 'immediately take the train to the asylum'.[19] According to William Daunt,

a close ally of the now dead Daniel O'Connell, the anti-Catholic vitriol of
the Protestant press and some evangelical preachers at this time arose
from fear of the fact that, 'The Protestant Repealers, possessing ability,
respectable position and a powerful case, were beginning to produce a
strong case on the mind of their fellow religionists of the humbler class'.[20]

By the end of July, divisions within Protestantism appeared as irrecon-
cilable as those between Old Ireland and Young Ireland. Similar to the
Confederate clubs, a number of Orange lodges were arming and preparing to resist an uprising by force. A number had appealed to the
government to supply them with arms and ammunition, as had occurred
during the 1798 rebellion.[21] Publically, Clarendon declined their offer of
help. Privately, the Prime Minister, Lord John Russell, had advised
Clarendon '*in extremis* not to rebuff offers of help from Orange associations, and to envisage arming the Protestants'.[22] Such advice was not
necessary as, secretly, Clarendon was arranging for arms to be shipped to
Orange lodges in Belfast.[23]

The sectarian spirit evinced by Orangemen on 12 July disturbed
Sharman Crawford, impelling him to write to John Beck, Secretary of the
Belfast Repeal Association. He asked that his letter be made public. In it,
he claimed that the last two sessions of parliament had convinced him that
the 'centralisation of imperial legislation [was] unfit for Ireland'. He
rejected the idea that independence would threaten the Protestant
Ascendancy. Instead, he accused the British government of encouraging
Protestants to believe 'that their security rested on Catholic oppression'.
The Union had rescued Protestants at a time when Catholics were getting
power and they were told that they needed this protection, but 'now
Catholics and Protestants alike have become slaves of British power'.
Since the Union, 'Protestants have held a nominal ascendancy by the sacrifice of all national rights', but he believed it to be 'the ascendancy of
injustice'. Yet, he added, the sectarian violence that had accompanied the
recent 12 July marches 'leaves me small grounds for hope that the
Protestant mind will be brought to the views which I have suggested',
because 'they have successfully raised the old no popery cry'. His conclusion was pessimistic, suggesting that 'the Orangemen are deluded into the
suicidal course of becoming the forgers of their own chains. The separation of Protestants and Catholics, if continued, will give power to the
enemies of Ireland to uphold abuses'. Beck agreed with these sentiments
and issued an address 'To the Orangemen of Ulster' accusing them of
dishonouring the name of William of Orange and displaying ignorance of
their own history.[24] The disillusion evinced by Beck and Sharman
Crawford provided a dismal counterpoint to the aspirations of the
Protestant Repeal Association, whilst highlighting the deep-rooted suspicions that were undermining their attempts to create a united political
movement.[25]

Clubs

The Irish Confederation hoped that the clubs would provide the basis for new nationwide organization of united Repealers when the Irish League was fully established.[26] Throughout 1848 the number of clubs had been increasing and the government's treatment of Mitchel gave a further boost to the numbers enrolling. On 12 June 1848, Thomas Halpin, the Secretary of the Irish Confederation, informed O'Brien that the organization of clubs was proceeding 'astonishingly fast', with twenty-six clubs in Dublin City and eight in its suburbs. Optimistically, he predicted that the 'whole country' could be organized by the end of the month.[27] All club members were asked to enrol a new recruit each week. They were also asked to take the teetotal pledge before the harvest was over. On 1 July, Halpin claimed that in the previous three weeks the number of clubs had doubled. The *Nation* calculated that there were now 52 clubs in the Dublin area, each with approximately two hundred members, while the two Belfast clubs each had 300 members. They warned, with some prescience, that this could be the last week for club organization as the government wanted to suppress them.[28] Inevitably, the clubs had become a focus of government attention. Consequently, the activities of each of the Dublin clubs were being monitored, with one policeman usually standing at the door during each meeting, sometimes with attendants. Less visibly, the government's informers were encouraged to attend the meetings of as many clubs as possible.[29]

While Dublin continued to be the centre of club activity, at the beginning of July there were fifteen clubs in Cork City, seven in Limerick City and additional ones in the county; eight in Waterford, four in Kilkenny City, one in County Clare, two in Belfast and a further two or three in the process of being formed, three in Country Tipperary, and an undisclosed number in counties Galway, Kerry, Kings, Louth, Mayo, Meath and Sligo.[30] Nor was the spread of clubs confined to Ireland. The subscriptions received by the Confederation from 9 to 28 June, which totalled £262-7-6, included donations from London, New York, Liverpool, Birmingham, Rochdale, Staffordshire, Glasgow, Cincinnati, New Orleans and Edinburgh.[31] The support extended beyond mere financial involvement. A letter to the *Nation* from a Confederate supporter in Leeds said that immediately after the French Revolution Irishmen there had started to collect arms. They now had 300 guns and pistols hidden in Yorkshire 'waiting for us, and we [are] waiting for you'. The writer said the same was true in Birmingham, Manchester and Liverpool. The response of the paper's editor was to say that it hoped that the writer was not 'a boaster or braggart'.[32]

At the beginning of July, a number of leading Confederates, including O'Brien, undertook a tour of the country with the aim of establishing new clubs outside Dublin and thus creating a more truly national movement.[33]

They were aiming to establish a club in every parish, O'Brien averring that, 'it is in those clubs public opinion will be concentrated; it is through them every grand object can be obtained; it is through them the country can be brought into immediate action'. Before leaving, he appeared optimistic that a union of Repealers was imminent, claiming that the differences between the two groups had been 'settled'. Provocatively, he added that when the alliance was complete 'then we may defy the treachery of a British government'.[34] Similarly, the behaviour of the Confederates who visited the country appeared to be deliberately confrontational. They each took a tricolour, which they had adopted as the national flag. They also urged every club member to arm. Despite the public optimism of the Confederate leaders, they were aware that opposition to their aims remained entrenched. In addition to the government's opposition, they found that the local gentry and sometimes the local Catholic clergy were actively discouraging the people from joining the clubs. In Coolock, a local man had been dismissed after he attended a club meeting. A deputation of fellow Confederates agreed to pay him a weekly wage until he got alternative employment.[35]

O'Brien's tour of the south commenced in Cork: a city that already possessed a network of clubs. On 10 July, the local Confederates held a soirée to honour 'the prosecuted Patriots', which was attended by about 500 people. O'Brien, the guest of honour, was toasted for being 'devoted, chivalrous, uncompromising'.[36] During his tour, O'Brien estimated that he met 15,000 clubmen, many of whom paraded before him in military formation, some carrying arms.[37] At this stage, it was clear that O'Brien did not believe that an uprising was imminent as he was privately planning to follow his trip to Cork with 'the pleasure of an excursion through Kerry and West Cork'.[38] Furthermore, he was unaware that the government had seized the initiative, taking advantage of the fact that many of the Confederate leaders were absent from Dublin, and arrested the editors of the radical press. The government had also taken action against the most prominent members of the newly-formed Inner Council of the Confederation, charging them with seditious activities. Additionally, various areas in the country, including parts of Cork, Drogheda, Dublin, Limerick, Tipperary and Waterford, had been 'proclaimed' as being 'disturbed' and stringent curfews were imposed. Amongst other things, these restrictions forbade the possession of weapons.[39] By taking these measures, the government had changed the timetable of any future revolution and recast the agenda on its terms.

Despite being a primarily Presbyterian town, which was regarded as possessing the most loyal population in Ireland, emergency measures were also put in place in Belfast. The local magistrates estimated that by July, there were five Confederate clubs in the town and that many of their supporters possessed arms. They therefore asked the Lord Lieutenant for permission to enrol Special Police Constables, while the Police Committee sought permission for the local constabulary to be 'immediately armed and trained to military discipline'.[40] As was the case elsewhere, the authorities employed informers to keep abreast of the activities of the local clubs. Based on these reports, a number of arrests were made, including that of John Rea, a successful solicitor and prominent Young Irelander, who was imprisoned in Kilmainham Jail in Dublin.[41] The fact that he was released without charge resulted in his being dubbed 'the Kilmainham Spy'; an accusation that was neither fully proven nor completely refuted.[42]

Although these actions marked the start of a sustained attack on the Confederation by the government, the radical press had not been suppressed. From their prison cells in Newgate, the editors continued to write for their respective journals, and thus remained in the vanguard of the revolutionary movement. An editorial in the *Nation* announced that, 'The long impending war with England has actually commenced ... the clubs have been told to disband and Dublin to give up its arms ... If England can commit these excesses with the impunity of a despot, Ireland is utterly and ignobly overthrown ... In revolutions, a retreat is fatal.' These sentiments were echoed by the usually cautious Duffy who, from his prison cell, wrote an article entitled 'Casus Beli', in which he stated, 'With me war was not a natural or instinctive resource: I accepted it only as the last resource; but I accepted it without reservation.'[43] On 22 July, Lalor writing in the *Felon*, asked, 'Who will strike the first blow for Ireland?'[44] The continued publication of the *Nation* resulted from the fact that the editorship had been taken over, initially by McGee and later by Margaret Callan and Jane Elgee (Speranza). Under their management, it published ever-more bellicose articles. Unaware that an uprising was taking place in County Tipperary, on 29 July the *Nation* appealed to both Catholics and Protestants to arm themselves.[45] The same edition included a provocative article called *Jacta Alea Est* (The Die is Cast), which appeared unsigned.[46] It was written by Speranza, and it amounted to a call to arms, challenging the men of Ireland to fight. The British government responded by immediately suppressing the paper.[47]

By mid-July, an altercation between the government and the Irish Confederation seemed inevitable. Clearly, waiting until the harvest was gathered to commence a rebellion was no longer an option. O'Brien responded to the news of the arrests by cutting his tour short and returning directly to Dublin. At this point, O'Brien, who for so long had been a reluctant rebel leader, now appeared to be publicly courting a confrontation. Privately, his doubts remained. Even following the arrest of his close political ally, Chares Gavan Duffy, O'Brien continued to hope that 'circumstances would render it unnecessary for me to call upon the country to take up arms'. Nonetheless, he believed that 'each new aggression of the government made it imperative upon me to place the country in a condition to protect itself and its most valued and gifted children'.

Reluctantly, he decided 'to place it in a state of preparation', although he felt that no action should be taken until they heard the outcome of Duffy's trial.[48] A few days later, a warrant for O'Brien's arrest was issued. The *Manchester Guardian*, which in common with the rest of the British press was following events in Ireland closely, prophesized that the leaders in Ireland had been 'fairly driven to the wall' and 'they must either fight or conceal themselves, or submit to being apprehended and lodged in prison'. The paper advised the men to allow themselves to be quietly apprehended, as the Irish people would come out worse if there was a collision with the troops. It predicted that while there might be local outbreaks, there would not be a national one.[49]

Regardless of their increasingly precarious situation, a number of Confederate leaders travelled to the countryside to visit the local clubs. Their destinations were partly determined by the government as many had been summoned to trial and they were required to attend court in different parts of the country. Meagher, who paid his bail before leaving Dublin, travelled to Limerick where he had to present himself at the local assizes. His reception in the city was 'enthusiastic'. In a gesture typical of his flamboyant style, on the night of his arrival he made a speech from the balcony of his hotel, saying, 'I know the hereditary heroines of the city – the women of Limerick will not disgrace the heroic character they have acquired.' He accused the government of deliberately making the leaders of the Confederation attend assizes in different parts of the country, saying, 'Their object in sending me here, in sending Mr Doheny to Nenagh and Mr McGee to Wicklow, and placing others in the felon's cell was, that by cutting off its leaders, they might throw the ranks into disorder.' During the course of his address, as many as thirty policemen marched 'ostentatiously' past the hotel.[50]

From Limerick, Meagher went directly to Slievenamon in County Tipperary, where he and Doheny had organized a mass meeting to be held on the mountainside on Sunday 16 July. In advance of the meeting, the local police and military had been placed under arms by the government. Doheny estimated that 50,000 people attended, which included supporters from Cork, Wexford and Waterford.[51] The Hugh O'Neill and the John Mitchel Clubs of Clonmel, followed by the Fitzgerald Caher Club, marched to the mountainside. At 4 o'clock, Doheny and Meagher arrived. Doheny was dressed in the uniform of the '82 Club while Meagher wore a green cap and a tricolour sash. They both carried the tricolour flag.[52] Doheny spoke first and asked the crowds, 'Will you continue to starve and beg?' Meagher, despite admitting to feeling exhausted, spoke with his usual passion and, like Doheny, referred to the ongoing famine, saying, 'The potato was smitten, but your fields waved with golden grain. It was not for you.' He added, 'There is a stain on the nation while [Mitchel] remains in Bermuda.' Meagher then left and went to Waterford, his home town, and from there he travelled back to Dublin.[53]

On Monday 17 July a number of leading Confederates met in Dublin. O'Brien reported favourably on his southern tour but, inevitably, the main topic was how to respond to the actions of the government.[54] That an insurrection was viewed as inevitable was evident from the creation of a Council of Five which, in reality, was a War Council. It comprised John Blake Dillon, Thomas D'Arcy McGee, Thomas Francis Meagher, Richard O'Gorman (junior) and Thomas Devin Reilly. O'Brien had asked not to be a member and on 23 July he left Dublin, to continue with his tour of southern counties.[55] The die, however, had already been cast due to the increasingly repressive actions of the authorities. Clearly, the British government had been planning their moves against the Confederation for some time, whilst the leaders of the Confederation had been taken by surprise.

Even more oppressive legislation was being prepared. On 24 July, Habeas Corpus was suspended in Ireland. The bill had been rushed through the Houses of Parliament during the weekend of 22 and 23 July. From its introduction, through six readings and up to receiving royal assent, the complete procedure took only 70 hours.[56] It provided for anybody suspected of treason to be imprisoned without trial. During the parliamentary discussion that preceded its introduction, it was suggested in the House of Lords that this measure was necessary on the grounds that, in addition to the military training taking place in Ireland, 'Attempts also had been made to promote excitement in foreign countries on the subject of this proposed insurrection. In America, regular subscriptions had been entered into for the purpose of obtaining arms for the Irish Confederation.'[57] In reality, the act had been passed at the insistence of Clarendon, although his earlier request had been refused. The bill was only finally introduced when Clarendon threatened to resign.[58] It was the third time that Clarendon had used the threat of resignation in order to get more support from the British government. Shortly after the rebellion had been put down, Clarendon admitted, 'I have been much bothered by the vacillation and timidity of our rulers on this occasion … it is not pleasant to have to poke a Cabinet into a sense of duty, to extract by threats, as if for a personal favour, that which should be readily acceded to when the public necessity for it was proved and manifest.'[59] His comments reveal that the nationalist threat was regarded differently by politicians in London and Dublin. Nonetheless, there was little opposition in parliament to these measures. An exception was the Irish MP, Henry Grattan. In a debate in the House of Commons of 24 July, Grattan lambasted the government for its recent actions, ranging from blatant jury-packing to the suspension of Habeas Corpus.[60] In regard to the latter, he accused the government of not observing due parliamentary process and passing it on a day (Sunday) when few Irish members could attend. The consequence had been that, 'in seven hours the liberties of the Irish people were taken away'. Just as damningly, he pointed out that instead of debating Irish civil liberties, the government should be concerned with giving the Irish poor food, medicine and clothes.[61] His latter point was sentient. The potato harvest of 1847 had been small, but relatively blight-free; in 1848 blight returned to Ireland and was almost as virulent as it had been in 1846, making more suffering, starvation and death inevitable.

The suspension of Habeas Corpus gave the Irish Lord Lieutenant the power to detain persons without trial until 1 March 1849. It was followed by a fresh wave of arrests that included the Irish Chartist leader, Patrick O'Higgins. The government also banned the distribution of the radical press, including the *Nation*, and arrested people who had been selling these papers, even though it had not previously been illegal to do so. Newgate Prison was put in a state of emergency and the editors imprisoned inside it were forbidden to send writings outside. A fresh Proclamation was issued on 26 July, which was accompanied by a letter from the Lord Lieutenant saying that he was going to use his new powers to close the clubs and thus end treason in the country. On the same day, the secretaries of many clubs were arrested. In anticipation of their suspension, a number of clubs in the countryside voluntarily dissolved, including ones in Kerry, Mayo and Tipperary.[62]

Following the news of the suspension of Habeas Corpus, the Council of the Irish League voted on whether or not to rise, and only by a small majority they voted against rising. Some of the opponents argued that they should wait to get a better opportunity to strike against the government as so many of their leaders were in prison or scattered around the country. However, when members of the War Council heard of the suspension of Habeas Corpus, they made plans for an immediate uprising, fearing that any delay would allow even more of their supporters to be arrested. Thomas D'Arcy McGee was sent to Glasgow to raise an Irish army, which would then seize a number of ships and sail them to Ireland. When he arrived in Glasgow on 25 July, he was informed that there were as many as 500 armed nationalists who were ready to sail to Ireland to support the rising.[63] Another Confederate, Martin MacDermott, was despatched to Paris 'to represent in Paris the political leaders of 1848'.[64] MacDermott was charged with seeking general support for a 'military intervention'.[65] According to Meagher, the arguments used by the emissary were so persuasive that the French government agreed to intervene once an insurrection had got under way.[66] French intervention never materialized, but MacDermott remained in Paris, continuing to act as the *Nation*'s correspondent.[67]

O'Brien was not in Dublin when news was received of the suspension of Habeas Corpus. Nor was he aware that a warrant had been issued for his arrest. Meagher and Dillon travelled to Wexford, via Killiney, to inform him of the latest government actions. They used false names, knowing that they were being sought by the police. O'Brien was asleep in bed when they arrived. In the discussion that followed they agreed that three options were open to them: 'be arrested or . . . to escape. The third, to throw ourselves upon the country and give the signal of the insurrection.' The three Confederate leaders chose the final option. The most moderate of the group, O'Brien, suggested that the suspension of Habeas Corpus justified the recourse to an armed insurrection. Meagher, despite being the youngest of the group, realized that the rising had 'no hope of success . . . [but] the leading men of the Confederation were bound to go out and offer to the country the sword and banner of Revolution, whatever consequences might result to themselves for doing so'.[68]

Overseas support

The increase in radical activities was not confined to Ireland. In July, a number of Chartist leaders were arrested in England, suggesting that Chartism continued to be a potent force there, even after the failure of the meeting on 10 April.[69] The Irish Confederates, however, were perceived to be an even greater threat. News received from Ireland throughout July alarmed the British public, with the recently-introduced electric telegraph providing up-to-date accounts of events there. Thus, on 26 July the *Manchester Guardian* reported the 'probability of a collision between the authorities and the populace'. It was still believed that the conflict would take place at the harvest period. The paper pointed out that the exceptionally wet weather meant that the prospects for the harvest were poor, which would further exacerbate tensions in Ireland.[70] Even more worryingly, the British newspapers reported that agitators in Dublin had been urging their supporters in Manchester and Liverpool to create a diversion by setting fire to factories and warehouses. The authorities in Liverpool were particularly alarmed because the city not only contained a large Irish population, but was the main port of disembarkation from Ireland and from North America. By 25 July, a large police force had been put under arms and more military reinforcements had been sent for to defend the dock area. A military encampment had been established in Everton, a suburb of Liverpool, some weeks earlier and 4,000 Special Constables had been enrolled.[71] The Mayor had sent a 'special train to Chester Castle' to obtain more artillery and all sales of gunpowder in the town had been stopped and existing supplies taken into the Town Hall.[72] Despite these precautions, the local magistrates and merchants remained nervous, and sent a memorial to the government asking for a suspension of Habeas Corpus in the city, similar to the new legislation in Ireland. They pointed out that any unrest would not only be bad for business, but might encourage arsonists and other disaffected groups to behave badly. The *Manchester Guardian* was dismissive of the actions of the Liverpool authorities, regarding them as 'unreasonable and exaggerated'. While the paper did not doubt that Confederate supporters were active in both

Liverpool and Manchester, they were confident that 'the parties disposed to listen to their suggestions are few in number'. They expressed their confidence in the vigilance of the Manchester magistrates to frustrate the 'villainous schemes of the traitors in Dublin'.[73]

The assuredness of the *Manchester Guardian* was undoubtedly helped by the fact that by July parts of the north of England were under virtual martial law. Birkenhead, which was on the other side of the River Mersey to Liverpool, had enrolled 1,000 Special Constables.[74] In Manchester, the authorities had already enrolled 12,000 'Specials'.[75] Since April also, Special Forces had also been present in the major towns and cities of Britain, including London, Birmingham, Bradford, Glasgow and Edinburgh. They proved to be a powerful augmentation to the New Police, the military, and the network of government informers. The government's skilful deployment of these forces of order, rather than lack of a radical spirit, was a major factor in the fact that there was little violence in Britain in 1848.[76]

Of just as much concern, if not more, to the British government were developments in the United States, over which they had no control. The increased militancy evident in Ireland in the summer of 1848 had been mirrored by Irish nationalists 3,000 miles away in the United States. Unaware of the latest round of arrests and legislation, preparations were still being made in America for a rising. Yet the distance between the countries meant that while Ireland was on the brink of a rising, plans were still being made for an outbreak after harvest. The revolutionary fervour had been kept alive over the summer by the arrival in the United States of two representatives of Young Ireland and of John Mitchel's brother, all of whom confirmed that an uprising would take place after the harvest. Following the arrival of the Young Irelanders in New York, a 'Directory' was established that comprised 'eminent Americans and eminent Irishmen to co-operate with the Confederates'. They quickly raised £10,000 following which the two Young Irelanders returned separately to Ireland with part of the money and the promise of more to follow.[77] Inevitably, the 4 July became the occasion of mass meetings, when the success of American republicanism could be allied with Irish republican aspirations. In Boston, an immense meeting took place on the eve of 4 July in the Melodeon Hall, which was so full that people had to be sent away. A number of Senators were present. An even larger meeting was held in Fanueil Hall (the Cradle of Liberty) on 10 July, which voted to support Irish independence.[78]

New York had become the centre of Irish activities. A monster meeting of the Irish Republican Union was held on 4 July, on a field north of Williamsburg, near New York. The meeting was attended by 'many thousands of exiled Irishmen'. M.T. O'Connor said the time for speech-making had passed – he was going to Canada to win support for Irish independence, even though he knew he would be arrested. If so, he expected that would mark the beginning of the battle. As usual, a large portion of the meeting was devoted to discussing the role of the Irish Brigade. O'Connor reported that subscriptions had started and 'very many ladies subscribed to the funds for sending men to Ireland'.[79] The star attraction of the meeting, however, was William Mitchel and the newly-formed Irish Brigade, replete with pikes and tricolours, paraded in his honour.[80] His message was optimistic, predicting that Ireland would get its freedom after the harvest and he stated, 'In the crisis that is coming you Irishmen in America will do your duty.' When questioned, he minimized the differences within the Repeal movement in Ireland, telling his audiences to, 'Act boldly and wisely and unitedly, for there is no disunion amongst us at home.'[81]

The arrival of Irish nationalists in the United States coincided with news reaching Britain that Irish-Americans were sailing to Ireland. Throughout July, British newspapers devoted extensive coverage to the imminent arrival of an Irish Brigade. Liverpool was believed to be the central stage in the journey from New York to Ireland. These reports confirmed what the government had been told by its network of informers in the States. They were further verified by the American Consul who – based on the information provided by informers – provided descriptions of three of the alleged sympathizers.[82] Again, the authorities acted decisively to the perceived transatlantic threat. In July, Metropolitan Police were sent to Liverpool. By the end of the month, the port was virtually under martial law with an additional 2,000 troops stationed in the district, 5,000 Special Constables and 2,000 pensioners having been sworn in.[83] Police officers were permanently located at the local docks in order to monitor all arrivals from America. The Liverpool authorities also attempted to establish a telegraph link with Dublin for the rapid transmission of information to and from the Lord Lieutenant.[84] Rumours and misinformation abounded. A number of Irish newspapers reported that the *John R. Skiddy*, which was sailing from New York to Liverpool, was carrying 'a brigade of sympathizers with the rebels in Ireland [and] subscriptions and arms'. Before it could dock in Liverpool, the ship was boarded by detectives but none of the sympathizers were on board.[85] Nonetheless, the threat of American intervention remained, demonstrating that the desire for Irish independence extended far beyond the island of Ireland.

The rising

In July 1848 the men of words became men of action – a transformation that only twelve months earlier had appeared highly unlikely. Their rhetoric in the early months of 1848 made action unavoidable if they were not to lose face and honour. In the end though, it was the actions of the government that made a rising inevitable. The suspension of Habeas Corpus amounted to a call to arms. Those who answered did so with little chance or expectation of success. Despite the activities of the clubs in the weeks preceding the rebellion, the Confederates were ill-prepared and poorly armed, and while many of their leaders were sincere patriots, they were reluctant rebels.

The sudden departure of the remaining Young Ireland leadership to the country created a problem for the Confederate clubs in Dublin who were left without leaders and, it seemed, with no instructions as to what role they should play in any planned rising. Consequently, shortly before the rebellion, Halpin travelled to the countryside to seek out O'Brien and ask what the 'poor club men of Dublin' should do. At this stage, O'Brien was preoccupied with disarray amongst the clubmen in Tipperary and the decision by the local priests to oppose a rising.[86] Moreover, it is unlikely that he was fully aware of what was going on as he had left Dublin before the suspension of Habeas Corpus. According to Meagher, however, before leaving Dublin he (Meagher) had visited Duffy in Newgate to explain the role of the Dublin clubs in the rising. Halpin was to disseminate the plan to the local clubs. Duffy and Halpin later denied any knowledge of the scheme.[87] Both Michael Cavanagh and John O'Mahony verified Meagher's account, with the former attributing the inactivity of the Dublin clubmen to Halpin's failure to pass on important information, due to his fear of being arrested.[88]

The location chosen for the commencement of the rising was Kilkenny, not Dublin, which was under heavy police and military protection. The number of troops in Dublin was estimated to be 14,000.[89] It was intended for the first outbreak to be partly diversionary, to draw troops and attention away from the capital city. The plan was for a larger uprising to then take place in Dublin *after* the troops had been sent to cope with the outbreaks elsewhere.[90] However, the final days before the uprising were marked by confusion and subsequent accounts written by those involved reflected these discrepancies. The vacillation of the local leadership and lack of support in Kilkenny resulted in relocation to County Tipperary, the home of Michael Doheny. Consequently, the location remained unknown to O'Brien as he traversed the countryside seeking support. This meant that a number of Dublin Confederates who wanted to join O'Brien found it difficult to do so, not knowing which part of the south-east he was agitating in.[91] Some supporters came from outside Ireland. On 24 July Terence Bellew MacManus, a Liverpool merchant and Confederate, sailed to Dublin in order to support the uprising, even though he was unaware of its location. Unbeknown to him, he had been tagged by a detective from Liverpool who intended to arrest him in Dublin, but lost sight of him after landing. MacManus was next sighted marching towards Ballingarry in County Tipperary.[92] When the two emissaries sent by the Confederation to America returned to Ireland at the end of July they found that during their absence Habeas Corpus had been suspended and that 'every American was subject to strict scrutiny'. One of them avoided arrest and joined O'Brien in Ballingarry, but the American money arrived too late for the purpose intended. The second representative was advised to immediately return to the States for safety, which he did.[93]

While O'Brien and other Confederate leaders were travelling around the south-east of the country in the hope of initiating a rising, John O'Connell was in Cork from where he published an address to the Repealers of Cove in which he re-iterated his adherence to moral force agitation, condemning all other approaches as 'not only opposed to prudence, but also religion'.[94] However, at this stage it was becoming evident that the Confederates would have to deal with an Irish enemy that was more influential than either John O'Connell or the Orange Order – namely, the Catholic Church. The local priests in the various locations where the rebel leaders amassed publically admonished their flocks and told them to return home. Their words were a powerful deterrent. To some extent, their disapproval was not unexpected, especially in the aftermath of the June rising in France. More surprising was the defection of two radical priests who had been consistent supporters of the Irish Confederation and advocates of physical force, but who now declined to join the Confederates. Both Father Kenyon and Father Birmingham refused to give any support to the insurgents, on the grounds that their bishops had forbidden any involvement.[95] In the case of Father Kenyon, a close friend and champion of John Mitchel, this was particularly surprising as he had frequently declared his support for an armed uprising. In fact, his militancy had resulted in his being suspended by his bishop in the summer of 1848. Yet, when the rising commenced, Kenyon did not even allow his chapel bell to be rung, which was to be a sign that the rebellion was under way.[96] Furthermore, according to *The Times*, Father Kenyon, who was well known for his uncompromising pronouncements, had given Lalor, a former friend, 'a cool reception', when the latter visited him.[97] The loss of Father Kenyon was undoubtedly a blow to the movement and was probably influential in persuading some of the younger priests not to become involved.

The arrival of Meagher and O'Brien at Carrick-on-Suir provoked a lot of interest, with an estimated 2,000 people turning out to support them. But the men decided not to act at this stage and much of the goodwill dissipated. Instead, the various Confederate leaders gathered at Ballingarry in County Tipperary by accident, rather than by design. They continued to disagree about tactics, although the other leaders deferred to O'Brien. O'Brien, who had for so long been a reluctant rebel leader, now proved to be an inappropriate one. While his bravery and honour were not in doubt, his tactics were badly chosen: he advised married men to return home to their families, and he told his followers not to fell trees (for building barricades) without first seeking the owner's permission. He also insisted that all provisions had to be paid for, even paying for supplies for his followers from his own resources.[98] Only a few hours before the rising commenced, O'Brien wrote a formal letter to the Director of the local Mining Company, promising to do everything to prevent the local people from suffering inconvenience. He also politely suggested that the price of coal should be lowered. The response of the Director of the Company was to give the letter to the constabulary, who immediately forwarded it to Dublin Castle.[99] As many as 2,000 people, which included an equal number of women, initially turned out to support O'Brien in Ballingarry, but the number quickly dwindled to an estimated 300. They were armed only with 'reaping hooks, scythes and forks stuck on hand staves'. Throughout the day preceding the rising, the parish priest drove slowly through the crowd in his carriage and his presence 'seemed to freeze the people's hearts when he passed through them'. O'Brien was informed that Father Morrison and Father Comerford had gone from house to house telling the people not to stir without permission, until the harvest was ripened, when the priests would lead them.[100]

In Ballingarry, O'Brien was accompanied by MacManus, Patrick O'Donoghoe, and the young James Stephens. Meagher, Dillon and Doheny, who all enjoyed a lot of personal popularity, had gone to other parts of the county to try to start simultaneous insurrections. At this stage, most of the local supporters had left and of the men and women who had stayed with him, only about thirty possessed firearms. Others had pikes, pitchforks or just sticks. In contrast, the south-east of the country had been flooded with additional constabulary and troops. This included four companies newly arrived from England who had been sent directly to Kilkenny, 1,500 additional troops who had been stationed in Carrick-on-Suir, 500 marines who had been dispatched to Waterford, and a naval squadron which was anchored off the Cork coast.[101]

Further military preparations were being made. On 28 July, the Duke of Wellington, who had been put in overall charge of military operations in Ireland, issued a memorial for the government recommending the formation of a special corps comprised of 6,000 troops, including artillery and cavalry, 2,000 armed police and 2,000 armed pensioners, who should be 'rendered moveable', that is, provided with camp equipment, provisions and fuel, and transport to carry it. This was because he and Sir Edward Blakney, the Commander in Ireland, were concerned about military transport and food supplies as the population in the south of the country had decided not to cooperate with the military. According to a confidential report by Sir Henry Hardinge, 'the resistance to assist the army was decisive and universal'. One baker's shop that had sold bread to the army had been 'demolished by the mob'. Moreover, the police and JPs in the southern counties concurred that 'whenever a general uprising may take place, no assistance but, on the contrary, every resistance to the government will be offered by the peasantry in the country and the tradesmen in the towns'. He warned:

Such is the prevailing disaffection that our possession of the southern part of the Country depends at this moment on the military and police forces. In short, the Army is in an enemy country with the great and additional disadvantage that the Officer commanding the troops cannot take beforehand, those preventative measures which he would in prudence take if he were in an enemy's country. The law to the last moment of the rebellion bursting forth protects the traitor, while the law hampers the army.[102]

The two reports not only reveal the concerns of the British military authorities, but demonstrate that support for O'Brien was widespread, although it was uncoordinated, largely unarmed, and lacked decisive leadership. Ironically, only a day after Wellington issued the memorial the rising was over, without the army having to fire a shot.

The actual conflict when it occurred was swiftly over, resulting in a resounding defeat for O'Brien. It was precipitated by the actions of the local constabulary who took the initiative forcing O'Brien to act. On 29 July, under the command of Sub-Inspector Trant, forty-six armed policemen marched towards Ballingarry. Near to the local town they encountered a barricade. A shot was fired and Trant and his men retreated, pursued by O'Brien and his supporters. The constabulary took shelter in the home of Widow McCormack, who was in the house with her six children. When O'Brien heard that the family were still present, risking his own safety he approached the house and asked Trant and his men to surrender. They refused. A stone was thrown by an insurgent, which resulted in the police firing on the insurgents, with O'Brien caught in the cross-fire. The firing continued for two hours by which time O'Brien's followers were almost out of ammunition. Stephens, despite being wounded, attempted unsuccessfully to set fire to the house. The priests, led by Reverend Fitzgerald, intervened telling the local people to return to their homes. The approach of police reinforcements effectively marked the end of the conflict. The people fled and the leaders, including O'Brien, went on the run.[103] None of the constabulary had been injured, although two insurgents were reported to have been killed.[104] One of the alleged victims, James Stephens, appeared in Paris shortly afterwards.

What happened next was disjointed, with no coordination between the Confederate leaders. Some, such as McGee in Sligo, were still trying to arrange risings in other parts of the country, unaware that O'Brien had been so swiftly and comprehensively defeated.[105] The first news to arrive in Dublin regarding the insurrection was vague and unsubstantiated: on 28 July the second edition of the *Examiner* reported at 5.30 pm that they suspected the rebellion had commenced as soldiers were on the move in the Carrick-on-Suir region. Bugles were sounding in the area and a number of families had fled from the district. The paper reported that O'Brien had announced that he would not be taken alive.[106] The reality was more prosaic.

Charles Gavan Duffy, who had been in prison since early July, believed that the uprising had taken place three months too late. O'Mahony, however, who had accompanied O'Brien throughout Tipperary, blamed the failure on a number of factors including poor leadership and clerical intervention. In his opinion, the apathy of the Ballingarry population, and the absence of arms amongst those who did support them, meant that 'O'Brien could not have commenced in a much worse place'. Ultimately, he regarded the role of the clergy as pivotal in persuading the people not to support the Confederate leader. Many of the local clubs had been led by young Catholic priests who had supported the call for an armed struggle. Yet, when O'Brien appealed to them in late July 1848, they universally refused to support him on the grounds that a rising was premature and should not take place before harvest. A number subsequently admitted that they had been forbidden from further participation by their superiors.[107] Whatever their reasons for opposing O'Brien the outcome was that the priests provided a powerful barrier between the Confederate leaders and the Tipperary clubmen, with disastrous consequences for the former. O'Mahoney's claim that the intervention of the local priests was a major factor in the failure of the uprising was supported by many other Confederate leaders. In the immediate aftermath of the Ballingarry uprising, though O'Donoghoe and Reilly blamed O'Brien's lack of tenacity and poor leadership skills, with Reilly even allegedly suggesting that O'Brien should be shot.[108] In his defence, Michael O'Farrell suggested that O'Brien – against his better judgement – had been coerced into taking action by Dillon and Meagher, only leading the rebellion out of a sense of duty and honour.[109]

Even before they knew the outcome of the rising, the British press, led by *The Times*, had been deriding the Irish leaders. O'Brien was described thus: 'Poor O'Brien, if it is allowable to pity so perverse and mischievous an animal, is evidently beside himself, if indeed he ever enjoyed an English average of sanity.' They referred to him as being 'armed with pike and pistol, muttering broken sentences, and with a reckless swaggering gait'.[110] O'Brien was not their only target: they also claimed that, 'No one appears to know where Meagher is flourishing his sword, but if he is fighting anything, it must be the air.'[111] The newly-installed electronic telegraph meant that news of the defeat of the uprising first appeared in *The Times* on Tuesday 1 August, only two days after it was over.[112] The immediate response of the British authorities and the press was to treat the uprising with scorn. The proximity of a cabbage patch provided an ongoing source of amusement and derision. *The Times* took glee in pointing out that 'King Charles hid himself in the oak, and King O'Brien in the cabbages' and the paper reminded its readers that 'if he crept out the way of the bullets, [he] betrayed no fear of the slugs'.[113] Undoubtedly, the rebellion, which was over in less than four hours, was an anti-climax. Months of speculation and anticipation ended ignominiously for the insurgents: a situation that was at once exploited by the authorities and the conservative press, which immediately, and memorably, characterized it as 'an affray in Widow McCormack's cabbage patch'.

After the rising

Following the defeat at Ballingarry, the insurgents did not know what to do next, although some attempted to escape from Ireland. Immediately, proclamations were issued and rewards offered for their capture. Five hundred pounds was offered for the capture of O'Brien. Arrests continued for weeks after the uprising. Journalists sympathetic to the insurgents were imprisoned, including Mr Killiloe, the proprietor of the *Waterford Chronicle*.[114] In late August, Irish newspapers reported the arrest of a man who had been wounded at Ballingarry. James Dwyer was taken to Clonmel and put in jail. He had a 'dreadful' wound in his right breast. Dwyer had been hiding in a pit, but the government had received information on his location.[115] Although the majority of state prisoners were men, those arrested included some women, generally for harbouring men. In Carrick-on-Suir, two young women, Miss Jane Ryan and Miss Eliza Power were committed to Clonmel jail and charged with being engaged in treasonable practices. Miss Ryan was charged with hiding her brother and Mr Mahoney, who were wanted for their part in the uprising.[116]

The arrest of the leaders was treated with scorn by the conservative press. The fact that some of the leaders of the uprising did not resist arrest led the London *Times* to disparage the ultimate seriousness of the actions, describing their reactions in the wake of Ballingarry as 'all panic, dispersion, concealment and surrender'.[117] Two weeks after the rising, Meagher, O'Donoghoe and Maurice Leyne (the only member of the O'Connell family who fully identified with Young Ireland) were apprehended, probably deliberately, on a railway bridge near Holy Cross in Thurles. The correspondent for the *Times* described Meagher as looking 'more like a "swell" rather than a gentleman', and O'Donoghoe as having a look of 'savage obstinacy [which would] look well on a prison barricade', while Leyne had no features worth noting apart from 'an expression of silly enthusiasm'.[118] A more sympathetic account in an Irish newspaper reported that the three men, who were not attempting to disguise themselves, were arrested by a large party of police, while walking down a high road. They did not resist arrest. Meagher was reported as looking in good health, and smoking a cigar on his way to the train station, from whence he and his colleagues were taken by special train to Dublin.[119] The search for O'Brien extended to his home at Cahirmoyle, although none of his family were at home.[120] He was eventually captured at Thurles train station on 5 August from where he was attempting to return to his home. He did not resist arrest either.

A number of Confederate leaders avoided capture, including Dillon, Reilly, O'Gorman and Doheny, and even their former colleagues and

families were not sure of their whereabouts.[121] While on the run, Dillon
secretly wrote to his wife outlining what had happened to him after he had
left O'Brien. On that day, 28 July, he had travelled to Thurles where he
had been concealed by 'a patriotic young lady'. He had then moved to
Eva's house on 8 August. She said that he was a 'finished priest'. He had
shaved off his whiskers to make this more plausible. At this point, he was
still hopeful that further insurrection would take place. When he left Eva,
he went to various priests' houses looking for shelter, but found that
many of them were nervous about shielding a felon as a new proclamation had denounced everyone harbouring an outlaw. He stayed on the
Arran islands for some days, hiding in the rocks when the police searched
the islands. He went on the run again until he was given shelter at St
Jarleth's College near Tuam, where he remained for a fortnight. His plan
was to escape from Galway to New York, again disguised as a priest, and,
if he reached the United States then 'I regard my career as a patriot is
almost closed'. He hoped his wife and family would join him the following summer. The President of St Jarleth's College had asked all the priests
and nuns in the area to offer Masses and novenas for his safe escape.
Apart from missing his wife, his main regret was not seeing O'Brien and
Meagher again, averring, 'If I had these two with about a dozen others in
the same ship with me, I would depart with a light heart, with a prospect
of never setting foot on Irish soil.' His anger, however, was directed at his
fellow countrymen, rather than the British government, leading him to
assert, 'As for the people, I have lost all faith in them. They are treacherous and cowardly, and if Ireland is ever destined to be free, her freedom
must be the gift of a stranger. That's why my career as a patriot is almost
over.'[122] Dillon did eventually escape to the United States. Other
Confederates who made it there included McGee, Cavanagh, Reilly, P. J.
Smyth, O'Gorman and Doheny, some disguised as priests, O'Gorman as
a woman.

One of the participants in Ballingarry was not so fortunate. Terence
Bellew MacManus had travelled from Liverpool in order to participate in
the rising. Like the other leaders, he had gone into hiding after
Ballingarry, hoping to escape to the United States. He was on board an
American ship when he was arrested, resulting in a diplomatic standoff
between the American Embassy and the British government. MacManus
had written from aboard the ship to Duffy, asserting that by the time the
letter arrived he would be on his way 'to a free country'. Despite the uprising having failed and his Liverpool business being ruined, he stated, 'I
regret nothing I have played and ... will be ever ready to play it over
again.' He believed they had learned a lot from the 'last campaign' and so
still had 'high hopes – more so than when I stood on the hill of Tara in
1843'. Of his colleagues who had been captured he commented, 'Freedom
must have its sacrifice.'[123] He was unaware that within a few days his
own freedom would end and instead of escaping to the United States he

would be transported to the penal colony at Van Diemen's Land. In contrast, the young James Stephens, who had been shot in Ballingarry, escaped to France, allegedly disguised as a maid. His departure was helped by the fact that Irish newspapers reported in mid-August that he had died of his wounds. He was commended for his loyalty to O'Brien and his behaviour as a good son and brother.[124] His escape proved to be particularly momentous as less than ten years later, he established the Fenian movement from his base in Paris.

Post-Ballingarry unrest

The defeat and capture of O'Brien did not mark an end to unrest in Ireland. Despite the public assurances made by the government and the conservative press, suggesting that the revolutionary threat had been extinguished, it took a long time for Ireland to be tranquil following the rising at Ballingarry. The British authorities had hoped that the arrest of O'Brien, the 'Rebel Chief' at the beginning of August would mark an end to agitation. However, Sir Henry Hardinge, an experienced soldier and former Chief Secretary, who had been appointed by the Duke of Wellington to assess the military situation in the country, was pessimistic. He regarded the military transport system as 'hopeless' and warned that 'in three-quarters of Ireland we are in an enemy's country'.[125] The actions of the government suggested that they concurred with his assessment. A naval cordon remained in place around the Irish coast. In mid-August, the officers were told to search all ships near to the shoreline – even those with a British flag. The purpose of the exercise was to 'seize all arms and ammunition attempted to be landed in any part of the country by Americans'. According to the Irish press, the government was acting on information received regarding the involvement of Irish-American sympathizers.[126] The network of informers remained in place and the government persisted in its close surveillance of all former members of the clubs, especially in Dublin, Liverpool and London.[127] In September 1848, the counties of Kilkenny, Tipperary and Waterford were proclaimed following a series of anti-government meetings.[128] Habeas Corpus had been suspended in July 1848 for a period of six months, but the Queen's speech on the opening of parliament on 1 February 1849 announced that the legislation was to be extended.

Regardless of the continuation of repressive measures, and the fact that so many leaders of the Confederation were in prison or in exile, further nationalist outbreaks took place in late 1848 and in 1849. McGee, a wanted 'felon' who had travelled circuitously from Glasgow to Sligo at the end of July, continued to hope that the Glasgow Repealers and the local Ribbonmen would add their support to the rising.[129] It was only when he was informed of the extent of the failure of O'Brien's rising that he decided to escape to America.[130] In the Abbeyfeale region of County

Limerick, Richard O'Gorman led a series of skirmishes and raids on the local towns. On 12 August the police received a report from Abbeyfeale, stating that O'Gorman, an escaped Confederate leader, accompanied by 700–800 men, had attacked the commissariat store. He and his followers also robbed the Royal Mail. Despite an increase in local constabulary, O'Gorman remained at large.[131] A constable who had been sent to apprehend him was captured by O'Gorman and his followers, who then destroyed the warrants for their arrest.[132]

A few weeks later, Irish newspapers reported that a further rebellion had taken place in September, under the command of Michael Doheny, who was still on the run and described as 'a leader more capable of conducting it than Smith O'Brien'. The rebels were alleged to have ransacked Lord Waterford's mansion at Curragh-More looking for arms, fired on a police barracks and taken control of the town of Carrick.[133] A more sustained outbreak took place in October 1848 centered on the Valley of Suir in the south-east of the country. It was led by Michael Doheny and John O'Mahony. They hoped that the commencement of the state trials in Clonmel would induce the people to rebel. When one American newspaper heard of these activities, it reported, 'A real rebellion has come at last.'[134]

Over the course of three days, there were isolated uprisings in parts of the south-east, but they were not coordinated and were mostly over within a day. O'Mahony attributed their failure to impatience and lack of skills among the leaders, lack of weapons, internal divisions and infiltration by 'emissaries' working for the British government.[135] During one conflict, a man was killed when a police station was attacked. The rebels were alleged to have been dressed in the uniform of the '82 Club, a society formed by Daniel O'Connell in memory of the establishment of Grattan's parliament in 1782.[136] In January 1849, O'Mahony fled to Paris and from there he moved to the United States where he later founded the American branch of the Fenian Brotherhood. Doheny also escaped to the United States and immediately wrote an account of the 1848 rising.[137] According to Michael Cavanagh, before leaving for France, O'Mahony had 'laid the foundation of a secret revolutionary organization in the Vale of the Suir', appointing a Central Directory comprised of James Fintan Lalor, Thomas Clarke Luby, Philip Gray and Joseph Brenan.[138] All of these men showed more skill in fighting as guerrilla leaders than they had done during the rising in July.[139] The *Dublin Freeman* viewed this unrest as 'arising from poverty and not a manifestation of political discontent'.[140] Poignantly, the backdrop to activities was the reappearance of potato blight, as virulent as it had been in 1846. However, the fact that these outbreaks took place during the state trials probably hardened the resolve of the government against the insurgents.

Unrest was not confined to Ireland. In the north-west of England many meetings had continued throughout July between Chartists and Repealers with intermittent talk of an uprising.[141] One of the most militant speakers was an Irish woman, Mrs Theobald, who frequently spoke in the Stockport area, urging defiant action while suggesting that her gender protected her from arrest.[142] The Stockport authorities wanted to arrest the leaders, but they were advised by the government to wait until the outcome of the Irish rising was known.[143] Following the Ballingarry episode though, they were told to proceed with the arrests. In other parts of Britain, the authorities responded to the news of the failed uprising in Ireland by banning public meetings.[144] Arrests were also made. In Liverpool, John Cuddy and James O'Brien were in custody charged with supplying arms to the Irish rebels. They were in touch with the Dublin Confederates and accused of selling pikes for 'the notorious Dr Reynolds'.[145]

Chartist and Confederate activities continued for a number of months after Ballingarry, even though the government was ruthless in suppressing such activities. The authorities, through their network of spies, were aware of these meetings in advance, including a planned outbreak in Ashton, near Manchester, on the night of 13 August. Although there was no outbreak, a meeting of Confederates and Chartists did take place, following which they marched in 'military order' towards Manchester. *The Times* reported that following this, 'the mob' chased the policemen with pikes. A few days later, a midnight meeting was to be held in Stevenson Square in Manchester. The local magistrates knew that this meeting would be held and were determined to deliver a fatal blow. Three hundred police and four companies of troops were brought to the town. At 10 pm they entered the local clubs concurrently and captured eleven of the leaders, including James Leach, who had been active in promoting a Chartist and Confederate alliance.[146]

A report, received from Manchester in the middle of August, stated that the local Chartists, assisted by Irish Confederates, would attack the town.[147] Responding to information that on 15 or 16 August the city would be burned and magistrates shot, '300 police simultaneously arrested a clutch of leading Chartists and Confederates, dealing the movement a severe blow at a crucial moment'.[148] The arrests were followed by a confrontation with the local police. It was only due to the intervention of the Special Constabulary that the authorities 'at length, succeeded in driving off the mob'.[149] On the same day, police in Liverpool, who were described as being 'well armed for an encounter', undertook a surprise attack on the Chartist club in Blackfriars where they found pistols, pikes, daggers, swords and gunpowder. Fourteen men were arrested.[150] Unbeknown to the Chartists in Liverpool and Manchester, since 1 April the local authorities had not only been surreptitiously attending their meetings, but had kept detailed accounts of the speakers, their personal lives and what they had said.[151] From September, the meetings became less well attended than previously, possibly because of the activities of informers and Special Constables. At the end of 1848, the government felt confident enough to take action against the local leaders in Liverpool and Manchester. Forty-six men were accused of having 'on many occasions unlawfully assembled and made seditious speeches and excited discontent and advice on procurement of arms'. Examples of their support for the Confederates, especially John Mitchel, were also cited.[152]

Support for the Confederates was not only evident in the north-west of England. On 16 August, a number of joint Chartist and Confederate uprisings were planned to take place in various locations in London. However, the government had received information concerning these plans, which meant that the police were able to break them up. In addition, the military in London were placed under arms. Police action included the arrest of Chartist leaders in the Orange Tree pub in Holborn in London. These men were alleged to have had powder and fire balls in their possession and, again, the police were acting on information that they had received from informers. The local division of police, armed with cutlasses, was joined by a magistrate, 150 constables, a sergeant, plus other local police divisions. When a magistrate and the police entered the building, the men offered no resistance. Pikes, daggers, pistols and swords were found. At a separate meeting of Chartists and Confederates at the Blue Anchor Yard near Westminster, a magistrate, accompanied by police, was confronted by a gang of armed Chartists. According to official reports, 'the Chartist and Confederate clubs intended to march out well armed, as they did some weeks back, and attack such buildings as might be pointed out to them'.[153] Overall, these activities demonstrated the extent and depth of dissatisfaction with the authorities. That the British government survived these challenges, unlike rulers in other parts of Europe, was largely due to the astute – and ruthless – deployment of the various forces of law and order at their disposal. Clearly, they took the threat of an Irish uprising very seriously in 1848.

Notes

1 *Tyrawley Herald*, 13 July 1848.
2 *Nation*, 1 July 1848.
3 'Address of the Council of the Irish Confederation to the Irish People', reprinted in Savage, *'98 and '48*, Appendix XI, p. 404.
4 Duffy, *Four Years*, p. 609.
5 *Tyrawley Herald*, 18 May 1848.
6 'The Protestant Repeal Association to the Protestants of Ulster, Adopted at a meeting of the Protestant Repeal Association, held in the Music Hall, Dublin, May 30 1848. J. Nuttall, M.D. presiding', reprinted in Savage, *'98 and '48*, Appendix X, pp. 399–402.
7 *Nation*, 15 July 1848.
8 *Belfast News-Letter*, 12 July 1848.
9 *The Tablet*, 8 July 1848.
10 Daunt, *Eighty-Five Years of Irish History*, p. 276.

11 *Warder*, 10 July 1848.

12 *Belfast News-Letter*, 11 July 1848.

13 *Warder*, 10 July 1848, 17 July 1848.

14 *Warder*, 10 July 1848.

15 *Belfast News-Letter*, 11 July 1848.

16 Ibid., 12 July 1848.

17 Ibid., 14 March 1848.

18 Davis, *Young Ireland*, p. 228.

19 *Northern Whig*, cited in *Wexford Independent*, 19 July 1848.

20 Daunt, *Eighty-Five Years of Irish History*, *p.* 278.

21 A Petition from Orange Lodge No. 12, National Archives of Ireland, Outrage Papers for County Down, 1848, 29 July 1848.

22 Russell to Clarendon, 17 July 1848: Bodleian Library, Clarendon Letter Books.

23 John Mitchel writes of this in his *Last Conquest*, p. 175. His accusation was verified by other sources, including Clarendon himself.

24 *Wexford Independent*, 29 July 1848.

25 Letter to Dr J.W. Beck, Secretary of Belfast Protestant Repeal Association from Sharman Crawford, dated 15 July 1848, *Nation*, 22 July 1848.

26 Colman O'Loughlen to O'Brien, 4 June 1848: Smith O'Brien Papers, NLI, MS 442. f.2465.

27 Thomas Halpin to O'Brien, 12 June 1848: ibid., f.2473.

28 *Nation*, 3 July 1848.

29 Reports of CD, TCD, MS 2038/9.

30 *Nation*, 1 July 1848; *Tyrawley Herald*, 3 August 1848.

31 *Nation*, 1 July 1848.

32 O'Brien, Memorandum, Smith O'Brien Papers, NLI, MS 442, n.d.

33 Ibid.

34 Ibid.

35 Ibid.

36 *Nation*, 15 July 1848.

37 O'Brien, Memorandum, Smith O'Brien Papers, NLI, MS 449, n.d.

38 O'Brien, Cahirmoyle, to un-named correspondent, 29 June 1848. Letters written by O'Brien between 1844 and 1850, NLI, MS 10515.

39 R.W. Russell, *America Compared with England: The Respective Social Effects of the American and English System of Government and Legislation* (London: J. Watson, 1849), pp. 141–3.

40 Belfast Petty Sessions to Chief Secretary, Dublin Castle, Outrage Papers for County Antrim (1848), NAI, 26 July 1848; Ibid., Town Clerk, Belfast on behalf of Police Committee to Chief Secretary, Dublin Castle, 26 July 1848.

41 George Bentinck, R.M., Belfast to Dublin Castle, 29 July 1848: ibid.

42 Brian Griffin, *The Bulkies: Police and Crime in Belfast, 1800–1865* (Dublin: Irish Academic Press, 1997), p 127.

43 *Nation*, 10 July 1848, 17 July 1848.

44 *Irish Felon*, 22 July 1848.

45 *Nation*, 29 July 1848.

46 McGee, *The Men of '48*, p. 284.

47 *Nation*, 29 July 1848; Kinealy, 'Invisible Nationalists' in Boardman and Kinealy, *The Year the World Turned?*, p. 138.

48 O'Brien, Memorandum, Smith O'Brien Papers, NLI, MS 449, n.d.
49 *Manchester Guardian*, 16 July 1848.
50 *Nation*, 3 July 1848.
51 Michael Doheny, *The Felon's Track: History Of The Attempted Outbreak In Ireland, Embracing The Leading Events In The Irish Struggle From The Year 1843 To The Close Of 1848* (first pub. in New York in 1849: reprinted in the UK in 1867, 1875), with preface by Arthur Griffith (Dublin: Gill, 1914), p. 155.
52 Cavanagh, *Memoirs of Meagher*, pp. 236–9.
53 *Nation*, 15 July 1848, 22 July 1848.
54 Cavanagh, *Memoirs of Meagher*, p. 244.
55 Ibid., p. 224.
56 Mitchel, *Jail Journal*, p. 68.
57 *Hansard*, House of Lords, 21–22 July 1849, pp. 618–23.
58 Maxwell, *Life and Letters*, p. 290.
59 Clarendon to Charles Greville, August 1848: ibid., p. 290.
60 Grattan was the son of Henry Grattan, whose name was immortalised in Grattan's parliament of 1782–1800. From 1831–1852, Henry Grattan, jr. was Whig MP for Meath.
61 Henry Grattan speaking in House of Commons, 24 July 1848, quoted in *Wexford Independent*, 29 July 1848.
62 *Tyrawley Herald*, 27 July 1848, 3 August 1848.
63 Wilson, *McGee*, pp. 215–6.
64 MacDermott, *Songs and Ballads*, p. 366.
65 Sloan, *O'Brien*, p. 247.
66 Meagher, 'Memoir of '48' in Cavanagh, *Memoirs of Meagher*, p. 245.
67 MacDermott, *Songs and Ballads*, p. 366.
68 Meagher, 'Memoir of 48' in Cavanagh, *Memoirs of Meagher*, p. 245.
69 *Nation*, 22 July 1848.
70 *Manchester Guardian*, 26 July 1848.
71 *Tyrawley Herald*, 27 July 1848.
72 *Wexford Independent*, 26 July 1848.
73 *Manchester Guardian*, 26 July 1848.
74 Ibid., 22 July 1848, 26 July 1848.
75 Pickering, *Chartism in Manchester*, p. 176.
76 Roger Swift, 'The "Specials" and the Policing of Chartism in 1848' in Boardman and Kinealy, *The Year the World Turned?* pp. 48–56.
77 Duffy, *Four Years*, p. 693.
78 *New York Herald*, 5 July 1848, 12 July 1848; *Boston Pilot*, 12 August 1848. One of the Young Ireland emissaries was Martin O'Flaherty: Duffy, *Four Years*, p. 693.
79 *New York Herald*, 5 July 1848.
80 *Boston Pilot*, 8 July 1848.
81 *Liverpool Mercury*, 21 July 1848.
82 Abstract of Constabulary Reports, TNA, (ACR), HO 45 2416A, 21 July 1848.
83 For more on Liverpool in 1848, see Kinealy, *1848 in Liverpool*.
84 Daily Reports of Horsfall, TNA, HO 45 2410B, August 1848.
85 *Liverpool Mercury*, 4 August 1848.
86 'Narrative of 1848 by John O'Mahony', NLI, MS 7977.

87 Meagher, 'Memoir of '48' in Cavanagh, *Memoirs of Meagher,* pp. 247–8.
88 Ibid., p.258.
89 Balch, *Ireland As I Saw It*, p. 384.
90 Meagher, 'Memoir of 48' in Cavanagh, *Memoirs of Meagher*, p. 247.
91 Ibid., p. 258.
92 *New York Nation*, 4 November 1848.
93 Duffy, *Four Years*, p. 693.
94 *Cork Examiner*, 26 July 1848.
95 Duffy, *Four Years*, p. 638.
96 Gwynn, 'The Priests and Young Ireland', 594–5.
97 *The Times*, 31 July 1848.
98 O'Brien, Memorandum, Smith O'Brien Papers, NLI, MS 449, n.d.
99 Copy of O'Brien's Letter to the Colliers, forwarded to the Lord Lieutenant on 29 July 1848, Bodleian Library, Clarendon Papers, Irish Box 33.
100 'Narrative of 1848 by John O'Mahony' on 1848 uprising, NLI, *Narratives,* MS 7977.
101 *Wexford Independent*, 29 July 1848.
102 Confidential Report by the Duke of Wellington, 28 July 1848, contained in Confidential Report of Henry Hardinge, Bodleian Library, Clarendon Papers, Irish Box 16, 24 August 1848.
103 This is based on reports of Father Fitzgerald, John O'Mahony, Terence MacManus, Richard Gorman and O'Brien.
104 According to a biographer of Clarendon, three of the insurgents were killed: Maxwell, *Life and Letters*, p. 290.
105 Wilson, *McGee*, pp. 216–9.
106 *Examiner* reported in *Wexford Independent*, 29 July 1848.
107 'Narrative of 1848 by John O'Mahony', NLI, MS 7977.
108 Davis, *Young Ireland*, p. 162.
109 Ibid., p. 160.
110 *The Times*, 31 July 1848.
111 Ibid.
112 Ibid., 1 August 1848.
113 Ibid., 2 August 1848, 3 August 1848.
114 *New York Nation*, 28 October 1848.
115 *Cork Examiner*, 21 August 1848.
116 *New York Nation*, 28 October 1848.
117 *The Times*, 11 August 1848.
118 Ibid., 15 August 1848.
119 *Tyrawley Herald*, 17 August 1848.
120 Ibid., 10 August 1848.
121 William Mitchel wrote to his brother, John, informing him that O'Gorman had escaped to Bretagne, although he later heard it was Constantinople: Mitchel, *Jail Journal*, p. 78.
122 John Dillon to his wife, Ady, 30 August 1848, 2 September 1848: Dillon Papers, TCD (f.68).
123 MacManus to Duffy, n.d., *c.* August 1848: ibid., TCD (F. 79).
124 *Tyrawley Herald*, 24 August 1848.
125 Report of H. Hardinge, 6 August 1848: Bodleian Library, Clarendon Papers, Irish Box 16.

126 *Cork Examiner*, 21 August 1848.
127 Spy Reports, TCD, MS 2038/9: Report of police informer, K division, PROL, HO 45 OS 3136, 1 January 1849.
128 Clarendon to Home Secretary, September 1848: Bodleian Library, Clarendon Papers, Irish Box 33.
129 Ribbonism was a secret agrarian movement that had been formed in the early nineteenth century to defend the rights of Catholics. It had traditionally had an ambivalent relationship with Repeal, due to the disapproval of Daniel O'Connell.
130 Wilson, *McGee*, pp. 212–14.
131 *Frazer's Magazine*, October 1848, vol. xxxviii, p. 475.
132 Clarendon to Home Secretary, 6 August 1848: Bodleian Library, Clarendon Papers, Irish Box 33.
133 *Frazer's Magazine*, October 1848, vol. xxxviii, p. 475.
134 *Northern Journal*, 3 October 1848.
135 John O'Mahony, 'Report on Proceedings in the Valley (Vale) of Suir in the autumn of 1848', NLI, MS 7977.
136 *Tipperary Vindicator*, 16 September 1848, 24 September 1848.
137 Doheny, *Felon's Track*.
138 Cavanagh, Life of Joseph Brennan, NLI, MS 3225, p. 36.
139 Davis, *Young Ireland*, p. 162.
140 *Dublin Freeman* quoted in *Northern Journal*, 3 October 1848.
141 Disturbances in 1848, Part Three, TNA, f.270, HO 45 2410, 4 August 1848.
142 Clerk of the Court House in Stockport to George Grey, 5 August 1848: ibid., f.229.
143 5 August 1848: ibid., f.265. Mrs Theobald was sometimes accompanied by Mrs Kellet, who chaired the meetings for her.
144 Proclamation from Mayor of Edinburgh, 1 August 1848: ibid., f.752.
145 *The Times*, 16 August 1848.
146 *Boston Pilot*, 12 August 1848; Duffy, *Four Years*, p. 693; *The Times*, 17 August 1848.
147 *Northern Star*, 19 August 1848.
148 Pickering, *Chartism in Manchester*, p. 177.
149 *The Times*, 16 August 1848.
150 Reported in *Northern Journal*, 5 September 1848.
151 Evidence of Treasury Solicitor, TNA, HO, TS 11. 137, pack 2. Liverpool Winter Assizes, 1848.
152 Ibid.
153 *The Times*, 17 August 1848.

7

'Graves which their own cowardice has digged': the aftermath

The trials of the state prisoners commenced a month after their capture. During this time, they were imprisoned in Kilmainham, Richmond or Newgate jails in Dublin, or in the Old Gaol at Clonmel. Apart from being bored and lonely, a number of them were sick, at one point Duffy fearing that he had contracted cholera. The prisoners communicated with each other by letter, some surreptitiously carried by their visitors, to avoid being read by the authorities. With so many men on the run, in prison, or under threat of arrest, women played an important role in visiting the men in jail and keeping their spirits up, and passing on confidential information.[1] The young poetess Eva, in particular, acted as a conduit for passing on secret correspondence.[2] Meagher charged her with smuggling out of his cell and looking after a letter he had written while in hiding, when he had been in secret negotiations with the authorities in Dublin Castle. In it, he said that he and his colleagues would surrender if they were allowed to leave the country. The Under-Secretary responded by offering to spare the lives of the leaders if they surrendered, but only if they also told their sympathizers to give up their weapons, and pleaded guilty to high treason. Meagher refused, saying that he had only made the initial offer because 'we had heard of the arrest of the poor fellows at Ballingarry [and] by making it, we might save these poor fellows, and their families, from destruction'.[3] Following the failure of these negotiations, Meagher can have been in little doubt that his capture would result in the Young Ireland leaders being sentenced to death. The letter remained in Eva's possession until her death.[4] While visiting the prisoners, Eva met and fell in love with the young medical student, Kevin O'Doherty, who had been imprisoned for promoting rebellion in his paper, the *Irish Tribune*.[5]

Despite their defeat, many of the arrested Confederates remained positive, believing that their actions had been honourable. On the eve of his trial, Richard Dalton Williams, a student who had used the pseudonym 'Shamrock', wrote to Martin saying:

Yes, our bungling at Ballingarry and elsewhere led many to believe that we were arrant cowards, but our greatest enemies admit that we have a high sense of honour and abundance of moral courage. Our small and young party held admirably together: there was no treachery within it and even now, while we appear vanquished and bleeding, the silent suffering of our captive leaders, from Mitchel to yourself, to the least amongst us, speaks powerfully to the hearts of thousands, and will bear worthy fruit at no very distant day.[6]

The prisoners were returned to Clonmel for the state trials in September. The continuing agitation in parts of Ireland possibly hardened attitudes to those who were being tried. O'Brien paid for legal assistance for the state prisoners who could not afford it themselves. Privately also, part of the money raised by the Directory in New York was used for their defence.[7] The judges were Chief Justice Blackburne, Chief Justice Doherty and Judge Moore, which one nationalist newspaper described as being 'all names of ill omen to the cause of Ireland'.[8] This prediction was prescient. The opening request of the defence lawyer, that the prisoners have the same rights as English prisoners who were being tried for high treason, was denied. An objection was made to the religious imbalance of the jury: out of the panel of 288 persons for O'Brien, only sixteen were Catholics.[9] The panel for John Martin contained thirty Catholics and 100 Protestants, while O'Doherty's panel comprised 134 Protestants and only forty-two Catholics.[10] The defence repeatedly protested against the preference given to Protestant jurors, with the panels from which the jury was chosen being overwhelmingly Protestant. Although requests for a change were made, the judges refused to accede to any of these. Moreover, the Protestant jurors were hand picked for their conservative political views.

In the trials of the editors convicted of treason-felony, John Martin, Kevin O'Doherty and Richard Dalton Williams, there was also careful jury selection. O'Doherty and Williams, the two young medical students who had edited the *Irish Felon*, were offered their freedom if they informed on their friends, but they refused to do so. O'Doherty was judged by his friends to have had 'a diabolically bad jury' and was found to be guilty.[11] Williams, who was defended by Samuel Ferguson, was acquitted: the sympathy of the jury allegedly being won over when Ferguson (himself a talented poet) read some of the poetry written by Williams.[12] Martin and O'Doherty were both sentenced to be transported for ten years. In his statement before the dock, Martin reiterated his belief in the inalienable right of all citizens to bear arms. He also said that he had been driven to make a political stance because he felt compelled to do something 'to make an end of the horrible scenes the country presents – the pauperism, the starvation, and crime and vice, and the hatred of all classes towards each other ... This is the reason I engaged in politics.'[13]

Duffy was tried five times in total, although he was eventually acquitted in April 1849. He was defended, brilliantly, by Isaac Butt. One of the charges against Duffy related to the article published on 29 July, *Jacta Alea Est*, which had appeared unsigned. On the eve of the trial Speranza disclosed to the Solicitor General her authorship, but he took no action. During the trial she announced that, 'I am the culprit if a crime there be. I wrote that article.'[14] Again, no action was taken, leading *Saunders' News-letter* to claim that her gender and her class had protected her from prosecution.[15] Nevertheless, the incident alarmed her sufficiently for her to declare that 'I shall never write sedition again.'[16]

Some junior members of the Confederation believed that Duffy had won his freedom by compromising his principles and endangering the freedom of others. John Mitchel, who was no admirer of Duffy, was sceptical when he read from his prison hulk in Bermuda that Duffy had produced people to provide evidence of his character at his trial. Moreover, he scorned the fact that Duffy had denied that he was the author of some of the inflammatory articles in the *Nation*. Mitchel, who deemed that British law had no legitimacy in Ireland, believed that Duffy had allowed himself to be 'cowed and prostrated to the earth'.[17] Mitchel was even more scathing when a petition was sent to the government pleading for Duffy not to be prosecuted if he agreed to withdraw from politics, which Mitchel regarded as 'miserable grovelling'.[18] In contrast, O'Brien and the other state prisoners defended Duffy's behaviour as being appropriate and beyond reproach.[19]

Using information provided by informers was an integral part of government strategy during the trials, despite the fact that it was notoriously unreliable. One of the first witnesses was John Hodges who, posing as a reporter, had been admitted to all of the Confederation meetings. During the trial he confirmed that O'Brien's speeches proved him to be 'a seditious and turbulent person'.[20] Informers and people who gave evidence against their former colleagues were disliked, with rumours that traitors were being paid £400 and given a free passage to America if they gave information to help the prosecutions.[21] Two witnesses refused to give evidence against O'Brien. John O'Donnell, a small farmer, declined to be sworn in 'under any circumstances', adding, 'Bring me out with a file of soldiers, and put a pile of bullets in me, I will never swear.' He gave his reason as being, 'My brother is concerned in this case: and I could never go home with the infamy of an informer on my brow.'[22] Richard Shea also refused to be sworn in, on the grounds that he would not give evidence 'against such a gentleman'.[23] Both O'Donnell and Shea were placed in custody for their actions.[24] Throughout the trials, the propaganda war continued. Duffy had sent a letter to the *Freeman*, which was reprinted widely, refuting a claim made in the *Daily News* that he was going to plead guilty. Duffy responded that this suggestion was 'a lie from beginning to end' and that its purpose was 'to sow dissention between me and my dear and honoured friend, Smith O'Brien'.[25]

Inevitably, public interest centered on the trials of O'Brien, Meagher,

MacManus and O'Donoghoe for high treason. O'Brien was the first prisoner to be tried on this charge and, like the other prisoners, he pleaded not guilty. O'Brien had been told by his brother, Sir Lucius O'Brien, that if he admitted unconditionally that his actions had been wrong and that he would renounce politics for ever, his treatment would be more lenient.[26] O'Brien refused to conciliate, leading his defence team to suggest their strategy would be:

> As long as you are convinced of the moral rectitude of what you have done, simply to set public opinion and feeling right as respects some important points in your character and history, and thus to make leniency of the part of the government not a matter of <u>mercy</u> but of <u>necessity</u>.[27]

O'Brien proved defiant to the end. He objected to the jurors returned by the Sheriff, as only one-eighteenth of them were Catholics which, he believed, would prejudice his case.[28] James Henry Monaghan, the Attorney General, responded that the selection was 'equally and impartially made'.[29] The trial of the young and dashing Meagher undoubtedly attracted the most attention. In a speech, delivered at the close of his trial and while awaiting sentence, he said, 'Having done what I felt to be my duty – having spoken what I felt to be the truth – I now bid farewell to the country of my birth, my passion, and my death ... Pronounce, then my Lords, the sentence which the law directs. I am prepared to hear it. I trust, I shall be prepared to meet its execution.'[30]

Although the four prisoners were convicted, the juries asked that the men be shown mercy. The first verdict to be made was on O'Brien. It stated that, 'The sentence is that you, William Smith O'Brien, be taken from hence to the place from whence you came, and be thence drawn on a hurdle to the place of execution, and be there hanged by the neck until you are dead; and that afterwards your head shall be severed from your body, and your body divided into four quarters, and be disposed of as Her Majesty shall think fit. And may God have mercy on your soul.' The same sentence was passed on Meagher, MacManus and O'Donoghoe, but the jury, when pronouncing MacManus to be guilty added, 'We earnestly recommend the prisoner to the merciful consideration of the crown.'[31] O'Brien responded to the verdict simply by stating that he had done his duty. It was left to Meagher to make a speech. He predicted that people in Ireland 'will judge of those sentiments and that conduct in a light far different from that in which the jury by which I have been convicted will judge them'.[32] Copies of Meagher's speeches during the trial were printed and displayed throughout Ireland.[33]

The behaviour and comportment of the four men throughout the trial and when the sentences were passed gave them nobility that counterbalanced the fiasco of the rising. Following their sentencing, O'Brien, Meagher and MacManus all privately suggested that although they had failed, some good would eventually come out of their actions. On the evening that the sentence of death was passed on Meagher, O'Brien wrote him a letter of consolation which ended with the words 'never despair'.[34] He wrote similar messages to both MacManus and O'Donoghoe. Meagher's response was typically ebullient and gracious, sending regards to O'Brien's wife and sister. More seriously, he added, 'we have done our parts' and that ultimately success would come from their failure.[35] MacManus's response was similar, confiding in O'Brien of 'the satisfaction I feel in my own mind of having discharged my duty to my country ... I am of opinion that the English government must someday negotiate ... Whatever errors we have committed we have acted our part. Let those who come after us do the same, and do it they will.'[36] Of the four convicted men, O'Donoghoe seemed to have been most affected by his time in jail, with his appearance at trial being described as 'pale and [he] seemed to have suffered in bodily health from his imprisonment'. His jury had been composed entirely of Protestants.[37]

The news of the trials was followed in the United States by former colleagues. John Dillon, one of the escaped leaders, regarded Meagher's speech as 'superior, vastly superior, to Tone's or Emmet's'. O'Brien's defence was viewed as an attempt to vindicate his actions and to protect other people involved.[38] While imprisoned in Bermuda, Mitchel heard of the convictions of O'Brien and his other colleagues. He was particularly impressed by Meagher's conduct and words and wrote in his diary, 'I have a hope that will not leave my soul in darkness – a proud hope that Meagher and I together will stand side by side on some better day – that there is work for us yet to do.'[39] He did not realize that their next meeting would be as exiles in Van Diemen's Land.

The Irish state prisoners found support at the highest political level. President Polk asked his Secretary of State, James Buchanan, 'to interpose in a delicate way and intimate to the British government that it would be very gratifying to the Government and people of the U.S. if that Government could, consistently with its own sense of duty, extend a general amnesty or pardon to English [sic] subjects in Ireland, who had recently attempted by a revolution to free themselves of the oppression of the government'. He went on to say, 'We have no right to make such a demand, but simply to request it, and appeal to the magnanimity of Great Britain not [to] execute Mr Smith O'Bryan [sic] and other Irish Patriots who are understood to be under arrest for Treason.'[40] Polk believed that this action would be popular because 'the whole American people with rare exceptions deeply sympathize with the oppressed and suffering people of Ireland, and if by interposing our good offices the lives of O'Bryan [sic] and other leading patriots can be saved, I am sure we will do an act of humanity, and discharge a duty which will be acceptable to our own country and, indeed, to the civilized world, wherever liberal principles are cherished'.[41]

The nationalist press overseas was outraged. The London *Tablet* claimed, 'Never was there a more disgraceful exhibition than the government has made of itself in this great trial.' Even more critically, the *New York Truth Teller* stated that if the men were hanged 'it is a confession of weakness on the part of the Government, and an act that will render England odious to all mankind'.[42] The New York *Nation* called on readers in America to, 'Admire, free citizens, the elaborate ceremonial of this new massacre by the English in Ireland.' They went on to say that those who questioned why these men had acted so irrationally 'may well ask these questions who never saw years of famine ... who know not how low the heart of a nation could fall, through the trials of hunger, poverty and public alms'.[43] In contrast, some sections of the British press continued to mock the state prisoners. As early as November 1848, *Frazer's Magazine* predicted that O'Brien would be shown mercy 'because both his character and his actions had inspired in this country a mixed feeling of pity and contempt'.[44]

Within Ireland there was outcry against the harshness of the sentences and the methods employed by the government to bring them about. Even some Orangemen demanded that the four men should receive a reprieve.[45] The government had lost respect due to the fact that they had 'packed' the juries. At the end of 1848, a petition signed by 41,000 people was presented by the Reverend Spratt to the Lord Lieutenant, protesting against the deliberate exclusion of Catholics at the political trials. The petition was signed by prominent Protestant church leaders and peers, including Lord Ffrench. The Lord Lieutenant's response was that it was the duty of the public prosecutor to exclude persons 'of whatever religious persuasion they might be, who could only on reasonable grounds be supposed to be under the undue influence of such opinions and such views'.[46] Mitchel, however, believed that the packing of juries with 'Castle Protestants' had 'exasperated religious animosities in Ireland' by emphasizing differences between the religions.[47]

Events in Ireland overshadowed what was happening in England to the supporters of the Irish Confederates. At the end of 1848, a Special Commission was held in Liverpool to try the men who were referred to as 'the English Confederates'. Two of the Confederate leaders in Liverpool, Dr Reynolds and Thomas O'Brien, had already escaped to the United States, despite a countrywide search for them. Nine men were found guilty of having conspired to 'purchase arms to transmit for rebellious purposes to Ireland; and also an intent to raise an insurrection in Ireland, and to procure arms for the purpose of obstructing the law in this country'. Their sentences ranged from three months to two years' imprisonment.[48]

O'Brien, Meagher, MacManus and O'Donoghoe were not hanged, but were kept in jail not knowing what their fate would be. In correspondence with fellow Confederates, Meagher continued to style himself either as 'Member of the Council of Five' or President of the Grattan Club. He referred to his own career as being 'short and sorrowful'.[49] Nonetheless, he maintained that he had hope in the Celtic race and for 'my country, her peace, her liberty, her glory'.[50] Eleven months after the sentence was passed the government suggested that if the four men asked for pardons, their sentences could be reduced. The four state prisoners refused to ask for pardons, thereby forcing the government to pass legislation allowing treasonable sentences to be commuted to transportation, without a pardon being requested. Each of the prisoners objected to this being done. The legislation provided for the four state prisoners awaiting execution to be sent to Van Diemen's Land, which was also to be the destination of Martin and O'Doherty.

When it was announced that the state prisoners were to be transported, a number of militant supporters, led by Edward O'Donoghoe, brother of Patrick, wanted to rescue them. He persuaded a reluctant Fintan Lalor to support them, although the latter believed that the attempt would end with them getting their 'skulls split'.[51] Little came of the rescue plans. On his prison hulk in Bermuda, Mitchel heard of his former colleagues being transported. He drew comfort from the fact that half of the transported felons were Catholic and half were Protestant, believing that this circumstance, 'will surely help to convince the North (if anything can ever teach the blockhead North) that our cause is no sectarian cause'.[52] Within a year, for reasons outside the control of the British government, Mitchel would join his former friends and colleagues in Van Diemen's Land.

American support

As the state trials were commencing in Ireland, revolutionary activities were continuing in the United States. The lack of synchronization between events in Ireland and America had become most acute in the wake of the failed uprising. Throughout August, as news trickled through to the States of the arrest or escape of many Confederate leaders, it was accompanied by reports suggesting that the rebellion was far from over. Some of the information was erroneous. An article that appeared in the *Boston Courier* and other newspapers, based on a letter from Ireland dated 2 August, described a battle that had allegedly taken place between 5,000 British troops and 2,000 Repealers in County Derry.[53] Ironically, as some of the Irish Confederate leaders were escaping to America, large numbers of Irish nationalists were reported to be sailing the other way.[54] Therefore, despite the easy defeat of the uprising in Ballingarry, the government was privately concerned that the nationalist threat was not over.[55] They were particularly worried that the arrival of the Irish Brigade from the United States might rekindle the republican flame. This fear was given substance when, at the beginning of August, an address was circulated in parts of Ireland which was attributed to 'The Friends of Ireland in New York', suggesting that support was on its way.[56]

Throughout the summer months, elaborate preparations for a brigade to be sent to Ireland from New York intensified. Moreover, many of the differences which had plagued the various Repeal organizations in the United States appeared to have been temporarily overcome. The Directory, which was coordinating the activities of the disparate groups, had appointed fifty men to tour the States and establish a national network.[57] It had also initiated a fund-raising drive with the aspiration of raising $1million for a forthcoming struggle. To promote its work, it convened a monster meeting in Vauxhall Gardens in New York, which was judged to be the largest political meeting ever to have taken place in the city.[58] Even moderate nationalists appeared to be caught up in the revolutionary fervour. Bishop Hughes of New York, previously a supporter of moral force, contributed to the fund with the proviso that his $500 donation should be used to buy shields, not weapons.[59] On 7 August, he addressed a meeting in New Orleans, which raised almost $6,000 for Ireland.[60]

Throughout August, further meetings took place in Boston and New York on behalf of Ireland.[61] Reports from Ireland that the rebellion was under way had added more ardour to these meetings and, on 14 August, the New York Directory issued an address, which was printed in many newspapers, saying that 'the blow is struck'. It reported that, 'O'Brien has taken a strongly fortified position with a force of one hundred thousand, and a score of the Irish leaders are already in the field with a force of arms and courage at heart sufficient to meet all opposition'. It chided Irish-Americans, asking:

> Why sleeps the Irish blood in America? Precious hours are being wasted; precious blood flowing. The Dying call for Vengeance. The Living Hope of Ireland implores your aid. Let us promptly answer that call. Awake to instant action! Ask no questions, but remit funds at once to Robert Emmet, our Treasurer. Trust to our zeal, determination and prudence, and neither you nor Ireland shall be disappointed.[62]

The British government watched the activities of the Directory with growing concern. Moreover, a new threat had emerged which greatly alarmed them. The war between the United States and Mexico had ended in July and it was followed by reports of veterans of the war being recruited into the Irish Brigade.[63] The government's concern was exacerbated by the fact that their main spy, Samuel Saunders, had been exposed.[64] The Consulate in New York, however, informed them that on 2 August seventy-five men who had recently returned from Mexico had boarded a packet ship bound for Liverpool.[65] At the beginning of September, the same Consulate reported that during the previous five days over 2,000 Irish men – principally veterans of the Mexican War – had sailed for Ireland.[66] They warned that every ship from the States that was destined for either Liverpool or Ireland carried a member of the Irish Brigade and possibly a veteran from Mexico. Lord Palmerston also informed the Home Office that he had received information from New York that 'emissaries continue to sail from that port with a view of insti-gating rebellion in Ireland. They are sent by the Irish Republican Union – within the last five days, over 200 have gone to Liverpool or Ireland'. He believed they would be easy to recognize because they had been previously fighting in Mexico, which meant 'their complexions are swarthy'. The names and descriptions of some of the men who had sailed were provided.[67] Furthermore, the government suspected that the Irish Brigade was chartering vessels, ostensibly to take corn supplies to Ireland but, in reality, carrying arms and ammunition there.[68]

The public dissemination of this information led the *Dublin Evening Post* to observe that, in regard to support from America, the British government had been 'made minutely acquainted, long before they sailed, with the points of departure, the names of the vessels, the nature of the freight, the sympathizers on board, and the number and names of the captains and crew, all written in the United States'.[69] Despite this flow of information, the British government was alarmed by developments in America and they issued a formal diplomatic protest concerning 'the assis-tance in skilled military Instruction, in money and in Arms, which has been sent, from the United States to the traitorous conspirators in Ireland, and you will observe that such open encouragement to rebellion in a Country with which the United States are at peace is not consistent with international Duties'.[70]

Despite the government's alarm, it soon became apparent that reports concerning the Irish Brigade had been greatly exaggerated and that much misinformation was being provided. At the end of July, an American liner was captured by two English frigates and it was found to be carrying 50 sacks of weapons disguised as 'relief flour' for distribution to the destitute in Ireland.[71] Three veterans of Mexico were arrested in County Carlow in September 1848 and they admitted that they had come 'to assist in the rebellion', but that they were 'disappointed' by the lack of agitation in the country.[72] Yet arrests and seizures of ships were rare despite the vigilance of the Liverpool and Irish authorities and, by the end of September, the government were beginning to believe that the threat from America had been exaggerated.[73] Moreover, when news of the easy defeat of the upris-ing in Ballingarry reached the States in mid-August, it undermined support for the activities of the Irish Brigade. In October, the British Consul in Washington informed the British government, with undisguised delight, that the outcome of 'the entire failure of the attempted uprising under Smith O'Brien' had 'even more than their anticipated effect of damping the enthusiasm which was felt in this country for the expected Irish rebellion, for it seems to have put a stop to the movement of the sympathizers altogether'.[74]

Although by October the transatlantic revolutionary threat appeared to be over, the events of the previous few months had strained relations between the governments of the United States and Britain. Since July, a small number of Americans or Irishmen returning from America had been arrested in Ireland, although many of them had been subsequently released.[75] Two leading members of the Irish Republican Union, however, James Bergin and Richard Ryan, had been detained on charges of treason. They were both imprisoned in Newgate prison in Dublin where every night Bergin would sing the 'Star Spangled Banner'. When his singing was banned by the governor of the jail he continued to sing and the other prisoners joined in.[76] Information concerning Bergin's journey to Ireland had been provided to the British government by one of their informers in New York, Joseph Pinkerton, who claimed that Bergin was a leader of the Irish Brigade. He was described as being 'in appearance stout, dark complexion, large black whiskers which he wears around his chin, voice rather husky, and has a slight inclination to stoop'.[77] The detention of Bergin, who claimed American citizenship, was objected to by the American authorities, with the ambassador in London demanding that he be returned to the United States immediately.[78]

The detention of Ryan proved to be even more complicated. Ryan, who claimed that he was a naturalized American citizen and had been illegally arrested, appealed directly to the American President to intervene on his behalf.[79] When the American Ambassador enquired about the case and the grounds for arresting him, the Lord Lieutenant explained that Ryan had been detained under the Treason Felony Act of 1848 'as being concerned in treasonable practices, and from the facts that have come to his knowledge, the Lord Lieutenant entertains no doubt of his guilt, or of his being a subject of Her Majesty'. He included a privately written note in which he stated that Ryan was an English subject and had been charged with treasonable practices.[80] However, the American Embassy in London made an official protest about the treatment of American citizens in Ireland which they described as 'arbitrary and offensive'. In particular, they objected to two memoranda issued in August; the first one had ordered that all American citizens be observed and detained, whilst the second, more moderate, one had restricted detention to returned migrants. The Ambassador claimed that naturalized American citizens should not be treated in this way, pointing out that, 'The subjects of other countries who from choice have abandoned their native land, and, accepting the invitation which our laws present, have emigrated to the United States and become American citizens, are entitled to the very same rights and privileges as if they had been born in this country. To treat them in a different manner would be a violation of our plighted faith, as well as our solemn duty.'[81]

The American Ambassador in London asked the Home Office to explain the regulations that had been adopted by authorities in Ireland relative to American citizens. Thomas Redington of Dublin Castle responded that due to the disturbed state of the country he had called 'the particular attention of the magistrates and constabulary to those provisions of the law in this country affecting strangers who, being found in any district, and being brought before a magistrate, may be unable to render a satisfactory account of themselves'. He admitted that some people had been arrested:

In consequence of the information which reached the Irish Government, of the active steps being taken in the United States for the purpose of overturning Her Majesty's dominion in Ireland, and the means which it was openly stated as well as secretly arranged should be adopted for that purpose, it became the duty of the Lord Lieutenant to take special precautions regarding persons arriving from the United States; and instructions were accordingly issued by the Inspector General of the Constabulary, with the approval of the Lord Lieutenant, directing that a particular surveillance should be exercised as regarded them; and that the provisions of the law which have reference to the detention of strangers, should be rigidly enforced in such cases, until a communication had been made to the government. It is possible that in carrying out the precautionary measures, some individuals may have suffered temporary inconvenience; but if these stringent regulations have been a source of annoyance to the citizens of the United States visiting Ireland, it must be remembered that this has been occasioned by the conduct of their fellow citizens at home, who under the protection of American laws have openly plotted for the overthrow of Her Majesty's authority in Ireland and the Lord Lieutenant has only adopted measures in order to check those treasonable designs. His Excellency desires at the same time to add that he is not aware of the regulations issued by the Inspector General having been carried out in a harsh and arbitrary manner. In one instance only is he aware of complaints having been made by American travellers of the regulations referred to; and the most prompt steps were taken for the discharge of those gentlemen on it being ascertained that their movements were unconnected with the proceedings of the disaffected in this country.

Furthermore, the Lord Lieutenant was insistent that there existed 'no ground for directing any relaxation of the measures put in force for frustrating the treasonable objects which may be contemplated either by the subjects of Her Majesty or the citizens of a foreign state'. He also refused to provide copies of any order issued by the Inspector of the Constabulary on this subject to those who demanded them, 'not feeling it could be required of any government to communicate the instructions which they may have issued to their officers relative to the enforcement of certain statutes – and has referred those persons who may consider themselves aggrieved to the provisions of the law which has been put in force'.[82]

The activities of the British government regarding American citizens had come to the notice of the Secretary of State, James Buchanan.[83] In August, at the instigation of the British Foreign Secretary, Lord Palmerston, the British Consul in Washington had called on Buchanan to draw his attention to 'the unjustifiable proceedings of certain citizens of the United States who openly encourage and assist rebellion against Her

Majesty's government in Ireland by sending skilled military assistance, arms and money to the rebels, as well as by the use of the most inflammatory language at public meetings and in newspapers'. Buchanan did not deny that this was the case, but he stated that the United States would abide by their neutrality laws. He added that, as a lawyer, he recognized that the language of the Irish Republican Unions was 'violent and threatening' but insisted that they had done nothing illegal, therefore 'any prosecutions which the United States government might now institute against persons composing these societies would result in the acquittal of those persons'. Buchanan warned that the prosecution of American citizens would only serve to increase the existing support for Ireland. Moreover, 'such a proceeding would be made a handle for attacking the present administration with a view to influence the coming Presidential election, by thousands who otherwise never would have dreamed of troubling themselves of the affairs of Ireland'.[84] He further surprised the British diplomat by admitting that he personally 'sympathized' with the Irish Republican Union and had attended some of their meetings.[85] When he was asked to intervene, Buchanan concurred that Ryan was a naturalized American citizen and he pointed out to British officials that 'treason cannot be committed by a citizen of the United States against a foreign government'. The lack of support from Buchanan led the Foreign Office to advise its representatives in the United States not to approach him 'in a formal matter' on this topic again.[86] The British Ambassador agreed that it would be unwise to prosecute any Americans but hoped that when news of O'Brien's easy defeat was circulated, interest and support for Ireland would fall away.[87]

The American government's stance in regard to Irish nationalism annoyed the British authorities. Palmerston was particularly peeved, on the grounds that:

> it is notorious to all the world that proceedings of the most hostile character toward the British government have of late taken place in the United States; that not only private associations have been formed, but that public meetings have been held for the avowed purpose of encouraging, assisting and organizing rebellion in Ireland, with a view to dismember the British Empire ... These associations and public meetings have been composed not only of Irish citizens, but also of natural born citizens of the United States ... These conspirators in the United States have sent to Ireland, to assist the rebellion which they had intended to organize, money, arms ammunition and active agents ... Some of the agents have been arrested, and must be dealt with according to their deserts.[88]

Despite Palmerston's aggressive assertions, in November 1848 both Bergin and Ryan were released. By this stage, the insurrectionary threat had passed in Ireland.

In New York, the leaders of the Directory attempted to redirect their energies by suggesting that they should utilize their resources for an invasion of Canada, which would force the British government to deploy troops from Ireland.[89] As Michael O'Connor explained, 'If Irish independence was to be achieved it would be necessary to attack England in her dominions ... Canada must and will be invaded whenever Ireland rises.'[90] For the time being, an uprising in Ireland appeared to be unlikely and the enthusiasm and support that had manifested itself in the summer of 1848 quickly evaporated. Nonetheless, the constant waves of impoverished Irish poor emigrating to the United States, together with the arrival of escaped leaders of the Confederation, ensured that anti-British feeling and the desire for Irish independence did not disappear. In turn, nationalist activities in the United States continued to concern the British government who, at the beginning of 1849, confiscated copies of McGee's *New York Nation* that were being sold in Ireland.[91] The events of 1848 had demonstrated that Irish independence had become a transatlantic issue, and that America, rather than France, had become the natural ally of nationalists.

Post-rising rebellions

Despite the absence of so many Confederate leaders and the continuation of famine in many parts of the country, in 1849 there were signs of a resurgence in radical activities in the south-east of Ireland. One of the main forces behind the renewed agitation was James Fintan Lalor, whose radical writings on the need for a social revolution had greatly influenced John Mitchel. Lalor had been imprisoned in July 1848 but was released shortly afterwards due to ill-health. Following this, he, supported by Thomas Clarke Luby and encouraged by Father Kenyon, prepared to found a new radical newspaper in Dublin. He also tried to revive the clubs. His main purpose was to plan for a further uprising. Lalor's supporters were all '48 men', whom he described as 'bold, young fellows not wanting in zeal and energy'.[92] During the summer of 1849, he travelled around Ireland, mostly Munster, in order to spread support for his organization.[93] Lalor's activities in 1849 were all the more remarkable given that he was suffering from recurring bronchitis.[94]

Lalor was supported by Joseph Brenan. The two men had met when writing for the *Irish Felon*. Brenan had been arrested in July 1848 for selling copies of the paper. He was unofficially engaged to the radical female poet, 'Mary', Ellen Downing, who had contributed to his earlier paper, the *Cork Magazine*.[95] When released from jail in March 1849, Brenan was appointed editor of the radical *Irishman*. He was supported by Jean de Frazer and James Clarence Mangan.[96] The *Irishman* had been founded in June 1848 by Bernard Fulham, who had been the registered publisher of the *Nation*. It was inspired by the politics of John Mitchel, whom it described as 'the most practical and clear-sighted member of the Confederation'.[97] Most of the writers associated with the *Irishman* had belonged to the radical wing of the Irish Confederation. The paper was disliked by Duffy and more conservative former members of the Confederation, who accused Fulham of being opportunistic. The new paper combined nationalist and socialist aspirations, going even further than the ideas of land redistribution that had been propagated by Lalor. The front page of its first edition consisted of a eulogy to Mitchel, describing him as 'one of those men rarely met with in the pages of history. He possesses the most vigorous political sagacity and a courage that no danger could daunt.'[98] By the third edition, the circulation had reached 15,000 weekly. Outside Ireland, it had sales in Glasgow, London, Newcastle-Upon-Tyne, Barnsley, Bradford and Liverpool.[99] Despite the repression of other nationalist newspapers in 1848, the *Irishman* continued to be published throughout that year and until September 1849. The paper, therefore, became an important vehicle for keeping revolutionary ideals alive. On 8 September, as final preparations were being made for a rising, Brenan urged the people to hold on to the harvest. Those who refused to, he suggested, should be 'spurned from the doors of the nation – may they be cast forth from the family of man, and consigned to the famine graves which their own cowardice has digged'.[100]

Since the beginning of 1849, the government had been receiving information that the Dublin clubs were undergoing a revival and their members were in constant communication with the state prisoners.[101] They had even started their own newspaper, *The Clubbist*. Although it was supposed to be secret, the government received copies of it from its informers.[102] The trigger for a rising was to be Duffy's conviction.[103] His eventual acquittal, and the transportation of the state prisoners in the summer of 1849, diffused some of the revolutionary ardour. Given the poverty of the country, the absence of so many leaders, and the measures put in place by the government, a large-scale insurrection was unlikely. A small uprising did take place on 16 September 1849, but not in Dublin. It was located in Cappoquin in west Waterford.

The Cappoquin rising was led by Lalor and Brenan and supported by John O'Leary, John Savage and Thomas Clarke Luby, a Protestant law student. They attacked the local constabulary barracks. In total, seventy men took part, most of whom were armed only with pikes. They had sought the blessing of the local Prior in advance, but he refused to give it. He also refused to lend the insurgents his gun. The small number of armed police within the barracks was able to defeat the group, killing two of the rebels. The next day, Special Constables were sworn in and the Royal Fusiliers were sent to Cappoquin. Despite the heavy police presence, Brenan escaped and, like so many of his fellow Young Irelanders, he went into exile in the United States. He ended up in New Orleans, where he worked as a journalist and met up with Mitchel, his hero. Although most of the leaders escaped, arrests continued in Cappoquin for a number of weeks. The town remained under military occupation until September

1852.[104] Lalor did not escape, but was, again, arrested. He died of bronchitis in December 1849 while in prison. Fourteen other insurgents were sentenced to be transported, although only eleven were actually sent. On 13 September 1850, the first seven men were transported to Van Diemen's Land. While there, they appeared to have no contact with the original Young Ireland exiles, nor did they feature in Mitchel's *Jail Journal*. The Cappoquin rising marked the end of the revolutionary cycle in Ireland that had commenced in July 1848. In November 1850, Clarendon wrote that, 'Upon the whole I should say that this country is in a more tranquil, progressive and satisfactory state than we have ever known it.'[105] Yet it was not until August 1853 that he agreed to reduce the extra police force that had been located in County Kilkenny since 1848.[106]

Post-1848 Ireland

Although it concerned the government, the flurry of revolutionary activities after July 1848 was for the most part isolated and unnoticed by the majority of Irish people. The activities of Lalor, Brenan and others took place against the backdrop of hunger and social dislocation caused by the reappearance of potato blight in the previous year. It meant that, yet again, there was extensive starvation and homelessness in the country, with one million people depending on the draconian Poor Law for survival. The political agitators who escaped to America travelled on the same ships that carried hundreds of thousands of famine-worn Irish out of Ireland. For those who remained in the country, years of political agitation had ended in failure, in 1843 as well as in 1848. The decade which had commenced with the formation of the Repeal Association had ended with both constitutional and physical force nationalism in tatters.

In Ireland, the defeat of the uprising and disappearance of so many of the former leaders left a vacuum in popular politics. Furthermore, Irish society was demoralized following three consecutive years of famine. The rapid demise of the Repeal Party after 1848 effectively ended an Irish parliamentary presence, even though the Franchise Act of 1850 had increased the electorate. A more radical variety of the nationalist press had briefly been kept alive by the *Irishman*, although the paper had been dogged by financial problems and it disappeared following the defeat of the Cappoquin rising. Nor did the demand for parliamentary reform disappear altogether after 1848 despite the wholesale arrest of many of its leaders. In Ireland, radical politics were kept alive by the emergence of the Irish Democratic Association, which was also associated with Bernard Fulham.[107] Like the *Irishman*, it attempted to fuse nationalist with socialist politics. Although the alliance did not have the populist appeal or mass support of earlier movements, its public meetings in 1850 were well attended. It also had support in Britain.[108] By the end of the year though, the political initiative had passed to the Tenant League movement. Sixty years later, James Connolly acknowledged his ideological debt to the work of Fulham and others.[109]

The most senior member of the Confederation to remain in Ireland after 1848 was Charles Gavan Duffy. He had been tried a total of five times, but each time was acquitted. He was finally freed in April 1849, when he was found innocent by an independent jury. The nationalist *Irishman* averred that since the previous year feeling against jury-packing had been so strong that the government could no longer resort to such actions with impunity.[110] On 1 September 1849, Duffy revived the *Nation*, albeit in a modest form. From the start, he used the paper to advocate a return to constitutionalism. The paper's previous objective of gaining national independence was less prominent and the language used was more temperate. Instead of preaching separation from Britain, the economic improvement of Ireland and the amelioration of relations between landlords and tenants were Duffy's primary objectives.[111] The post-1849 journal also lacked the spirit and confidence of the pre-1848 paper. Significantly, many of its finest writers were in prison, in exile or overawed by their political rout in the previous year. Consequently, political polemic was replaced by news from the exiles in Van Diemen's Land, an American letter and Meagher's account of why the 1848 uprising had failed.[112] The new *Nation* included poems by Eva and Finola, who had been regular contributors in the heady days of 1848. Although Speranza occasionally contributed, she avoided political topics.[113] Mitchel was scathing about the political intentions of the new *Nation*, particularly Duffy's rejection of physical force. He believed that the true spirit of the former *Nation* was being represented by the underfunded and thinly staffed *Irishman*, edited by Joseph Brenan, which (to Mitchel's amusement) claimed to be preaching his doctrines.[114]

Apart from reviving the *Nation*, Duffy, together with Maurice Leyne, attempted to re-unite the remnants of Old and Young Ireland in a new organization, the Irish Alliance. Duffy described the Alliance as continuing the work of the short-lived Irish League. As had been the case with the League though, John O'Connell refused to support it. In answer to critics that the League had ended in the fiasco of the uprising, Duffy responded that despite the 'shadow of Ballingarry ... When another generation comes to review the history of these times, I am well convinced there is nothing they will pause upon with such fond pride and pity as the noble devotedness which, in the midst of mean men and the meanest motives, had still preserved the old heroic instinct –the grand-martyr faith that could die for the truth.'[115] From his exile in Van Diemen's Land, Mitchel was a harsh critic of these developments, describing the Alliance as providing a 'humble imitation' of Conciliation Hall, and warning that 'though fresher now than the real old Hall, is destined, I think, to decompose and putrefy even sooner'.[116] Nonetheless, Mitchel did have some sympathy with his former supporters in Ireland, observing, 'Those refugees are exiles, too – have suffered, as well as we, the demolition of home, of means, and hopes. Moreover, they are still present in the scene of our failure; still stung by the coward taunts of our enemies, and feeling the onus on them to do something.'[117]

Inevitably, the failure of 1848 changed the nature of political debate in Ireland and Duffy showed himself willing to adapt to the new climate. In November 1849 Duffy, helped by Frederick Lucas of the *Tablet* newspaper, organized a national conference, which laid the foundation for a tenant right movement in the 1850s. Following this, Duffy focused his energies on tenant rights, which gave an early recognition to the centrality of the land question in the struggle for independence. As a consequence, the political focus changed with the demand for national independence being muted, while demands for land reform appeared more in the foreground. Significantly, the movement had the backing of the outspoken Archbishop of Tuam, John MacHale. Archbishop Paul Cullen, however, was unwilling to support Duffy, regarding him as the 'Irish Mazzini'. Duffy's approach was less radical than that proposed by Lalor and Brenan, whose ideas were a central component of the Land League almost thirty years later. Rather, it was more in keeping with the Ulster Tenant Right Association which had been founded in May 1847 by William Sharman Crawford and James McKnight, both liberal Protestants.

Between 6 and 9 August 1850 a Tenant Right conference was held in Dublin, which concluded with the formation of the Irish Tenant League. The Tenant League brought together Catholics and Protestants and representatives from the north and the south, giving it a national unity that had been the elusive ideal of Young Ireland. One of its first aims was the adoption of the 'Ulster Custom' throughout the country, which would provide security of tenure and the freedom of sale for all tenants. A few weeks later, the editorial in the *Nation* declared that the League was going to give a new message to the people, namely, that the land question would be central to its new philosophy.[118]

Despite the Irish Tenant League having few charismatic personalities, in 1852 it returned forty candidates to Westminster, which almost equalled what Repeal had achieved in its heyday of 1832. To some extent, this was partly an anti-landlord vote, but it was an indication of the centrality of the land question in parliamentary politics.[119] Nonetheless, the result disguised underlying tensions and problems. Apart from being disliked by republicans, democrats and constitutional nationalists, the League was opposed by landlords and by militant Protestants. Only one Tenant League candidate was returned in Ulster, with even the elder statesman of the movement, William Sharman Crawford, being defeated in County Down. Duffy was elected for New Ross in County Wexford. His success was largely due to local clerical support. In the wake of the election, Duffy formed the Independent Irish Party, which he led in Westminster. Duffy's activities did not impress his exiled former colleagues, notably, John Mitchel in Van Diemen's Land and Thomas Devin Reilly in the United States. When the latter heard that Duffy was standing for election in New Ross he nicknamed him 'Mr Give-in Duffy'.[120]

If Irish politics were less radical after 1848, they were no less divisive, and the tensions between the remnants of Old Ireland and Young Ireland remained. While the rising had been a defeat for Young Ireland, Old Ireland was not the beneficiary. Although John O'Connell attempted to revive the meetings of the Repeal Association, both the membership and the Repeal Rent had fallen dramatically. Consequently, he had to resort to making a special financial appeal in order to keep possession of Conciliation Hall. O'Connell also persisted with his isolationist policy, thus limiting support for the Repeal movement further. In August 1850, he informed a meeting that he would *not* be joining the Tenant League, on the grounds that he believed that there would be Repeal in under ten years' time.[121] He even went as far so to describe the Wexford Tenant Right Committee as 'illegal and dangerous'.[122] At the beginning of 1851, John O'Connell announced he was standing for parliament and was looking for support. The *Nation*, which continued to be an implacable enemy, mocked the fact that he was seeking support:

> from the country whose factions and divisions he has promoted by the meanest artifices and foulest lying, from the country whose martyrs and patriots he reviled and betrayed, from the country for whose shame he bargained with the Whigs, till he sunk too low to be pensioned or purchased.[123]

It took pleasure in pointing out that at a meeting in Conciliation Hall in February, the weekly Repeal Rent had only amounted to nineteen pounds. O'Connell responded by continuing to attack Young Ireland, blaming them for the ills of the country.[124]

In addition to divisions amongst nationalists, the 1850s was marked by increasing religious tensions in Ireland, which occasionally descended into sectarian conflicts. On St Patrick's Day 1849, a confrontation between Catholics and local Orangemen took place at Crossgar, near Belfast, resulting in the deaths of a man and a woman.[125] A more serious conflict took place on 12 July 1849 at Dolly's Brae, near Rathfriland, when the local Orange Order decided to re-route its annual parade to go through an exclusively Catholic village. This decision was prompted by their anger at the nationalist rising in the previous year. The resulting deaths of five Catholics, ranging from a ten-year-old boy to an eighty-five-year-old woman, were indicative of a new militancy amongst hard-line Protestants.[126] After 1848, therefore, the non-sectarian ideals of Young Ireland were replaced by more polarized divisions between Catholics and Protestants, especially in the north-east of the country. The achievement of a non-sectarian, inclusive movement proved as ephemeral after 1848 as it had before.

Religious tensions were inflamed when Russell's Whig government introduced the ill-advised Ecclesiastical Titles Act in 1851. The legislation was a response to Pope Pius IX's attempt to re-establish a hierarchy of Catholic bishops in England, similar to that which had existed before the Reformation. He misjudged the resistance to this measure and the anti-Catholic feelings that it would revive. The opposition was led by the Prime Minister, Russell, who wrote an open letter to the Bishop of Durham, denouncing 'the aggression of the Pope upon our Protestantism', adding that Englishmen 'looked with contempt on the mummeries of superstition, and with scorn at the laborious endeavours ... to confine the intellect and enslave the world'.[127] While Clarendon condemned the Pope's action, he opposed an extension of the act to Ireland and tendered his resignation when this occurred.[128] He regarded the Irish legislation as particularly dangerous because it would increase sectarian tensions, which had already been exacerbated by the conflict at Dolly's Brae. He declared that the response of Catholics had been that 'their fury exceeds all bounds'. Furthermore, he opined, 'I fear we are going to have a regular phase of sectarian bitterness, and that we shall never see things as peaceable again as they were last week.'[129] In the short term, the Act alienated Catholics; in the longer term, it contributed to a split in the Tenant League. Anger at the Act had resulted in an alliance between some Irish Catholic MPs, including John Sadleir and William Keogh, and the Tenant League. They agreed that they would not enter into an alliance with a British political party. The unity was short lived, with the alliance fragmenting when Sadleir and Keogh supported Lord Aberdeen's ministry in 1853, accepting appointments within it. As had been the case with the O'Connells only a few years earlier, Irish political unity had been undermined by the desire for personal advancement.

The introduction of the Ecclesiastical Titles Act and the aftermath of dissent damaged the Tenant League movement. Furthermore, disillusioned and disheartened, Duffy emigrated to Australia in August 1855. Despite the success of some of his political activities after 1849, his personal reputation had never recovered from his earlier disputes with John Mitchel.[130] His departure marked an end to an important phase in Irish political and literary development. Regardless of internal divisions, the Irish Independent Party survived, although its impact was negligible. A few decades later, Charles Stewart Parnell confessed that he had got the idea of creating an independent parliamentary party from Duffy's activities in 1852 and his vision to establish a party that reflected 'the ideas of the masses of the people, free from the influence of either English political parties, pledged not to take office or form any combination with any English political party until the wants of Ireland had been attended to'.[131] Duffy's initiative, therefore, helped to lay the foundations for the later Home Rule movement.

1848: Dillon Papers,

ted to visit 'poor, darling Meagher and O'Brien'

Notes

1 Ady [or Addy] Dillon to John Dillon, 13 September 1848: Dillon Papers, TCD (f.69). She had attempted to visit 'poor, darling Meagher and O'Brien' in Clonmel Jail, but they had already been moved to Dublin.
2 Meagher to Dillon, including information for Eva, 23 January 1849: ibid., (f.92).
3 Meagher to Father Markey (the go-between), 12 August 1848: T.J. Kiernan, *The Irish Exiles in Australia* (Melbourne: Burns and Oates, 1954), pp. 60–1.
4 Ibid., p. 61.
5 Meagher to Dillon, 23 January 1849: Dillon Papers, TCD (f.92).
6 R.D. Williams, Newgate Prison, to John Martin, 31 October 1848: R.D. Williams Papers, NLI, MS 10519.
7 Duffy, *Four Years*, pp. 694–5. The Executive Directory in New York was willing to allow the money to be used for state trials but did not know how to get it to Ireland, eventually deciding to channel it through business ventures.
8 *New York Freeman*, 28 October 1848.
9 Ibid.
10 *New York Nation*, 6 January 1849.
11 R.D. Williams, Newgate Prison, to Martin, 31 October 1848: R.D. Williams Papers, NLI, MS 10519.
12 Williams had written in the *Nation* and in the *Irish Tribune* as 'Shamrock'.
13 Doheny, *The Felon's Track*.
14 Anon., 'Women of Young Ireland', NLI, MS 10906, pp. 16–17.
15 *Saunders' News-Letter*, 20 February 1949.
16 Melville, *Mother of Oscar*, p. 49.
17 Mitchel, *Jail Journal*, 12 April 1849, p. 129.
18 Ibid., 24 April 1849, pp. 144–5.
19 O'Brien, Richmond Prison to Isaac Butt, 9 December 1848: O'Brien Papers, NLI, MS 442, f.2520.
20 *New York Nation*, 28 October 1848.
21 Ibid., 6 January 1849.
22 Evidence of John O'Donnell: John George Hodges, *Report of the Trial of William Smith O'Brien for High Treason at the Special Commission for the County Tipperary held at Clonmel, September and October 1848, with the Judgment of the Court of Queen's Bench, Ireland and of the House of Lords, on the Writs of Error* (Dublin: Hodges and Smith, 1849), p. 359. O'Donnell was later commemorated in a poem by Eva, *Poems by 'Eva' of the Nation* (San Francisco, 1877) p. 45.
23 Evidence of John Shea, Hodges, *Report of the Trial*, p. 381.
24 Ibid.
25 *New York Nation*, 28 October 1848.
26 Lucius O'Brien to O'Brien, 8 August 1848: Smith O'Brien Papers, NLI, MS 442, f.2493.
27 John Mansell, Ballycastle, to O'Brien, 23 August 1848: ibid., f.2497.
28 Hodges, *Report of the Trial*, p. 60.
29 Ibid., p. 61.
30 Speech Delivered by Thomas Francis Meagher in the Court House at Clonmel, at the close of the Special Commission, October 23 1848, New

York Public Library (NYPL), Madison Collection, 23 January 1849.
31 *New York Nation*, 4 November 1848.
32 Quoted in Lyons, *Speeches and Writings*, p. 17.
33 Poster of Speech of Meagher, NYPL, Thomas Meagher Letters, NYPL, Madison Collection, October 23 1848. Meagher sent a hand-signed copy to 'Eva of the "Nation" in grateful acknowledgement of her noble sympathy for those who have been proud to suffer for the cause which her poetry has ennobled'.
34 O'Brien to Meagher, 9 October 1848: PRONI, Papers of John Martin, D. 2137/1/12.
35 Meagher to O'Brien, 26 October 1848: Letters of Smith O'Brien, NLI, MS 442, f.2505.
36 MacManus to O'Brien, 27 October 1848: ibid., f.2507.
37 *New York Nation*, 4 November 1848.
38 Dillon, New York, to his wife, Ady, 14 November 1848: Dillon Papers, TCD (f.71a).
39 Mitchel, *Jail Journal*, 7 November 1848, p. 75.
40 5 September 1848: Milo Milton Quaife, *The Diary of James K. Polk, During his Presidency 1845–49* (Chicago: McClurg, 1910, 4 vols), p. 118.
41 Ibid., 5 September 1848, pp. 118–9.
42 Reprinted in *New York Nation*, 4 November 1848.
43 *New York Nation*, 28 October 1848.
44 *Frazer's Magazine* (November 1848) pp. 593–4.
45 Davis, *Young Ireland*, p. 165.
46 *New York Nation*, 6 January 1849.
47 Mitchel, *Jail Journal*, p. 116.
48 *New York Nation*, 6 January 1849; *Freeman's Journal*, 9 December 1848, reprinted in *Nation*, 6 January 1849.
49 Meagher to James Supple, President of Wolfe Tone Club, 9 December 1848: NYPL, Madison Collection, Thomas Francis Meagher Letters.
50 Meagher to unidentified person (fragment), Clonmel Gaol, 8 November 1848: ibid.
51 'The Intended Rescue of the State Prisoners of 1848' by Thomas Clarke Luby, in *Irish Nation* (New York), 28 January 1882.
52 Mitchel, *Jail Journal*, 21 November 1848, pp. 76–7.
53 This story was reprinted in *Northern Journal*, 29 August 1848.
54 The *Liverpool Mercury* of 11 August 1848 reported that 'large numbers of club leaders have left from Cork for America'.
55 Secret questionnaire to Magistrates, TNA, HO, TS 11. 137, pack 2, Liverpool Winter Assizes, 1848.
56 Ibid., Constabulary Reports (ACR), HO 45 2416A, 2 August 1848.
57 *Boston Pilot*, 12 August 1848.
58 George Potter, *To the Golden Door: The Story of the Irish in Ireland and America* (Boston: Little, Brown and Company, 1960), suggests (p. 506) that this was the largest meeting held by Irish-Americans for overseas revolution.
59 *Boston Pilot*, 19 August 1848.
60 *Northern Journal*, 22 August 1848.
61 British Consul in Boston, to Addington, 29 August 1848: ibid., FO, HO 45 2391.

62 The Address was signed by 'Robert Emmet, C. O'Conor, H. Greeley, F. Ingoldsby, James W. White, M.T. O'Connor, Thomas Hayes, B. O'Connor, John McKeon', *Northern Journal*, 22 August 1848.

63 Addington, FO, London, to Barclay, Consulate, New York, Secret Dispatch, 25 August 1848: TNA, FO 5/488.

64 Barclay to Addington, 18 September 1848: ibid., FO.

65 Barclay to Palmerston, 2 August 1848: ibid., HO 45 2391.

66 Barclay to Palmerston, 8 September 1848: ibid., 45 2391.

67 Addington, FO to Waddington, HO, 26 September 1848: ibid., HO 45 2391.

68 Barclay to Palmerston, 8 September 1848: ibid., FO 5/488.

69 *Dublin Evening Post* cited in *Liverpool Mercury*, 15 August 1848.

70 Palmerston to Crampton (Chargé d'Affaires) 4 August 1848: TNA, FO 5/483.

71 Report of CD, 5 August 1848: TCD, MS 2039, p. 58.

72 Sworn statement of John Anderson, Sub-inspector of the Constable Station at Borris, 23 September 1848: TCD, MS 9932/102.

73 Horsfall, Liverpool, to Clarendon, 27 September 1848: Bodleian Library, Clarendon Letters.

74 J. Crampton, Washington, to Viscount Palmerston, 9 October 1848: TNA, HO 45 2391.

75 Ibid., Details of some of the arrests are provided in the Constabulary Reports (ACR) for August 1848, in HO 2416.

76 Duffy, *Four Years*, p. 631. R.F. Ryan was a member of the Maryland Bar. James Bergin (or Bergen), was described as a merchant who looked like Shakespeare.

77 Pinkerton to Palmerston, 11 July 1848: TNA, HO 45 2391.

78 Reddington, Dublin, to Waddington, 19 September 1848: ibid., FO 5/487.

79 Dispatch of Crampton, 6 November 1848: ibid., FO 5/487.

80 Redington, Dublin, to Waddington, 19 September 1848: HO 45 2416A; Duffy, *Four Years*, p. 591.

81 Belchem 'Nationalism', 63.

82 Redington to Waddington, 19 September 1848: TNA, HO 45 1416A.

83 James Buchanan became the fifteenth President of the USA, 1857–61.

84 John Crampton, Washington, to Palmerston, 8 August 1848: TNA, HO 45 2391.

85 A. Barclay New York to J. Crampton, marked Confidential, 8 July 1848: ibid., FO, HO 45 2391.

86 Addington, FO, to Waddington, HO, 2 November 1848: ibid., HO 45 2391.

87 Ibid., Dispatch of Crampton, FO 5/487.

88 *New York Commercial Advertiser*, 15 January 1849.

89 Barclay to Palmerston, 30 August 1848: TNA, FO 5/488.

90 Belchem, 'Nationalism', 58, observed that such a project fitted in with America's programme of republican expansion.

91 Report of CD, 22 February 1848: TCD, MS 2039, p. 212.

92 *Irish Nation*, 25 February 1848.

93 Ibid., 28 January 1882.

94 Ibid., 25 February 1882.

95 Cavanagh, Life of Joseph Brennan, pp. 9–11.

96 Ibid.

97 *Irishman*, 21 April 1849.
98 Ibid., 10 June 1848.
99 Ibid., 1 July 1848.
100 Ibid., 8 July 1849.
101 Reports of CD, TCD, MS 2039: 16 February 1849, p. 211; 27 February 1849, p. 215.
102 Ibid., 3 March 1849, p. 3.
103 Ibid.
104 Kiely, *The Waterford Rebels, pp.* 18–21.
105 Clarendon to Charles Wood, 29 November 1850: Maxwell, *Life and Letters*, p. 317.
106 *The Times*, 11 August 1853.
107 *Nation*, 7 September 1850.
108 Vincent Geoghegan in George Boyce, *Political Thought in Irish Society Since the Seventeenth Century* (London: Routledge, 1993), pp. 116–17.
109 James Connolly, *Labour in Irish History* (first pub. 1910, reprinted Dublin: New Books, 1973), Chapter XV.
110 *Irishman*, 21 April 1849.
111 *Nation*, 1 September 1849, 8 September 1848.
112 Ibid., 11 January 1851.
113 Ibid., 5 October 1850.
114 Mitchel, *Jail Journal*, 26 October 1849, pp. 207–8.
115 *Nation*, 8 December 1848, reprinted in *New York Nation*, 12 January 1849.
116 Mitchel, *Jail Journal*, 26 April 1850, p. 242.
117 Ibid., p. 243.
118 *Nation*, 7 September 1850.
119 Hoppen, *Elections, Politics and Society*, p. 161.
120 Reilly to Mitchel, Mitchel, *Jail Journal*, 8 January 1853, p. 297.
121 *Nation*, 31 August 1850.
122 Ibid., 28 September 1850.
123 Ibid., 11 January 1851.
124 Ibid., 1 February 1851.
125 *Armagh Guardian*, 26 March 1849.
126 Christine Kinealy, 'A Right to March? The Conflict at Dolly's Brae, 1849' in George Boyce and Roger Swift, *Problems and Perspectives in Irish History* (Dublin: Four Courts Press, 2004).
127 Lord Clarendon to Lady Clarendon, 2 September 1850: Maxwell, *Life and Letters*, p. 314.
128 *Nation*, 25 January 1851.
129 Clarendon to Lady Clarendon, 26 November 1850: Maxwell, *Life and Letters*, pp. 314–15.
130 O'Sullivan, *Young Irelanders*, p. 105.
131 R. Barry O'Brien, *The Life of Charles Stewart Parnell* (New York: Harper and Brothers, 1898), vol. 1, p. 289.

8

'The chained wolves':
the 1848-ers overseas

The decision not to execute the leaders immediately following their conviction in October 1848 was taken for pragmatic reasons, the government preferring to create fools rather than national martyrs.[1] In July 1849, on the eve of Queen Victoria's visit to Ireland, the death sentence on the four leaders of the 1848 uprising was commuted and they were transported to Van Diemen's Land (Tasmania). This island had been utilized initially as a penal colony to relieve the pressure on Port Jackson in Botany Bay (Australia). Because of its remoteness and lack of internal development, it was viewed as ideal for 'the most turbulent and rapacious' of British and Irish convicts, making it 'the Botany Bay of Botany Bay'.[2] It was also used intermittently by the government for political prisoners, some of the first of whom had been involved in the 1798 rebellion in Ireland.[3] In 1849, O'Brien, Meagher, MacManus and O'Donoghoe were transported to Van Diemen's Land for life. John Martin and Kevin O'Doherty were also transported, but for ten years. Despite the differences in age and religion, the two men became firm friends, with O'Doherty nicknaming John Martin, 'John Knox' and Martin retaliating by calling O'Doherty 'Saint Kevin'. O'Donoghoe was referred to as 'Denis' by the other prisoners.

The four men convicted of high treason sailed together on the *Swift*. The journey took 110 days. The arrival of the men in the colony coincided with demands for the end of transportation. The Launceston Association for Promoting the Cessation of Transportation of Convicts to Van Diemen's Land had been formed in May 1847, and by 1850, it had expanded into the 'Australasian League' to end transportation.[4] This movement was not confined to Australasia but was strongest in the Cape. The protests there coincided with the arrival of John Mitchel in the colony.

At the beginning of 1849, following weeks of illness caused by asthma, John Mitchel was persuaded by the medical superintendent to ask the Governor of Bermuda to relocate him to a healthier climate.[5] On 12

February 1849, he heard that he was being transferred to the Cape of Good Hope, with a number of other convicts, where they would be allowed to roam free but under police surveillance. Mitchel was glad to leave Bermuda.[6] However, his medical attendant thought that Mitchel was so ill it was unlikely that he could survive the long journey. This sentiment was echoed in a debate in the House of Commons, when the Home Secretary stated that it was unlikely that Mitchel would outlive the journey to the Cape.[7] On 22 April 1849, however, Mitchel left Bermuda on board the transport ship *Neptune*; he and the other convicts were bound for the Cape of Good Hope.

On arrival at the Cape, the ship was caught up in protests when the settlers refused to allow any of the Irish convicts on board to disembark. At that stage, Mitchel had been at sea for months as the *Neptune* had been, according to *The Times*, 'roaming nobody knows where', even appearing at Pernambuco near Brazil on 11 August.[8] The arrival of the convict ship at Cape Town had been long anticipated and the local population were prepared to resist its landing. The Cape Town municipality described the convicts on board the *Neptune* as 'avowed and determined enemies of the constitution, who are not infrequently possessed of great talent, energy and enterprise'.[9] Mitchel's presence, moreoever, created excitement amongst the protesters and the Anti-Convict Association, who proposed to the Governor that Mitchel should be allowed to stay there as a free settler. The request was refused, but Mitchel apparently responded to it by saying, 'Bravo, men of the Cape.'[10] Mitchel also learnt that the *Swift*, carrying his former colleagues, O'Brien, Meagher, MacManus and O'Donoghoe, had arrived in the Cape a week earlier to take fresh provisions on board.[11]

The *Neptune* spent almost six months at the Cape while the conflict ensued, awaiting orders from the government in London.[12] Mitchel, who sympathized with the colonists, subsequently published an account of their resistance in the *Colonial Times*, as a further way of exposing British misrule.[13] On 13 February 1850, instructions arrived from London that the vessel was to proceed to Van Diemen's Land and, as compensation for the hardships of the voyage, the convicts were each to receive 'conditional pardons': all, that is, except for Mitchel.[14] The *Neptune* finally sailed to Hobart in Tasmania on 19 February 1850.[15] Mitchel was ill for most of the journey.[16] After a further forty-two days at sea, the *Neptune* arrived in Derwent, near Hobart, on 6 April. The anti-convict movement had spread to the Australian colonies and the arrival of the *Neptune* was described by the *Hobart Town Advertiser* as 'a new insult to Van Diemen's Land'.[17] The local population objected on the grounds that they did not want the 'refuse of the mother country'.[18] In Hobart, all of the prisoners whose conduct had been good while on board ship, with the exception of John Mitchel, were granted conditional pardons, instead of the usual tickets-of-leave.[19] Mitchel was offered a ticket-of-leave, giving him more freedom than he had had in

Bermuda. The British government had debated whether such a privilege should be afforded, but the Home Secretary argued that Mitchel could not be treated more harshly than O'Brien. He reassured Clarendon that 'you are mistaken as to his wish to renew his endeavours to revolution. From what we have heard of him while at Bermuda he seems to be deeply sensible of the extreme folly of his former violence and is thoroughly disgusted with his old associates'.[20] Inadvertently, the protests of colonists in the Cape and other British colonies meant that Mitchel was again joined with his fellow Young Irelanders, including his life-long friend, John Martin. As his *Jail Journal* suggested, his desire for revolution appeared undiminished by three years of exile.

The seven state prisoners were separated by class, religion, economic status and political objectives, yet their experiences in July 1848 and later in Van Diemen's Land created strong and enduring ties between them. Sir William Denison, the Governor of Van Diemen's Land, had wanted to treat the exiles as common convicts and deny them all privileges, but he was over-ruled.[21] Consequently, they were each offered a ticket-of-leave, which, if accepted, amounted to a promise not to escape. In return, they were allowed to live in relative liberty, but had to remain within their own separate districts. Meagher, MacManus, O'Donoghoe, Martin and O'Doherty accepted the tickets-of-leave, but O'Brien refused to do so. Meagher regarded the enforced segregation as unnecessarily vindictive, writing in a local newspaper that 'having separated us by so many thousand miles of all that was dear, consoling, and inspiring to our hearts, they should have still further increased the severity of this sentence by distributing us over a strange land'.[22] They kept in touch by letter, although in the early months they had little news of O'Brien.

A few of the Tasmanian colonists shunned the company of the exiles, but most of the Irish settlers made them welcome, treating them differently from the other convicts. Within a short time, however, they each admitted that they were shocked by the amount of in-fighting amongst the colonists and the prevalence of gossip. The transported men found it difficult to recreate the lives they had left behind, partly because they were all constantly short of money.[23] Meagher was frequently unable to pay his bills, surviving on credit and good will, while O'Brien was subsidized by income from his estate at Cahirmoyle in Ireland. In 1851, he took a job as a personal tutor. O'Donoghoe, who was the least affluent and well-connected of the group, was initially given money by the other prisoners.[24] He attempted to resolve his financial problems by establishing a newspaper, *The Irish Exile and Freedom's Advocate*, shortly after his arrival on the island.[25] The other exiles disapproved, fearing that he would become embroiled in the petty squabbles of the colonists.[26] O'Doherty, who had been a medical student prior to his arrest, was eventually allowed to work as an apothecary and then in a hospital.

The prisoners were all desperate for news of Ireland and any newspaper that they received from home was circulated amongst them, even though it was months out of date.[27] One piece of information that raised their spirits was that John O'Connell, whom Meagher described as 'a curse upon our country', was retiring from politics.[28] In general, though, the political news from home added to their despondency. When Mitchel and Meagher first met again they became sad when they spoke of Ireland, deprecating, according to Mitchel, 'the miserable debris of her puny agitators, who are fast making the name of Irishman a word of reproach all the world over'.[29] In August 1851, Meagher, who had just received copies of the *Weekly Freeman*, informed O'Doherty that 'The Irish news is utterly unattractive. The Tenant League even seems to have disappeared. There has been an election for Dungarvan ... The parish priest standing "neutral", that is, deserting the popular party. Damn him and his neutrality ... England is full of the Great Exhibition – an immense piece of London Puffery.' The only news item he found of interest was the 'popery' debates, concerning the introduction of the Ecclesiastical Titles Act.[30]

When O'Brien arrived in Van Diemen's Land, he refused to promise not to escape, thus he was not eligible for a ticket-of-leave. Consequently, the Governor of the colony, Sir William Denison, sent him to the Probation Station at Maria Island, a punishment usually reserved for the most hardened criminals. He was only allowed to walk the island accompanied by an armed constable and all of his correspondence was opened. The other exiles protested against his harsh treatment.[31] While there, he kept a journal and wrote poetry. The latter included a poem entitled, 'To My Country', which revealed his love for Ireland and his continuing defiance:

> When foes upon me lour
> In exiles darkest hour
> Whilst I defy their power
> Still pines my heart for thee
>
> In loneliest solitude
> By dastard spite pursued
> Silenced but not subdued
> Still pines my heart for thee

Although he sent a copy to a friend, he asked that his poetry should not be published until after his death.[32] The combination of solitary confinement and the fact that he was only allowed limited exercise had a detrimental effect on his health.[33] Meagher suggested that O'Brien should challenge the legality of the authorities in treating him in this way.[34] In his usual insouciant way, Meagher also wrote to Sir Denison, appealing to his 'sense of common justice and humanity' to remove the restriction on O'Brien.[35] Mitchel and Martin asked him to reconsider and accept a ticket-of-leave, which O'Brien only did at the end of 1850, when he was moved to New Norfolk.[36]

The Irish press reported regularly on the health and treatment of O'Brien and within the columns of the relaunched *Nation* it became a rallying point for the remnants of the Repeal movement. The debate was given fresh impetus when Robert Potter, O'Brien's friend and attorney, gave a letter by O'Brien to *The Times*, at the beginning of 1850, in order to place the matter before the English public. In the letter, O'Brien admitted to Potter that banishment was worse than he had feared. After only two months of solitude, his health had broken down, but this was insignificant 'compared with the separation from my family'. Nevertheless, he was adamant that his family should not join him.[37] *The Times*, far from showing sympathy, responded to O'Brien's letters by calling him a 'petulant puppy'.[38] The press in Van Diemen's Land had initially been hostile to the Young Irelanders but, within a few months, it had become more sympathetic to the men, deprecating their actions but recognizing that they arose from a deep sense of patriotism and anger at the British government's indifference during the Famine.[39]

On 12 August 1850, O'Brien attempted to escape.[40] He was the first state prisoner to do so and he was also the only one to be unsuccessful. His friends had arranged for a schooner to collect him from Maria Island, but the captain of the vessel allegedly informed on him and he got no further than clambering onto a boat near the shore before he was arrested. The attempt was made more difficult as O'Brien was always accompanied by a constable, who drew his gun on the fleeing O'Brien and the boatman who was collecting him. According to the *Irish Exile*, O'Brien's attempt to escape failed because he had been surrounded by government informers who had betrayed him. The paper believed that his action was not a violation of honour as he had not accepted a ticket-of-leave.[41] More surprising was the sympathy expressed in the *Launceston Examiner*, which averred:

> In common with the colonists generally we were gratified to hear that this gentleman had escaped from the colony. The attempt was no violation of honour for he declined to accept the usual terms, which accompanied the tender of a ticket-of-leave. We learn with regret he has been recaptured, but in the name of the community we protest against the exhibition of a spirit of revenge which petty souls, dressed in a little brief authority, are apt to display.[42]

Some time later, following his escape to San Francisco, MacManus arranged a 'kangaroo court' to try the captain who had allegedly betrayed O'Brien, but he was freed due to lack of conclusive evidence.[43]

As punishment for his unsuccessful attempt, on 21 August O'Brien was transferred to the probation station at Port Arthur, which contained a penitentiary considered to be for the most hardened of criminals. It also had a reputation for being impossible to escape from. During his stay there, O'Brien continued to receive special treatment. He was allowed to reside in a cottage, which was a converted stable. However, he was placed in virtual solitary confinement. The *Nation* was indignant that, despite O'Brien's poor health, he was to be moved from Maria Island to Port Arthur, and housed in a former stable.[44] O'Brien remained in Port Arthur for only three months. At the end of 1850, he applied for a ticket-of-leave. It was an admission that he would not attempt to escape again. It was granted and he was allowed to move to New Norfolk. While travelling there, he passed through Hobart where he received a standing ovation from the local population.[45] He was also secretly visited by MacManus, O'Doherty and O'Donoghoe. When the Governor heard of this, he sentenced the three men to three months' hard labour. MacManus was released on a technicality and took advantage of his freedom to escape from Van Diemen's Land. The treatment of the prisoners caused outrage, and it resulted in the dismissal of Governor Denison.[46] Following his removal, the state prisoners were treated more leniently.

O'Brien stayed at New Norfolk only a short time, moving on to Avoca, where he had taken a job as a private tutor. En route to his job at Avoca, O'Brien had requested permission to stay with Mitchel and Martin, and then Meagher, but the Governor refused to allow him to travel by that route.[47] Thereafter, although he was allowed to mix socially with the local population, he was forbidden from meeting his former colleagues. He did, however, join some of them at illicit meetings at Lake Sorrel.[48] O'Brien used his time studying the Classics, gardening and latterly, tutoring. Although he initially enjoyed teaching, he believed he could not be truly happy until he was reunited with his family.[49] Like many of the men involved in the uprising, he began to pen his account of what had happened in 1848. Despite the outcome of the events, and his own personal unhappiness, he remained convinced of the appropriateness and honourable nature of his actions.

Meagher's flamboyance did not appear to be diminished by exile. He decided that while in Van Diemen's Land, he would render his surname as 'O'Meagher'. Meagher lived initially at Campbell Town and then at Ross. Because he had accepted a ticket-of-leave, he enjoyed relative freedom of movement, although this did not include meeting his former colleagues. One of the first things Meagher did was to have a boat built in Hobart, which was then hauled by six bullocks the seventy-five miles to Lake Sorrel. He named the vessel *Speranza*, possibly in memory of his former colleague and friend at the *Nation*. He sailed it under the American flag.[50] Meagher was assiduous about staying in touch with his fellow prisoners and with his friends and family in Ireland, even sending presents home despite being constantly short of money.[51] The territories where Martin, Meagher and O'Doherty lived all adjoined Lake Sorrel and Meagher arranged for the three men to meet secretly each week on the edge of the Lake, although this was forbidden by the terms of their parole. However, Meagher had used his charm to persuade the local boatmen not to inform on them. He also organized frequent picnics, ordering the other men to bring mutton chops, ale, brandy, cigars and a back-gammon board.[52] Terence MacManus, who lived at Launceston, was too far away to be involved in these gatherings. Although Meagher stayed in touch with O'Brien and MacManus by letter, he seemed to have little contact with O'Donoghoe.

Regardless of Meagher's apparent cheerfulness, he was frequently frustrated by the petty restrictions imposed on him and his friends. When he was denied permission to visit O'Doherty at his residence in Oatlands, he complained that the refusal had been made in 'a very snobbish colonial style'. He believed, however, that 'the chained wolves must have patience, and put up for a short while at all events with the grimaces and worrying of the most contemptible of the Quilps, whether they be in or out of office'.[53] Moreover, because he had so much time on his hands, Meagher was restless, although for a while he planned to manage a farm. According to the unsympathetic London papers, Meagher was 'in excellent health, but not spirits'. He was building a house on Lake Sorrel and desired to decorate it with pictures of Ireland. According to the report, he believed society in Van Diemen's land to be comprised of 'snobs, traps and demons' and had come to despise 'this English-organised hell on earth'.[54]

Clearly, Meagher was lonely for female companionship. Before leaving Ireland, he had had a close relationship with a 'Miss O'Ryan', with whom he continued to correspond. However, she was forced to end the association when her parents intercepted a letter and thus discovered the engagement. They ordered her to cease corresponding with Meagher. According to Meagher, their reason was that they could 'never sanction an engagement which would be sure to end in disappointment in never being realised, since there was little or no prospect of my return to Ireland'. They asked that all of their daughter's letters be returned, which Meagher did.[55] Only a few weeks later, in February 1851, he married Katherine (Kate or Bennie) Bennett, the daughter of a convict. He was angered by the fact that many newspapers had been reporting his new relationship for a number of weeks. Meagher realized that 'in the opinion of the frivolous, the fashionable, the sordid, the worshippers of the dollar, and of the flimsy phantom known as Birth', he had married beneath him, but he didn't care. The ceremony was simple: in Meagher's words there were to be 'no gloves, no cards, everything quite quiet', although Mitchel, Martin and O'Brien attended.[56] Meagher regarded the marriage as his salvation, confiding in O'Doherty that he hoped that matrimony would help him to:

> forget the ruins that were behind me, and the waste in which I was idly living on, from day to day – feeling too every incentive to useful and elevated pursuits hourly subsiding and life becoming to me a sickening stagnation, in which the best sympathies and tendencies of my nature were drooping into death, having no object to attract them, no vital purpose to sustain and

quicken them … it is no wonder that my heart should have turned to one, in whose love it felt assured that peace and health and gladness would be returned to it – on which its earlier action might be re-inspired, and its old ambitions to do something upon this earth, for the good to bless and the free to glorify, might be disengaged from the indifferent emptiness.[57]

The arrival of John Mitchel, shortly followed by Jenny Mitchel, helped to raise Meagher's spirits. Jenny had brought with her copies of the nationalist newspapers from the period leading up to 1848 and Meagher began using them to write a book of the events that had led to the uprising. In addition to setting the record straight, he hoped that it would provide him with an income admitting that, 'I have set to work with the rascally intention of making it vastly marketable.'[58] The need to make money was an important consideration as by the middle of 1851 he was forced to sell his pony to raise cash and apologised to O'Doherty for not paying him money that he owed him. Regardless of his marriage, and the fact that by the end of the year Kate was pregnant, Meagher was finding life in Van Diemen's Land increasingly intolerable. His relationship continued to be the subject of 'wicked gossip' with stories circulating that he had been neglecting his wife, even though she had not been well. As usual, he confided in O'Doherty: 'What a detestable country it is! What depths of selfishness, insincerity, treachery, falsehood … How my heart beats and pants for a quick deliverance from the abominable captivity, yearning for some other land, built up with sounder stuff and radiant with a purer destiny.' At the end of his long letter, he made an oblique reference to the fact that he was considering escaping: concluding his letter by saying 'Could the "bolt" be managed?'[59] The significance of this question was apparent a few months later when Meagher escaped from Van Diemen's Land.

Kevin O'Doherty found exile especially difficult, even though he had accepted a ticket-of-leave and had relative freedom. One reason was that, while in prison in Dublin, he had become close to Eva, the nationalist poet. She had promised to wait for him but he was pessimistic about their meeting again. During one of their illicit meetings, Mitchel noted that he was 'gloomy and desponding' guessing that he was depressed because in Ireland there was 'a dark-eyed lady, a fair and gentle lady, with hair like blackest midnight'.[60] In May 1850 O'Doherty informed O'Brien that he still hadn't heard from his family, but that 'our youthful poetess Eva, the only person I have heard from, desired to be remembered in the kindest manner to you'.[61] Eva also kept in contact with Meagher and Martin, often providing them with news from home. O'Doherty had not completed his medical studies in Ireland and hoped to take his final exams while in exile. The authorities refused to allow him to do so, without copies of his certificates. He suspected them of being 'particularly stringent in this case'.[62] Nonetheless, in November 1850 he was made manager of a dispensary in Hobart. Shortly afterwards, he was allowed to work as a surgeon in a hospital. When O'Doherty moved to Hobart Town in order to practise medicine, he was missed at the illicit meetings at Lake Sorrel.[63]

The older men protected and nurtured O'Doherty, financially and in other ways. Meagher, who was the same age (they were both born in 1823), was especially protective, frequently sending him short notes (which were rarely answered) and making arrangements to meet him. On one occasion, O'Doherty had failed to attend a meeting with Meagher and Martin, who had waited five hours for him. The former gently berated him, asking 'What's the matter with you? – Sick? Crippled or disconsolate? ... You're going to Old Nick straight.'[64] Even following Meagher's marriage, his hospitality to O'Doherty continued: at one point he even offered to build him a cottage on the grounds of his home.[65] Following Meagher's escape, O'Brien took over the role of O'Doherty's mentor, lending him money and telling him to keep his spirits up.[66] Following his appointment as a tutor, O'Brien used part of his income to finance O'Doherty's medical studies.[67] In 1851, O'Doherty was discovered visiting the newly-arrived Mitchel without permission. He was accused of breaking his parole and was punished with four weeks' penal servitude, with hard labour. Meagher was outraged and even considered breaking his own parole, but he was talked out of it by Mitchel and Martin. He wrote to Duffy though, urging his former colleague to publicize how O'Doherty had been treated.[68]

Patrick O'Donoghoe, together with Terence MacManus, was one of the least well known of the exiles. Socially, he had little in common with the other Young Irelanders. He was also more politically radical. O'Donoghoe had first introduced himself to O'Brien in May 1848, informing him, 'I believe you are the political instrument he [God] has destined to achieve the political redemption of Ireland.'[69] Almost immediately upon landing O'Donoghoe established a newspaper, called the *Irish Exile*. The other prisoners disapproved of this undertaking. When Mitchel arrived in Hobart he received a letter from O'Donoghoe asking him to join him in the venture, but Mitchel doubted O'Donoghoe's competence to run such a paper and he refused to be involved.[70] John Martin, however, contributed a series of articles justifying the 1848 rebellion. Moreover, the paper was successful, with distribution outlets in Sydney, Melbourne and New Zealand. It also attracted attention in Ireland, with the *Nation* reporting that the paper was getting hundreds of subscribers.[71] O'Donoghoe's continuing interest in nationalist politics was evident in the first edition, which declared 'we are, in fact, very green – as green as the shamrock that grows in our own native Isle of the Ocean'. His radicalism was also apparent and he promised that the paper would defend oppressed people everywhere 'whether they be free or in chains'.[72] In keeping with this promise, he was a consistent defender of the rights of Tasmanian Aborigines [sic].[73] Initially, he ran articles deprecating the treatment of O'Brien, but the Governor banned O'Donoghoe from including these reports.

O'Donoghoe's professional success was not mirrored in his personal life. He had accepted a ticket-of-leave but it was revoked following a drunken brawl with a friend. A failed escape attempt and a further drunken brawl resulted in his being sentenced to hard labour, which entailed working on a treadmill.[74] Despite these drunken episodes, in mid-1852 O'Donoghoe gave a public lecture in which he warned his audience 'to be on their guard against the foul friend of drunkenness'. He was described as being 'a true disciple of Father Mathew'.[75] O'Donoghoe's second escape attempt was successful and he arrived in New York in 1853. He was not feted like Meagher or Mitchel. He died, in relative oblivion and poverty, in January 1854.

Following Mitchel's arrival in Van Diemen's Land, the doctor on board the *Neptune* persuaded the governor that Mitchel should be offered a ticket-of-leave. Largely for health reasons, he chose to accept it.[76] Also, because of his 'shattered health', the doctor suggested that Mitchel be allowed to reside with his friend, John Martin.[77] This too was granted and so, after two years being confined on board a convict ship, Mitchel was again able to live on land, in relative freedom. Mitchel and Martin resided in the village of Bothwell, which was about forty-six miles from Hobart Town. Martin had already lived there alone for five months. While travelling to Bothwell, Terence MacManus had an illicit meeting with Mitchel. MacManus filled him in about what had happened in Ireland since his deportation and following their arrival in Van Diemen's Land. Mitchel was shocked to hear of O'Brien's treatment and wrote to him immediately, admitting that such communication was 'unsatisfactory'.[78] MacManus also persuaded Mitchel to extend his stay and meet illicitly with Meagher and O'Doherty.[79] Within a short time of arriving in Van Diemen's Land, therefore, Mitchel was reunited with Meagher and O'Doherty at their secret meeting place near Lake Sorrel. Mitchel described the two men as looking 'fresh and vigorous' and O'Doherty, whom he had hardly met before, as 'a fine, erect, noble-looking man'.[80] According to Mitchel, 'five Irish rebels [were] together again in order to shoot ... ducks'.[81] Following the meeting, Mitchel recorded that he was pleased to find that his friends were 'unsubdued', adding, 'The game, I think, is not yet over.'[82] While he was at Bothwell, Mitchel's health improved.[83] This led one London newspaper to report that Mitchel had grown 'fat and strong' since coming ashore.[84] Former colleagues in Ireland rejoiced that the exiles were all together especially as, regardless of their former differences, 'they all love Mitchel'.[85]

Mitchel, like O'Brien and O'Donoghoe, had a wife and children and he agonized as to whether he should ask his family to join him. Within a few months of being in Van Diemen's Land he had decided to invite them to do so.[86] He was unaware that his wife, Jenny, accompanied by their children, had already sailed to the Cape to join him, unaware of the local situation.[87] At the Cape, she chose to continue on to Van Diemen's Land. Jenny's unilateral decision to join her husband won her the admiration of the nationalist press in Ireland.[88] It was not until 25 May 1851 that Mitchel heard that his family were sailing from Adelaide in South Australia to a port near Launceston.[89] Only a few weeks earlier, MacManus had escaped and his whereabouts remained unknown. Therefore, Mitchel was required to spend a night in jail, the local police magistrate fearing that he was following MacManus's example.[90] Mitchel's family arrived in Van Diemen's Land on 18 June 1851. On this day, the usually garrulous Mitchel simply noted in his journal, 'These things cannot be described.'[91] Because the house he had shared with Martin was small, Mitchel rented the nearby Nant Cottage, a farm of 200 acres. Following his family's arrival, he was allowed more freedom to travel and to see his former colleagues. In early July 1851 Meagher and his wife stayed at the Mitchels' home for two days. He described Jenny as 'looking extremely well … and in the highest possible spirits'. He also suggested that she was pregnant.[92]

In August, Mitchel and his wife visited O'Brien. Meagher had warned him that O'Brien's appearance had deteriorated. The two men had not seen each other for over three years and at first Mitchel did not recognize O'Brien. Although O'Brien looked older and desolate, Mitchel believed that he was 'a man who cannot be crushed, bowed or broken' as his principles were 'anchored immovably upon his own brave heart within'.[93] In spite of past ideological disagreements, their pleasure at meeting was genuine. Mitchel reported that their reunion was warm, even though their last meeting in Ireland had not been so cordial. O'Brien, in turn, recorded that he had 'rejoiced' at meeting Mitchel 'and his charming family'. He even suggested that both Mitchel and Martin should move their homes closer to his.[94] After visiting O'Brien and Meagher, Mitchel became bored and depressed, feeling lonelier than before, and so he did not write in his journal for fifteen months.[95] Instead, he wrote angry letters to the Irish press, venting his frustration and referring to the Britain as the 'Carthaginian government'.[96] Part of his anger derived from his belief that he had never been tried by his countrymen but by 'a foreign tyrant'.[97] His spirits were lifted by the fact that the exiles continued to meet unofficially, notwithstanding the risks. Mitchel was secretly visited by O'Doherty who was now resident surgeon in Hobart, and both men also visited O'Brien regularly.[98]

A bitter-sweet development occurred while the Irish rebels were in exile. In the autumn of 1851 the first election of representatives took place under the new Constitution, which had granted Van Diemen's Land their own legislature.[99] O'Brien had contributed to the drafting of the Constitution through his friendship with a member of the new legislature. His writings were published in 1856 as *Principles of Government or Meditations in Exile*. While in Van Diemen's Land, the prisoners unexpectedly met a former acquaintance. John Balfe, a former radical member of the Irish Confederation who had become a government informer in 1848, arrived in Van Diemen's Land in 1850. He was employed initially as Comptroller of the Convict Department. In 1851 he became proprietor of the *Hobart Town Advertiser*. By this stage, the *Nation* had exposed him as a spy, working for Lord Clarendon, whose undercover name had been 'the General'.[100] For most of the period from 1857 until his death in 1880, Balfe served in the House of Assembly. Unlike the men that he had betrayed, he was buried in Tasmania.[101]

Overseas support

The seven exiles, rather than being regarded with ignominy or disappearing from public view, continued to attract attention not only amongst the residents of Van Diemen's Land and Australia, but also in Ireland, Britain and the United States. That these men were not forgotten or despised was evident in a number of petitions collected on their behalf, and from the support that each one received. Not all of the publicity was positive. *The Times* suggested repeatedly that the people of Ireland did not like or respect O'Brien and the paper continued to include articles denigrating him.[102] Their claim was difficult to sustain as he continued to command respect in his home country and even further afield. This was evident immediately following O'Brien's sentencing, when a petition was commenced in Ireland asking for clemency. In total, over 80,000 signatures were collected.[103] Additionally, in May 1849 a memorial was sent to the government asking for mercy for the four state prisoners.[104] Only a few weeks later, the government announced that the death sentence was to be commuted to one of transportation for life.

The treatment of the prisoners in Van Diemen's Land angered nationalists in Ireland. On 27 June 1850, there was a meeting of the citizens of Cork to adopt a petition to Queen Victoria to mitigate the suffering of O'Brien. Cork Corporation adopted a similar resolution. Even the *Dublin Evening Packet*, which did not support O'Brien, joined in and denounced the cruel treatment meted out to him.[105] The Grand Juries of Counties Limerick and Clare also petitioned the government on his behalf.[106] In 1851, a further petition was collected in Ireland asking for 'leniency to Smith O'Brien and the men who had led the 1849 rising in Carrick-on Suir'.[107] An even larger petition was sent to the British government at the beginning of 1852, which briefly raised O'Brien's hopes that he and the other prisoners would be released. When he was informed of its unequivocal rejection, O'Brien confided in O'Doherty that, 'It leaves me no reason to hope that I shall ever return home to Ireland.'[108] A petition submitted in 1853 was similarly unsuccessful. Regardless of his disappointment, O'Brien remained punctilious in publicly thanking those who had petitioned on his behalf.[109]

Nor were such activities confined to Ireland. On 24 July 1850 there was a meeting in London to denounce the government's cruelty towards O'Brien.[110] A few weeks later, a meeting was held in Tammany Hall in New York to express 'indignation at the treatment of O'Brien by the English government, and to sympathise with his family'. About 1,000 persons were present, most of whom were natives of Ireland. Horace Greeley, the newspaper proprietor, was in the chair. He had first joined the Repeal movement in the United States in 1842 as an admirer of O'Connell, but by 1848 had come to believe that an uprising was necessary. The meeting was unanimous in expressing both its admiration for O'Brien, saying that his malicious treatment had elicited 'universal and heartfelt indignation at the perfidy of England', and the hypocrisy of those who 'saved him from death but inflicted worse on him' – and they sent him their sympathy.[111] In February 1851, Thomas O'Kane, a politician in Boston, wrote to the British Prime Minister, Lord John Russell, asking that O'Brien and the other prisoners be allowed to emigrate to the United States.[112] This request was taken up in the Senate by General James Shields, the Senator for Illinois.[113]

The imprisonment of Mitchel in June 1851, when he travelled to Launceston to meet his family, provoked a strong response in the colony, the general consensus being that he had been harshly treated. The most vociferous paper, the *Colonial Times*, suggested that the colonists in both Van Diemen's Land and Australia should hold meetings and organize petitions asking that the state prisoners be pardoned. Mitchel publicly responded to the proposal by asking that his name should not be included as he refused to beg pardon or to ask anybody to do so on his behalf. He also exonerated the magistrate who had arrested him on the grounds that he had only carried out his duty. [114] However, O'Brien was concerned that some of Mitchel's angry letters to the press had hardened attitudes within the government towards the exiles.[115] At this stage, MacManus and Meagher had already escaped from Van Diemen's Land, which was a public humiliation for the authorities both there and Britain.

By 1854, only three of the seven Young Irelanders remained in Van Diemen's Land. At the beginning of the year, Isaac Butt, who had so skilfully defended Duffy in 1848 and had championed their cause in the British parliament, contacted the Foreign Secretary, Lord Palmerston, directly. He asked that a pardon should extend to all three men equally. In Martin's case, he argued that at the beginning of 1848, Martin had attempted to dissuade his party from physical force 'but in the progress of events, he was unhappily drawn in, lending his money and talents to establish a newspaper and to advocate different doctrines'. He believed that O'Doherty had similarly been persuaded to preach radical doctrines in his newspaper by events in Ireland. Butt did not believe that any of the men were hardened revolutionaries but that they were acting out of a misguided sense of honour.[116] A few months later, the British Foreign

Secretary recommended that the remaining Young Ireland and Chartist prisoners should be granted conditional pardons. On 9 May 1856, to celebrate the end of the Crimean War, they were granted full pardons.

Escape from Van Diemen's Land

The seven state prisoners only spent a few months together in Van Diemen's Land because in the latter part of 1851 Terence MacManus escaped from the island. He successfully reached San Francisco, where he remained until his death in 1861. The other men knew of his plans. O'Brien admitted that 'my mind will <u>not</u> be at ease until I hear he is safe in California'.[117] In the United States, he became involved in Irish politics, attending meetings of the local branch of the 'The Sons of the Emerald Isle'. At the St Patrick's Day celebrations in 1854 he toasted to O'Brien, who had 'forfeited everything for his home and his country'.[118] When MacManus escaped, he had left his shaggy greyhound, Brian, in Meagher's care.[119] However, in January 1852 Meagher escaped. Two more Young Irelanders followed. In December 1852 O'Donoghoe escaped and he was followed by Mitchel, in June 1853. The arrival of the four men in the United States ensured that Irish nationalism remained at the forefront of political debate there.

Following MacManus's escape, the remaining prisoners were more closely monitored, making further attempts difficult. Undaunted, in January 1852 Meagher withdrew his parole, thus alerting the authorities to the likelihood of his intentions, immediately after which he shaved off his moustache and fled to the United States.[120] His wife was pregnant at the time. At first, O'Brien did not approve as he was concerned that Meagher had not honoured the terms of his parole.[121] From his new home in America, Meagher sent letters to various newspapers, including to the *Colonist*, explaining his actions.[122] It was later shown that a number of newspaper articles which had accused Meagher of being 'ungentlemanly' had been written by Balfe, using the pseudonym, 'Dion'.[123] O'Donoghoe responded by writing an article denouncing Balfe, which was published in the *Launceston Times*. It resulted in O'Donoghoe being sent to the Cascades Probation Station for three months.[124] Shortly after his release, he escaped to the United States.

O'Brien's anger with Meagher was short lived; he admitted to O'Doherty that he 'rejoiced' in their friend's escape.[125] Upon hearing that Meagher had arrived in the United States, he wrote, 'the reception with which Meagher has been greeted in America has been to me a source of unmixed satisfaction ... and I am rejoiced to see that the brilliance of his oratory has been in no respect diminished by the long eclipse which has endured in Irish prisons and in the forests of Van Diemen's Land'.[126] He was similarly pleased when he heard that Mitchel had arrived safely.[127] At the beginning of 1853, Meagher's wife left Van Diemen's Land, initially travelling to Ireland to meet his family. Before she left, O'Brien bought her 'a little keepsake' from his meagre resources.[128]

In January 1853 Mitchel received surprising news from O'Doherty. A colleague from the Irish Confederation, Patrick (or P. J.) Smyth had come to Van Diemen's Land at the bidding of the New York Directory, to help the remaining exiles escape to San Francisco. Smyth himself had fled to the United States in 1848, disguised as a drover.[129] Like many of his colleagues, he had found employment as a journalist, initially in Pittsburgh and then in New York, where he was a correspondent for the *New York Tribune*. This paper was owned by Horace Greeley, who had been a founding member of the New York Directory in 1848. Smyth and Mitchel had been close friends in Ireland, but Smyth did not recognize Mitchel when they first met, mistaking him for a detective.[130] Both Smyth and Mitchel wanted O'Brien to escape first as his sentence was for life, but O'Brien declined on the grounds that he had had his chance and had failed. If he was captured, he feared that he would never be allowed to return to Ireland. It was therefore decided that Mitchel should be the first to go, accompanied by Martin, although this plan was changed. Jenny Mitchel and the children would be left behind but would follow at some later stage.[131] O'Doherty, now working as a surgeon, did not seem to be part of the plan.[132]

Mitchel's escape was typically dramatic. He needed a fast horse to help his get-away and he mischievously purchased one from the police magistrate.[133] However, the authorities were fully informed of the escape plans and extra police were sent to Bothwell, while Smyth was arrested briefly. Despite these problems, neither man would contemplate escaping without first withdrawing their parole. At this point, Martin decided not to go as it would be more arduous than had originally been thought. Mitchel was undaunted and on 12 June 1853, he resigned his ticket-of-leave in person and, with Smyth, departed from Bothwell on horseback. Mitchel had already made the decision not to be taken alive.[134] Because of the delays, the escape ship had already left and so Mitchel had to spend some time in hiding. He shaved off his whiskers and disguised himself as a priest. Even O'Doherty did not recognize him when they met in Hobart. The second vessel Mitchel was to meet did not stop as planned, because the captain wanted to avoid being searched, which the government was doing to all ships that docked in Van Diemen's Land. Although Mitchel attempted to join the ship, it was too far from the coast. He eventually escaped by being smuggled on board by moonlight on 19 July. He had been in hiding for five weeks. From Van Diemen's Land he sailed to Sydney. Although his ship was searched by the police authorities, he was not discovered. He then sailed to Tahiti, where he joined a ship going to San Francisco. Unknown to either side, it was the same one that his wife and family were on, together with Smyth.[135] At this stage, he felt safe enough to cast off his disguises and to become John Mitchel again and openly join his family.[136] O'Brien rejoiced in Michel's safe escape but was disappointed that he had been unable to say farewell to Jenny Mitchel before her departure. He had charged O'Doherty with buying her a present on his behalf, up to the value of £10.[137] However, without the company of his friends and political allies, O'Brien was even lonelier than he had been previously.

While Mitchel was escaping, it was announced that Van Diemen's Land was no longer going to be a penal colony. As he approached the United States, Mitchel heard that a war in Europe was likely to erupt, probably between Britain and Russia. He wondered whether this conflict would result in the re-emergence of nationalist struggles and whether Ireland would participate. Mitchel and Smyth arrived in San Francisco on 9 October and they immediately looked for MacManus, who was now living on a ranch fifty miles out of town. When MacManus heard the news, he travelled to meet his friends. For three weeks, Mitchel and Smyth were honoured guests of the town, with celebrations that included a banquet from the Governor of the State. They then left for New York where Mitchel was planning to meet his friends from 1848, including Reilly, Meagher, Dillon, O'Gorman, Doheny and others. More importantly, he was looking forward to seeing his mother who had travelled to the United States to be with him.[138] Significantly, Mitchel's narrative of his experience – the *Jail Journal* – ended when he arrived in New York on 29 November 1853. Meagher and William, Mitchel's brother, were there to meet him, but, despite spending months at sea, he went straight to Brooklyn to see his mother.[139]

The three exiles who remained in Van Diemen's Land were granted conditional pardons in early 1854. One of the conditions was that they were not allowed to return to the United Kingdom. O'Brien, therefore, took up residence in Brussels where he could be visited by his family. Despite these restrictions, O'Brien expressed relief that he had not been asked to apologize for his actions in 1848, stating that he would have refused to do so. En route to Europe, O'Brien first visited Australia where he was feted as a hero. In July, for example, the gold miners at Ballarat presented him with a gold cup.[140] Martin chose to live in Paris following his release. O'Doherty briefly broke the conditions of his release, returning to the United Kingdom where he married Eva, who had stayed faithful to her promise made in 1848. In 1856, they were given full pardons, following which O'Brien and Martin went back to Ireland. On their return, they were welcomed as heroes. In 1855 also, the British government issued a general amnesty to the men who had left Ireland to escape arrest in 1848. A number returned to Ireland, including John Blake Dillon.

Life in the United States

When MacManus, Mitchel, Meagher and O'Donoghoe arrived in the United States they were joining colleagues who had already been living there for over three years, with mixed success. Despite the convincing defeat of the 1848 uprising in Ireland and the failure of the 1849 rising in Waterford, within the United States support for Irish nationalism continued, most evidently in New York City. Dreams of Irish independence were kept alive by the presence of so many members of Young Ireland, together with that of thousands of famine emigrants, many of whom viewed themselves as economic refugees. Anger at the British government was further fuelled by the arrival of two American citizens, Richard Ryan and James Bergin, who had been imprisoned in Ireland in 1848. Their release was regarded as a victory for Irish patriots and Irish-America, with plans made at the end of 1848 in New York for a 'grand banquet' on their return.[141]

For some of the 1848 exiles, the United States offered not only a sanctuary from the British government, but also a refuge from politics within Ireland. Dillon had arrived in New York in October 1848, after seven weeks at sea. He was greeted by the 'sad news' that O'Brien had been sentenced to death 'and the cowards around him are behaving like women so that their lives might be spared'.[142] Their actions made his exile easier to bear as he was 'grateful for being separated from a people amongst whom I could no longer live without a constant loathing'.[143] He also admitted that he was glad to have escaped 'not so much the vengeance of the British government, as on being rescued for ever from the contaminating society of its slaves'.[144]

Some of the former Young Irelanders were regarded as heroes, even if their actual involvement in the events of July 1848 had been minimal. *The Spirit of the Times* in Philadelphia, for example, welcomed the arrival of Thomas D'Arcy McGee, who had been in Scotland at the time of the Ballingarry uprising, as 'a distinguished Irish patriot ... a refugee from the land of his birth and his glorious endeavours'. The *Boston Pilot* averred that 'these gifted, self-sacrificing, but unfortunate, patriots deserve our most generous sympathies'. The welcomes were often tied in with anti-British sentiment. The *New York Tribune* for example, stated that, 'England, with all her boasted power, has crushed a starving people, she may pronounce it a "glorious victory" , but it is not sufficient to deter the fearless and noble-hearted people of this country from expressing their sympathies in favour of those who have struggled ... though vainly for a time ... against tyranny.'[145]

McGee, an experienced journalist, founded his own newspaper, the *New York Nation*, in October 1848. He declared that its main purpose was to advance 'the liberation of Ireland'. He called on all exiled Irishmen, especially Irish-Americans, to continue to pursue this goal, stating that, through his paper, 'by impregnating the Irish mind with large and heroic views of duty we conceive we will be doing substantial service to this commonwealth'.[146] However, McGee, and his ally Duffy, had represented the moderate wing of Young Ireland and he had been disliked by Mitchel, Doheny and Reilly. The old enmity continued in the United

States, with McGee using the columns of his paper to criticize some of his former colleagues. Doheny responded to claims that he was an alcoholic by physically assaulting McGee in the streets of New York.[147] When Meagher arrived in New York, his opinion of McGee was similarly low; he disliked the fact that McGee had exaggerated his role in the 1848 uprising. This resulted in the usually warm-hearted Meagher describing McGee as a 'mere trickster in politics'.[148] Not surprisingly, the conservative press in Ireland and Britain were keen to report these instances of division amongst the exiles.[149]

The *New York Nation* gave regular updates about Young Irelanders overseas. The early arrivals included 'Mr Treanor of Stalybridge, and Dr Reynolds, of Liverpool, the two most active Confederate-Chartist leaders, Messrs Drumm, O'Byrne, Cantwell and Crean of Dublin, Messrs Hennessy and Maguire of Cork, and some Tipperary, Limerick and Galway gentlemen, all active agents in the late revolutionary preparations in Ireland, and all men worthy of the most liberal confidence and the largest sympathy'. The new arrivals were advised 'never to join in a joke at Ireland's expense; never to stifle truth for the sake of gain; never to eat borrowed bread (which never fattens nor fills); sedulously to avoid the prevalent practices of drinking and swearing; and never to speak largely on their own praise'.[150] Some of the exiles were honoured with dinners, including relatively humble men such as Michael Crean, a mechanic from Dublin.[151] Not all of the men were what they appeared, however. *The New York Nation* reported on the arrival of 'Mr Fitzgerald and Mr Mansfield', who both claimed to be Young Irelanders fleeing from government prosecution. It was later shown that they had nothing to do with the group.[152]

Nonetheless, especially after the initial interest had subsided, some of the exiles in America did experience difficulties, the main one being poverty. Shortly after arriving, therefore, part of the reality of their new life was the need to find an income. They were helped by the fact that the Irish community in the United States looked after each other and, regardless of their poverty, some of the exiles mixed in exalted circles. Robert Emmet used his influence to get Dillon admitted to the American bar immediately, rather than having to wait the usual period of five years.[153] Horace Greeley of the *New York Tribune* and Charles O'Conor, a prominent lawyer whose father had been involved in the 1798 uprising, also intervened to help them.[154] In May 1849, Greeley used his influence to find a job for some Young Irelanders, including William Mitchel, who only a year earlier had been courted as the brother of John. Greeley warned William that his previous fame would count for little and hoped that 'for the sake of his many friends, he will do his utmost to deserve the place by resolute energy and the most observable devotion to his duties'.[155] William appeared to heed the advice and got a job working for the American government in Washington.[156]

Not all of the exiles fared as well. Thomas Devin Reilly, a brilliant young graduate of Trinity College, who had been a journalist in Dublin, writing for the *Nation*, the *United Irishman* and the *Irish Felon*, found the transition difficult. In the United States, he remained true to his radical politics. He was an admirer of Wolfe Tone and the democratic principles of 1798 and he had been a close friend and political ally of Mitchel. They remained in contact even following Mitchel's transportation. In 1848, due to his political activities, he was forced to flee to New York. In 1849 he founded his own paper, *The People*, in which he wrote of the need for American intervention to bring about a successful republican uprising Ireland. He was scathing about Duffy, who had remained in Ireland where he was promoting constitutionalism. Reilly also championed the rights of labour. However, he found little support for his radical ideas within the Irish community and the paper folded within six months. Moreover, because he had offended the Catholic Church he was threatened with excommunication.[157] When *The People* ceased circulation, he worked briefly in Boston, writing for a labour union. Subsequently, he made a meagre living contributing to various journals. When the Hungarian nationalist, Lajos Kossuth, visited the United States, Reilly interviewed him, but criticized the fact the he had allied himself with the English Liberals.[158]

Reilly's financial situation improved when he got a job for the *American Review*, but he found himself unemployed when the editorship changed. He then wrote for the *Democratic Review*. Although he mostly lived in a few rooms in New York and later in Washington, with no direct access to water, Reilly frequently entertained both his former colleagues and American politicians in his humble lodgings.[159] In spite of his brilliance, his descent into poverty continued.[160] Reilly died prematurely in 1854, aged only thirty, and was buried in Mount Olive Cemetery. He was survived by a wife and a daughter, two other children having died in infancy.[161] Some members of the Irish-American community established a testimonial fund for his child.[162] Even in exile, and while enduring poverty and suffering from ill-health, Reilly had remained committed to the idea of a democratic, republican Ireland.[163] Moreover, Reilly's admiration and affection for Mitchel never diminished.[164] His deceased son had been named after John Mitchel.[165] The *New York Times* when reporting his death described him as a 'distinguished Irish patriot'.[166]

Reilly's criticisms of Duffy, and McGee's criticism of Doheny, were a microcosm of wider tensions that had existed in the Irish Confederation prior to 1848. These divisions re-emerged amongst supporters of Young Ireland in the United States. At a meeting held in New York in the summer of 1850 to express support for O'Brien the divisions came to a head between those who continued to favour direct action against Britain and those who preferred constitutional tactics. Horace Greeley, who chaired the meeting, admitted that he had recently come to realize that 'there are very serious divisions among Irishmen as to the policy of holding any meeting on the subject, and ... some have declared that, if such a meeting were held, it should be broken up by violence'. Greeley, a supporter of the Young Ireland rising in 1848, believed that in the short term winning Irish independence was unlikely: 'after her tame surrender of her noblest patriots to a felon's doom, without a blow, I can no longer believe her people capable of winning their rights by the strong hand. I shall therefore bear no part in any future agitation looking to the recovery of her liberty by force'. Instead, Greeley placed his hopes for Ireland's future redemption in education, tenant right and the fusion of Catholics and Protestants. Michael Doheny, who was present, opposed these sentiments, arguing that here was no virtue in supporting peaceful tactics. Rather, he suggested that more arms should be sent to Ireland, citing the success of the American struggle for independence. He suggested that, 'If you wish to send comfort to Smith O'Brien, tell him there are 100,000 Irish men in America ready to fight the battle of freedom.' Not surprisingly, the meeting ended in confusion.[167]

For the most part, while in the United States, the various emigrants and exiles remained in contact with each other. There were even some marriages. Joseph Brenan married John Savage's sister.[168] They also helped each other financially.[169] Thus, in 1853, Brenan, who had been plagued by illness during his stay in New Orleans, was helped by his colleagues. Meagher visited him and made him a present of his speeches, while Mitchel offered him a job on his New York paper, the *Citizen*.[170] The sense of displacement felt by many Irish political exiles was summed up by Mitchel. He admitted that since his transportation in 1848 much in Ireland had changed as a consequence of famine, emigration and the defeat of the uprising. He believed that mass emigration to the United States had broken the spirit of the country because 'Ireland without the Irish – the Irish out of Ireland – neither of these can be *our country*'.[171]

The popularity of the convicted leaders of 1848 endured during their exile in Van Diemen's Land, and so when MacManus, Meagher and Mitchel escaped to the United States, they were each given a hero's welcome.[172] However, as Mitchel approached New York he wrote, 'I am going to be a demigod for two or three weeks – so my American friends warn me with many a prudent caution.' [173] Inevitably, life in the United States was not the panacea that the 1848–ers hoped it would be and, inevitably, some of the old tensions and divisions emerged. O'Donoghoe, who had been largely invisible to the outside world during his exile in Van Diemen's Land, and had been marginalized by his fellow prisoners, was similarly disregarded during his brief stay in the United States. His one public appearance took place when he attended a dinner to celebrate the arrival of John Mitchel in New York. Shortly afterwards, in January 1854, O'Donoghoe died from diarrhoea. He had been ill for a number of weeks. At that stage, he was living in lodgings in Brooklyn, with people he had known in Ireland. He died on the day that his wife and daughter arrived from Ireland, but before they were able to meet. The inquest suggested that the people with whom he lodged had taken large amounts of money from O'Donoghoe and following his death refused to give his family his personal papers. Although none of his fellow lodgers attended the funeral, some of his former colleagues from Young Ireland did, including Michael Doheny, John O'Mahony and Michael Cavanagh. They had only heard of his death by accident. When Cavanagh realized that only one funeral carriage had been ordered, paid for from charity, he ordered five more, at his expense. According to Doheny, O'Donoghoe's unpopularity in the United States had arisen from the fact that 'he had told stories about the other Irish patriots, and I did not care to meet a man who would repeat such stories, whether true or false; however, any feelings of an unpleasant nature ceased with his death'.[174] O'Donoghoe was the first of the state prisoners to die. In death, much as during his life, his role in the events of 1848 remained largely unnoticed.

The second escaped state prisoner to die in the United States was Terence Bellew MacManus. He passed away in January 1861 in San Francisco, where he had been living since his escape from Van Diemen's Land in 1851. His death was particularly mourned by Meagher, who had struck up a friendship with him while in Van Diemen's Land.[175] However, apart from brief period of notoriety in 1848, MacManus achieved more attention following his death than during his life. Local Fenians, with the support of the Irish organization, decided to remove his body to Ireland for burial in Dublin. The idea probably emanated from John O'Mahony, a former Confederate and co-founder of the Irish Republican Brotherhood. The long journey was to be broken by a stop in New York, the heartland of much Irish nationalist activity. The Fenians asked John Hughes, the Irish-born archbishop of New York, if the coffin could be displayed in his cathedral. He complied, which was in contrast to the Irish Catholic Church's condemnation of the Fenian movement by the Catholic hierarchy in Ireland. Thus, in September 1861, MacManus's casket was laid in the centre of St Patrick's Cathedral. Following the requiem mass, Hughes made an address 'on the nature of lawful resistance to the state within the context of Catholic doctrine ... [His] central purpose was to harmonise MacManus's actions with Catholic teachings according to the precepts of St Thomas Aquinas. His main argument focused upon MacManus's love of his country.' [176] To his predominantly Fenian audience, Hughes's comments demonstrated how physical force and Catholicism could be compatible. The archbishop's involvement was surprising because apart from briefly supporting a nationalist rising in 1848, he was critical of members of Young Ireland now resident in the United States, including Meagher and Mitchel, whom he accused of having 'red' republican sympathies.[177] Moreover, the Pope and leading members of the Catholic Church in Ireland were opposed to nationalism in general and Fenianism in particular.

On 18 October, MacManus's remains were taken to the dockside for transport to Ireland. The accompanying procession through the streets of New York attracted thousands of observers, with Irish delegations from California, Philadelphia and Boston. Meagher and O'Mahony were present.[178] Archbishop Hughes's response contrasted sharply with the actions of Cardinal Cullen in Ireland who refused to allow MacManus's body to be laid in the Pro-Cathedral in Dublin. Nonetheless, the burial of MacManus on 10 November in Glasnevin Cemetery was attended by thousands of people. James Stephens wrote the oration. The funeral of the Young Irelander, MacManus, which took place over two continents, scored a massive propaganda victory for the Fenians, while demonstrating the links between the two nationalist movements. For the next four years though, the activities of Irish nationalists, especially those in the United States, were overshadowed by the Civil War.

Meagher was warmly welcomed in the United States, where his reputation as a charismatic and uncompromising nationalist preceded him. Like his colleagues, he primarily made a living by lecturing and writing on the events of 1848 in journals published as far away as Australia.[179] He also studied law. Although courted by both men and women he found life in New York as unfulfilling as life in Van Diemen's Land. He quickly became fed up with being asked to lecture about 1848 and its aftermath, suggesting that he be allowed to talk on different topics.[180] Within a few months of his arrival, Meagher fell foul of the Catholic Church in the person of the influential archbishop of New York, John Hughes. Briefly, in 1848, Hughes had supported an uprising in Ireland, but he subsequently embraced the new conservatism promoted by Pope Pius IX. He later labelled Meagher, Mitchel and other Irish radicals 'red republicans' because they supported Italian nationalism and were admirers of Garibaldi.[181] Undeterred, Meagher frequently spoke out in defence of the rights of the poor and of religious liberty. By 1856 though, he was again reconciled with the Catholic Church.[182] He even gave the proceeds of a lecture in Philadelphia for the building of a new church.[183] Meagher's wife, Bennie, never joined him in the United States: she died while visiting his family in Waterford. Their child survived. He was a son and so while in the United States Meagher seemed to be responsible for a child being reared by his family in Ireland. Meagher subsequently married a wealthy American woman.

Meagher appeared as restless in the United States and he had been in Van Diemen's Land.[184] He remained unwavering in his love for Ireland and desire for Irish independence, but he did not support the Fenian movement, which had been founded in 1858. The founders of this organization were James Stephens and John O'Mahony, members of Young Ireland who had fought in the various uprisings in 1848 and 1849. Ironically, fifteen years after he made his famous 'Meagher of the Sword' speech, Meagher appeared to find fulfilment when he participated in another national struggle, not on behalf of Ireland but in the United States. He became captain of a company of Zouaves in the exclusively Irish Sixty-Ninth Regiment.[185] He subsequently formed a New York Irish Brigade, who fought bravely – and suffered many losses – in all of the major battles,[186] and he himself was wounded at the battle of Fredericksburg. During the American Civil War Meagher demonstrated his prowess as a soldier and as a leader of men. He resigned in 1863 when he failed to gain promotion, but his resignation was cancelled. Although he may have lost the support of some of his superiors, he never lost the loyalty of his men.[187] Ironically, Meagher of the Sword, who never got a chance to fight for his country's independence in 1848, fought brilliantly and valiantly on behalf of his adopted homeland.

Following his military career, Meagher was offered the Secretaryship of the Territory of Montana. Before travelling there, he wrote to his father explaining that the position would be 'a profitable one to me, and ... it will enable me to pay you visits in France next summer'. As was his custom, he enclosed presents for some of his family, including 'dear little Bernie', who was possibly his child from his first marriage. He also sent his love to his aunts.[188] Two years later, Meagher wrote to his father from Montana, describing some of the problems he was having with 'the Indians on our Eastern Settlements [as] these gentlemen have been displaying for some months a very hostile spirit'. The irony of his role did not seem to strike him. In his letter, Meagher talked of visiting Europe the following year and meeting with his father and daughter. He even considered travelling to Ireland.[189] He died two weeks later, drowning in mysterious circumstances, with his detractors claiming that he was either drunk or deranged at the time. He was aged only 44.

Meagher had been the youngest leader of the 1848 uprising. Regardless of the vicissitudes of his career, he was widely mourned.[190] The Irish community in America were devastated by the news, with the *Irish People* in New York proclaiming 'Meagher of the Sword is dead' and adding it was 'the saddest news that has befallen our lot since we made an appearance in the journalistic world'.[191] Mass meetings were held on the eastern seaboard, from Washington to Boston, with an estimated 8,000 present in the latter.[192] Following the unexpected death of Meagher, Mitchel wrote a tribute to his erstwhile colleague in the American press. It showed that regardless of ideological differences, which had been evident in 1848 and during the American Civil War, their relationship was underpinned by enduring affection.[193]

Mitchel's life in the United States was not without controversy either; he maintained the same outspoken declamation of what he perceived to be injustice that had marked his career in Ireland. Amongst his first targets was the anti-Catholic Know Nothing Party. This party, which had originated in 1849, was opposed to Catholic immigrants, who it suggested were loyal only to the Pope. By 1856 it was at the height of its power, even fielding a candidate in the presidential election. Later, Mitchel was similarly critical of some of the showier and more bombastic elements within the Fenian movement, believing their policy of secret conspiracy to be seriously flawed.[194] He made it clear that while he was a nationalist, he did not espouse either republicanism or sentimentalism in the abstract. Mitchel's championing of the Southern States in the Civil War lost him support in the United States, although he appeared shocked that 'in a "land of liberty" a man was supposed to conceal unpopular opinions'.[195]

In the United States Mitchel seemed afflicted with the same restlessness as Meagher, moving around and starting a number of short-lived ventures, including some political publications.[196] Following his arrival in New York one of the first things he did was to start his own newspaper, the *Citizen*, which was dedicated to Irish affairs. In it, he published a weekly account of the events of 1848, commencing with his transportation in May of that year. It was based on the journal he had kept while in exile. This series was reprinted in some Irish newspapers, thus providing an early alternative version of events, while keeping the memory of 1848 alive.[197] It was later published as *The Jail Journal*. Mitchel's fame and popularity – and reputation as an unrepentant critic of British rule – were kept alive in Ireland by the serialization of his *Jail Journal* in the United States and Ireland.[198] The *Citizen* was critical of the authoritarianism of the Catholic Church, which lost him Catholic support, notably that of Archbishop Hughes of New York. His paper was equally disparaging about the Know Nothing Party.[199] As had been the case in 1848, he demonstrated his willingness to endure personal opprobrium in pursuit of his political beliefs.

In 1856, Mitchel purchased a farm in Knoxville, Tennessee. As his experience in Van Diemen's Land had suggested, he was not a good farmer. Regardless of his notorious support for slavery he did not utilize slave labour.[200] In 1857 he started the *Southern Citizen*, which also failed. While in Tennessee, Mitchel was visited by James Stephens, founder of the Fenian Brotherhood, who was seeking his support. Mitchel wrote to Horace Greeley asking if the money that had been raised by the New York Directory in 1848 could be given to the new republican organization. He explained that:

> I think the time has come when the Directory may discharge itself of the remainder of its funds fully and strictly in pursuance of its original objects. Mr Stephens has himself made great exertions and sacrifices to create so perfect an Organisation looking to the speedy revolutionizing of that country ... I have systematically refused to join in any of the organisations calling on the people for subscriptions, because there was no feasible occasion for using them, and because such funds, when collected, have always been mismanaged. But I am now fully satisfied ... I would earnestly ask the Directory to place their fund at Mr Stephens' disposal.

Shortly afterwards, Mitchel went to Paris, probably on Fenian business, but he returned to the United States when the Civil War commenced. His defence of the Confederacy in the American Civil War lost him some friends and support, and it also resulted in the death of two of his children. His son John was killed at Fort Sumter in 1863, and William was killed at Gettysburg in 1864. Mitchel had offered his services to the Confederacy, saying that he was willing to run the blockade, but he was turned down.[201]

Mitchel's outspokenness during the Civil War resulted in his imprisonment for the second time in his life. The opening passages of his *Jail Journal* described how, in May 1848, because of his revolutionary preachings in the *United Irishman*, he had been led, in chains and manacles, into exile. His adversary was the British government. In 1865, as a result of his unwavering support for the Confederacy, he was placed under military arrest by the American government and he was taken under armed guard to a military stronghold at Fort Munroe, where he remained a prisoner for two months. The intervention of the Irish Republican Brotherhood helped to bring about his release.[202] After the war, Mitchel returned to Paris as an administrator for the Fenians, where he was visited by John Martin and Father Kenyon. His disapproval of the fund-raising activities of the Fenians resulted in his return to New York. In March 1867 he asked for a letter to be published in the New York press in which he stated his support for the general principles of Fenianism, but added 'I disapprove strongly of claim upon people for large contributions of money under the delusion that anything important could be effected'. He was adamant that unless Britain was at war with France or the United States, no Fenian uprising could succeed.[203]

In 1874, Mitchel visited Ireland, after an absence of twenty-six years. Wherever he went, he was treated as a hero. Despite being in ill-health, before leaving he issued an address to the electorate in Tipperary, where a by-election was to be held.[204] In February 1875, Mitchel was elected unopposed as MP for County Tipperary, the location of the 1848 uprising. Since he was a convicted felon, the result was invalidated by the British government. A further election was held and he was re-elected with a larger majority. Regardless of his chequered career, his controversial support for slavery, and his long absence from Ireland, he had not been forgotten in his native land. Moreover, in the spirit of Young Ireland, his Ulster and Protestant origins did not matter to the voters of Tipperary. Following his election he returned to Ireland, as MP in a parliament he refused to recognize and had spent most of his adult life criticizing. While there, he dined with his former colleague, Speranza, and her husband, Sir William Wilde. Fittingly perhaps, Mitchel died in March 1875, in the land of his birth. His death saved the British government from the indignity of having to hold a third by-election.

In Ireland, even those who disagreed with Mitchel mourned his death. He was buried in Newry and on the day of his funeral, the local businesses closed and the mills stopped working. All flags were flown at half mast. An estimated 10,000 people attended. Sixteen Roman Catholic clergy preceded the hearse, while it was followed by ministers from the Presbyterian Church. It was a fitting tribute to Mitchel's advocacy of non-sectarianism. Mitchel was buried with his father and his beloved mother.[205] His close friend John Martin attended the funeral, but caught a cold while there. It proved to be fatal. Consequently, within only nine days of each other, two men who had been life-long friends, political allies and exiles in Van Diemen's Land, died and were buried in Ireland. Their deaths marked the end in a chapter of Irish nationalism that had been characterized by non-sectarian ideals and an adherence to their principles, no matter how unpopular they were. As the relationship between the two men showed, Mitchel was a loyal friend and devoted family man. The friendship between John Mitchel, John Martin and Father Kenyon had endured, surviving even Mitchel's exile and political disagreements. In late life they met in France on a number of occasions. Martin also visited New York in 1869 and shared a platform with Mitchel, in which they both praised the patriotism of William Smith O'Brien.[206] Mitchel's relationship with Martin was further consolidated when the bachelor married Mitchel's sister. A telling indication of the enduring ecumenicalism of both Mitchel and his fellow Young Irelander, William Smith O'Brien, was their support when they each had a daughter who converted to Catholicism.[207]

In death, as in life, Mitchel proved to be a controversial figure. His detractors referred to the confusing circumstances when he surrendered parole on Van Diemen's Land over twenty years earlier.[208] In the United States, his commitment to Irish nationalism was overshadowed by his later espousal of the institution of slavery. The *New York Times* judged his life to have been a failure, averring that, 'He was undoubtedly a man of undaunted courage, but he lacked judgement and discretion ... His career in this country proved a complete failure.'[209] Some Irish constitutional nationalists, including Duffy and his protégé A.M. Sullivan remained harsh in their assessment of Mitchel's life. Duffy and Mitchel had fallen out in 1847 and almost fifty years later, Duffy was unusually critical of Mitchel's political and literary judgements.[210] The writings of these two men – which in many ways were diametrically opposed – were widely read and influenced subsequent interpretations of the 1848 rising. It was Mitchel, rather than Duffy or any of his fellow Young Irelanders, who influenced the next generation of Irish republicanism at the beginning of the twentieth century, with both constitutionalists and 'advanced nationalists' borrowing from his writings. Arthur Griffith regarded Mitchel as 'the greatest figure in Irish history', while Patrick Pearse ranked him as one of 'the four apostles' of Irish nationalism.[211] His death marked the close in an important phase in the history of Young Ireland.

Later lives

Many Young Irelanders had illustrious careers after 1848, with their influence extending far beyond Ireland. Ironically, the most experienced parliamentarian, William Smith O'Brien, who had been an MP in Westminster prior to his involvement in the 1848 rising, never formally became involved in politics again. Nonetheless, he wrote profusely on political topics, taking a particular interest in the struggle for Hungarian independence. He visited the United States in 1859 where he was an outspoken critic of slavery. Although he disliked the Know Nothing Party, he suggested that the behaviour of some Irish immigrants had contributed to a general anti-Irish feeling in the country.[212] He opposed slavery, but deprecated the outbreak of civil war in 1861 and publicly criticized Meagher for offering to fight in it. He offered his services as a mediator in the conflict.[213] Following the death of O'Brien's beloved wife Lucy in 1861, his own health declined. This may have been expedited by financial wrangles with his son, who had totally rejected his father's politics. Even in old age, he defended the actions that he had taken in 1848 when he was a 'Middle-Aged Irelander'. When he heard that Sir Robert Peel's son had, in the House of Commons, referred to O'Brien and his colleagues as 'the cabbage patch heroes of 1848', he challenged him to a duel.[214] When Peel failed to respond, O'Brien described him as a coward as well as a bully.[215] O'Brien died in June 1864 in Wales. His remains were returned to Ireland where they received a hero's welcome. In the eyes of some of his family, however, his participation in the 1848 rising continued to blight his memory, and his son did not attend his funeral service.

John Martin had been introduced to nationalist politics by John Mitchel, but his involvement was sustained after he was allowed to return to Ireland in 1856. Although a landlord himself, he immediately became involved in the Tenant Right League. Like Mitchel, he supported the South in the American Civil War, but he did not receive the same public opprobrium as his friend.[216] Martin opposed the Fenian movement, believing that peaceful tactics were preferable to violent ones.[217] Moreover, he considered that the Fenian plan of 'a combined insurrection and invasion while England is at peace with both France and America' was 'mad'.[218] Nonetheless, in December 1867 he spoke at a meeting in Dublin to protest at the hanging of the 'Manchester Martyrs', three young Fenians, a month earlier.[219] Martin was an early supporter of Isaac Butt's Home Government Association and he was elected a Home Rule member for Meath in 1871.[220] He was victorious in spite of the opposition of many local priests.[221] As a consequence, Martin became the first Home Rule MP in the British parliament. He was re-elected in the General Election in 1874. A year later, he died, succumbing to an illness contracted when attending Mitchel's funeral. He died in relative poverty, having refused to take rent from his tenants during years of poor harvest.

Until their deaths, the lives of John Martin and John Mitchel had remained entwined. As northern Protestants, they were outsiders in mainstream nationalist politics, which, regardless of interventions of Young Ireland, had been slowly moving towards a Catholic view of Irish identity since the time of O'Connell.

One of the most enigmatic of the Young Ireland exiles was Kevin O'Doherty. His later life was inextricably linked with that of his fellow nationalist, 'Eva' (Mary Anne Kelly). Following the granting of his conditional pardon in 1854, he went to Paris to continue his medical studies. During this time, he made an illegal visit to London to marry Eva, to whom he had become secretly affianced before being transported from Ireland. He received an unconditional pardon in 1856, and completing his studies in Dublin, graduated in 1857. He practised in Dublin, but in 1862 he and Eva moved to Brisbane where he became a leading physician. His interest in politics continued and, in 1867, he was elected to the Legislative Assembly. In 1872 he was responsible for a Health Act being passed. In 1877 he transferred to the Legislative Council, but resigned in 1885 as he intended to return home. Even when living in Australia, he retained his interest in Irish politics, and for some years was president of the Australian branch of the Irish National League. In Ireland O'Doherty was welcomed as a hero of 1848, and he was returned unopposed to the House of Commons for Meath North in November. However, he did not seek re-election in 1886, and returned to Brisbane. Although he attempted to take up his medical practice, he was not successful. He died in relative poverty in July 1905. Eva and one daughter survived him. A fund was raised by public subscription to provide for them.[222]

Charles Gavan Duffy outlived most of his colleagues from Young Ireland and he had a long and distinguished political career. After 1848, he became involved in various constitutional activities in Ireland, notably the Tenant League. Many were undermined by internal division and external apathy. Despite his election to parliament in 1852, the following year he confided to Kevin O'Doherty that 'the public spirit of Ireland is so low it disgusts me to live here'.[223] He emigrated to Australia in 1855, disillusioned with Irish politics. He maintained his interest in politics and was appointed Prime Minister of Victoria in 1871. His Catholic origins, however, seemed to alienate some of the Protestant population.[224] Nonetheless, he was knighted in 1873. When he eventually returned to Ireland he decided not to re-enter political life, but instead he wrote the history of Young Ireland and the uprising 'to make known the men of a past era, as they thought and acted, to the men of the present time'.[225] His various accounts of events were influential, even though he had been in jail for much of 1848. Duffy died in 1903 aged 86. While his political contribution to the events of 1848 was doubtful – and later questioned by critics such as Mitchel and Reilly – his literary contribution was impressive. The *Nation* not only provided a vehicle for the most gifted Irish writers of the 1840s, but it also laid the foundations for a cultural and literary revival later in the century.

Apart from Duffy, a number of other Young Irelanders who had attempted to end British rule in Ireland in 1848 were, in their later lives, elected to the imperial parliament in Westminster. Martin and O'Doherty, both convicted felons who had been transported to Van Diemen's Land, sat in the British parliament. P. J. Smyth, a school friend of Meagher who had helped Mitchel to escape from Van Diemen's Land, was elected as a Home Rule MP for Westmeath, shortly after Martin.[226] He had the support of the Catholic clergy and was elected due to his 'impeccable nationalist record, with an unnerving support for the political policies of the Catholic Church'.[227] While in Australia organizing Mitchel's escape, he met the woman whom he subsequently married. John Blake Dillon, one of the founders of the *Nation*, continued to follow Irish politics until his death. He escaped to the United States in 1848 following his conviction for treason. In the United States, he practised law. He returned to Ireland in 1855 as a result of a general political amnesty. In 1865, he was elected to parliament for the Home Rule Party. His son, also John Dillon, was an ardent supporter of Charles Stewart Parnell. Dillon and Duffy had always been close friends and when Dillon died of cholera in 1866 his mother asked if Duffy would write a history of his life. She lamented the fact that as young men, Dillon, Duffy, Mitchel and John Pigot had been such close friends, but circumstances had forced them to live apart, on three separate continents. [228]

Other Young Irelanders proved to be more controversial. Thomas D'Arcy McGee had an illustrious, but ultimately tragic, life. Following his escape in 1848, he was a successful journalist in the United States. However, his politics were increasingly overshadowed by his increasing devotion to Catholicism. When Meagher arrived in New York he warned his fellow Young Irelanders that McGee should not be trusted. [229] Shortly afterwards, McGee moved to Canada to take up a new political career. He quickly emerged as a leading politician in the Federation of Canadian States, serving in the Ministry of Agriculture and of Emigration, and as Commissioner to Europe. He helped to establish the Confederation of Canada in 1867. As his politics became increasingly conservative and Catholic, McGee explained why he had supported the 1848 rising thus: 'when I saw in Ireland the people perish of famine at the rate of five thousand souls per day; when I saw children and women, as well as able-bodied men, perishing for food under the richest Government within the most powerful empire of the world, I rebelled against the pampered state church – I rebelled against the bankrupt aristocracy – I rebelled against Lord John Russell, who sacrificed two millions of the Irish people to the interests of the corn buyers of Liverpool. At the age of twenty-two I threw myself into a struggle ... which was not directed against the government, but against the misgovernment, of that day.'[230] However, like Duffy, he had not been present during the rising, but was travelling to Scotland seeking support. While serving in the Canadian parliament, McGee became a supporter of the imperial connection. He was assassinated, probably, by a fellow Irishman, in Ottawa in April 1868.[231] He was aged 42. McGee's assassin was allegedly a Fenian, who regarded McGee as having betrayed his country.[232] His murder divided public opinion, with his being described alternately as 'Canada's martyred hero' and a 'traitor to Ireland'.[233]

Other Young Ireland exiles made successful careers outside Ireland. Richard O'Gorman became a judge of the Supreme Court in New York.[234] John Pigot achieved both wealth and success at the Indian bar, but he refused a judgeship on the grounds that he would not accept such a role until Ireland had her independence.[235] Notoriety of a different kind was achieved by James Stephens and John O'Mahony. They were both young men in 1848, who were responsible for founding the Fenian Brotherhood in Ireland and the United States respectively. A confidential report on the activities of Fenians in 1861 referred to O'Mahony as 'the Garibaldi of Ireland' and warned that he was willing to lose his life on behalf of his native country.[236] As a young man, he had studied Classics at Trinity College and had been regarded as the most brilliant scholar of his generation. Despite having raised thousands of pounds for the Fenian Brotherhood, he died in poverty in New York in 1877. His remains were brought to Ireland for burial. An estimated 100,000 people lined the streets of Dublin to watch his funeral procession. Cardinal Cullen, who was vehemently opposed to Fenianism, refused to allow O'Mahony's coffin to enter the Cathedral in Dublin or to allow him a Christian burial.[237] While Stephens's reputation had been tarnished by his political vacillations, in the United States O'Mahony was remembered as 'the father of Fenianism'.[238] Michael Doheny, who had also taken part in the 1848 rising, had been a prominent member of both Young Ireland and the Fenian movement. Apart from Meagher, a number of Young Irelanders were commended for their involvement in the American Civil War, including Dr Reynolds, a former Young Irelander from Liverpool and John Cavanagh, who lost his life. Ironically, men who attempted to rebel against the British government in 1848, with such little effect, displayed bravery and military skill when fighting in somebody else's war.

Those who stayed in Ireland also made a mark. John O'Hagan, a Catholic barrister from Belfast, whose first contribution to the *Nation* had been *Ourselves Alone*, a philosophy subsequently adopted by Sinn Féin, had a successful career as a barrister. In 1848 he had been retained by the Crown, but he asked to be excused from this brief due to his friendship with Duffy.[239] In 1881, was appointed Chairman of the Irish Land Commission.[240] Throughout, O'Hagan continued to write and translate poetry that reflected his love of Ireland.[241] The outspoken Father Kenyon, who was sometimes regarded as having deserted his comrades at the last

minute and criticized for refusing shelter to some of those involved in the
rising, remained firm friends with both John Martin and John Mitchel.
Neither Mitchel nor Martin, who suffered years of imprisonment for their
actions, believed that Kenyon's actions were inconsistent with his beliefs.
Thomas Clarke Luby, who first met Kenyon in 1849, on the verge of
another uprising, explained that Kenyon himself feared arrest at this time
and therefore could not have hidden the fugitives, although a number,
including Meagher and John Dillon, had visited him looking for
support.[242]

It was not only the men of Young Ireland who led impressive lives after
1848; many of the women associated with the *Nation* contributed to
Ireland's subsequent political development. In the wake of the Ballingarry
rising, Eva had visited the state prisoners frequently, passing on secret
messages and keeping their spirits up. In keeping with her promise, she
waited for Kevin O'Doherty to be released, marrying him upon his return
to Europe. Throughout her later life, she continued to write poetry,
usually with a nationalist message. Both she and Mary wrote for the
Fenian newspaper, the *Irish People*. One of her poems appeared in the
final edition, before the paper was suppressed by the government. It was
entitled 'To our beloved dead'.[243] Nor was Eva's admiration and support
for the Young Ireland uprising diminished by time. When the first edition
of her poetry was published in the United States in 1877, the introduction
read, 'To the memory of John Mitchel and John Martin, "felons" of 1848.
These poems (associated with the cause for which they suffered) are dedicated by their friend and compatriot, Eva.'[244] The dedication in the
extended edition, published in Ireland in 1908, however, simply read 'To
the Memory of the Dead'.[245] In Australia Eva occasionally contributed to
Queensland journals, and one of her poems was included in *A Book of
Queensland Verse*. Following O'Doherty's death she lived in relative
poverty in Australia with her daughter, publishing a further collection of
her work in order to raise money.[246] She died in Brisbane on 21 May
1910.[247] Olivia Knight, who had written in the *Nation* as Thomasine,
emigrated to Queensland, Australia with her husband, Hope Connolly,
where they continued to support Irish nationalist causes.[248] A collection
of her poetry, *Wild Flowers from the Wayside*, was published in 1883,
and it included an introduction written by Sir Charles Gavan Duffy.[249]

Ellen Downing, or 'Mary of the *Nation*', never recovered from her
disappointment at the arrest and conviction of John Mitchel, whom she
greatly admired. Following this she stopped writing poetry.[250] She was
also disappointed in love, with her engagement to Joseph Brenan being
broken off. After 1848 Mary's patriotic energy was channelled into religious piety. In October 1849 she entered a convent, but had to leave due
to bad health. She became a lay sister and worked for some years as
matron of Cork Fever Hospital.[251] Although she continued to write
poetry, it was mostly based on religious themes. She died in 1869.[252]

Unusually, Mary had little contact with her former colleagues on the *Nation*, not even her former close friend, Eva.[253] Ethna (Marie Thompson) was also a friend and admirer of Mitchel. In a collection of her poems published in 1915, the dedication explained, 'She owes the impressions of early youth and her ardent patriotism, then and since, to the brilliant literary movement of Young Ireland, and to those gallant men of 1848 who breathed a new soul into Ireland. She still fervently hopes that her aspirations for Ireland may yet be realised, and she would there-fore dedicate this little volume to all who have preserved the old traditions and in sincerity are striving to lift their country to a position of honour and renown.' She died in January 1916, on the eve of another nationalist uprising.[254]

Ellen Magennis from County Monaghan, who was born in 1828, was a teenager when she first contributed poetry to the *Nation* and to the *Dundalk Democrat*. Like many of her former colleagues, she continued to write poetry and be to be involved in radical politics although, after 1848, she used her married name, Ellen Forrester. She emigrated to England as a young woman, living initially in Liverpool and then Salford, where she worked as a seamstress. Following the death of her alcoholic husband she raised their five children alone. She was unusual amongst the Young Irelanders in being working class. Despite her poverty and ill-health, two books of her poetry were published: *Simple Strains* in 1863 and *Songs of the Rising Nation* in 1869. The latter was a collaboration with her son, who was arrested twice for his involvement with the Fenian movement.[255] Her daughter Fanny, a dye-worker in Lancashire, had over sixty of her poems published. Ellen worked with John Martin to help raise money for the Manchester Martyrs.[256] In 1872, she applied to the Royal Literary Fund for financial support. In her application she described herself as 'a cripple' who was in 'deep poverty' and supported by her daughters. Her application was refused.[257] She died, destitute, in England in January 1883. Although the Ballymena family of Elizabeth Treacy ('Finola') had Orange sympathies, she was a nationalist sympathizer throughout her adult life. She assisted the Fenians, and took part in the Home Rule and the Land League movements. She lectured into her sixties in both Ireland and Britain on her support for Irish independence.[258] She married a fellow Young Irelander, Ralph Varian, in 1871.[259]

One of the most talented, prolific and colourful of the women contrib-utors to the *Nation* was 'Speranza', or Jane Elgee. In July 1848 Speranza had risked prosecution for treason for the publication of her call to arms *Jacta Alea Est*, although the British government had insisted on blaming the imprisoned Duffy for its publication.[260] Even more than the other female contributors, her background had little prepared her for national-ist politics as she came from an upper-class, Protestant, unionist family, which had no social contact with Catholics. The outcome of the 1848 rising had clearly alarmed Speranza yet she continued to write for the newly-constituted *Nation*, but she did so under the pseudonym 'A' and her articles had little political content.[261]

In 1851, she married William Wilde, a successful oculist who was largely responsible for the census of that year. They had two sons, William and Oscar, the latter following in his mother's footsteps as a writer.[262] In 1864, William Wilde was knighted, following which Speranza used her title, although she maintained her link with her radical past by writing as Lady Francesca Speranza Wilde.[263] However, Speranza never lost her love of Ireland or her interest in nationalist politics.[264] When a collection of her poetry was published in 1864 it was dedicated to 'My sons, Willie and Oscar Wilde'. When it was re-issued some years later, the dedication read 'For Ireland'.[265] Speranza moved to London following the death of her husband in 1876, where she maintained their Dublin tradition of hosting salons for the literati of the day. However, she never felt comfortable in England. She admitted privately that her poetry was 'not suited to *English* taste as you may suppose. Oh, what an incubus this English government is on our country. It strangles all life.'[266] Her interest in feminist issues, about which she had written in the original *Nation*, also persisted and she and her husband attended the first suffrage meeting to be held in Dublin in 1870.[267] In later life she became interested in Irish folklore. Despite being a talented linguist, typically for somebody of her age and background she could not speak Irish, and so relied on translators for her research. In 1887 Speranza published *A Batch of Irish Legends: Ancient Legends, Mystic Charms and Superstitions of Ireland*, which was well received, especially in the United States. She described her reason for publishing this collection as being to give 'the expression of my love for the beautiful island that gave me my first inspiration, my quickest intellectual impulses, and the strongest and best sympathies with genius and country possible to a woman's nature'.[268] Although it is widely assumed that as she became older Speranza moved away from the nationalism of her youth, the reality is more complex. In 1875, when John Mitchel returned to Ireland as MP for Tipperary, he dined with her and her family in Dublin.[269] The odd coupling of a society hostess with an unrepentant rebel lay in their comradeship before and during the 1848 rising. Moreover, a little-known book written by Speranza in her later in life, *The American Irish*, demonstrated that her political fervour on behalf of Ireland had not dimmed. She regarded the demand for Home Rule as a 'hollow fiction', and based on 'feudal distinctions of class and caste'. Rather, she sided with 'the advanced party in Irish politics' and with Irish-Americans who argued for total and permanent independence and a parliament based on universal suffrage. Overall, she felt that a simple Repeal of the Union was insufficient, and that only a republic could give Irish people true freedom.[270]

Nor was Speranza forgotten by the people who had been inspired by her writings in the lead-up to the 1848 rising. When her son Oscar arrived in the United States at the beginning of 1882, references were repeatedly made to his mother's contributions to the *Nation*.[271] He was described in the nationalist press as 'Speranza's son', and his lecture on the 'The English Renaissance: the Utterness of Aesthetics', was criticized for 'phrasing about beauty while a hideous tyranny overshadows his native land'.[272] Oscar Wilde was repeatedly asked about his views on Irish national issues, leading Davis Coakley to suggest that, 'It was his lecture tour in North American that brought Wilde face to face with his Irishness.' Significantly, three months into his tour, he gave a lecture entitled 'The Irish Poets of 1848' in which he praised, amongst others, the writings of his mother.[273] In San Francisco, he referred to Speranza as 'a young girl who had been brought up in an atmosphere of alien English thought ... far removed from any love or knowledge of those wrongs of the people to which she afterwards gave such passionate expression'.[274] The influence of Speranza on later generations of nationalists was apparent at the end of the century, with Maud Gonne being hailed as 'the new Speranza'.[275] Notwithstanding her glittering career and lifestyle, Speranza died in poverty in London, much of her wealth having been squandered by her husband. She was buried without a headstone, away from the land of her birth. Her beloved son Oscar, who was in jail for homosexual offences when she died, paid for her funeral expenses.[276]

While the rising in 1848 may have been brief, inglorious and unsuccessful, the subsequent lives of the people who had supported it, both directly and indirectly, was a testament to the vision and courage of the Young Irelanders. Even in middle and old age they did not lose their love of Ireland or their desire for their country's independence. Moreover, their actions and writings both inspired and informed subsequent generations of nationalists. Their influence, however, extended beyond far the field of politics and far beyond the defeated uprising in Ballingarry in July 1848.

Notes

1 *The Times*, 8 August 1848, 10 August 1848.
2 John West, *The History of Tasmania* (Launceston: Henry Dowling, 1852), p. 30.
3 In total, the political prisoners sent to Van Diemen's Land amounted to about 2,000 (of 160,000 convicts) and included Irish insurgents from 1798 and 1803, the Cato Street conspirators from 1819, the Tolpuddle Martyrs in 1834, Chartists in 1842 and Irish 'felons' in 1848: see West, *History of Tasmania*, pp. 39, 652. West estimates (p. 675) that a quarter of all transported Irish prisoners were 'political' ones.
4 West, *History of Tasmania*, pp. 219–28.
5 Mitchel, *Jail Journal*, 4 December 1848, pp. 110–11.
6 Ibid., 12 February 1849, p. 125.
7 Ibid., p. 157.

8   *The Times*, quoted in Alan F. Hattersley, *The Convict Crisis and the Growth of Unity: Resistance to Transportation in South Africa and Australia 1848–1853* (Cape Town: University of Natal Press, 1965), p. 2.

9   *Freeman's Journal*, 14 December 1849; Reports on Cape Town Anti-Convict Movement, BPP, 1849, xliii, (217) p. 22.

10 Mitchel made his support for the protest widely known: *Jail Journal*, 27 September 1849, p. 190. He, in turn, was excluded from the boycott – the colonists supplying him with locally produced wine: ibid., 12 October 1849, p. 195.

11 Ibid., 19 September 1849, pp. 176–7.

12 Ibid., 21 September 1849, p. 180.

13 Ibid., 18 October 1851, p. 273. This was the first public appearance of what later was to be the *Jail Journal*.

14 Ibid., 13 February 1850, pp. 217–18.

15 West, *History of Tasmania*, p. 225.

16 Mitchel, *Jail Journal*, 4 April 1850, p. 221.

17 Hattersley, *The Convict Crisis*, p. 89.

18 *Nation*, 31 August 1850.

19 West, *History of Tasmania*, p. 617.

20 George Grey, London, to Clarendon, December 1849: Bodleian Library, Clarendon Papers, Irish Box 34.

21 Carmel Heaney, 'William Smith O'Brien in Van Diemen's Land', *History Ireland* (Autumn 1998), 29.

22 *Launceston Examiner*, 25 September 1850.

23 Mitchel admitted he had no money: Mitchel, *Jail Journal*, 21 April 1848, p. 136.

24 O'Donoghoe to O'Doherty, 9 November 1849: reprinted in Kiernan, *Exiles*.

25 Dunya Lindsay, 'A Fanatic Heart', *National Library of Australia News* (August 2006).

26 Kiernan, *Exiles*, pp. 26–7.

27 Meagher, Ross, to O'Doherty, 12 December 1849: NYPL, Madigan Collection.

28 Meagher, Ross to O'Brien, 11 May 1850: Smith O'Brien Papers, NLI, MS 4444 f. 2690.

29 Mitchel, *Jail Journal*, pp. 275–9.

30 Meagher to O'Doherty, 15August 1851: NYPL, Madigan Collection.

31 Mitchel, *Jail Journal*, p. 270.

32 'To My Country' by William Smith O'Brien, Darlington Probation Station, Maria Island, 7 January 1850. Smith O'Brien Collection, NLI, MS 10515.

33 O'Brien wrote to Mitchel saying that despite all the restrictions he did not regret his decision not to take a ticket-of-leave. Mitchel, *Jail Journal*, p. 240.

34 Meagher to O'Brien, 11 May 1850: Smith O'Brien Papers, NLI, MS 444, f. 2690.

35 Meagher to O'Brien, 17 January 1850: Kieran, *Exiles*.

36 Mitchel, *Jail Journal*, p. 241.

37 *Nation*, 12 October 1850.

38 *The Times*, 28 February 1850.

39 See for example *Launceston Examiner*.

40 Mitchel, *Jail Journal*, p. 268.

41 *Nation*, 18 January 1851.
42 *Launceston Examiner*, quoted in Kiernan, *Exiles*, pp. 53–5.
43 Mitchel, *Jail Journal*, 15 October, pp. 268–9. Mitchel recounts how the captain who betrayed O'Brien was brought before a 'kangaroo' court in San Francisco by MacManus but acquitted through lack of evidence.
44 *Nation*, 31 August 1850.
45 Heaney, 'O'Brien', 30.
46 Blanche M. Touhill, *William Smith O'Brien and his Irish Revolutionary Companions in Penal Exile* (Missouri: University of Missouri Press, 1981).
47 Mitchel, *Jail Journal*, 26 August 1851, pp. 260–1.
48 O'Brien to O'Doherty, 25 January 1851: NLI, MS 10515 (3).
49 O'Brien to Dunne, 15 March 1851: Smith O'Brien Correspondence, NLI, MS 10515.
50 Mitchel, *Jail Journal*, p. 274.
51 Meagher to O'Doherty, 14 July 1851: NYPL, Madigan Collection.
52 Meagher, Hopes Hotel, Ross, to O'Doherty, Saturday Morning [possibly Dec. 1849]: ibid. 10 January 1850: ibid.
53 Meagher, Ross, to O'Doherty, Saturday, November 1849: ibid.
54 Quoted in *Nation*, 25 January 1851.
55 Meagher, Ross, to O'Doherty [n.d. – early 1851?]: NYPL, Madigan Collection.
56 Meagher, Ross to O'Doherty, Thursday [n.d. – early 1851?]: ibid.
57 Meagher, Ross, to O'Doherty [n.d. – early 1851?]: ibid.
58 Meagher to O'Doherty, 14 July 1851: ibid.
59 Meagher to O'Doherty, 15 August 1851: ibid.
60 Mitchel, *Jail Journal*, 21 May 1851, p. 254.
61 O'Doherty to O'Brien, 27 May 1850: Smith O'Brien Papers, NLI, MS 444 f.2691.
62 O'Doherty to O'Brien, 27 May 1850: ibid.
63 Mitchel, *Jail Journal*, 8 May 1851, p. 249.
64 Meagher, Hopes Hotel, Ross, to O'Doherty, 12 December 1849: NYPL, Madigan Collection.
65 Meagher, Lake Sorrel, to O'Doherty, 30 June 1851: ibid.
66 O'Brien to O'Doherty, 11 October 1852, 29 December 1852: Smith O'Brien Letters, NLI, MS 10515 (3).
67 O'Brien to Dunne, 15 March 1851: ibid.
68 Meagher to O'Doherty, [n.d. – early 1851?]: NYPL, Madigan Collection.
69 P. O'Donoghoe to O'Brien, 2 May 1848: Letters of Smith O'Brien, NLI, MS 442, f.2430.
70 Mitchel, *Jail Journal*, 8 April 1850, p. 227.
71 *Nation*, 31 August 1850.
72 Lindsay, 'A Fanatic Heart'.
73 Davis, *Young Ireland*, p. 204.
74 Lindsay, 'A Fanatic Heart'.
75 O'Donoghoe Papers, NLI, MS 770.
76 Davis, *Young Ireland*, p. 226.
77 Mitchel, *Jail Journal*, 8 April 1850, p. 225.
78 Mitchel, Bothwell, to O'Brien, June 1850: Smith O'Brien Papers, NLI, MS 444, f.2696.

79 MacManus, traveling under the pseudonym of Dr Smith, went 65 miles in order to meet his former colleagues.

80 Mitchel, *Jail Journal*, 15 April 1850, p. 235.

81 Ibid., 22 July 1850, p. 246. Although initially such meetings were in a remote district and kept clandestine, by the following year, they were less cautious, even sometimes dining out in hotels: ibid., 21 May 1851, p. 254.

82 Ibid., p. 238.

83 Ibid., 13 April 1850, p. 230.

84 *Nation*, 25 January 1851.

85 R.D. Williams to Eva, 1 October 1850: 'Letters of Eva', MS 10520.

86 Mitchel, *Jail Journal*, 22 July 1850, p. 246.

87 *Irishman*, 19 May 1849.

88 Ibid.

89 Mitchel, *Jail Journal*, 25 May 1851, p. 255.

90 MacManus had escaped a few weeks earlier. Mitchel had travelled so quickly to Launceston that the papers authorizing his journey had not been received: Mitchel, *Jail Journal*, 9 June 1851, p. 256.

91 Ibid., 20 June 1851, p. 259.

92 Meagher to O'Doherty, 14 July 1851: NYPL, Madigan Collection.

93 Mitchel, *Jail Journal*, 15 October 1851, pp. 266–7.

94 O'Brien to John Martin, 1 December 1852: Letters of Smith O'Brien, NLI, MS 10515.

95 Mitchel, *Jail Journal*, 1 January 1853, p. 278.

96 Ibid., p. 274.

97 Ibid., 15 October 1851, p. 268.

98 Ibid., p. 278.

99 One-third was to be nominated by the Crown and two-thirds were to be elected.

100 *Mercury* (Tasmania), 26 November 2005.

101 Ibid.

102 O'Brien to Martin, 26 October 1850: Letters of Smith O'Brien, NLI, MS 10515.

103 The O'Brien Petition was circulated between October 1848 and May 1849.

104 *Irishman*, 26 May 1849.

105 *Dublin Evening Packet*, 4 July 1850.

106 O'Brien to Martin, 11 January 1851: Letters of Smith O'Brien, NLI, MS 10515.

107 Petition from Carrick-on-Suir, TNA, HO 12/2/81, 1851.

108 O'Brien to O'Doherty, 14 September 1852: Smith O'Brien Papers, NLI, MS 10515 (3).

109 O'Brien to O'Doherty, 28 December 1853: Smith O'Brien Papers, NLI, MS 10515.

110 *Nation*, 11 January 1851.

111 *New York Tribune* quoted in *Nation*, 5 October 1850.

112 Thomas O'Kane, Boston to Lord John Russell, 18 February 1851: TNA, HO 12/2/81.

113 O'Brien to O'Doherty, 2 October 1852: Smith O'Brien Papers, NLI, MS 10515 (3).

114 Mitchel, *Jail Journal*, 9 June 1851, p. 258.

115 Ibid., 2 October 1852.
116 Butt to Palmerston, 25 February 1854: TNA, HO 12/2/81.
117 O'Brien to Dunne, 15 March 1851: Smith O'Brien Letters, NLI, MS 10515.
118 *Cork Examiner*, 19 May 1854.
119 Mitchel, *Jail Journal*, p. 273.
120 Ibid., January 1853, p. 280.
121 O'Brien to O'Doherty, 2 October 1852: Smith O'Brien Letters, NLI, MS 10515 (3).
122 Ibid.
123 *Mercury* (Tasmania), 26 November 2005.
124 Lindsay, 'A Fanatic Heart'.
125 O'Brien to O'Doherty, Smith O'Brien Letters, 2 October 1852: NLI, MS 10515 (3).
126 O'Brien to John Martin, 1 December 1852: Smith O'Brien to Letters, NLI, MS 10515.
127 O'Brien to O'Doherty, 16 August 1853: ibid.
128 O'Brien asked O'Doherty to buy a present on his behalf in Hobart, up to a value of £1: O'Brien to O'Doherty, 26 January 1853: Smith O'Brien Letters, NLI MS 10515 (3).
129 *Dictionary of National Biography* (London: Smith Elder, 1898), pp. 188–9.
130 Mitchel, *Jail Journal*, p. 301.
131 Ibid., pp. 302–4.
132 Ibid., 13 January 1853, p. 300 (note: Mitchel refers to 'the four of us').
133 Ibid., 12 February 1853, pp. 304–5.
134 Ibid., 12 June 1853, pp. 310–12.
135 Ibid. A full account is provided pp. 308–39.
136 Ibid., 13 September 1853, p. 349.
137 Ibid., 21 July 1853, 16 September 1853.
138 Ibid., 1 November 1853, p. 350.
139 Ibid., 29 November 1853, p. 363.
140 Lindsay, 'A Fanatic Heart'.
141 *New York Nation*, 30 December 1848.
142 Dillon, New York, to his wife, Ady, 30 October 1848: Dillon Papers, TCD (f.69a).
143 John Dillon to his wife, Ady, 30 October 1848: ibid., (f.70).
144 Ibid.
145 All reprinted in *New York Nation*, 28 October 1848.
146 *New York Nation*, 28 October 1848
147 Davis, *Young Ireland*, p. 258.
148 Quoted in Wilson, *McGee*, p. 18.
149 *Dublin Evening Mail*, 3 October 1849.
150 *New York Nation*, 28 October 1848.
151 Ibid., 4 November 1848.
152 Ibid., 28 October 1848.
153 Dillon, New York to his wife Ady, 14 November 1848: Dillon Papers, TCD (f.71a).
154 Dillon to Ady 22 November 1848, 4 December 1848: ibid., (f.73a, 74).
155 Horace Greeley to W.E. Robinson and T.D. Reilly, 11 May 1849: NYPL, Greeley Papers.

156 Mitchel, *Jail Journal*, 10 August 1849, p. 161.
157 Ibid., Reilly to Mitchel, 8 January 1851, pp. 294–5.
158 Ibid., Reilly to Mitchel, 24 April 1852, 7 January 1853, p. 288.
159 P.A. Sillard, *The Life and Letters of John Martin: With sketches of Thomas Devin Reilly, Father John Kenyon, and other 'Young Irelanders'* (Dublin: J. Duffy and Co., 1893), p. 93. Guests at the O'Reilly home included Dudley Mann, the Secretary of State and Thomas Francis Meagher, following his escape from Van Diemen's Land.
160 Mitchel, *Jail Journal*, p. 118.
161 Devin Reilly to John Mitchel, 24 April 1852: P. A. Sillard, *The Life of John Mitchel: With an Historical Sketch of the '48 Movement in Ireland* (Dublin: J. Duffy and Co., 1889), pp. 90–2.
162 *The Irish American*, Lenon Manuscripts, NLI, MS 19941, 20 September 1856.
163 Mitchel, *Jail Journal*, 8 January 1853, pp. 296–7.
164 Ibid. Reilly wrote to Mitchel before his death on 24 April 1852, although the letter took 8 months to arrive. Mitchel described the style of the letter as full of 'wild, rollicking eloquence, melting with brotherly tenderness', 7 January 1853, p. 287.
165 Ibid., Reilly to Mitchel, 24 April 1852, p. 292.
166 *New York Times*, 7 March 1854.
167 *Nation*, 5 October 1850.
168 Cavanagh, Life of Joseph Brennan, p. 40.
169 Dillon, New York, to Ady, 14 November 1848: Dillon Papers, TCD, MS 6457, (f.71a).
170 Cavanagh, Life of Joseph Brennan, pp. 48–56.
171 Mitchel, *Jail Journal*, 19 November 1853, pp. 356–7
172 Ibid., pp. 349–50.
173 Ibid., 22 November 1853, p. 362.
174 *New York Times*, 1 February 1854.
175 Ibid., 3 April 1861.
176 Louis R. Bisceglia, 'The Fenian Funeral of Terence Bellew McManus' in *Eire-Ireland* (vol. 14, no. 3, 1979), pp. 54–5.
177 *New York Times*, 19 October 1861.
178 Ibid.
179 In July 1854, he received $45 for an article published in the *Australasian*: Meagher, William Street, New York to Mr Didd, 3 July 1855: NLI, Madigan Collection.
180 Ibid., Meagher, 37 Ninth Street, to John Fresner, 22 December 1853.
181 William Dillon, *Life of John Mitchel* (London: Kegan Paul, 1988), pp. 50–51.
182 *New York Times*, 30 October 1857.
183 Meagher was introduced by Robert Tyler: *The Irish American*, Lenon Manuscripts, NYPL, MS 19941, 15 March 1856.
184 Lyons, *Speeches and Writings, p.* 58.
185 Ibid., p. 80.
186 Ibid., p. 82.
187 Ibid., pp. 32–5.
188 Meagher, New York, to his father in Waterford, 17 July 1865: NYPL, Madigan Collection.

189 Meagher, Virginia City, Montana, to his father, 15 June 1867: ibid.
190 *New York Times*, 8 July 1867.
191 *Irish People*, 13 July 1867.
192 Ibid., 20 July 1867, 3 August 1867.
193 J. Mitchel, *Shamrock*, July 1867.
194 Griffith, preface to 1913 edition of Mitchel, *Jail Journal*, p. 370.
195 Ibid., p. 369–71. For a defence of Mitchel's views on slavery see Griffith, p. 371.
196 For example, on 19 October 1867, he commenced publishing *The Irish Citizen*, of which he was both proprietor and editor.
197 *Cork Examiner*, 6 February 1854.
198 John Mitchel, Knoxville, to Horace Greeley, 22 October 1858: NYPL, Horace Greeley Papers.
199 *The Citizen*, 9 September 1854.
200 *New York Times*, 24 May 1875.
201 Martin to Eva, 25 September 1862: Letters of Eva, NLI, MS 10520.
202 Mitchel, *Jail Journal* (1982 reprint), pp. xiii–xiv.
203 *New York Times*, 17 March 1867.
204 Sillard, *The Life of John Mitchel*, pp. 258–60.
205 *New York Times*, 5 April 1875.
206 Ibid., 17 November 1869.
207 'Women of Young Ireland', NLI, MS 10906, pp. 46–7.
208 *New York Times*, 21 April 1875.
209 Ibid., 24 May 1875.
210 Duffy, *Four Years*, pp. 96–7.
211 Mitchel, *Last Conquest*, pp. xxvi–xxvii.
212 *New York Times*, 8 December 1859.
213 Ibid., 4 November 1861.
214 O'Brien to Peel, 22 February 1862: Dillon Papers, TCD, MS 6457 (f.337).
215 O'Brien to Dillon, 28 February 1862: ibid. (f.338).
216 Martin to Eva, 25 September 1852: Letters of Eva, NLI, MS 10520.
217 *New York Times*, 17 November 1869.
218 Martin to Eva, 18 September 1865: Letters of Eva, NLI, MS 10520.
219 A.M. Sullivan and T.D. Sullivan, *The Wearing of the Green, or the Persecuted Funeral Procession* (Dublin: J. Duffy, 1882).
220 Duffy, *Four Years*, p. 250.
221 Michael Hurst 'Ireland and Ballot Act of 1872' in *The Historical Journal* (vol. 8, no. 3, 1965), 334.
222 *Australian Dictionary of Biography Online*: www.adb.online.anu.edu.au/biogs/A050406b.htm (accessed 10 October 2007).
223 Duffy to O'Doherty, 12 July 1853: Letters to Eva, NLI, MS 10520.
224 MacDermott, *Songs and Ballads*, p. 352.
225 Duffy, *Four Years*, p. vii.
226 A.M. Sullivan, *The Story of Ireland: A Narrative of Irish History, From the Earliest Ages to the Insurrection of 1867* (Dublin: M.H. Gill, 1894), chapter mcl.
227 Hurst, 'Ireland and Ballot Act', 340.
228 Mrs Dillon, Adelaide, to Duffy, Melbourne, n.d.: Dillon Papers, TCD (f378); Duffy to Mrs Dillon, December 1867: ibid.

229 Davis, *Young Ireland*, p. 258.

230 McGee quoted in Lady Ferguson, *Sir Samuel Ferguson*, p. 151.

231 MacDermott, *Songs and Ballads*, p. 370.

232 Davis, *Young Ireland*, p. 167.

233 Wilson, *McGee*, p. 9.

234 MacDermott, *Songs and Ballads*, p. xxiv.

235 Davis, *Young Ireland*, p. 167.

236 Information respecting association of Irishmen in the US entertaining designs hostile to the British government, NLI, Larcom Papers, MS 7697, June 1861.

237 *New York Times*, 19 March 1877.

238 Ibid., 24 November 1884.

239 The O'Hagan Papers are in the Public Record Office of Northern Ireland. For an introduction to these records see: www.proni.gov.uk /introduction__o_hagan_papers_d2777.pdf (accessed 2 December 2007).

240 Morash, *Hungry Voice*, p. 288.

241 MacDermott, *Songs and Ballads*, p. xii.

242 *Irish Nation*, 11 February 1882.

243 'Women of Young Ireland', NLI, MS 10906, pp. 8–12.

244 Eva, *Poems by 'Eva' of the Nation* (San Francisco, 1877).

245 Seamus MacManus (ed.), *Poems. By 'Eva' of 'The Nation'* (Dublin: M. Gill, 1909).

246 Letters of Eva, NLI, MS 10520.

247 *Australian Dictionary of Biography*.

248 Anton, 'Women of the *Nation*', 34–8.

249 Thomasine, *Wild Flowers from the Wayside* (Dublin: James Duffy and Sons, 1883).

250 Mary to Eva, 18 June 1848: Letters to Eva, NLI, MS 10520.

251 MacDermott, *Songs and Ballads*, p. 349.

252 Anton, 'Women of the *Nation*', 34. In 1874, her *Voices from the Heart*, a collection of religious poetry, was published.

253 Williams to Eva, 1 October 1850: Letters to Eva, NLI, MS 10520.

254 'Women of Young Ireland', NLI, MS 10906, p. 25.

255 Florence S. Boos, 'The "Homely Muse" in Her Diurnal Setting: The Periodical Poems of "Marie," Janet Hamilton, and Fanny Forrester' in *Victorian Poetry* (39.2, 2001), 255–85.

256 'Women of Young Ireland', NLI, MS 10906, p. 23.

257 Boos, 'The Homely Muse', 255–85.

258 O'Sullivan, *Young Irelanders*, p. 129.

259 Ibid.

260 *Nation*, 29 July 1848.

261 O'Sullivan, Young *Irelanders*, p. 99.

262 T.G. Wilson, 'Sir William Wilde and Speranza' in *Irish Journal of Medical Science* (November, 1933) 636.

263 Kinealy, 'Invisible Nationalists', in Boardman and Kinealy, *The Year the World Turned?* p. 139.

264 Wilson, 'Sir William Wilde', 634–6.

265 Lady Wilde, *Poems by Speranza (Lady Wilde)* (Dublin: James Duffy, 1864).

266 Jane Wilde to Olivia Rosacrona, 23 March 1865: Laurence Flanagan, *Irish Women's Letters* (Stroud: Sutton, 1997), p. 126.

267 Carmel Quinlan, '"Onward Hand in Hand": the nineteenth century Irish campaign for votes for women', in Louise Ryan and Margaret Ward, *Irish Women and the Vote* (Dublin: Irish Academic Press, 2007), p. 22.

268 *New York Times*, 20 June 1887.

269 Sillard, *The Life of John Mitchel*, p. 278.

270 Lady Wilde, *The American Irish* (Dublin: William McGee, n.d.) pp. 243–5.

271 *New York Times*, 3 January 1882.

272 *The Irish Nation*, 14 January 1882.

273 I am grateful to Steven Butler, a PhD student at Drew University, NJ, for sharing his research with me.

274 Melville, *Mother of Oscar*, pp. 13–17.

275 Gonne in Maud Gonne MacBride, *The Autobiography of Maud Gonne: A Servant of the Queen* ed. A. Norman Jeffares and Anna MacBride White (Chicago: Chicago University Press, 1995), pp. 8–9.

276 Melville, *Mother of Oscar*, p. 275.

9

'Dreams and delusions': the legacy of 1848

In 1861, on the eve of Queen Victoria's third and penultimate visit to Ireland, the London *Times* wrote an article suggesting that now, forty years since George IV had visited the country, Ireland was no longer a source of 'trouble and anxiety', but had become 'an increasing hope of union and prosperity'. The character and leadership of Queen Victoria were praised for contributing to this change but, according to the paper:

> The turning point was reached in the abortive rebellion of 1848 ... The rebellion of Smith O'Brien exposed and exploded the corresponding sham of a baseless political agitation. Since that time Ireland has been guided by reason instead of the imagination, by reality and possibility instead of by prejudice and poetry ... the dreams of Repeal, the delusion of a separate Government and nationality.[1]

The Times was wrong. Only six years later, the country was in the grips of another violent rebellion, which this time was associated with the Fenian movement. It was led by men who had been youthful participants in the 1848 uprising. Moreover, as Fenianism powerfully demonstrated, the demand for independence was not confined to the island of Ireland, but it had powerful support in Britain and North America. Furthermore, while the 1848 rebellion in Ballingarry had lasted for only a few hours, its impact and legacy was evident for decades, stretching far beyond the nationalist revolts in 1867.

In the short term, the failure of Young Ireland in 1848 appeared to be complete. Within two weeks of the rising, the main leaders had been arrested and, two months later, they had been convicted of high treason and sentenced to be hanged. Why had the insurgents been so easily and totally defeated? The answer is complex and many of the factors were beyond the ability of the Confederate leaders to foresee or control. The British government and the conservative press were keen to attribute the failure to two main reasons: the weakness of the Confederates and the strength of the government. However, indecisive leadership, lack of weapons, failure to win the support of landlords or large farmers, the hunger of the people and the opposition of the clergy were each significant factors individually, and collectively, they were fatal.

In the Queen's Speech proroguing parliament on 5 September 1848, the Queen referred to the role that Lord Clarendon had played in suppressing the Irish rebellion, averring, 'The energy and the decision shown by the Lord Lieutenant of Ireland deserve my warmest approbation.'[2] Privately though, the government acknowledged that the failure of the rising had depended on a traditional opponent of the British government: that is, the Catholic Church. The inability of the Confederation to win the support of the priests was critical. Although the insurgents lacked both food and arms, a key factor rested in whether the priests would assist or oppose them.[3] The consensus of the participants, the government and the British press, was that the local clergy played a major role in deterring people from involvement in the rising. Privately, Lord Clarendon admitted that the Catholic clergy had supported the government 'without exception'.[4] John O'Mahony, who was present at Ballingarry, wrote that the local clergy's insistence that the people should not participate in the rebellion was a crucial factor in its failure, particularly when combined with O'Brien's poor leadership and the unpreparedness of his supporters.[5] *The Times* informed its readers that, 'It is most gratifying to hear – and we are anxious to do all justice to the fact – that the Roman Catholic clergy have interfered with great earnestness and effect to save the poor creatures from the doom that awaited them.'[6] It added that even Father Kenyon, who was well known for his uncompromising pronouncements, had given Lalor 'a cool reception'.[7] Only two weeks later though, *The Times* chided the Catholic clergy for seeking a prominent role in the negotiations between government and the prisoners, and between government and the Irish people.[8]

To some extent, the Church's disapproval was not unexpected, especially in the aftermath of the violent 'June Days' in France. Moreover, throughout the nineteenth century, the Irish Catholic Church hierarchy had proved to an implacable enemy of all radical movements.[9] A surprising defection, however, was that of the Catholic priest Father Kenyon, a friend and advocate of John Mitchel. Kenyon's militancy had resulted in his being suspended by his bishop in the summer of 1848. Consequently, he refused to support his former colleagues in any way, even to the extent of declining to allow his chapel bell to be rung, a signal that had been agreed on in advance.[10] The loss of Father Kenyon was a blow to the movement and probably influential in persuading some of the younger priests not to become involved. In the longer term, the events of 1848 drew a large wedge between nationalists and the Catholic Church. As a result of the activities of Italian nationalists in 1848, Pope Pius IX was forced to flee from Rome. He was restored due to the intervention of the

British and French governments. To show his gratitude, Pius IX directed the Sacred College to issue a Rescript forbidding the Irish clergy from 'taking a prominent or violent part in future nationalist agitation'.[11] Within Ireland, this pronouncement was viewed as 'the death blow of Repeal, and it trumpeted forth the above resolution as the dividing wedge between the priesthood and the people'.[12] The impact of this position was evident during the Fenian uprisings in 1867. Nationalists in both 1848 and 1867 were fighting a powerful enemy that vied with them for leadership of the people.

In the spring of 1848, in the wake of the revolution in France, the Confederate leaders had decided that a rising was inevitable, but that it should not take place until the harvest had been gathered. Would they have succeeded if it had occurred either earlier or later? Clearly, the decision to revolt was triggered the by government's suspension of Habeas Corpus on 22 July. When Mitchel heard of the uprising on his prison ship in Bermuda, he lamented that O'Brien had been driven into taking precipitative action – adding that Lord Clarendon would thank him heartily for doing so.[13] Duffy, who was in prison when the rebellion took place, believed that the revolution had failed because it took place three months too late, on the grounds that the leaders should have capitalized on the revolutionary fervour following the conviction of John Mitchel. The nationalist historian, P.A. Sillard, writing at the end of the nineteenth century, concurred with Duffy. But if the Confederates had acted in May, would they have had more popular support?[14] The absentee Mitchel regarded the decision of the Confederate leaders *not* to allow the Dublin Clubs to rescue him, and to wait until harvest for a rising, as 'fatal'.[15] A similar viewpoint was expressed by the Irish Lord Lieutenant. In a personal letter to his friend, Henry Reeve, written on the eve of John Mitchel's trial in May, Lord Clarendon confided that an uprising had only been averted by the prompt action of the government. He averred:

> Two hours fighting in the streets of Dublin would have sufficed to cause a general uprising in the country; and, looking at the strange and unexpected events on the Continent, and the Catholic composition of our army and constabulary, it would have been impossible to predict the issue.[16]

In contrast, Thomas D'Arcy McGee claimed that the leaders should have held out for three more months on the grounds that, 'It was evident enough, if Ireland had taken and kept revolutionary ground for three months, American officers and American gold would not be wanting. It ended otherwise: and dense clouds of despair covered all the horizon of the Irish in America.'[17] His suggestion, which was written while he was in exile in the United States, was disingenuous in light of the wholesale arrests of Confederates that had taken place since the beginning of July. Moreover, McGee, who was in Glasgow when the uprising was taking place, demonstrated that his interpretation of the events of 1848 was not consistent but reflected his own, increasingly conservative and Catholic, political outlook. Thus, he had initially blamed the intervention of Catholic priests for the rising's failure, but by 1853, as his own politics became more right-wing, he blamed Irish Protestants for their failure to support Irish nationalist aspirations.[18]

An alternative view was taken by the moderate John O'Connell, son of Daniel, who believed that a rebellion had taken place five years too late.[19] He suggested that a rising would have succeeded if his father had called for one in 1843. He claimed that:

> At any moment that Mr O'Connell had chosen during that year, and, indeed, for long afterwards, he could have raised them in insurrection, as one man throughout the entire country; and however bloody, wasting, and desolating might have been the struggle, it is utterly impossible but that the result would have been a violent separation from England.[20]

O'Connell's opinion was shared by an adversary of both himself and his father: John Mitchel. Despite having publicly called for a revolution since the beginning of 1848, he believed that after three years of famine, Ireland 'did not then possess the physical resources or the high spirit which had "threatened the integrity of the Empire" in '43'. Regardless of the country being 'depopulated, starved, cowed and corrupted, it seemed better that she should attempt resistance, however heavy the odds against success, than lie prostrate and moaning as she was'. He based his argument on his conviction that, 'Better that men should perish by the bayonets of the enemy than by their laws.'[21]

Was defeat inevitable when set against the might of the British government? A leading historian of the 1848 revolutions, Jonathan Sperber, has argued that Britain was well placed to deal with any conflict in that year. He suggested that, 'The greater ability of the liberal state in Great Britain, with its parliament and elaborate legal system, to enforce its will, when compared with the surprisingly feeble forces of repression in the absolutist monarchies on the continent also helps explain why the United Kingdom rode out the revolutionary wave with little rocking of the boat.'[22] The power of the British state was particularly evident in the overt and covert measures used to defeat both the Chartists and the Irish nationalists. Within Ireland, the British authorities moved decisively and comprehensively to counter the nationalist threat. The fact that the Irish uprising occurred relatively late in the timetable of European revolutions meant that the British state had time to prepare to meet the insurrectionary threat. Throughout spring and summer, a package of repressive legislation was introduced, which included a new Treason Felony Act. These measures culminated in the suspension of Habeas Corpus, which forced the insurgents to choose between taking immediate action or risking arrest. The hope of waiting until after the harvest period, to ensure the people had food, disappeared at this point. Wholesale arrests had depleted the leadership of the Confederate clubs and had undermined the morale of the remaining confederates. Additionally, the government was kept informed about the activities of the clubs through a network of informers. Moreover, the practice of packing juries helped to ensure the convictions that the government desired. All of these measures suggested that the British government took the threat of a Confederate uprising very seriously.

The repressive legislation was backed up by armed force. By the summer of 1848, there were over 100,000 troops and 13,000 police in Ireland, all of whom were armed. Consequently, there was one member of the crown forces for every 500 people, which was fourteen times as many as the number per head of population in Prussia, and four times the level in France – the most heavily policed country in continental Europe.[23] Unlike the police force in Britain, the Irish constabulary were trained to use arms and, according to General Hardinge, they were 'loyal and in a high state of discipline ... the finest corps I ever saw, and fit for every description of service'.[24]

Despite the extensive preparations of the British government, their success was not a foregone conclusion. In reality, the outcome was less certain than the subsequent bravado of the British government and the conservative press would suggest. Their unease was expressed privately by Lord Clarendon. In August, he confided:

> We have had a narrow escape. The organization was nearly complete; and if the insurgents had been permitted to select their own time, instead of being forced to take ours, we must have had a long and bloody struggle, the issue of which would, I hope, not have been doubtful, but there would have been a loss of life and property, and an amount of individual suffering, terrible to contemplate.[25]

Was the location of the rising a contributory factor in its failure? In general, the 1848 revolutions in Europe originated in the cities, especially capital cities. Ireland did not conform to this trend. Although the authorities had feared that Dublin Castle would be the target of an initial insurrection, the city remained untouched in both 1848 and 1849. The real strength and support for Young Ireland had resided in the Dublin clubs, although they played no part in the rebellion. Meagher later claimed that before leaving the city in pursuit of O'Brien he had given instructions for the Dublin clubmen to join in after the initial rising had commenced in the country. These instructions were not conveyed. Michael Cavanagh, the friend and biographer of Meagher, subsequently tried to exonerate the Dublin clubmen from accusations of cowardice, believing the fault lay with the Secretary of the Confederation, Thomas Halpin, and the imprisoned Duffy. Their failure to convey the relevant information was attributed to fear, for themselves and their families, of being arrested.[26]

Did the decision to rise in the countryside contribute to the failure of the rising? Writing from his exile, Mitchel not only claimed that the insurrection had taken place too late; he argued that it should have taken place in Dublin on the grounds that, 'In the present condition of the island, no rising must begin in the country. Dublin streets are for that.'[27] However, following his removal from the country in May, further military reinforcements had been sent to the city, supervised by the Duke of Wellington. In June and July the leaders of the Confederate clubs and the radical press had been systematically arrested. The absence of O'Brien, who was in Wexford when Habeas Corpus was rushed through parliament, created a dilemma for Meagher and Doheny, both of whom had remained in Dublin. They knew that a rising had to take place either immediately or never, and that the south-eastern counties were more difficult for the authorities to monitor. County Kilkenny was the first choice for O'Brien, but lack of support meant that he moved on to County Tipperary. The final location was precipitated by the action of the local constabulary in Ballingarry, and, according to Michael Cavanagh, it was the worst possible location. Subsequent events consolidated O'Brien's reputation for bravery and honour, but they also confirmed his lack of suitability to lead a rebellion.

Famine

For John Blake Dillon, who was present in Ballingarry, the failure of the rising lay in the actions of the Irish people, whom he described as 'treacherous and cowardly'.[28] His harsh assessment was written in the immediate aftermath of the rising, when he was trying to avoid capture. Writing over fifty years later, Maud Gonne, an 'advanced nationalist', was more forbearing of the actions of the people in 1848. Gonne, who had achieved notoriety for her searing article, 'The Famine Queen', in which she blamed Victoria personally for much of the death and suffering during the Famine, suggested that:

> When one realises the condition of the country at that time, there is little wonder the Young Irelanders failed. It is a fallacy to think that the poorer and more miserable a people are the better they will fight; there is a degree of misery and poverty which saps all energy, moral and physical.[29]

She was echoing the sentiments of Speranza's poem 'The Famine Year' which appeared in the *Nation* in 1847:

> Weary men, what reap ye?—Golden corn for the stranger.
> What sow ye?—Human corpses that wait for the avenger.
> Fainting forms, hunger-stricken, what see you in the offing?
> Stately ships to bear our food away, amid the stranger's scoffing.
> There's a proud array of soldiers—what do they round your door?
> They guard our masters' granaries from the thin hands of the poor.

Pale mothers, wherefore weeping?—Would to God that we were dead—
Our children swoon before us, and we cannot give them bread ...

No; the blood is dead within our veins—we care not now for life;
Let us die hid in the ditches, far from children and from wife ...
Accursed are we in our own land, yet toil we still and toil;
But the stranger reaps our havest—the alien owns our soil.
O Christ! how have we sinned, that on our native plains
We perish houseless, naked, starved, with branded brow, like Cain's?
Dying, dying wearily, with a torture sure and slow—
Dying, as a dog would die, by the wayside as we go.[30]

What was the impact of the Famine? While the February Revolution in France was undoubtedly an important catalyst in the decision to rebel, the Confederate leadership was angered by the British government's management of three years of famine. Throughout Europe, the year 1847 had been marked by poor harvests, industrial recession, and a credit crisis. Nonetheless, the poor of no other European country were undergoing such a sustained period of food shortages as the Irish people were in 1848. In Ireland, the Famine made a rising imperative, yet it simultaneously was the main reason why the leaders delayed any action until the harvest was in. At this stage, Ireland was entering its fourth consecutive year of shortages, which meant that the potential foot- soldiers of the uprising were depleted and exhausted, and preoccupied with survival or preparing to emigrate. For Mitchel, the choice between dying of starvation, and dying in an attempt to liberate their country, was simple. He asked:

tell me which is better, to pine and whiten helplessly into cold clay, passing slowly, painfully through the stages of hungry brute-ferocity – passionless, drivelling, slavering idiocy, and dim awful unconsciousness, the shadow-haunted confines of life and death, or to pour out your full soul in all its pride and might with a hot torrent of red raging blood ... to scourge the stranger from your soil?[31]

A similarly impassioned sentiment was expressed by Speranza, in her article *Jacta Alea Est*, which the authorities regarded as treasonable.

The unfavourable conditions within the country made external intervention even more significant. The Confederate leaders were young (mostly in their twenties) and were comprised of middle-class writers, lawyers, poets and idealists. They had no experience of fighting or of military strategy; nor had many of their followers. The possibility of foreign intervention alarmed the British government, who passed the draconian 'Aliens Act' in April 1848. By that stage, it was becoming increasingly apparent that the new French government would not intervene in an uprising in Ireland: Britain used her diplomatic leverage (backed by threats of war) to ensure such a response. The lack of military knowledge amongst the Confederate leaders was commented on by their supporters in the United States, who suggested that the formation of an Irish Brigade would provide the rising with 'men of science' who were hardened fighters. This support never materialized. The need to have military expertise was a lesson that was adopted by the Fenians when they were planning the next phase of nationalist rebellion. Nevertheless, they were to be equally unsuccessful, in the face of determined opposition by the British government, the Catholic Church and militant Protestants.

What was the role of religion in the failure of the 1848 uprising? While the leadership of the Confederation differed on a number of ideological issues, they were consistent in their support of non-sectarianism. Unlike many nationalists before and after them, they made a concerted attempt to woo Protestants, including members of the Orange Order. They met with mixed success, although the formation of a Protestant Repeal Association in May 1848 was a significant development. In the 1798 rebellion, the newly-formed Orange Order had been supplied with arms by the British government to act as a counter-insurgency force. In 1848, they wished to replicate this role, seeing themselves as a 'native garrison' in Ireland. Clearly, the authorities saw them as a reserve force to be deployed against the insurgents if the rebellion spread. The easy defeat of the Confederates at Ballingarry made their intervention unnecessary. Despite playing no part in putting down the 1848 rising, the role of Orangemen in defeating it quickly became part of Protestant mythology. At the twelfth of July parades in 1849, numerous speeches lauded the role of Orangemen in defeating the disloyal rebels.[32] More worryingly, the anti-Catholic violence that was evinced at Dolly's Brae on that day, when the Orangemen provocatively decided to route their parade through the village, was intended to act as a warning to all nationalists.[33] By the twentieth century, historians of the Orange Order accepted this version of history. Thus, writing in 1939, R.M. Sibbett asserted that 'The Orangemen saved Ireland for the British Crown in 1848'.[34] This interpretation not only reinforced a sectarian view of the Irish national struggle, but it suggested that the British presence in Ireland depended on the loyalty of Orangemen. Paradoxically, what was intended to be an inclusive, non-sectarian, struggle in 1848 was subsequently used to exacerbate divisions along religious and political lines. Despite the appeal of Young Ireland to non-sectarianism, their actions had angered the more militant members of the Orange Order who increasingly characterized the outcome of the 1848 rebellion as simply a victory of Protestantism over Catholicism. Consequently, the rising contributed to the emergence of a more belligerent and violent form of loyalism. An unlooked-for aspect of the 1848 rising, therefore, was its contribution to the emergence of militant unionism.

The political legacy of 1848

The 1848 rising was over within a few hours, but its legacy was wide ranging, long term, and far-reaching. The political lessons of 1848 were

especially significant in shaping the longer-term political development of
Ireland. The writings of Young Irelanders laid the foundations of the
tenant league movement, initially through the involvement of Charles
Gavan Duffy, who used his energy and the columns of the *Nation* in the
years immediately following the Ballingarry uprising to promote the cause
of tenant right. James Fintan Lalor, despite a brief life, left a wealth of
writings relating to the land question, most of which appeared in the
Nation and the short-lived *Irish Felon*. He used his ideas on tenant right
to briefly mobilize people in Tipperary in 1847. His ideas had a profound
influence on the later writings of John Mitchel and a number of them were
developed by Duffy in the 1850s. They also directly influenced the period
of agricultural and social unrest from 1879 to 1882, known as the Land
War. During this struggle, Lalor's philosophy of combining political and
social revolution and his tactics of non-cooperation found a wider and
more appreciative audience than they had done during his lifetime.[35]
During this period the writings of both Mitchel and Lalor were widely
reprinted in Ireland and the United States.[36] Thomas Clarke Luby, who
had been involved with Young Ireland in his youth, and knew Lalor
personally, reminded some of the hot-heads involved in the Land War that
they would do well to remember his advice.[37] Michael Davitt, mastermind
of the Land War, declared, speaking in New York in 1887, that his principles were derived from the writings of James Fintan Lalor, and he
quoted frequently from Lalor's short-lived paper, the *Irish Felon*. He
further claimed that the programmes of both the Land League and the
National Leagues of 1879 to 1887 had their origins with Lalor in 1848.[38]
Lalor's writings continued to inspire the next generation of radical nationalists, including James Connolly and Patrick Pearse.[39] Connolly adopted
some of Lalor's words as the motto for his Irish Citizen Army, while Lalor
was identified by Pearse as one of the four creators of Irish nationalism.[40]

   The 1848 rising paved the way for the next phase of physical force
nationalism, that is, Fenianism. The two founders of the Fenian
Brotherhood, James Stephens and John O'Mahony, had taken part in the
1848 rebellion, following which they had escaped to Paris. Mahoney
subsequently moved to the United States. The international support for
the Fenians had its roots in 1848. In 1861, when Fenian activity was
increasing in Ireland, Britain and the United States, a report to the
constabulary at Dublin Castle warned that in 1848 'steps were taken by
"patriots" here to aid in the expected movement of that day. Money was
collected and men said they were volunteers.'[41] This activity had created
a precedent and a model for subsequent Irish-American involvement. The
mass emigration that resulted from the Famine not only gave Irish nationalism an international base of support, but it provided a further
compelling example of British misrule.

   In 1848, many Fenians looked upon France and America as their
natural allies, believing that external aid was necessary to achieve inde-

pendence.[42] For some of the Fenian leadership, however, the failure of the 1848 rising had provided a number of lessons. One was that outside support should not be relied on but the Irish people should learn to fight for themselves. For Jeremiah O'Donovan Rosa, this was highlighted by the response of the French government to the Irish delegation in 1848, leading him to write in his *Recollections* that:

> It was that 'unmeaning reply' of Lamartine's that the English government placarded all over Ireland overnight in 1848. It was that poster I saw my mother tear down next morning. It is that memory, implanted in my mind very early in my life, that makes me take very little stock in all the talk that is made by Irishmen about France or Russia, or any other nation doing anything to free Ireland for us. They may do it, if it will be in their interest to do it.[43]

For John Devoy, architect of the New Departure, even more stark lessons had been learned. He recognized that Young Ireland had been rushed into an insurrection for which they had no military training, while the people had no arms and many were hungry. Consequently, they were bound to fail.[44] Nonetheless, the fact that the leaders of the rebellion had been unwilling to fight to the death was a mistake because, 'A physical force movement in Ireland which ends without a fight has a more demoralising influence on the people than a fight that fails.'[45] Apart from the political failure, Devoy believed that the 1848 rising 'disheartened the people, whose spirit had already been shattered by the Famine, and the exodus had already begun'.[46]

Although many of the Fenian leadership had been involved in the 1848 rebellion, some of the leadership of Young Ireland remained ambivalent in their support for this movement. For the most part, they watched the emergence of Fenianism with both bemusement and sadness, while publically distancing themselves from it. Mitchel, who was the most senior of Young Irelanders to be involved with Fenianism, even acting as their agent in Paris for a short time, remained pessimistic about their chances of success. As late as November 1866 he warned that an insurrection would fail: Ireland was at peace and, without external intervention, the Irish Fenians could not succeed. He further believed that Stephens was deluding himself (and others) about the extent of support for the movement.[47] After 1848, a number of Young Irelanders renounced physical force tactics, although they remained unrepentant for their actions in that year. John Martin and P.J. Smyth contributed to the emergence of the constitutional Home Rule movement, and they were important figures in the early Irish Parliamentary Party, from which Charles Stewart Parnell derived much of his support and power.

Subsequent generations of physical force nationalists clearly identified with the men of 1798 and 1848, rather than with the constitutional tactics of Daniel O'Connell. One man in particular was viewed as exceptionally

inspirational; John Mitchel, who had not been in Ireland during the 1848
uprising, and whose views on Fenianism oscillated, was remembered as a
hero of republicanism. Writing in 1896, John O'Leary, a leading Fenian
who had taken part in the 1848 uprising as a young man, recalled his days
in the Irish Confederation, saying that, 'Many, if not most, of the younger
amongst us were Mitchelites before Mitchel, or rather before Mitchel had
put forth his programme.'[48] Furthermore, he believed that, 'Fenianism
was the natural, or at least a natural, outcome of Young Irelandism.'[49]
For the generation of 'advanced nationalists' who were active at the
beginning of the twentieth century, Mitchel was seen as the important
ideologue in showing the limits of constitutional nationalism. In 1901,
Maud Gonne offered her own assessment of the legacy of 1848, writing
that, 'Though John Mitchel failed in his manly and fearless teaching, he
prepared the way for the Fenian movement. He cleared the air of the
miasma of the decadent doctrine of peaceful agitation. Mitchel rendered
James Stephens' organisation possible.'[50]

Women and 1848

The involvement of women in the 1848 revolutions was diverse although,
in the short term, their contribution did not change the position of women
in society. Throughout Europe, women's participation in the uprisings
had been mostly limited to an auxiliary one – sewing flags, collecting
money – with few playing a direct part in the revolutionary activities in
their own right, only occasionally speaking at political meetings or taking
part in street fighting.[51] The question of women getting the vote was not
an issue in 1848, and even universal male suffrage was rarely a central
demand of the revolutionaries. Only in France did women participate as
equals in republican clubs, although even the outspoken George Sand
continued to publish her political tracts anonymously, fearing a backlash
if her gender was known.[52] Nonetheless, throughout Europe in 1848
'women conquered for themselves a definite, if admittedly limited, portion
of the public sphere'.[53]

In Ireland, women nationalists had attended meetings of both the
Repeal Association and the Confederation, even if they did not speak. The
nationalist press referred to these women as 'fair confederates'.[54] Even
more importantly, women nationalists were given a voice in the columns
of the *Nation* and other radical papers, even if their identity was disguised
by pseudonyms. As the writings of Eva, Mary and Speranza demonstrated, women were as well informed, militant and brave as their male
colleagues. They were also interested in questions relating to the rights of
women although, like later Irish activists, they believed that winning
national independence was more important in the short term.[55]

Although many of the women who had contributed to the *Nation*
seemed to fade from political involvement after1848, a high portion, in

fact, reappeared in later nationalist movements. Their contributions to the *Nation* also paved the way for succeeding generations of female nationalists. The female supporters of the Fenians and the Land League, however, formed their own committees and associations, parallel to those run by the men, and they were able to use their own names, rather than having to use pseudonyms, as did the women of 1848.[56] Speranza, in particular, was regarded as an inspiration to the next generation of female 'advanced' nationalists, including Alice Milligan, Maud Gonne and Countess Markievicz. In their journals, such as the *Shan Van Vocht*, *Bean na hÉireann* and the *United Irishman*, they recounted tales of earlier generations of female activists, from Brigit to Speranza.[57] Milligan, a Protestant nationalist and feminist who was active in the Irish literary revival, wrote, just a month after Speranza's death, that because of her range of activities it was impossible to do full justice to her contribution but that:

> Today the best we can do is draw attention to her life, to the persistent and consistent course which she followed to the risks that she dared and the matchless spirit which in a time of doubt, danger, and despair, she brought to the service of Ireland.[58]

For this generation of republican nationalists, Speranza, an upper-class Protestant woman, provided a model of how cultural activities could be linked with direct action.[59]

Literary legacy

The contribution of Young Ireland was not confined to politics; their intellectual and literary legacy, both within Ireland and amongst the Irish diaspora, was considerable. Although it only survived for six years in its original form, the *Nation* revolutionized the way in which Irish literature, history and culture were written and viewed. According to Terry Eagleton, 'Few groups of intellectuals have had such a spectacular impact on politics as Young Ireland ... and not many pieces of newsprint have created such historical turmoil as the *Nation*.'[60] The writings of Young Irelanders contributed to the emergence of cultural nationalism in Ireland, which sowed the seeds for the later Gaelic revival. W.B. Yeats, who was a great admirer of John Mitchel's writing skills, regarded him as 'the only Young Ireland prose writer who had a style at all'.[61] When Queen Victoria visited Ireland in 1900, Yeats publicly read Mitchel's condemnation of the Act of Union which, he believed, still had resonance fifty years later.[62]

One of the most talented poets associated with the *Nation* was the eccentric, but tragic, James Clarence Mangan. In his best known poem, 'My Dark Rosaleen', he pictured Ireland as a sorrowful woman, a theme later explored by W.B. Yeats and Lady Gregory in the play *Cathleen ni Houlihan*. Unlike many of the other writers, he was not middle class, but had been born in poverty and, regardless of his talent, died in poverty in 1849, of a combination of cholera and malnutrition.[63] Despite his short and tragic life, James Joyce wrote of Mangan that he 'sums up in himself the soul of a country and an era'.[64] The premature death of Thomas Davis in 1845 was a further loss to Young Ireland literature, especially the way in which he had woven non-sectarian themes into his poetry and politics. One of his poems, 'A Nation Once Again' has survived in the guise of a rousing song, which was adopted as an unofficial nationalist anthem by many republican nationalists. Davis, who, throughout his short life, promoted inclusive politics, would probably not have approved. In 2002 'A Nation Once Again' was voted the world's most popular song in a poll carried out by the BBC World Service.[65]

The literary legacy of the women who had contributed to the *Nation* was also considerable. The poetry of many of them was published in their lifetimes, not only in Ireland, but in the United States and Australia. Speranza was particularly prolific and her writings extended beyond her poetry. As Lady Wilde, she achieved notoriety by hosting literary salons in Dublin and London, leading the *Irish Times* to describe her home in Merrion Square as 'the house where a guest met all the Dublin celebrities in literature, art and the drama, as well as any stray literary waif who might be either sojourning or passing through the city'.[66] One such visitor was the young W.B. Yeats who greatly admired Speranza's work and pondered before he met her, 'I wonder if I will find her as delightful as her book – as delightful as she is certainly unconventional?'[67] Speranza was a gifted linguist and her earlier writings included translations from Latin, French and German. Like many educated people of her generation she did not speak Irish, but in her later years she wrote on Irish history and folk-lore.[68] Her contribution to the Gaelic revival may have been overlooked due the spectacular and public fall from grace of her son, Oscar Wilde. For many Irish people though, it was her early writings that made the most lasting impression.[69]

1848: memory and memorialization

During their own lifetimes, the 1848 rebels were respected, and this admiration was not tarnished by their failure in Ballingarry in 1848. The way in which the state prisoners conducted themselves during their trials and imprisonments meant that they achieved in exile dignity and influ-ence, despite being thousands of miles away. This was evidenced by the frequent petitions gathered for O'Brien and the other state prisoners. In 1850, the Iowa State Legislature appointed a committee for the purpose of giving names to its counties. They decided to name a number of them after the Irish 'patriots', including O'Brien County and Mitchel County.[70] Nor was the approbation limited to Ireland or the United States. When O'Brien, Martin and O'Doherty received their pardons, 268 inhabitants of Sydney in Australia signed an address of congratulations that was endorsed by seven members of the Legislative Council, six Roman Catholic and five Protestant clergymen.[71]

When relatively old men, John Martin and John Mitchel were both elected as MPs to the Westminster parliament. Mitchel's election was particularly remarkable given that he had not lived in Ireland since his transportation in May 1848, and during the intervening period his reputation had been tarnished by his support for the American Confederacy. Clearly, during his long absence from the country, he was neither forgotten nor despised. Moreover, both men were Ulster Protestants who were elected in overwhelming Catholic constituencies in counties Meath and Tipperary respectively. Within Ireland, the popularity of the exiled Young Irelanders, especially those in the United States, irritated both the conservative Protestant and conservative Catholic newspapers.[72]

Following their deaths, the Young Irelanders were memorialized in a number of visible ways. O'Brien, a Protestant landlord and the anti-hero of the 1848 rebellion, was remembered by the people of Ireland who erected a marble statue of him in Sackville Street (now O'Connell Street) in 1870.[73] It was paid for by public subscription and it was the first public monument to be erected in Dublin to a person who had tried to overthrow British rule.[74] It was a further hundred years before another 1848 statue would be put up in Dublin. On the centenary of Thomas Davis's death in 1945, it was decided that he should be honoured in this way, although it was not until 1966 that the statue was completed.[75] It was unveiled in the presence of President Eamon de Valera, who was a veteran of the 1916 Rising.

Unlike many of his fellow exiles, Meagher never got a chance to return to Ireland: he died mysteriously and prematurely in Montana in 1867. As a tribute to his role as Acting Governor, Meagher County in Montana was named after him. In 1905, almost forty years after his death, a statue of Meagher was erected in front of the main government building in Montana. Poignantly, 'Meagher of the Sword', who never got a chance to fight on behalf of Ireland in 1848, was depicted on horseback and brandishing a sword. Given his record in the American Civil War, however, it was appropriate. The changing way in which he was remembered is reflective of changes in Irish and in Irish-American nationalism. His statue was unveiled on 4 July 1905. It cost twenty thousand dollars, which was paid for by public subscription. The various speakers extolled Meagher's love of liberty and his Irish heritage, stating that, 'More than for any direct contribution to Montana, Thomas Francis Meagher owes his place on the Capitol grounds to his Irish Catholic heritage and Irish nationalist politics.' The statue was dedicated before a crowd of over fifteen hundred people.[76] At a rededication of the Meagher statue in July 2005, the emphasis was different. Meagher was no longer characterized as an Irish nationalist, but as somebody who had played a crucial role in defining

Irish-American identity not only in Montana, but throughout the United States.[77] In contrast, in Ireland 150 years after his death, Meagher is now remembered as Waterford's favourite son.[78]

Memories of John Mitchel continued to be polarized. Of all of the Young Ireland leaders, he has been respected and reviled in equal measure, making him the most controversial of nineteenth-century nationalists. Nevertheless, his name and notoriety lived on more than any others – not just due to the popularity of his writings, but to the proliferation of political clubs and sports societies that were named after him. A statue of Mitchel was also erected in Newry, the town where he grew up and died. Ironically, Mitchel, who was ensconced in Bermuda at the time of the 1848 uprising, was the man who has been indelibly linked with it. Writing in 1913 Arthur Griffith, the founder of Sinn Féin, identified Mitchel as the one person who 'met the crisis of 1848 with a policy' because he 'preached to Ireland a passive resistance reinforced at strategic points by aggressive action'. Griffith believed that this approach was adopted by Charles Stewart Parnell, 'the man whose career Mitchel's writings moulded'. Writing three years before the Easter Rising, Griffith believed that despite Mitchel's failure in 1848 he had sowed the seeds for the next struggle, opining that 'out of that degradation and misery and ruin new forces grow to encounter and defeat English policy in Ireland'.[79]

Historians have been more divided about his political legacy. In 1965, Kevin Nowlan described Mitchel as 'a man of remarkable political stature', but later, more conservative, historians were less flattering about his role in Irish nationalism. Inevitably, they were influenced by the conflict in Northern Ireland after 1969, and the anti-nationalist revisionist orthodoxy that dominated Irish history. Mitchel's enduring reputation amongst Irish republicans and his uncompromising style of writing made him an obvious target for opponents of nationalism, who lampooned him for his political fanaticism. According to Roy Foster, the writings of Mitchel and other extremists in the *United Irishman* were rooted in 'an almost psychotic Anglophobia'.[80] Mitchel, however, consistently made a distinction between the British government and its institutions and the British people, claiming that it was only the former that he hated and wanted to overthrow.[81] He repeatedly justified his unrelenting opposition to British rule by citing the Famine, 'the reeky shanks and yellow chapless skulls of Skibbereen'. His polemical *Jail Journal* has to be judged not only in the context of his own imprisonment following an unfair trial, but also against the backdrop of the Famine, leading him to state: 'At the end of six years I can set down these things calmly: but to see them might have driven a wise man mad.'[82] Clearly, like many of the leading Young Irelanders, he was not a social radical, his conversion to democracy only coming at the end of 1847, following which he allied closely with the British Chartists. Nonetheless, far from being regarded as Anglophobic, Mitchel was respected by British radicals, and when they received news of his conviction, thousands took to the streets, leading to days of rioting in London.[83] Mitchel was unequivocal about distinguishing between his support for republicanism and his dislike of socialism, stating that, 'Socialists are something worse than wild beasts.'[84] He also made it clear that he was a nationalist and did not approve of political sentimentalism in the abstract.[85] Mitchel's championship of the Southern States in the Civil War lost him support in the United States and he appeared shocked that 'in a "land of liberty" a man was supposed to conceal unpopular opinions'. Nonetheless, Mitchel's defence of slavery cast a long shadow over the memory of one of the most brilliant Irishmen of his generation.

1848: a year to remember?

The men and women who inspired and led the 1848 rising were not perfect and their ideas and ideals often appeared to lack coherence or consistency. Inevitably, in a group so large and drawn from such diverse backgrounds, politically, economically and socially, there were differences and contradictions. Like many nineteenth-century nationalists, they were ambivalent towards the British Empire, some like O'Brien favouring benign imperialism. Many were latecomers to democracy, even John Mitchel, persuaded by events in Europe in 1848. With some exceptions, notably Michael Doheny and Patrick O'Donoghoe, they followed the O'Connell line of disliking Chartism, which only changed at the beginning of 1848 much to chagrin of the British government, who feared an alliance between Irish and the British radicals. For most of the period up to 1848, the leaders of Young Ireland hoped that landlords would lead the revolution in Ireland. Mitchel, influenced by Lalor, only converted to the idea of a social revolution in 1847, while his colleagues only came to this viewpoint in 1848. There is no doubt that the Famine in Ireland angered and radicalized the politics of Young Ireland. An important legacy of this group is that they politicized the Famine, especially the human cost of mortality and emigration.[86]

Events in Ireland in 1848 cannot be divorced from events in other parts of Europe in the year of revolutions. In the longer term, the outcome of the risings was not what revolutionaries had hoped for. By the end of 1848, liberal movements throughout Europe were in retreat. In Germany and Hungary, Italy and Poland, establishing a nation state had been one of the central aims of the revolutionaries, but in each case they lacked the military and political power to achieve their ends.[87] Ireland fitted into this general pattern.

As has been pointed out by a historian of the 1848 revolutions in Europe, 'It was a year full of promise, but the promise was not realized ... The paradox of these myths, by which politicians and activists found in 1848 the heroes and defining moment of their movements, was that in all cases 1848 failed them.'[88] When viewed within the spectrum of other

292 Repeal and revolution

European nationalist movements, the abortive uprising in Ireland was not so unusual. In fact, as early as autumn 1848, the tide was turning against the revolutionaries throughout Europe as the forces of tradition regrouped. By spring 1849 it was clear that many of the nationalist revolutions had 'failed miserably'.[89] By 1851, conservative regimes had been reinstated. Even in France, republicanism had not survived and Louis Napoleon (soon to be Emperor) was in power. Moreover, Pope Pius IX had been reinstalled in Rome, and he was in the vanguard of a sustained Catholic assault on revolutionaries and nationalists.

The 1848 uprising in Ireland was defeated, but did it fail? An early evaluation of the 1848 rising was provided by a sympathetic John Savage, writing in 1856. He opined that, 'Young Ireland was "legally and constituently" banished and exiled, but was not defeated.' More importantly, he believed that, 'Young Ireland did revolutionize the country [and] it had the daring to win sectional Ulster back to the national position it assumed under Munroe and McCracken.'[90] Writing over a hundred years later, the Irish historian Kevin Nowlan stated that the contribution of Young Ireland to Irish nationalism lay in 'its doctrine of a comprehensive Irish nationalism, which could not be compromised, superior to religious differences and group prejudices. This belief, expressed with eloquence in the pages of the *Nation* newspaper, was to become in due time part of the common inheritance of Irish nationalism.'[91]

In the short term, Young Ireland was no more successful than O'Connell in uniting landlords with their tenants, or in bringing Catholics and Protestants together. Instead, in the second half of nineteenth century these social and political fault lines widened further. Nonetheless, their vision of an inclusive, united and independent Ireland, in which the poor would be protected, went far beyond the aspirations of many nationalists who came before or went after them. The fact that this aspiration proved to be elusive was the fault of men and women with less vision and honour than those who led the 1848 rising in Ireland.

Notes

1 *The Times*, 21 August 1861.
2 5 September 1848, quoted in Maxwell, *Life and Letters*, p. 293.
3 Gwynn, 'The Rising of 1848', 17.
4 Lord Clarendon to the Home Secretary, 3 August 1848, 6 August 1848: Bodleian Library, Clarendon Box, Irish Box 33.
5 O'Mahony, 'Narratives of 1848', NLI, MS 797.
6 *The Times*, 31 July 1848.
7 Ibid.
8 Ibid, 16 August 1848.
9 A sophisticated analysis of their opposition to radicalism in Cork is provided in Maura Cronin, *Country, Class or Craft: The Politicization of the Skilled Artisan in Nineteenth-Century Cork* (Cork: Cork University Press, 1994).

10 Gwynn, 'The Priests and Young Ireland', 594–5.
11 Gwynn, *Young Ireland*, p. 123.
12 Ibid., p. 125.
13 Mitchel, *Jail Journal*, p. 72.
14 Sillard, *Life of Martin*, p. 116.
15 Mitchel, *Jail Journal*, p. liv.
16 Clarendon to Reeve, 10 May 1848: Laughton, *Memoirs of Henry Reeve*, p. 200.
17 McGee, *History of Irish Settlers*, p. 134.
18 Wilson, *McGee*, p. 30.
19 *Frazer's Magazine* (October 1848), p. 475.
20 O'Connell, *Recollections of a Parliamentary Career*, p. 246.
21 Mitchel, *Jail Journal*, pp. xlix–l.
22 Sperber, *European Revolutions*, p. 242.
23 Ibid.
24 General Hardinge to Sir Edward Blakney, Confidential, 24 August 1848: Bodleian Library, Clarendon Papers, Irish Box 16.
25 Clarendon to Reeve, 17 August 1848: Laughton *Memoirs of Henry Reeve*, p. 202.
26 Cavanagh, *Memoirs of Meagher*, p. 258
27 Mitchel, *Jail Journal*, pp. 72–3.
28 Dillon to his wife, Ady, 2 September 1848: Dillon Papers, TCD (f.68).
29 Maud Gonne, 28 September 1901: Karen Steele, *Maud Goune's Irish Natonalist Writings 1895–1946* (Dublin: Irish Academic Press, 2004).
30 Lady Jane Wilde, *Poems* (Glasgow: Cameron and Ferguson 1881, 2nd edn), pp. 10–11.
31 Mitchel, *Jail Journal*, p. 87.
32 *Warder*, 16 July 1848.
33 Kinealy, 'A Right to March', in Boyce and Swift, *Problems and Perspectives*.
34 R.M. Sibbett, *Orangemen in Ireland and Throughout the Empire* (Belfast: Henderson and Co., 1914, 2 vols), vol. ii, p. 346.
35 Philip H. Bagenal, *The American Irish and the Influence of Irish Politics* (London, 1882), pp. 168–9.
36 *Irish Nation*, 18 February 1882.
37 Ibid., 28 January 1882.
38 Davitt, quoted from the *Irish Felon* of 24 June 1848, in which Lalor explained the need for a social revolution based on changing the structure of landholding in Ireland. For more on Davitt's address, see the *Irish World*, 29 January 1887. Davitt also possessed a first edition copy of Mitchel's *Jail Journal* and had marked the sections relating to the struggle for land in Ireland. I am grateful to Sheelagh Davitt, grand-daughter by marriage, for showing me his personal possessions.
39 Daly, 'James Fintan Lalor' in Brady, *Worsted in the Game*, p. 111.
40 Ibid.
41 Police Information, Dublin Castle, Report on Fenianism, June 1861: NLI, Larcom Papers.
42 John O'Mahony, Fenian Headquarters New York, to Mitchel, 10 November 1865: CUA, Fenian Collection.
43 Rossa, *Rossa's Recollections*, p. 134.

44 John Devoy, *Recollections of an Irish Rebel: The Fenian Movement, its Origins and Progress: Methods of Work in Ireland and in the British Army, Why it Failed to Achieve its Main Object, but Exercised Great Influence on Ireland's Future* (New York: D. Young, 1929), p. 290.
45 Ibid., pp. 10–11.
46 Ibid., p. 10.
47 J. Mitchel to M. Moynahan, CUA, Fenian Brotherhood Collection, 17 November 1866.
48 O'Leary, *Recollections of Fenians*, p. 4.
49 Ibid., p. 8.
50 Gonne, 28 September 1901: reprinted in Steele, *Maud Gonne.*
51 Sperber, *European Revolutions*, p. 174.
52 Gabriella Hauch, 'Women's Spaces in the Men's Revolutions of 1848' in Dowe *et al.*, *Europe in 1848*, p. 643.
53 Sperber, *European Revolutions*, p. 177.
54 *United Irishman*, 4 March 1848.
55 Kinealy, 'Invisible Nationalists' in Boardman and Kinealy, *The Year the World Turned?*, pp. 130–145.
56 In 1867 for example, female supporters of Fenians in Dublin formed a Ladies' Committee which raised money in Britain, the US and Australia for the families of Fenian prisoners: see *Irish People*, 20 July 1867.
57 Karen Steele, *Women, Press, and Politics During the Irish Revival* (New York: Syracuse University Press, 2007), pp. 11, 58.
58 *Shan van Vocht*, March 1896, quoted in Steele, ibid., p. 59.
59 Ibid.
60 Terry Eagleton, *Scholars and Rebels in Nineteenth-Century Ireland* (Oxford: Blackwell, 1999), p. 141.
61 W.B. Yeats, *The Autobiography of William Butler Yeats* (New York: McMullen Books, 1953), p.136.
62 John Kelly, *Collected Letters of Yeats* (Oxford: Oxford University Press, 1986), p. 503.
63 Morash, *Hungry Voice*, pp. 22, 282.
64 Quoted in Melville, *Mother of Oscar*, p. 33.
65 https://news.bbc.co.uk/l/entertainment (accessed 20 December 2002).
66 *Irish Times*, 11 March 1848.
67 Quoted in Melville, *Mother of Oscar*, p. 217.
68 Lady Jane Wilde, *Irish Cures, Mystic Charms and Superstitions* (New York, c. 1891).
69 Gonne quoted in Jeffares and White, *Maud Gonne*, pp. 8–9.
70 O'Brien County History website, Iowa: http://obriencounty.com/history.htm?lmo=2 (accessed 10 November 2007).
71 *Sydney Freeman*, reported in *The Citizen*, 3 February 1855.
72 For example, the editorials of the *Belfast News-Letter* consistently attacked Mitchel in 1854 and 1855, which Mitchel complained of in his New York paper, *The Citizen*, 17 February 1855.
73 Peter Harbison, Homan Pottterton and Jeanne Sheehy, *Irish Art and Architecture from Prehistory to the Present* (London: Thames and Hudson, 1978), p. 233.
74 Historical monuments on the O'Connell street area, Dublin City Council

website: http://Dublincity.ie (accessed 3 November 2007).
75 Yvonne Whelan, 'The Construction and Destruction of a Colonial Landscape: Monuments to British Monarchs in Dublin Before and After Independence' in *Journal of Historical Geography* (vol. 28. no. 4, 2002), 524.
76 See website of Montana: www.montanacapitol.com/exhibits/exterior /meagher.htm (accessed 19 November 2007).
77 Ibid.: http://governor.mt.gov/speeches/ltgov/speeches.asp?ID=124.
78 'Waterford's favourite son', at: www.ricksteves.com/plan/destinations /ireland/meagher.htm (accessed 10 November 2007).
79 Arthur Griffith, Preface to 1913 Edition, Mitchel, *Jail Journal* (re-pub. 1982), pp. 368–70. Griffith ranked Mitchel with three other great Irishmen: Sean O'Neill, Jonathan Swift and Charles Parnell.
80 Roy Foster, *Modern Ireland* (London: Penguin, 1989), p. 316. Foster's account of the 1848 rising contains factual inaccuracies. For example, he states that Meagher was in jail when the rising took place, (p.314), and that the *United Irishman* was the newspaper of the Confederates (p. 316).
81 Mitchel, *Jail Journal*, pp. 82–3.
82 Ibid., pp. 86, xlviii.
83 Goodway, *London Chartism*, pp. 116–20.
84 Mitchel, *Jail Journal*, p. 78.
85 Arthur Griffith in Preface to 1913 edition of *Jail Journal*, pp. 369–71. For a defence of Mitchel's views on slavery see p. 371.
86 Donnolly, *Potato Famine*, p. 207.
87 H. Haupt and D. Langewiesche, 'The European Revolutions of 1848' in Dowe, *Europe in 1848*, p. 19.
88 Robert Gildea '1848 in European Collective Memory' in Evans and Von Strandmann, *Revolutions in Europe*, p. 208.
89 Arthur James May, *Contemporary American Opinion of the Mid-century Revolutions in Central Europe* (PhD, University of Philadelphia, 1926), p. 19.
90 Savage, *'98 and '48*, p. xv.
91 Nowlan, *Politics of Repeal*, p. 14.

Appendix:
The Council of the Irish
Confederation

The council consisted of:
William Smith O'Brien M.P.; John Shea Lalor, J.P., Gurteenroe; John B. Dillon, barrister; Francis Comyn, J.P., Woodstock; Robert Orr, Bray Lodge; John Mitchel; Luke Shea, J.P., The Rennies, County Cork; Robert Cane, M.D., J.P., Kilkenny; Charles Gavan Duffy, barrister; James Haughton, merchant; Richard O'Gorman, sen., merchant; Denny Lane, barrister, Cork; Edward F. Murray, C.E., London; Thomas F. Meagher, Waterford; John Martin, Loughorne; M.J. Barry, barrister; George Smith, Liverpool; P. Brady, T.C., Cork; Richard O'Gorman, jun., barrister; James Cantwell; Joseph Duffy, M.D., Finglas; T.B. MacManus, Liverpool; Michael Crean; Michael R. O'Farrell, barrister; Martin MacDermott, architect; C.H. West, M.D.; James Keely; Isaac S. Varian, Cork; D.F. McCarthy, barrister; P. J. Smyth, Kilmainham; Charles Taffe, barrister; T. Devin Reilly; T.D. McGee; Patrick O'Donohoe; J. Gilligan, late Inspector of Dublin Repeal Wardens; and Nicholas Harding.

From Duffy, *Four Years of Irish History*, p. 406.

Bibliography

Manuscript Sources:

American Irish Historical Society, New York (AIHS)
Papers of Charles O'Connor (O'Conor).

Bodleian Library
Papers of the Earl of Clarendon.

British Library, London
An Adjourned Meeting of Loyal Irish Repeal Association of City of Toronto.
Microfiche. F. 232 (22 September 1843).

Catholic University of America, Washington (CUA)
Fenian Collection.

The National Archives, England (TNA)
TNA 30/22/7 C. Russell Papers.
HO/ 5/ 21. Removal of Aliens Act (1848).
HO 45 OS 3136. Chartist Papers.
HO 45 102. Chartist Papers.
HO 45 2391. Correspondence re. Irish Republican Union.
HO 45 2410. Disturbance Papers (1848).
F/O 5. Foreign Office Papers.
TS11. Treasury Solicitor's Papers.
TNA, HO 45/2369. Reports to Home Office from Informers.

National Archives of Ireland (NAI)
Outrage Papers.

National Library, Ireland (NLI)
MS 442. Letters of William Smith O'Brien.
MS 444. William Smith O'Brien Papers.
MS 449. William Smith O'Brien Papers. Narrative of 1847–1848.
MS 770. O'Donoghoe Papers.

MS 3225. Young Ireland Papers, including Life of Joseph Brennan [*sic*] by Michael Cavanagh.
MS 3486. Papers of Samuel Ferguson.
MS 5886. Narrative of Terence MacManus and Richard O'Gorman.
MS 7697. Larcom Papers.
MS 7977. Narratives of 1848, including that of John O'Mahoney (O'Mahony).
MS 8574 (1–4). Lalor Papers.
MS 10515(4). Nine Letters from William Smith O'Brien, 1844–5.
   Letters from O'Brien to John Martin.
   Letters from O'Brien to O'Doherty.
MS 10515. Correspondence of William Smith O'Brien.
MS 10519. R.D. Williams Papers.
MS 10520. Letters of 'Eva'.
MS 10906. Women of Young Ireland file (typed, anonymous).
MS 19840. Diary of a soldier in 1848.
MS 19941. Lenon Manuscripts.
MS 22345. William Smith O'Brien Papers.

New York Public Library, Manuscript Room (NYPL)
Madison Collection.
Horace Greeley Papers.

Public Record Office of Northern Ireland (PRONI)
D. 2137. Papers of John Martin.

Royal Irish Academy, Dublin (RIA)
MS 23.H.41. Correspondence of Confederate Clubs.
MS 23.H.43. Book of Expenditure of Irish Confederation.
MS 23.H.44. Minute Books of Council of Irish Confederation.

Trinity College, Dublin. Manuscripts' Room (TCD)
MS 6457. Dillon Papers.
MS 2038/2039. Reports of CJ (informer).

Windsor Castle
Journals and Papers of Queen Victoria.

Newspapers and Journals:

Armagh Guardian
Belfast News-Letter
Belfast Protestant Journal
Boston Pilot
Boston Weekly Globe
Cork Examiner
Dublin Evening Packet
Felon
Frazer's Magazine
Freeman's Journal

Globe
The Irish American (New York)
Irish Builder
Irish Citizen (New York)
The Irishman
Irish Nation (New York)
Irish People (New York)
Irish World (New York)
Journal of the British Empire
Launceston Examiner (Tasmania)
Liverpool Mercury
Manchester Times
Mercury (UK)
Mercury (Tasmania)
The Nation
The National Guard
New York Commercial Advertiser
New York Freeman and Catholic Register
New York Herald
New York Nation
Northern Journal (New York)
Northern Star
Shamrock (New York)
The Times
Tribune
Tyrawley Herald or Mayo and Sligo Gazette
United Irishman
The United States Magazine and Democratic Review
The Warder
Wexford Independent

British parliamentary papers:

Account of the Number of Cattle exported from Ireland to Great Britain from 1846 to 1849, BPP, 1850, 423, lii.

Debates of Seanad Éireann:

Adjournment Matters. Farrenrory (Tipperary) National Monument. vol. 154, 4 March 1998.

Contemporary publications:

Anonymous, *Revolt in the British Isles. How to Aid It* by the Son of a United Irishman (New York, 1848).

Bagenal, Philip H., *The American Irish and the Influence of Irish Politics* (London, 1882).

Balch, William S., *Ireland: As I Saw It: The Character, Condition, and Prospects of the People* (New York and London, 1850).

Bancroft, Elizabeth Davis (Mrs George Bancroft), *Letters from England, 1846–1849* (London: Smith, Elder & Co., 1904).

Benson, Arthur Christopher and Viscount Esher (eds), *The Letters of Queen Victoria: A Selection from Her Majesty's Correspondence Between the Years 1837 and 1861* (London: John Murray, 1908, 3 vols).

Brougham, Leech, H., *1848 and 1887: The Continuity of the Irish Revolutionary Movement* (London and Dublin, 1887).

Butt, Isaac, *A Voice for Ireland: The Famine in the Land* (Dublin: Thoms, 1847).

Carlyle, Thomas, *Reminiscences of My Irish Journey in 1849* (London: Sampson Low, 1882).

Cavanagh, Michael, *The Memoirs of Gen. Thomas Francis Meagher, Comprising the Leading Events of his Career* (Worcester, MA: The Messenger Press, 1892).

Comité National De Centenaire de 1848, *Documents Diplomatiques du Governement Provisoire et de la Commission du Pouvoir Exécutif* (Paris, 1953, 2 vols).

Cooke, Henry, *The Repealer Repulsed! A Correct Narrative of the Rise and Progress of the Repeal Invasion of Ulster: Dr. Cooke's Challenge and Mr. O'Connell's Declinature, Tactics and Flight. With ... Illustrations. Also, an Authentic Report of the Great Conservative Demonstrations in Belfast, etc.* (Belfast: William McComb, 1841).

Cullen, Rev. J.H., *Young Ireland in Exile: The Story of the Men of '48 in Tasmania* (Dublin and Cork: Talbot Press, 1928).

Daunt, William O'Neill, Esquire, *Personal Recollections of the Late Daniel O'Connell MP* (London: Chapman and Hall, 1848, 2 vols).

Daunt, William O'Neill, *Eighty Five-Years of Irish history, 1800–1885* (London: Ward and Downey, 1888).

Davis, Richard (ed.), *'To Solitude Consigned': The Tasmanian Journal of William Smith O'Brien, 1849–1853* (Sydney: Crossing Press, 1995).

Devoy, John, *Recollections of an Irish Rebel. The Fenian Movement, its Origins and Progress: Methods of Work in Ireland and in the British Army, Why it Failed to Achieve its Main Object, but Exercised Great Influence on Ireland's Future* (New York: D. Young, 1929).

Dictionary of National Biography (London: Smith, Elder and Co., 1898).

Dillon, William, *Life of John Mitchel* (London: Kegan Paul, 1888, 2 vols).

Disraeli, Benjamin, *Lord George Bentinck: A Political Biography* (London: Archibald Constable, 1905).

Doheny, Michael, *The Felon's Track: History Of The Attempted Outbreak In Ireland, Embracing The Leading Events In The Irish Struggle From The Year 1843 To The Close Of 1848* (first pub. in New York in 1849: reprinted in the UK in 1867, 1875), with preface by Arthur Griffith (Dublin: Gill, 1914).

Duffy, Charles Gavan, *Report of the Organization and Instructions for the Formation and Government of Confederate Clubs* (Dublin: William Holden, 1847).

Duffy, Charles Gavan, *The Use and Capacity of Confederate Clubs* (Dublin: James Charles, 1847).

Duffy, Charles Gavan, *Four Years of Irish History, 1845–1849, Being a Sequel to 'Young Ireland'* (London: Cassell, Petter, Galpin & Co., 1883).

Duffy, Charles Gavan, *Young Ireland: A Fragment of Irish History. Irish People's Edition* (Dublin: M.H. Gill, 1884–1887, 2 vols).

Duffy, Sir Charles Gavan, *My Life in Two Hemispheres* (London: T. Fisher Unwin, 1898).

Duffy, Charles Gavan, and others, *The Spirit of the Nation, 1845* (facsimile reproduction, Washington: Woodstock Books, 1998).

Eva, *Poems by 'Eva' of the Nation* (San Francisco, 1877).

Finola, *Poems by 'Finola'* (Belfast: John Henderson, 1851).

Fitzgerald PP, Rev. P., *Personal Recollections of the Insurrection at Ballingarry in July, 1848* (Dublin, 1861).

Gonne MacBride, Maud, *The Autobiography of Maud Gonne: A Servant of the Queen,* ed. A. Norman Jeffares and Anna MacBride White (Chicago: Chicago University Press, 1995).

Hansard.

Hassard, John R.G., *Life of the Most Reverend John Hughes D.D. First Archbishop of New York With Extracts From His Private Correspondence* (New York, 1866; reprinted Arno Press, 1969).

Hodges, John George, *Report of the Trial of William Smith O'Brien for High Treason at the Special Commission for the County Tipperary held at Clonmel, September and October 1848, with the Judgement of the Court of Queen's Bench, Ireland and of the House of Lords, on the Writs of Error* (Dublin: Hodges and Smith, 1849).

Hull, Hugh M., *The Experience of Forty Years in Tasmania* (London: Orger and Meryon, 1959).

Lamartine, Alphonse de, *History of the Revolution of 1848* (London: Henry G. Bohn, 1849, 2 parts).

Laughton, John Knox, *Memoirs of the Life and Correspondence of Henry Reeve* (London: Longman, Green and Co., 1898, 2 vols).

Levin, Lewis C., *A Lecture on Irish Repeal, in Elucidation of the Fallacy of its Principles, and in Proof of its Pernicious Tendency, in its Moral, Religious and Political Aspects* (Philadelphia, 1844).

Luby, Thomas C., *The Life and Times of Daniel O'Connell* (Glasgow: Cameron, Ferguson and Company, 1872).

Lyons, W.F., *Brigadier-General Thomas Francis Meagher: His Political and Military Career, With Selections From the Speeches and Writings* (London: Burns Oates, 1869).

M, 'Obituary for Lady Wilde' in *The Athenaeum*, 15 February 1896.

MacDermott, Martin, *Songs and Ballads of Young Ireland, with Portraits of Authors* (London: Downey and Co., 1896).

McGee, James E., *'The Men of '48. Being a Brief History of the Repeal Association and the Irish Confederation; with Biographical Sketches of the Leading Actors in the Latter Organization, Their Principles, Opinions and Literary Labours* (first pub. New York, 1874: Boston, 1881).

McGee, Thomas D'Arcy, *A History of the Irish Settlers in North America from the Earliest Period to the Census of 1850* (Boston: American Celt, 1851).

MacNevin, Thomas, *Young Ireland: A Few Words in Defence of the Party, its Principles and Practices* (Dublin: James Duffy, 1844).

MacNevin, Thomas, *To the Orangemen of Ireland* (Dublin: J. Browne, 1844).

Meagher, Thomas F. (ed.), *Letters of a Protestant on Repeal by the Late Thomas*

Davis (Dublin: The Irish Confederation, 1847).

Meagher, Thomas F., 'Speech on the Transportation of Mitchel, 1848' in W.F. Lyons, *Brigadier-General Thomas Francis Meagher: His Political and Military Career, with Selections from the Speeches and Writings* (London: Burns Oates, 1869).

Mitchel, John, *The Last Conquest of Ireland (Perhaps)* (Glasgow: R. and T. Washbourne, 1861).

Mitchel, John, *An Ulsterman for Ireland, Being Letters to the Protestant Farmers, Labourers and Artisans of the North of Ireland* (reprinted by Candle Press, Dublin, 1917, with a foreword by Eoin MacNeill).

Mitchel, John, *Jail Journal* (first pub. 1854; introduction by Thomas Flanagan, Dublin: University Press of Ireland, 1982).

National Repeal Convention of the Friends of Ireland in the United States of America, Held in the City of Philadelphia (Philadelphia, 1842).

Normanby, Earl of, Constantine Henry Philip, *A Year of Revolution: From a Journal Kept in Paris in 1848* (London: Longmans, 1857).

O'Connell, Daniel, *Liberty or Slavery? And Reply to O'Connell by Hon. S.P. Chase* (Cincinnati: Chronicle Print, 1863).

O'Connell, John, *Recollections and Experiences During a Parliamentary Career from 1833 to 1848* (London: Richard Bentley, 1849, 2 vols).

O'Connor, Thomas, Esq., *Address Delivered Before the Irish Repeal Association of the City of New York by Thomas O'Connor on Occasion of his Election to the Office of President* (New York: H. Cassidy, 1841).

O'Doherty, Mary Anne Kelly, *Poems. By 'Eva' of 'The Nation'* (Waterford: Gill and Son, 1909).

O'Leary, John, *Recollections of Fenians and Fenianism* (London: Downey and Co., 1896, 2 vols).

Proceedings of the Young Ireland Party at their Great Meeting in Dublin, December 2, 1846, With a Correct Report of the Speeches and Resolutions (Belfast: John Henderson, 1847).

Russell, R.W., *America compared with England: The Respective Social Effects of the American and English Systems of Government and Legislation* (London: J. Watson, 1849).

Sillard, P.A., *The Life of John Mitchel: With an Historical Sketch of the '48 Movement in Ireland* (Dublin: J. Duffy and Co., 1889).

Sillard, P.A., *The Life and Letters of John Martin. With Sketches of Thomas Devin Reilly, Father John Kenyon, and Other 'Young Irelanders'* (Dublin: J. Duffy and Co., 1893).

Speranza, 'Sympathies' in *The Dublin University Magazine* (Dublin, 1849), 429.

Speranza, *Poems by Speranza (Lady Wilde)* (Dublin: Gill and Son, n.d.). (see also Lady Wilde)

Sullivan, A. M., *New Ireland* (3rd edn, London: Collier Pub., 1878).

Thierry, Jacques-Nicolas-Augustin, *Dix ans d'études historiques* (Paris, 1835, pub. in English by Whittaker and Co., London, 1845).

Thomasine, *Wild Flowers from the Wayside* (Dublin: James Duffy and Sons, 1883).

Thomson, David and Moyra Gusty (eds), *The Irish Journals of Elizabeth Smith, 1840–1850* (Oxford: Clarendon Press, 1980).

Trant, Thomas, *Sub Inspector Trant's Reply to Father Fitzgerald's Pamphlet*

Entitled His 'Personal Recollections of the Insurrection at Ballingarry in July, 1848. With Remarks on the Irish Constabulary, and Hints to all Officials' (Dublin: McGlashan and Gill, 1862).

Ventura, Padre Gioacchino, translated by William B. McCabe, *The Funeral Oration on Daniel O'Connell Delivered at Rome on 28 June 1847* (Dublin: J.H. Scott, 1847).

West, John, *The History of Tasmania* (first pub. Launceston: Henry Dowling, 1852, reprinted, Sydney: A.G.L. Shaw, Angus and Robertson, 1971).

Wilde, Lady Jane, *The American Irish* (Dublin: William McGee, n.d.).

Wilde, Lady Jane, *Poems by Speranza (Lady Wilde)* (Dublin: James Duffy, 1864).

Wilde, Lady Jane, *Poems* (2nd edn, Glasgow: Cameron and Ferguson 1881).

Wilde, Lady Jane, *Irish Cures, Mystic Charms and Superstitions* (New York, *c.* 1891).

Wilde, Lady Jane, *Notes on Men, Women and Books* (first series, London: Ward and Downey, 1891).

Secondary published sources:

Ackroyd, Peter, *The Romantics* (Milton Keynes: Open University Press/BBC, 2006).

Beckett, J.C., *The Making of Modern Ireland 1603–1923* (London: Faber & Faber, 1966).

Boardman, Kay and Christine Kinealy, *1848: The Year the World Turned?* (Newcastle: Cambridge Scholars Press, 2007).

Boyce, D. George (ed.), *Political Thought in Irish Society since the Seventeenth Century* (London: Routledge, 1993).

Boyce, D. George and Roger Swift (eds), *Problems and Perspectives in Irish History* (Dublin: Four Courts Press, 2004).

Brady, Ciarán, *Worsted in the Game: Losers in Irish History* (Dublin: Lilliput Press, 1989).

Briggs, Asa, *Chartist Studies* (London: Macmillan, 1967).

Ceallaigh, Seán Ua, *Speeches from the Dock or Protests of Irish Patriotism* (Dublin: Gill and Son, 1953).

Claeys, George, *The Chartist Movement in Britain* (London: Pickering and Chatto, 1999).

Connolly, James, *Labour in Irish History*, (first pub 1910, reprinted Dublin: New Books, 1973).

Cronin, Maura, *Country, Class or Craft: The Politicization of the Skilled Artisan in Nineteenth-Century Cork* (Cork: Cork University Press, 1994).

Cronin, Mike, *A History of Ireland* (Hampshire: Palgrave, 2001).

Davis, Richard, *The Young Ireland Movement* (Dublin: Gill and Macmillan, 1988).

Davis, Richard, *Revolutionary Imperialist: William Smith O'Brien* (Dublin: Lilliput Press, 1998).

Davis, Richard (ed.), *'To Solitude Consigned': The Tasmanian Journal of William Smith O'Brien, 1849–1853* (Sydney: The Crossing Press, 1995).

Donnolly, James S., *The Great Irish Potato Famine* (Gloucestershire: Sutton, 2001).

Doughty, Sir Arthur G. (ed.), *The Elgin-Grey Papers* (Ottawa: J.O. Patenaude, 1937, 4 vols).

Dowe, Dieter, Heinz-Gerhard Haupt, Dieter Langewiesche, and Jonathan Sperber (eds), translated by David Higgins, *Europe in 1848: Revolution and Reform* (New York and Oxford: Berghahn, 2001).

Dunlop, Robert, *Daniel O'Connell* (London: Putnam, 1900).

Eagleton, Terry, *Scholars and Rebels in Nineteenth-Century Ireland* (Oxford: Blackwell, 1999).

Epstein, J., and D. Thompson (eds), *The Chartist Experience: Studies in Working-Class Radicalism and Culture, 1830–1860* (London: Macmillan, 1982).

Evans, R.J.W., (ed.), *The Revolutions of Europe 1848–1849* (Oxford: Oxford University Press, 2000).

Evans, R.J.W. and Hartmut Pogge Von Strandmann, *The Revolutions in Europe 1848–1849* (Oxford: Oxford University Press, 2000).

Ferguson, Lady Mary, *Sir Samuel Ferguson in the Ireland of His Day, etc.* (Edinburgh and London: W Blackwood and Sons, 1896).

Fitzpatrick, W.J., (ed.), *Correspondence of Daniel O'Connell* (London: John Murray, 1888).

Flanagan, Laurence, *Irish Women's Letters* (Stroud: Sutton, 1997).

Fogarty, L., *Father John Kenyon: A Patriot Priest of Forty-Eight* (Dublin: Mahon's Printing, 1921).

Foster, Roy, *Modern Ireland* (London: Penguin, 1989).

Geary, Laurence M., *Rebellion and Remembrance in Modern Ireland* (Dublin: Four Courts Press, 2001).

Gildea, R., *Barricades and Borders: Europe 1800–1914* (Oxford: Oxford University Press, 1996).

Goodway, David, *London Chartism, 1838–1848* (Cambridge: Cambridge University Press, 1982).

Griffin, Brian, *The Bulkies: Police and Crime in Belfast, 1800–1865* (Dublin: Irish Academic Press, 1997).

Grogan, Geraldine F., *The Noblest Agitator: Daniel O'Connell and the German Catholic Movement 1830–1850* (Dublin: Veritas, 1991).

Gwynn, Denis, *Young Ireland and 1848* (Cork: Cork University Press, 1949).

Harbison, Peter, Homan Potterton and Jeanne Sheehy, *Irish Art and Architecture from Prehistory to the Present* (London: Thames and Hudson, 1978).

Hattersley, Alan F., *The Convict Crisis and the Growth of Unity: Resistance to Transportation in South Africa and Australia 1848–1853* (Cape Town: University of Natal Press, 1965).

Heuston, Robert Francis, *The Catholic Press and Nativism* (New York: Arno Press, 1976).

Hoppen, K. Theodore, *Elections, Politics and Society in Ireland 1832–1885* (Oxford: Clarendon Press, 1984).

Houston, Arthur, *Daniel O'Connell: His Early Life and Journal 1795–1802* (London: s.n., 1906).

Jupp, P. and E. Magennis (eds), *Crowds in Ireland c. 1720-1920* (Basingstoke: Macmillan, 2000).

Kamenka, Eugene and F.B. Smith, *Intellectuals and Revolutions: Socialism and the Experience of 1848* (London: Edward Arnold, 1979).

Kelly, John, *Collected Letters of Yeats* (Oxford: Oxford University Press, 1986).

Kiely, Brendan, *The Waterford Rebels of 1849* (Dublin: Geography Publications, n.d.).

Kiernan, T.J., *The Irish Exiles in Australia* (Melbourne: Burns and Oates, 1954).

Kinealy, Christine, *This Great Calamity: The Irish Famine 1845–52* (Dublin: Gill and Macmillan, 1994; reprinted with a new Introduction, 2006).

Kinealy, Christine, *A Death-Dealing Famine: The Great Hunger in Ireland* (London: Pluto Press, 1997).

Kinealy, Christine, *The Great Irish Famine: Impact, Ideology and Rebellion* (Hampshire: Palgrave, 2002).

Kinealy, Christine, *Lives of Victorian Political Figures: Daniel O'Connell* (London: Pickering and Chatto, 2007).

Kinealy, Christine and Gerard MacAtasney, *The Hidden Famine: Poverty, Hunger and Sectarianism in Belfast c.1840-50* (London: Pluto Press, 2000).

Koseki, Takashi, *Dublin Confederate Clubs and the Repeal Movement* (Hosei University, Ireland–Japan Papers, no. 10, Japan, 1992).

Lane, Fintan, and Donal Ó Drisceoil (eds), *Politics and the Irish Working Class, 1830–1945* (Houndmills: Palgrave Macmillan, 2005).

Lydon, James, *The Making of Ireland from Ancient Times to the Present* (London: Penguin 1998).

MacAtasney, Gerard, *'This Dreadful Visitation': The Famine in Lurgan and Portadown* (Belfast: Beyond the Pale, 1997).

MacDonagh, Oliver, *The Hereditary Bondsman: Daniel O'Connell 1775–1829* (New York: St Martin's Press, 1987).

MacDonagh, Oliver, *The Emancipist: Daniel O'Connell 1830–47* (New York: St Martin's Press, 1989).

Macintyre, A., *The Liberator: Daniel O'Connell and the Irish Party 1830–1847* (London: H. Hamilton, 1966).

McKenna, Benjamin Vicuna, *The Girondins of Chile: Reminiscences of an Eyewitness* (first pub. 1876; Oxford: OUP, 2003).

MacManus, Seamus (ed.), *Poems. By 'Eva' of 'The Nation'* (Dublin: M. Gill, 1909).

Maxwell, Right Honorable Sir Herbert, *The Life and Letters of George William Frederick, Fourth Earl of Clarendon* (London: Edward Arnold, 1913, 2 vols).

Melville, Joy, *Mother of Oscar: The Life of Jane Francesca Wilde* (Edinburgh: John Murray, 1994).

Moley, Raymond, *Nationalism Without Violence: An Essay* (New York: Fordham University Press, 1974).

Monypenny, W.F. and G.E. Buckle, *The Life of Benjamin Disraeli, Earl of Beaconsfield* (London: John Murray, 1910–20).

Moody, T.W. and F.X. Martin, *The Course of Irish History* (Cork: Mercier Press, 1977).

Morash, Christopher, *The Hungry Voice: The Poetry of the Irish Famine* (Dublin: Irish Academic Press, 1989).

Newman, A., *Why the Manchester Martyrs Died* (Dublin: Whelan and Son, 1915).

Nowlan, K.B., *The Politics of Repeal: a Study in the Relations Between Great Britain and Ireland, 1841–50* (London: Routledge and Kegan Paul, 1965).

O'Brien, R. Barry, *The Life of Charles Stewart Parnell* (New York: Harper and Brothers, 1898).

Ó Cathaoir, Brendan, *John Blake Dillon: Young Irelander* (Dublin: Irish Academic Press, 1990).

Ó Cathaoir, Brendan (ed.) *Young Irelanders Abroad. The Diary of Charles Hart* (Cork: Cork University Press, 2003).

O'Connell, Maurice, R., *O'Connell, Young Ireland, and Violence* (Bronx: Fordham University Press, 1972).

O'Connell, Maurice (ed.), *The Correspondence of Daniel O'Connell* (Shannon: Irish University Press, 1972–80, 8 vols).

O'Conner, Rebecca, *Jenny Mitchel: Young Irelander: A Biography* (Tucson, Arizona: O'Conner Trust, 1988).

O'Ferrall, Fergus, *Catholic Emancipation: Daniel O'Connell and the Birth of Irish Democracy* (Dublin: Gill and Macmillan, 1985).

O'Rourke, Canon John, *The Great Irish Famine* (first pub. 1874, reprinted by Veritas, Dublin, 1989).

O'Sullivan, T.F., *The Young Irelanders* (2nd edn, Tralee: The Kerryman, 1945).

Parker, Charles Stuart, *Sir Robert Peel from his Private Papers*, (2nd edn, London: John Murray, 1899).

Pickering, Paul, *Chartism and the Chartists in Manchester and Salford* (Basingstoke: Palgrave Macmillan, 1995).

Potter, George, *To the Golden Door: The Story of the Irish in Ireland and America* (Boston: Little, Brown and Company, 1960).

Potter, Matthew, *A Catholic Unionist: The Life and Times of William Monsell 1812–1894* (Limerick: The Treaty Press, n.d.).

Quaife, Milo Milton, *The Diary of James K. Polk, During his Presidency 1845–49* (Chicago: McClurg, 1910, 4 vols).

Reinfeld, Barbara K., *Karel Havlicek (1821–1856): A National Liberation Leader of the Czech Renascence* (New York: Eastern European Monographs, 1982).

Robertson, Priscilla, *Revolutions of 1848: A Social History* (Princeton: Princeton University Press, 1952).

Ross, Patrick and Heather, *Exiles Undaunted: Irish Rebels Kevin and Eva O'Doherty* (Queensland: University of Queensland Press, 1989).

Rossa Jeremiah O'Donovan, *Recollections of Jeremiah O'Donovan Rossa, 1838–1898: Memories of an Irish Revolutionary*, with an Introduction by Seán Ó Lúing (Shannon: Irish University Press, 1972).

Ryan, Louise and Margaret Ward (eds), *Irish Women and Nationalism: Soldiers, New Women and Wicked Hags* (Dublin: Irish Academic Press, 2004).

Ryan, Louise and Margaret Ward, *Irish Women and the Vote* (Dublin: Irish Academic Press, 2007).

Savage, John, *'98 and '48. The Modern Revolutionary History and Literature of Ireland* (first pub. New York: Redfield, 1856: re-pub. New York: J.B. Aldem, 1884).

Saville, John, *1848: The British State and the Chartist Movement* (Cambridge: Cambridge University Press, 1990).

Sibbett, R.M., *Orangemen in Ireland and Throughout the Empire* (Belfast: Henderson and Co., 2 vols).

Simpson, William, and Martin Jones, *Europe 1783–1914* (Oxford: Routledge, 2000).

Sloan, Robert, *William Smith O'Brien and the Young Ireland Rebellion of 1848* (Dublin: Four Courts Press, 2000).

Sperber, Jonathan, *The European Revolutions, 1848–1851* (Cambridge: Cambridge University Press, 1994).

Steele, Karen, *Women, Press, and Politics During the Irish Revival* (New York: Syracuse University Press, 2007).

Steele Karen (ed.), *Maud Gonne's Irish Nationalist Writings 1895–1946* (Dublin: Irish Academic Press, 2004).

Strachey, Lytton and Roger Fulford (eds), *The Greville Memoirs 1814–1860*, vol. v, January 1842 to December 1847 (London: Macmillan, 1938).

Sullivan, A.M., *The Story of Ireland: A Narrative of Irish History, From the Earliest Ages to the Insurrection of 1867* (Dublin: M.H. Gill, 1894).

Sullivan, A.M. and T.D. Sullivan, *The Wearing of the Green, or the Persecuted Funeral Procession* (Dublin: J. Duffy, 1882).

Taylor, A.J.P., *Revolutions and Revolutionaries* (London: Hamish Hamilton, 1978).

Thompson, Dorothy, *The Chartists* (Hounslow: Temple Smith, 1984).

Thomson Guy (ed.), *The European Revolutions of 1848 and the Americas* (London: Institute of Latin American Studies, 2002).

Tipper, Karen Sasha Anthony, *A Critical Biography of Lady Jane Wilde, 1821?–1896, Irish Revolutionist, Humanist, Scholar and Poet* (New York: Edwin Mellen Press, 2002).

Touhill, Blanche M., *William Smith O'Brien and his Irish Revolutionary Companions in Penal Exile* (Missouri: University of Missouri Press, 1981).

Trevelyan, George M., *British History in the Nineteenth Century, 1782–1901* (London: Longmans, 1922).

Tyler, Lyon G., *Letters and Times of the Tylers* (Richmond: Whittel and Shepperson, 1885, 3 vols).

White, Terence de Vere, *The Parents of Oscar Wilde: Sir William and Lady Wilde* (London: Hodder and Stoughton, 1967).

Whitridge, Arnold, *Men in Crisis: The Revolutions of 1848* (New York: Charles Schribner and Sons, 1949).

Wilson, Alexander, *The Chartist Movement in Scotland* (New York: Augustus M. Kelly, 1970).

Wilson, David A., *Thomas D'Arcy McGee: Passion, Reason and Politics, 1835–57* (Montreal: McGill-Queens University Press, 2008).

Wyndham, Horace, *Speranza: A Biography of Lady Wilde* (London: Boardman and Co., 1951).

Yeats, W.B., *The Autobiography of William Butler Yeats* (New York: McMullen Books, 1953).

Articles and chapters:

Anton, Brigitte, 'Women of the *Nation*' in *History Ireland* (vol. 1, no. 3, Autumn 1993), 34–7.

Belchem, John, 'The Spy System in 1848: Chartists and Informers – An Australian Connection' in *Labour History* (vol. xxxix, 1980), 15–27.

Belchem, John, 'Nationalism, Republicanism and Exile: Irish Emigrants and the Revolution of 1848' in *Past and Present* (vol. 146, February 1995), 103–35.

Belchem, John, 'Liverpool in 1848: Image, Identity and Issues' in *Transactions of the Historic Society of Lancashire and Cheshire* (vol. 167, 1998), 1–26.

Bisceglia, Louis R., 'The Fenian Funeral of Terence Bellew McManus' in *Eire-Ireland* (vol. 14. no. 3, 1979), 45–64.

Boos, Florence S., 'The "Homely Muse" in Her Diurnal Setting: The Periodical Poems of "Marie," Janet Hamilton, and Fanny Forrester' in *Victorian Poetry* (39.2, 2001).

Cannavan, Jan, 'Revolution in Ireland, Evolution in Women's Rights: Irish women in 1798 and 1848' in Louise Ryan and Margaret Ward (eds), *Irish Women and Nationalism: Soldiers, New Women and Wicked Hags* (Dublin: Irish Academic Press, 2004).

Colantonio, Laurent, 'Daniel O'Connell : un Irlandais au cœur du discours républicain pendant la Monarchie de Juillet' in *Revue d'Histoire du XIX siècle* (Varia, 20/21, 2000). Available online at http://rh19.revues.org/document208.html (accessed 19 December 2008).

Cronin, M., 'Of one Mind? O'Connellite Crowds in the 1830s and 1840s' in P. Jupp and E. Magennis (eds), *Crowds in Ireland c.1720-1920* (Basingstoke: Macmillan, 2000).

Crouch, Charles, 'The Myth of the Dem-Soc Coalition: France in 1848' in Kay Boardman and Christine Kinealy (eds), *1848: The Year the World Turned?* (Newcastle: Cambridge Scholars Press, 2007).

Daly, Mary E., 'James Fintan Lalor and Rural Revolution' in Ciaran Brady, *Worsted in the Game: Losers in Irish History* (Dublin: Lilliput Press, 1989).

D'Arcy, F.A., 'The National Trades' Political Union and Daniel O'Connell 1830–1848' in *Eire-Ireland* (vol. 17, no. 3, 1982), 7–16.

Davis, Richard, 'The Reluctant Rebel: William Smith O'Brien' in *Tipperary Historical Journal* (1998), 46–55.

Davis, Richard, 'Young Ireland' in *Encyclopedia of 1848 Revolutions*: http://cscwww.cats.ohiou.edu (accessed 24 January 2005).

Gildea, Robert, '1848 in European Collective Memory' in R.J.W. Evans and Hartmut Pogge Von Strandmann, *The Revolutions in Europe 1848-1849* (Oxford: Oxford University Press, 2000).

Gladstone, W.E., 'Daniel O'Connell' in James Knowles (ed.), *The Nineteenth Century: A Monthly Review*, vol. xxv, January to June 1889 (New York and London: Kegan, Paul, Trench & Co.), 149–68.

Gwynn, Denis, 'The Priests and Young Ireland in 1848' in *The Irish Ecclesiastical Record* (vol. lxx, no. 38, 1948), 590–609.

Gwynn, Denis, 'The rising of 1848' in *Studies. An Irish Quarterly Review* (xxxvii, 1948), 7–17 and 149–60.

Gwynn, Denis, 'Father Kenyon and Young Ireland' in *The Irish Ecclesiastical Record* (vol. lxxi, no. 975, 1949), 226–46.

Heaney, Carmel, 'William Smith O'Brien in Van Diemen's Land,' in *History Ireland* (Autumn 1998), 29–32.

Hill, Jacqueline, 'The Intelligentsia and Irish Nationalism in the 1840s' in *Studia Hibernia* (no. 20, 1980), 73–109.

Hurst, Michael, 'Ireland and Ballot Act of 1872' in *The Historical Journal* (vol. 8, no. 3,1965), 326°35.

Kinealy, Christine, 'Food Exports', in Christine Kinealy, *The Great Irish Famine: Impact, Ideology and Rebellion* (Hampshire: Palgrave, 2002).

Kinealy, Christine, 'Les marches orangistes en Irlande du Nord. Histoire d'un droit' in *Le Mouvement Social* (no. 202, janvier–mars 2003), 165–81.

Kinealy, Christine, 'A Right to March? The Conflict at Dolly's Brae, 1849' in George Boyce and Roger Swift (eds), *Problems and Perspectives in Irish History*

(Dublin: Four Courts Press, 2004).

Kinealy, Christine, '"Brethren in Bondage": Chartists, O'Connellites, Young Irelanders and the 1848 Uprising' in Fintan Lane and Donal Ó Drisceoil (eds), *Politics and the Irish Working Class, 1830-1945* (Houndmills: Palgrave Macmillan, 2005).

Kinealy, Christine, 'Invisible Nationalists' in Kay Boardman and Christine Kinealy (eds), *1848: The Year the World Turned?* (Newcastle: Cambridge Scholars Press, 2007).

Lindsay, Dunya, 'A Fanatic Heart' in *National Library of Australia News* (August 2006). Available online at: www.nla.gov.au/pub/nlanews/2006/aug06/article3.html (accessed 19 December 2008).

Mansel, Philip, 'Nation Building: The Foundation of Belgium' in *History Today* (May 2005), 21-7.

McGrath, K.M., 'Writers in the *Nation*' in *Irish Historical Studies* (vol. vi, no. 23, March 1949), 189-223.

Mitchell, Leslie, 'Britain's Reaction to the Revolutions' in R.J.W. Evans and Hartmut Pogge Von Strandmann, *The Revolutions in Europe 1848-1849* (Oxford: Oxford University Press, 2000).

Nolan, William, 'The Irish Confederation in County Tipperary in 1848' in *Tipperary Historical Journal* (1998), 2-18.

Ó Fiaich, Tomás, 'The Northern Young Ireland' in *Tipperary Historical Journal* (1998), 19-31.

O'Higgins, Rachel, 'Irish Trade Unions and Politics, 1830-50' in *The Historical Journal* (vol. 4, issue 2, 1961), 108-17.

O'Higgins, Rachel, 'The Irish Influence in the Chartist Movement' in *Past and Present* (vol. 20, 1961), 83-96.

O'Neill, Thomas P., 'The Economic and Political Ideas of James Fintan Lalor' in *The Irish Ecclesiastical Record* (vol. 74, July–December 1950), 398-409.

Ó Snodaigh, Pádraig, 'The impact of the 1848 insurrection' in *Tipperary Historical Journal* (1998), 1.

Owens, Gary, 'Popular Mobilization and the Rising of 1848: The Clubs of the Irish Confederation' in Laurence M. Geary, *Rebellion and Remembrance in Modern Ireland* (Dublin: Four Courts Press, 2001).

Palmer, Stanley H., '"1848" in England and Ireland: A Revolution' in *Consortium on Revolutionary Europe, 1750–1850* (vol. 14, 1984), 424-33.

Petler, D.N., 'Ireland and France in 1848' in *Irish Historical Studies* (vol. 24, no. 96, 1985), 493-505.

Quinlan, Carmel, '"Onward Hand in Hand": The Nineteenth Century Irish Campaign for Votes for Women' in Louise Ryan and Margaret Ward, *Irish Women and the Vote* (Dublin: Irish Academic Press, 2007).

Quinn, John, 'The Rise and Fall of Repeal: Slavery and Irish Nationalism in Antebellum Philadelphia' in *Pennsylvania Magazine of History and Biography* (vol. 130, no. 1, January 2005), 45-78.

Robinson, Mary, 'Daniel O'Connell: A Tribute' in *History Ireland* (vol. 5, no. 4, Winter 1997), 26-31.

Swift, Roger, 'The "Specials" and the Policing of Chartism in 1848' in Kay Boardman and Christine Kinealy (eds), *1848: The Year the World Turned?* (Newcastle: Cambridge Scholars Press, 2007).

Taylor, Miles, 'The 1848 Revolutions and the British Empire' in *Past and Present* (vol. 166, 2000), 146–80.

Thompson, Dorothy, 'Ireland and the Irish in English Radicalism before 1850' in J. Epstein and D. Thompson (eds), *The Chartist Experience: Studies in Working-Class Radicalism and Culture, 1830–1860* (London: Macmillan, 1982).

Wangerman, Ernst, '1848 and Jewish Emancipation in the Hapsburg Empire' in Kay Boardman and Christine Kinealy (eds), *1848: The Year the World Turned?* (Newcastle: Cambridge Scholars Press, 2007).

Whelan, Yvonne, 'The Construction and Destruction of a Colonial Landscape: Monuments to British Monarchs in Dublin Before and After Independence' in *Journal of Historical Geography* (vol. 28. no. 4, 2002), 508–33.

White, J.H., 'The Age of Daniel O'Connell' in T.W. Moody and F.X. Martin, *The Course of Irish History* (Cork, Mercier Press, 1977).

Wilson, T.G., 'Sir William Wilde and Speranza' in *Irish Journal of Medical Science* (November 1933), 634–6.

Dissertations:

Collombier, Pauline, *Le discourse des leaders du nationalism constitutionnel irlandais sur l'autonomie de l'irlande: Utopies politiques et mythes identitaires.* Unpublished PhD, Sorbonne, Paris, 2007.

Kinealy, Siobhán, *1848 in Liverpool.* Unpublished undergraduate dissertation presented to Department of History, Essex University, 2007.

May, Arthur James, *Contemporary American Opinion of the Mid-Century Revolutions in Central Europe.* PhD, University of Philadelphia, 1926.

Index